The **Rosie's**
BAKER

All-Butter, Cream-Filled, Sugar-Packed Baking Book

The Rosie's BAKERY

All-Butter, Cream-Filled, Sugar-Packed Baking Book

By Judy Rosenberg
Written with Nan Levinson

WORKMAN PUBLISHING
NEW YORK

Library of Congress Cataloging-in-Publication Data is available.
ISBN 978-0-7611-5407-5

Some of the recipes in this book originally appeared in *Rosie's Bakery All-Butter,
Fresh Cream, Sugar-Packed, No-Holds-Barred Baking Book* and in *Rosie's Bakery Chocolate-
Packed, Jam-Filled, Butter-Rich, No-Holds-Barred Cookie Book*, both by Judy Rosenberg

Cover design by Raquel Jaramillo
Cover photos: (Front cover composite) Wooden spoon by flashgun/
istockphoto, chocolate drip by Nanka (Kucherenko Olena)/shutterstock
images, layer cake by Colin Cooke/©Stock Food; (Back cover) Brownies by
Jim Scherer/©Stock Food, Cupcakes by Jon Edwards Photography/
©Stock Food.

Book design by Jean-Marc Troadec
Interior illustrations by Tae Won Yu
Interior photos: p. xiv Michael Paul/©Stock Food, p. 8 Maura McEvoy/
Getty Images, p. 122 Clinton Hussey/age fotostock, p. 256 Brian Leatart/
Getty Images, p. 326 Brian Hagiwara/Getty Images.

Workman books are available at special discounts when purchased in bulk for
premiums and sales promotions as well as for fund-raising or educational
use. Special editions or book excerpts can also be created to specification.
For details, contact the Special Sales Director at the address below,
or send an e-mail to specialmarkets@workman.com.

Workman Publishing Company, Inc.
225 Varick Street
New York, NY 10014-4381
www.workman.com

Printed in the United States of America
First printing October 2011
10 9 8 7 6 5 4 3 2 1

To my mother and my father,
who endowed me with great taste buds and a lust for food
and who are now loving me from above . . .

I owe it all to them.

SPECIAL THANKS

TO NAN LEVINSON, whose humor, style, and good nature helped to make this book what it is.

TO ELIOT WINOGRAD, my business partner, for taking care of all the things that would drive me crazy if he wasn't there to do them.

TO MY EDITOR, SUZANNE RAFER, who patiently waited—and waited—while I perfected the manuscript. And to Kate Slate, Irene Demchyshyn, Ann ffolliott, Erin Klabunde, Barbara Peragine, and all the others at Workman who helped move the book along.

TO MY WONDERFUL STAFF, without whom Rosie's would be merely a concept.

TO MIMI SANTINI-RITT, my dedicated recipe tester, who is a joy to work with.

TO BEVERLY JONES, whose creativity and mastery of baking is an inspiration.

AND ESPECIALLY TO ALL MY WONDERFUL CUSTOMERS, who have remained true to Rosie's over the years and who have made my baked goods part of their children's childhood memories.

Contents

ROSIE'S

What is cooking on Chestnut Hill?
 Rosie is baking on Chestnut Hill!
Millions of mavens marvel and chatter,
 "See all that butter go into the batter!"
Out of the oven pops her poppy-seed pound cake,
 Her prize winning chocolate bound-to-astound cake,
The country's best brownies, on Chestnut Hill!

Why all the crowds on Chestnut Hill!
 Groupies and gourmets on Chestnut Hill!
The aroma of baking tells where Paradise is,
 Gluttony here is the nicest of vices,
So sample a sample, nibble a nibble,
 Once you have tasted, how can you quibble?
Critics will praise her, poets will scribble,
 "Rosie's is Heaven on Chestnut Hill!"

No one bakes bread on Chestnut Hill!
 Let 'em eat cake on Chestnut Hill!
Let 'em eat cake and have it, too
 For weddings, bar mitzvahs, a bris, a debut.
Rosie is ready, her pastries behind her,
 Her fan clubs have met and almost enshrined her,
So follow your palate, your taste buds will find her
 In Heaven at Rosie's on Chestnut Hill!

—MOM AND DAD, 1978

I can't say for sure that I came out of the womb on a diet, but it certainly wasn't long afterward that I was put on one. As far back as I can remember, it was a family ritual to climb on the scale each morning: first my father, who was blessed with a metabolism that burned up everything that he ate; then my mother, who had the will power to stay thin; and finally, me, their chubby child. No one would have guessed then that I'd end up a baker, least of all me.

We lived in a huge apartment in the middle of Manhattan. My mother was a theatrical agent, and my father quit teaching English to join her in the business. Our apartment was often full of people, all talking, making music, and eating. I heard the score for *A Funny Thing Happened on the Way to the Forum* way before anyone else. I remember Julie Andrews and Jean Stapleton coming over for auditions. Rob Reiner was at my third birthday party, and best of all, Marilyn Monroe lived in an apartment upstairs. It seemed ordinary to me.

It also seemed perfectly ordinary that my mother worked. I think of her as forever talking on the phone, making arrangements or organizing some event, so with all that, she didn't have a lot of time to spend in the kitchen. But that was never a problem. A master orchestrator, she'd go through cookbooks to pick out recipes for our housekeeper to make, and her instincts were unerring. Although my mother was anything but domestic, she knew exactly where to shop to get the best meats, the best fish . . . and the best desserts.

Sometimes, as a special treat for me, my mother baked brownies. It was the only thing she did bake, but her grandmother was reputed to have been a master baker in Czechoslovakia, so it may have been an inherited talent. In any event, those wonderful brownies were the stuff of my dreams from early childhood on. I still get a heightened physical reaction, a buzz, when I bite into a spectacular dessert, and lust is probably the only word that accurately describes my relationship to chocolate. So when people ask me how I came up with the name "Chocolate Orgasms" for Rosie's brownies, I don't know how to answer because it seemed the most obvious name in the world to me.

In the 1950s there weren't cookie shops or gourmet ice cream outlets on every corner, even in New York City, where you can get nearly anything you can imagine if you're willing to pay for it. But if you were as serious in your quest for the ideal dessert as I invariably was, you would be well rewarded. There were William Greenberg Jr.'s brownies made of that dense, not-too-sweet chocolate that I think of as pure American. There was Reuben's cheesecake, heavy enough to choke on if you didn't drink milk with it, and Serendipity's Frozen Hot Chocolate, which was so cold it gave me a headache, but so good I didn't care. Eclair made a chocolate cake with sour cherries, Ebinger's

had rugalah, Bonte's madeleines would have inspired Proust to write cookbooks, and even Schrafft's brownies were great in those days. On the home front, there were Hershey's Golden Almond Bars, which my mother hid in her stocking drawer for fear my father and I would consume them in a frenzy. A good number of my childhood memories, it seems, were chocolate-coated.

MAJORING IN DESSERT

Things didn't change much as I grew older. When I went away to college at the University of California at Berkeley in the late sixties, I continued my research into the ultimate dessert and added Crucheon's Fudge Pie, King Pin donuts, and See's candy to my pantheon. Officially I was studying French, but it was the era of the Free Speech movement, communes, and organic food, so I learned a lot of other things on the side. After graduation, I moved to Cambridge, Massachusetts, and looked for work. To no one's surprise, I gravitated toward food.

For a while, I waitressed in a coffeehouse in Harvard Square (which I loved and my parents hated), then I went back to school for another degree (which I hated and my parents loved), all of which qualified me to waitress at a classier restaurant and spend a year and a half at the Boston Museum of Fine Arts School (which, at last, pleased both my parents and me).

It was in those days that I developed my philosophy of food, an answer to every glutton's dream, because I figured out how to have my cake and eat it, too. It all had to do with balance, a kind of yin and yang of calorie consciousness. I lived on a strict diet of brown bread, cheese, fruit, nuts, and vegetables—sensible, healthy, balanced eating. Then I'd polish the meal off with a fat slab of cheesecake from Jack and Marion's, a now departed Brookline delicatessen. After all, guilty pleasures are still pleasures.

THE AWAKENING

Then on Valentine's Day, 1974, all those years of appetite and abstinence were vindicated. I was wondering about life after art school when it popped into my mind to create edible valentines. Until then I had done only the most basic baking: brownies and birthday cakes when the occasion demanded, not much more. Yet once I started, I found that this was how I loved spending the day: creating pastries that would delight the eye as well as the belly.

I baked heart-shaped sugar cookies, glazed them in lavender and pink, and decorated them with velvet flowers, miniature angels, silver sugar pearls, and colored crystals. They were elaborately campy concoctions that could have been eaten, I suppose, although I thought of them more as romantic gifts to be saved and savored. I arranged them on trays lined with purple satin, and trotted off to present my wares to four Cambridge art galleries and one food shop called Baby Watson Cheesecake.

The cookies were a hit, and Baby Watson called me early the next morning. "What else can you bake?" they demanded. I was on my way. There was the chocolate layer cake I made for birthdays, a carrot cake whose recipe had come from a friend's mother in California, and my own brownies, which I had perfected when I realized that I didn't want to go through life without a really good brownie recipe. Beyond that, I was starting from scratch. I began to investigate recipes, but I was seldom satisfied—too sweet, not chocolaty enough, too many additions. So I experimented and learned. I created Boom Booms, Harvard Squares, Chocolate Orgasms, Queen Raspberries . . . the names entered the Cambridge lexicon. I called them all my BabyCakes and went into the baking business.

I lugged hundred-pound bags of flour up to my second-floor apartment, where every doorknob was coated with chocolate. I learned to sleep with sugar in my bed and ignore that my floor crunched as I walked on it. I invested in a twenty-quart professional mixer and thirty-gallon trash cans to hold the sugar and flour. I woke at five in the morning and baked, took a quick run while the pastries cooled, then delivered them to Harvard Square, where customers lined up in anticipation. I must have been quite a sight, almost an emblem of the era, in my hot pants and platform shoes with a hairdo that stuck out about a foot from my head. I was having the time of my life.

Everything moved so quickly in the beginning that within six months I had outgrown the kitchen in my apartment. I built a new kitchen adjacent to Baby Watson, right in the heart of Harvard Square, and enclosed it in glass so that customers buying my goods could see the baking process. It was like a movie set, complete with custom-built cherry cabinets and cut-crystal knobs, an Art Deco lantern with satin shades, Edwardian botanical prints on the walls, and the insistent pulse of Toots and the Maytals in the background.

HELLO, ROSIE'S

After almost three years of working there and selling through Baby Watson, the next obvious step was to market my pastries myself. So I opened my own store in Inman Square in Cambridge and named it Rosie's as a declaration of independence. This new place was a full-range bakery where you could pick up a muffin and coffee on your way to work, a pie to take home for dinner, or a custom-made cake decorated for a special celebration. If you had the time, there were tables where you could indulge in a brownie and a cup of tea while discussing the soaps, a proposal for work, or the meaning of life. Over time Rosie's became the incongruous but appealing combination of a friend's kitchen, a neighborhood bar, and a thriving bakery.

In those first days, though, going from Harvard Square to Inman Square was a shock. The two neighborhoods are less than a mile apart, but when Rosie's arrived, Inman could be most charitably described as "funky." Since restaurants and jazz clubs were opening there, we did a lot of business late at night when people came from all over the city. During the day we were a neighborhood attraction and had our regulars. There was the professor who came in every morning to read his newspaper over coffee and a lemon poppy-seed muffin, and a guy writing his magnum opus—about what I never found out—in daily sessions at one of our tables. We had little kids counting out pennies to buy a treat, mothers with baby carriages converging every afternoon at about three o'clock, doctors and nurses from Cambridge City Hospital who never ordered fewer than twenty items for takeout, and the firemen of Cambridge Local 30 who gave us a plaque in appreciation of our hospitality and pastries after a particularly bad fire nearby.

Graduate students who had once gotten stoned to the strains of the Velvet Underground stood shoulder-to-shoulder with businessmen who had never heard of the rock group but hungered just as avidly for our dark chocolate cake of the same name. Genteel women ordered Chocolate Orgasms in elegant but unflinching tones, while our nonchocolate products developed equally loyal followings since rugalah, butter cookies, and shortbread seemed appropriate tributes to everyone's grandmother, no matter what her heritage.

In a neighborhood then short on decoration, the pink neon sign in our window drew people in, and, once inside, they stayed, mostly for the goodies but also for the homey atmosphere. I had determined from the first that Rosie's would be a treat not just for the taste buds but for all the senses, so I painted and decorated, lugged in overstuffed furniture, and made sure we had fresh flowers every week.

Since those early years, Rosie's has grown larger and more established. What began as a whim in Harvard Square now delights residents of Cambridge, Chestnut Hill, and Boston's South Station. In the intervening years, my first customers have cut their hair, put on suits, acquired kids, mortgages, and life insurance, and ventured beyond the rarified atmosphere of "the Square." But what hasn't changed is their desire for a little something from Rosie's, and they still indulge it, even if that now means having to go out of their way.

So it's sometimes tempting to view Rosie's as an inevitability—you know, the hand of fate gently nudging me in that direction from birth, all that lust and denial as a rite of passage. Or maybe it was bred in the bone, this taking my chocolate very seriously and insisting on the best. Not that it matters, really. When you're having so much fun, it seems greedy to question fate.

CHAPTER 1
Common Sense Baking

We all have certain conversations that get repeated so often we could conduct them in our sleep. Mine begins, "No kidding! You own Rosie's? Where did you study baking?" When I answer that I didn't but learned on my own, the response is often amazement. But what's amazing to me is that so many people don't believe it's possible. It makes me wonder who has been perpetuating this myth that baking involves a delicate chemical reaction that only the chosen few can control. And, more to the point, it makes me ask where all the hocus-pocus has gotten us. I mean, how many oh-so-stylish Baba au Hazelnut Tortes do we have to try before we admit that both Aunt Esther and our college roommate's mother could whip up better at a moment's notice?

I don't mean to denigrate expertise, but all this training business should be put in perspective. Baking does involve chemical reactions, but so does taking an aspirin. While you may not reach baker's heaven on your first try, if good food is important to you, if you like desserts, and if you can count, none of the recipes in this book are beyond you. It's as simple as that. Baking can also be fun; there are even those among us who find it more therapeutic than a hot bath or a session on the couch, and that's not even considering its more tangible rewards.

Now, about achieving those tangible rewards. Let's start with one basic rule I learned from my years on the baking front: Don't let yourself be intimidated. That may sound simple, but bear in mind that these are the words of a woman who used to panic whenever a recipe called for beaten egg whites. I was sure I had a genetic inability to tell if they were stiff or soft enough, and even if by some miracle I made it past that hurdle, who knew how gently I should be folding the stiff-soft whites into the batter? I had myself convinced that if I beat the egg whites one second too long, the entire enterprise would be a flop. And you know what? It often was, fear of failure being one of those things that fulfills itself with depressing regularity.

Only slightly daunted though, I remembered that old chestnut about learning from my mistakes, and I now stand before you a reformed egg beater. The moral of this story (and the trick with more than just egg whites) is to develop a feel for what you're doing and the confidence to make adjustments. That's where real creativity comes from, because when you're in control, you feel freer to experiment.

There's something to be said for serendipity, too. I've put too little flour in a cake only to find that it came out lighter, and the time I forgot to add the eggs to pumpkin bread, I ended up liking the texture better without them. Archimedes, on discovering the principle of displacement of water, was said to have run naked through the streets shouting, "Eureka! I have found it!" I merely file my discoveries in the back of my mind to use for future creations.

In addition to goofs, there are lots of factors that affect how a recipe comes out, and you can't be aware of all of them before you start. Your oven may bake differently from mine, your apples may be less juicy, or your eggs larger. That's where adaptability and experience come in.

First you learn that time-honored baking ritual in which you take something out of the oven, hit yourself on the forehead, and say, "Darn, I should have thought of that!" Next you figure out how to adjust your oven temperature so that your cake layers don't have a crust or how much juice to add to keep your apple pies from drying out. One of the joys of baking is that problems have solutions, and they're often a matter of common sense.

Aside from the power of positive thinking and the incantation I chant over each batch

BAKING TEMPERATURE AND TIMES

I can't emphasize enough how important it is to remember that oven temperatures vary greatly from oven to oven and sometimes even from week to week in the same oven. Consequently baking times will vary, too. Don't take the times suggested in the book too literally; rely on the visual descriptions of the various stages and finished product, as well as the techniques suggested to test for doneness.

of brownies that I'm not at liberty to disclose, I have a few suggestions that should help you avoid basic problems in baking and keep your frustration level within reason.

METHOD TO THE MADNESS

Soul and panache go a long way in making a good baker, but it helps to be organized and systematic, too, and I don't make that suggestion lightly. When I left home and my mother's compulsion for tidiness, I realized that by nature I'm a slob. So it wasn't until years later that I also realized my mother was on to something. Chaos makes baking twice as hard. I don't always practice what I preach, but nonetheless I'd like to pass on to you: *Rosie's Five Steps to Carefree Baking, Longer Life, and Gaining Permission to Use Your Mother's Kitchen:*

1. First, read the entire recipe so that there are no surprises. It's a pain to discover halfway through that you're out of an essential ingredient and can't finish baking without a trip to the store.

2. Line up, pour, measure, and count out all your ingredients in advance, replacing boxes and containers as you go along to avoid confusion (as in: Uh oh, is that white mound in the batter baking soda or baking powder?).

3. Avoid distractions: chatty phone calls, drop-in visits, disgruntled children pulling at your apron strings, the soaps, or Ellen DeGeneres. You may think you're concentrating, but sooner or later you will be rummaging through the garbage counting egg shells to figure out how many you've cracked.

4. Bake when you're not tense or in a hurry. Otherwise baking becomes a chore, not a pleasure, and you're more likely to make mistakes.

5. Make sure you understand basic baking techniques and try to become comfortable with the procedures explained in the recipes you use so that you can deepen your confidence and expand your creativity.

THE RIGHT STUFF

When you're stocking up on ingredients, keep in mind that it's hard to improve on nature when it comes to food, so you're on firm ground if you rely on fresh, pure items as much as possible. That doesn't mean that you have to buy the most expensive ingredients or that all things imported are heaven-blessed, despite what many gourmet shops would have us believe. But baking with second-rate ingredients is like playing a sonata on a kazoo; it's not the real thing and it's not as good.

Check the pantry box on page 4 for a list of all-important baking ingredients.

EQUIPMENT

As with ingredients, having the equipment you need on hand will make baking convenient and more spontaneous. It's easy to go overboard on kitchenware, though, what with those seductive displays at kitchen

ROSIE'S PANTRY

Most of my recipes call for ingredients that your supermarket stocks regularly, but if you want to be able to bake from this cookbook with a degree of spontaneity ("I think I'll whip up a little chocolate mousse cake tonight in case this blizzard lasts another week"), here are the ingredients you should keep in good supply in your pantry.

Unbleached all-purpose flour

Cake flour (not self-rising)

Baking soda

Baking powder

Cornstarch

Granulated sugar

Brown sugar (light and dark)

Confectioners' sugar

Molasses

Honey

Corn syrup (light and dark)

Unsalted butter

Unflavored gelatin

Fruit preserves

Raisins

Peanut butter (salted or unsalted)

Instant espresso or other good-quality coffee powder

Pure vanilla extract

Almond extract

Salt

Spices: ground ginger, cinnamon, nutmeg, mace, allspice, cloves

Sweetened shredded coconut

Semisweet chocolate chips

Unsweetened chocolate

shops and all the fads. Remember fondue pots and yogurt makers, those necessities of the seventies? And before you make major purchases, I suggest you shop around, because prices can vary widely. You might start at a commercial kitchen supply store. They usually offer a large selection, sturdy quality, and reasonable prices.

To make the recipes in this book easily and successfully, regardless of where you acquire your tools, I recommend that you equip your kitchen with as many of the following items as possible:

ELECTRIC MIXER with paddle and whisk attachments and two mixing bowls. If your budget allows, invest in a mixer mounted on a base, as opposed to a handheld one, for the simple reason that it leaves your hands free. The extra bowl is essential for cakes that require beaten egg whites. The KitchenAid mixer is the absolute best.

FOOD PROCESSOR. Great for preparing pie crusts, chopping nuts and chocolate, making Bavarians or fillings for tarts, and on and on. I don't know what I did without one.

TWO 8-INCH LAYER CAKE PANS (2 inches deep) of heavy metal.

TWO 9-INCH LAYER CAKE PANS (2 inches deep) of heavy metal.

ONE 9-INCH AND ONE 10-INCH SPRINGFORM PAN, although you can usually get away with only the smaller one.

STANDARD JELLY-ROLL PAN, 15 × 10¼ inches.

TWO SQUARE PANS: 8 inches and 9 inches.

TWO RECTANGULAR PANS: 11 × 7 inches and 13 × 9 inches.

SOME NOTES ON INGREDIENTS

BUTTER: Keep in mind as you follow these recipes that melted butter is not equal to solid butter in terms of measurement. For example, 6 tablespoons of melted butter equals approximately 5½ tablespoons of solid butter. Always remeasure the butter once it's melted to make sure you are using the correct amount.

CAKE FLOUR (NOT SELF-RISING): This flour is lighter than all-purpose flour because it contains less gluten. Although the standard wisdom says that 1 cup of all-purpose flour equals 1 cup plus 2 tablespoons of cake flour, I find that when I substitute all-purpose flour, I often have to adjust other ingredients to avoid getting a powdery texture. So to make life simple, I recommend using cake flour when it's called for. Convenience stores and smaller markets don't usually stock it, but you'll find it at large supermarkets.

SUGAR: Granulated and light and dark brown sugar differ in moisture and mass, though they are the same in weight. This means that the drier granulated sugar tends to produce crunchier cookies and slightly drier cakes when it is substituted for equal amounts of brown sugar. Also, dark brown sugar has a higher molasses content than light brown sugar, so the equivalent cup measure weighs more. When you substitute dark for light, you need smaller amounts. You can make accurate substitutions if you have an ounce scale. In other words, 6 ounces of granulated sugar equals 6 ounces of light brown sugar equals 6 ounces of dark brown sugar.

CHOCOLATE: I've spent my lifetime thinking and dreaming about chocolate, and I still swear by Baker's when it comes to baking chocolate. I find the taste to be real, unadulterated, and exactly what I think chocolate should be. You'll find a lot of cookbooks and chefs who recommend imported chocolate, but I haven't found any that's better than our homegrown variety for baking.

That said, I make two exceptions to the rule. For chocolate chips, I like Nestlé. Whatever brand you buy, make sure that they're real chocolate, not "chocolate flavored." And for making glazes, I've found that the more expensive chocolates do have a smoother texture, so I use Lindt bittersweet chocolate. Often, when a recipe calls for semisweet chocolate, I'll substitute bittersweet for one-third to one-half of the amount because I feel it adds more depth to the chocolate flavor.

EGGS: Uncooked eggs can be a source of *Salmonella* bacteria, which causes food poisoning. If you are unsure of the quality of the eggs you buy, avoid recipes that use them raw.

BUNDT PAN or **TUBE PAN** 10-inch-diameter with a removable bottom.

TWO LOAF PANS, about 9 × 5 × 3 inches.

TWO STANDARD PIE PLATES, 9 × 1½ inches.

DEEP-DISH PIE PLATE, 9 × 2 inches, usually made of Pyrex.

TWO BAKING SHEETS, 15 × 12 inches, standard, heavy weight. I don't care for the air-cushion baking sheets—they tend to take the crunch out and leave the cookies soggy. I'd use them only for baking cakelike cookies.

TWO COOLING RACKS.

TWO BAKING DISHES for puddings and custards, preferably ceramic: 1½ quarts and 2½ to 3 quarts.

DOUBLE BOILER, 3 quarts, heavy weight.

BARE ESSENTIALS

Having listed what may appear to be enough equipment to outfit Buckingham Palace, let me say that I know many bakers who wouldn't be able to fit into their kitchen if they followed my suggestions to the letter. Never fear, there's no question that you can bake successfully without purchasing a whole battery of equipment.

Of course, with less equipment you will have to make some common-sense recipe adjustments. For example, if a recipe calls for baking brownies in an 11 × 7-inch pan and you only have an 8-inch square pan, your brownies will be thicker and therefore should bake more slowly and at a temperature 25 degrees lower than the one called for. If you bake a recipe calling for 8-inch layers in a 9-inch layer pan, they will require a shorter baking time because the batter level will be lower. Use your judgment; if the results are less than perfect, you'll know to make further adjustments next time.

If you want to start off easy, here are the important items to have on hand:

1 electric mixer, stationary or handheld	1 measuring cup (2-cup size) for liquid ingredients
2 round layer cake pans, 8 or 9 inches	1 set measuring spoons
1 springform pan, 9 or 10 inches	1 set small, medium-size, and large mixing bowls
2 baking sheets	
1 standard pie plate, 9 × 1½ inches	1 rubber spatula
	1 handheld whisk
1 set graduated measuring cups for dry ingredients	1 wooden spoon
	1 rolling pin

SAUCEPAN, 3 quarts, heavy weight.

THREE OR FOUR SMALL BOWLS: 2 cup and 4 cup, for cracking eggs, sifting dry ingredients, and measuring nuts.

ONE LARGE BOWL, 12 to 14 cups, for sifting flour or folding ingredients together.

TWO ATTRACTIVE BOWLS for mousses, Bavarians, and puddings: 5 cups and 2 quarts.

TWO SETS OF GRADUATED MEASURING CUPS: ¼ cup, ⅓ cup, ½ cup, and 1 cup for dry ingredients. Metal ones with handles last longest.

PYREX MEASURING CUP, for liquids, 2 cup.

TWO SETS OF METAL MEASURING SPOONS.

TWO STURDY, STANDARD-SIZE RUBBER OR SILICONE SPATULAS, 9½ inches long (even better, make your second one commercial-quality, 13½ inches long—available at a kitchen supply store).

ONE VERY SMALL RUBBER SPATULA

STANDARD METAL SPATULA to remove cookies from baking sheets.

STANDARD METAL FROSTING (OFFSET) SPATULA, 10 inches long and 1½ inches wide, for icing cakes and for leveling off dry ingredients in measuring cups.

SMALL HAND WHISK, 8 inches long, and a standard whisk, 12 inches long, for beating by hand.

STANDARD SIZE OR LARGER ROLLING PIN.

PIE WEIGHTS.

LARGE WOODEN SPOON for mixing puddings and custards.

TIMER AND A CLOCK or watch with a second hand.

TWO STRAINERS, about 3 and 5 inches in diameter.

TWO SHARP KNIVES, one thin and one sturdy.

ONE 10- OR 12-INCH PASTRY BAG with writing tips for decorating cakes.

BAKING PARCHMENT for lining baking sheets and cake pans (also consider parchment cake pan liners).

PLASTIC WRAP OR WAXED PAPER for rolling dough.

A FINAL WORD

I confess that I began this book with grand ambitions. It was to be a cookbook that grew dog-eared and smudged with fingerprints from generations of use while the recipes wormed their way into family lore and got trotted out along with the old photos. You know, my recipes were the ones referred to in statements like: "I've still never run across anyone who can make brownies as scrumptious as my father's," or "Every time I visited my grandmother, she used to make this really incredible chocolate cake with raspberries."

I still hope for something like that. But, as I mentioned earlier, my more immediate goal is to demystify baking through common sense, because I'm convinced that that is the key to successful and happy baking. In an odd way I was lucky in my baking career. Lacking formal training, I learned what I know through passion,

SOME NOTES ON EQUIPMENT

ELECTRIC MIXERS: The recipes in this book were tested with a KitchenAid mixer, which is more powerful than a standard hand mixer, so your mixing times may vary from the ones noted. When you're mixing batters, use the paddle attachment, if you have one. Save the whisk for whipping cream and egg whites and yolks.

MICROWAVE OVENS: I'm crossing my fingers we won't discover someday that microwaves turn teeth green or make our great-grandchildren grow horns, because I use mine constantly in baking. It's wonderful for melting butter and chocolate; bringing eggs, cold butter, liquids, sour cream, or cream cheese to room temperature; and softening hard brown sugar. Test your microwave to find the best temperatures and times for the results you're looking for, since ovens vary. But, for the most part, avoid all high temperatures.

instinct, and trial and error, and these still seem to me to be the best teachers anyone—novice or pro—can find.

So my final advice is to trust my recipes but trust yourself as well. After all, the worst that can happen is that you make a mistake—and one of the joys of baking is that the majority of our mistakes are edible.

Cakes

1

CHAPTER 2

Piece of Cake

From birthday cakes adorned with plastic ballerinas or cowboys and Indians, to wedding cakes worthy of Claes Oldenburg, it's hard to imagine a proper anniversary or holiday as a cakeless event. So, early on, Rosie's started developing an array of cakes for every occasion.

I began with a little something chocolate, of course: Rosie's Famous Chocolate–Sour Cream Layer Cake, which, when topped with ice cream, was cause for celebration in its own right. That was

followed by the Snow Queen, inspired by the yellow cakes with white frosting and raspberry jam that are the perennial mark of an authentic birthday party among the under-ten crinoline set. Next came the Velvet Underground (as decadent as the group it was named after), the Mocha Cake, Queen Raspberry, Cold Fudge Sundae, and Texas Ruby Red, which have become the mainstays of Rosie's menu.

THEME AND VARIATIONS
I learned quickly an old baker's strategy of taking a basic recipe and adding one or two things to make it into a whole new cake. For instance, once you've perfected a simple chocolate cake, you can layer it with fudge,

preserves, whipped cream, mousse, fresh or frozen fruit, bananas and cream, or liqueur, and—voilà!—have seven additional cakes in your repertoire. Or take the humble pound cake, which, like one of those makeovers in a fashion magazine, can be plain at morning coffee, be dressed tastefully with fruit for afternoon tea, or be transformed into a rich layer cake for a ritzy dinner party. And you get to call the cake something different in each of its incarnations—naming is half the fun.

Since getting a cake just right can take some doing, you need something that comes easily at the beginning. Cake batters can be finicky, and a slight variation, such as the sequence in which ingredients are added, the mixing technique, or the baking time and temperature, can affect the outcome greatly.

Telling someone how to bake a cake gets complicated because nearly every rule has an exception. To try to simplify things in the following sections, I've identified basic rules. Where there are exceptions to the rules, I've noted in the recipe how to deal with them.

PREPARING THE PAN FOR EASY CAKE REMOVAL

LAYER CAKES: Do yourself a favor and line your baking pans with inserts made of baking parchment, which are larger versions of muffin papers and are usually available at kitchen stores. This way, you won't have to grease or flour your pans, and because the batter doesn't touch the sides of the pan, your cake edges come out moist and spongy.

If you don't have ready-made liners, I recommend making a partial liner for the bottom of the pan using parchment rather than waxed paper, which smokes as it heats.

To cut parchment circles from a larger roll, place the baking pan right side up on the paper and trace around the base of the pan with a pen or pencil. Cut out the shape with scissors just inside the outline and place the paper cutout in the bottom of the pan. Lightly grease the pan side.

Regardless of whether you grease the pan or use parchment, it's best to cool all your cakes on a cooling rack and to leave the layer in the pan until you're ready to frost the cake. If you leave it for any length of time, cover it with plastic wrap after it has cooled.

When you use a pan insert, after the layer has baked and cooled, pick it up by the edge of the insert and lift it out of the pan onto a plate. Remove the insert just before you frost the layers. When you've used circles cut out of parchment, after the cake has baked and cooled, run a frosting spatula around the edge to loosen it. Then turn the pan upside down at a 45-degree angle and allow the layer to drop onto your hand. Peel the parchment off with your other hand and flip the layer onto a plate.

If you have neither paper inserts nor baking parchment, use a small piece of paper towel to grease the pan lightly and thoroughly with vegetable oil or butter. Then, when the layer has cooled but is still slightly warm, run the spatula along the edge to loosen it, turn the pan over, and, holding the layer in place with your hand, tap the pan lightly on the counter as you rotate it. When the layer has loosened, let it fall onto your palm, then flip it over onto a plate.

TUBE AND BUNDT PANS: Parchment doesn't work here, so grease these pans lightly with butter or oil, paying special attention to where the center tube meets the bottom of the pan because cakes tend to stick there. Pans without removable bottoms require particularly thorough greasing.

When the cake has cooled in the pan, run a flat frosting spatula around its sides. If the bottom is removable, lift it out, then run the spatula between the cake and the bottom of the pan and leave it under one side of the cake. Place a second spatula or a knife under the opposite side of the cake and use both to lift the cake off the pan bottom. (I sometimes press my chin against the top of the tube to help release the tube from the cake, too.) Put the cake on a plate and cover it with plastic wrap until you're ready to frost or serve it.

For chiffon and angel food cakes, use a tube pan with a removable bottom and don't grease it because grease keeps them from rising. When cooling the cake, rest it upside down on the counter to prevent it from dropping back into the pan. If the tube pan isn't high enough to keep the top of the cake from touching the counter, stick a funnel or bottle into the hole of the pan, then turn it upside down and balance it on

the funnel. Either way, after the cake cools for about 1½ hours, run a spatula around the sides and bottom and remove it the same as you would above.

SPRINGFORM PANS: This is an either/or situation vis-à-vis inserts or greasing. If you've greased the pan, when the cake has cooled, run a spatula around its edge, release the pan's lock, and remove the side of the pan. Then run a spatula between the cake and the bottom of the pan and use the spatula and your hand or two spatulas to lift the cake onto a plate.

If you have time to chill the cake (for a minimum of 6 hours) after baking, it will be sturdy enough to invert out of the pan. In this case, you should line the bottom with a parchment circle. Chill the cake in the pan, then run a spatula around its edge and release the sides. Turn the cake upside down onto a plate or counter, remove the pan bottom, and peel off the paper. Then flip the cake right side up, if necessary (depending on the type of cake, the bottom can be more attractive than the top and easier to frost).

SQUARE AND RECTANGULAR PANS: If you plan to frost your cake in the pan and cut it into squares to serve, then it's best to grease the bottom and sides of the pan with butter or oil. If, however, you want to take the cake out of the pan in one piece and serve it on a plate, I'd go with a parchment liner. Let the cake cool, run a spatula around the edges, invert the pan onto a plate, drop the cake out, and then remove the parchment. When you don't have parchment but want to remove the cake, grease the pan and remove the cake from the pan while it is still slightly warm with the assistance of your trusty metal spatula.

MUFFIN/CUPCAKE TINS: You don't have to be a kid to love cupcakes. They're portion controlled, transportable, festive, and best of all, fun to eat. If you're a cupcake fan, keep a couple of muffin tins and a package of muffin cup liners on hand. I find that the paper liners keep the outside of the cupcake moist and make life very easy when it comes to removing the cupcakes from the tin. If you don't have liners, just be sure that each muffin cup is well greased with vegetable oil before pouring in the batter.

Once baked, cool the cupcakes in the pan. If you've used paper liners, the cupcakes should lift right out. If you've greased the pan instead, run a thin knife or spatula around the cupcakes and gently pick them up by their tops. Sometimes it's necessary to place the pan on an angle and tap it lightly on the counter to release the unpapered cupcakes.

LOAF PANS: To line a loaf pan, cut a piece of parchment paper big enough to overhang the sides and ends by a couple of inches when it is molded into the pan. After the loaf has cooled, lift up the overhang and slide a metal spatula along the inner edges of the pan. Use the overhang to lift the cake gently out of the pan. Loosen the parchment by holding the overhang and tipping the cake gently from side to side. Carefully slide the cake off the paper.

MIXING THE BATTER

So much depends on texture that, to me, it contributes as much to a cake's character as does its flavor. A cake's texture depends largely on the way you mix the batter, and there are basic rules for mixing that will stand you in good stead.

I've found it useful to divide mixing techniques into five categories, and once again, I suggest you find the one that applies to the recipe you're making. This system is imperfect, however (too much order makes me nervous), and a few recipes in this chapter blithely defy all my categories.

Before you begin to follow any of these methods, it's very important that all of your ingredients be at room temperature, unless the recipe specifies otherwise. This makes it easier to mix everything together thoroughly.

CREAMING METHOD: This is a standard method for mixing cakes, such as Poppy-Seed Pound Cake and Breakfast Coffeecake, that have a high fat content (for example, eggs, butter, and margarine). You alternate adding liquid and dry ingredients so that the flour helps the butter blend with the liquid. These cakes have a sturdy texture, but can vary in lightness and density.

1. Sift all the dry ingredients except for the sugar together into a small bowl.

2. Blend the butter and sugar with the paddle attachment of an electric mixer set on medium or medium-high speed until light and fluffy.

3. Add the eggs one at a time to the butter mixture (unless the recipe says otherwise) and beat at medium-low to medium speed until each one is distributed evenly. Scrape the bottom and side of the bowl with a rubber spatula once during the mixing. Then turn the mixer to medium-high speed and mix until light and fluffy.

4. Add the dry ingredients to the butter, sugar, and egg mixture, alternating with the liquid. To do this, set the mixer on low speed, add one-third of the dry ingredients, and mix just until they are blended. Scrape the bowl with the spatula each time new ingredients are blended in. Next add half the liquid; blend and scrape. Follow this with another one-third

SOME NOTES ON PROCEDURES

TO SEPARATE AN EGG: Hold a raw egg over a bowl and crack its shell open around the middle with a knife. Gently separate the two halves of the shell, keeping the yolk in one half while letting the white run through your fingers into the bowl. Take care not to allow any of the yolk to get into the white, then slide the yolk into a separate bowl.

TO DIVIDE A YOLK IN TWO (WHEN YOU WANT TO HALVE A RECIPE): Follow the procedure for separating an egg, but rather than sliding the yolk into a bowl at the end, slide it into the palm of your hand. With a sharp knife—careful, now—slice through the yolk's center and push half off your hand into the cake batter. Save the other half to scramble into your kid's eggs.

TO MELT CHOCOLATE IN A DOUBLE BOILER: Place the chocolate in the top of a double boiler; the water in the bottom shouldn't touch the top pan. Cover the top pot and allow the water to simmer until the chocolate is about two-thirds melted—the shape will still be discernible but the chocolate will be soft. Turn the heat off and let the chocolate continue to melt completely. Once melted, remove the top pot to allow the chocolate to cool, if necessary.

TO MEASURE DRY INGREDIENTS: This includes flour, sugar, cocoa, confectioners' sugar and others. Use individual measuring cups (1 cup, ½ cup, ⅓ cup, ¼ cup, ⅛ cup, and so on) and spoons (1 tablespoon, 1 teaspoon, etc.). Scoop the ingredients into the cup or spoon, then level the top by scraping off the excess with a frosting spatula.

of the dry ingredients; blend and scrape. Add the remaining liquid; blend and scrape. Then add the remaining dry ingredients and—do I sound like a caller at a square dance?—blend just until everything is incorporated and scrape again. If the recipe doesn't call for liquid, add the dry ingredients in two parts, mixing just until blended.

5. Use your spatula to complete the blending by hand.

6. Pour the batter into the prepared pan and bake the cake immediately.

CREAMING WITH SEPARATED EGGS METHOD:
This method is good for recipes such as Sour Cherry Fudge Cake and Pineapple Upside-Down Cake. Because the whites are beaten to a froth before being added to the batter, this method produces a lighter cake.

1. Follow the Creaming Method through step 2, but separate the egg yolks from the egg whites and set the whites apart in a grease-free bowl.

2. Add the egg yolks to the butter and sugar mixture and beat until incorporated, using the paddle attachment of an electric mixer set on medium-low speed.

3. Add the dry ingredients and liquid alternately as in the standard Creaming Method (step 4).

4. Whip the egg whites with a clean whisk attachment on medium speed until they are frothy. Gradually add the sugar reserved for the whites over a span of about 20 seconds. Increase the speed to high and beat until they form firm but not dry peaks. Add one-third of the egg whites to the batter and whisk gently to lighten the batter. Fold the remaining egg whites in with a rubber spatula.

5. Pour the batter into a prepared pan and bake the cake immediately.

STANDARD SPONGE METHOD: This type of cake, such as Lemon-Strawberry Sponge Roll and Chocolate Custard Sponge Roll, usually contains little or no butter or oil and gets its sponginess from the air in the eggs. The mixing process begins by foaming the eggs, that is, beating air into them with a whisk or paddle. Sometimes the whole egg is foamed, other times the egg yolks are foamed separately from the whites, or just the whites are foamed.

1. Sift the dry ingredients together into a small bowl.

2. Separate the egg yolks from the egg whites, and set the whites aside in a grease-free

mixing bowl. Put the yolks in a separate medium-size mixing bowl and, with the whisk attachment of an electric mixer, beat them with the sugar at high speed until they are thick and pale.

3. Sift the dry ingredients over the egg yolk mixture, then fold it in with a rubber spatula.

4. Whip the egg whites with a clean whisk attachment on medium-low speed until they are frothy. Increase the speed to medium and gradually add the sugar reserved for the whites. Beat until they form firm but not dry peaks. Fold the egg whites into the batter gently by hand right away.

5. Pour the batter into the prepared pan and bake immediately.

BUTTER SPONGE METHOD: This type of cake is similar to the one above but includes melted butter, producing a cake that is somewhat denser and richer. Desert Island Butter Cake, for example, uses this method.

1. Sift all the dry ingredients except for the sugar into a small bowl.

2. In a medium-size mixing bowl, beat the eggs and sugar with the whisk attachment of an electric mixer at high speed until the mixture is thick and pale, 4 to 5 minutes.

3. While the eggs and sugar are beating, melt the butter.

4. Sift the dry ingredients a second time over the egg and butter mixture and fold them in carefully with a rubber spatula.

5. Fold the melted butter in with the spatula.

6. Pour the batter into the prepared pan and bake immediately.

TWO-BOWL METHOD: Batters containing a lot of sugar and more liquid than usual (for example, eggs, milk, or juice) use this method. The batter is usually runny before baking, and the texture of these cakes can vary considerably. Rosie's Famous Chocolate–Sour Cream Cake Layers and Lemon-Glazed Orange Chiffon Cake both use this method.

1. Sift the dry ingredients together into a medium-size mixing bowl. Add the butter

or oil and mix on low speed, using the paddle attachment of an electric mixer.

2. If the recipe calls for melted chocolate, mix it in now.

3. Stir the eggs together with the liquid ingredients in a separate bowl and add the liquid in a stream to the dry ingredients, while mixing at low speed. Mix just until the batter is blended.

4. The batter will be thin, but pour it into the prepared pan and bake immediately.

ON THE WAY TO THE OVEN

Few recipes I've come across pay attention to the steps between mixing the batter and getting it into the oven. Yet how the batter sits in the pan is crucial to the baking process. Loose (thin) batters should be poured directly into a prepared pan by tipping the mixing bowl at a sharp angle and using your trusty rubber spatula to direct the flow and to scrape the bowl clean. The batter needs to be distributed evenly in the pan to bake well, so rock the pan gently from side to side to achieve this. With thicker batters, use a rubber spatula to scoop it from the bowl and to spread it evenly in the pan.

The tricky question though (and one my mother never really answered) is, when is enough enough? It's important to know how full a pan should be. Too much batter in the pan can overflow, and, even if it doesn't, the edges of the cake will overcook before the center is done. With too little batter, the cake won't rise or brown properly. Layer,

springform, and sheet cake pans should be between one-half and two-thirds full. Bundt and tube pans should be two-thirds full. So if you don't have a large enough pan, put the right amount of batter in the one you have and make cupcakes from what's left over. If you don't have a small enough pan, borrow one from your neighbor.

INTO THE OVEN

So now you've got the properly mixed batter properly poured into the proper size pan, and all that's left is to get the cake into the oven—properly. But oven temperature and the position of your oven racks are crucial to attaining the proper taste and texture. No matter what kind of cake you're baking, you want to place it in the center of a rack that is positioned in the center of the oven, where the heat is most even. When baking layer cakes, make sure that the pans are at least 1 to 1½ inches apart and arrange them on a slight diagonal so that they can both take advantage of this sweet spot in the oven.

The majority of cakes bake at 350°F, but several kinds require a slightly different temperature. When an oven is too hot, a cake rises too quickly, often forming an underdone mound at the center and a dark crust at the edges. When an oven is too cool, a cake, unlike the sun, never rises.

SPONGE ROLL: I bake this type of cake (such as Chocolate Custard Sponge Roll and Lemon-Strawberry Sponge Roll) at 400°F. Because there's usually less than an inch of batter in the pan, the cake can bake quickly and evenly without burning or drying out, even at this high temperature.

FLOURLESS AND CHIFFON CAKES: These cakes (such as Chocolate Truffle Soufflé Cake and Lemon-Glazed Orange Chiffon Cake) contain a number of beaten egg whites and often call for an oven set between 300°F and 325°F so that they will bake evenly and rise gently.

CHEESECAKES: Because cheesecake batter is heavy and doesn't rise much anyway, I use a lower temperature, usually 300°F. In this cooler oven, cheesecake bakes slowly and evenly and its surface is less likely to crack. Try putting a shallow pan of hot water on the oven rack below; its steam will keep the cake moist. You can turn the oven off when the cake is done and leave it inside to set for 1 hour. By avoiding a quick change in temperature, you can often keep your cake from dropping or cracking. Or you can cool it on a wire rack. I've had success both ways.

AND OUT OF THE OVEN

Ovens vary; that's one of those truisms like fish swim and birds fly, only with fewer exceptions. It's for that reason that I suggest you first look at your cake about 10 minutes before the end of the baking time suggested in the recipe. To tell if it's done then, consider three indicators in the following order:

1. How the cake looks.
2. What the cake feels like when you touch it lightly.
3. Whether a tester inserted into the center comes out clean.

Layers will spring back to the touch; cheesecakes will feel firm; Bundt cakes will have a rounded crisp top, and cakes baked in jelly-roll pans will be spongy in texture and almost level. Every recipe in this book

SPLITTING LAYERS

To split each layer in two through the thickness, put the full layers on a piece of waxed paper on a flat surface, such as a counter or table. Place the blade of a long, thin knife at the midpoint of the first layer. With your free hand resting lightly on the top of the layer, slice through the layer evenly, keeping the knife parallel to the flat surface. Repeat with the second full layer.

If you have a cake wheel or lazy Susan, follow these instructions, but turn the wheel carefully for a full revolution as you cut through the middle of the layer.

describes what the cake should look like when it's finished baking, but the most dependable test is to insert a tester or a long wooden skewer in the center of the cake when you think it's done. (I don't use the time-honored toothpick because it's seldom long enough to get to the bottom of the cake.) If the tester comes out dry or with a few crumbs on it, the cake is done. If it comes out at all wet, the cake isn't done and needs to be baked a little longer, after which you should test it again. Don't remove the cake from the oven when performing this test, just slide the cake forward on the rack or gently slide out the rack.

THE EYES HAVE IT

On more than one occasion I have argued for an anatomical connection between the eyes and the appetite, but even if there isn't one, there is surely a sensual relationship. So how your cake looks can add to its appeal. I'm partial to decoration that enhances the taste and appearance of the cake without overwhelming the cake itself. I find desserts that proclaim "Look at me!" are about as appealing as people who do, and it's been my experience that cakes with gobs of sugary frosting lose their allure shortly after one's tenth birthday.

The simplest decoration for a cake is a modest amount of frosting, although getting the frosting on evenly and neatly takes several steps. Before beginning make sure your cake has cooled to room temperature.

Filling and Frosting a Two-Layer Cake

1. To keep the plate clean, cut 4 strips of parchment or waxed paper, each 3 inches wide and 2 inches longer than the diameter of your cake. Arrange the strips around the edge of your cake plate to form a square with the ends of the strips overlapping. Put the plate on a cake wheel or lazy Susan, if you have one.
2. Place one layer right side up on the plate so that the strips of paper are under the outer edge of the cake with their ends sticking out.
3. Using a frosting spatula, spread frosting ¼ inch thick over the top of this layer and then stack the second layer on top.

4. Apply a thin layer of frosting to the top and sides of the cake to form a base coat that seals the cake, contains the crumbs, and makes it easier to frost.

5. Spread another layer of frosting, no more than ¼ inch thick, over the sides of the cake and smooth it out with the long, thin edge of the spatula.

6. Spread the remaining frosting over the top of the cake, smooth it out, then glide the rounded tip of a frosting spatula across the top of the cake on a diagonal to form parallel ridges. Trim off excess frosting by passing the long edge of the spatula around the circumference of the cake's top.

   If you have a cake wheel or lazy Susan, you can add a swirl by centering the cake on the wheel and spinning the wheel slowly while holding the top of the spatula at a 45-degree angle to the cake and gliding it toward the center of the cake in a continuous stroke.

7. Pull the paper strips out carefully. If there are any frosting or finger smudges on the plate, wipe them off with a damp paper towel.

If you were working on a cake wheel, ease your spatula underneath the cake and gently lift it. Use both your free hand and the spatula to support the cake as you move it to a cake plate.

Frosting a Four-Layer Cake

Follow the directions for frosting a two-layer cake, but in step 2, carefully slice each layer horizontally through its middle (see the box, page 18, on splitting layers). In step 3, spread frosting on the top of each layer before stacking on the next one. Then continue on to the next step.

Writing on a Cake

Use a #14 or #15 star tip and a 10- or 12-inch pastry bag. All of the items needed for writing are available at a cake-decorating store or online. Before beginning, write your message down on a piece of paper. Check the spelling of all words, especially names.

1. If the pastry bag is new, clip just enough of the tip off so that the plastic cone fits securely, and insert the cone. Put the metal writing tip over the end of the cone and secure it by screwing the ring in place.

2. Fold the top of the bag down once over your left hand and hold it there. With a

rubber spatula, fill the bag one-third full with frosting, then pull the collar back into place.

3. Gather up the top of the bag with your right thumb and forefinger and squeeze out any air bubbles with your palm.

4. Use your left thumb and forefinger to support and guide the bag as you write. If you're left-handed reverse these directions.

5. Again, practice writing on a piece of parchment or waxed paper before you tackle your cake; it's not erasable.

Making a Chain of Rosettes

Fit a 10- or 12-inch pastry bag with a large star tip. All the items needed to make rosettes are available at a cake-decorating store or online.

1. Remove all parchment paper strips from under the cake.

2. Follow steps 2 and 3 for writing on a cake but fill the bag half full of frosting.

3. Hold the bag as you would for writing, but keep it at a 45-degree angle with the tip touching the outer edge of the top of the cake. Squeeze the bag enough for a single rosette, then slowly pull the bag away while releasing the pressure. Continue this rocking motion until you have a chain of rosettes around the edge of the entire cake.

4. Repeat this process around the base of the cake, pointing the tip at the edge where the cake meets the plate.

Fresh Flowers

Not all decorations have to be edible. When I first started adorning my cakes, I had no idea how to make those pink, sugary roses bakeries use, and I waited for someone to discover my secret and say, "And you call yourself a baker!" So in self-defense, I found the one lavender plastic orchid in a five-and-ten that didn't look tacky and stuck it on top of a chocolate–sour cream layer cake whose rich brown frosting showed it off to distinction.

Then it dawned on me that there is an alternative to plastic, and I began to decorate cakes with real flowers. I've learned how to make the bakery buds since then, but why bother when a bouquet of fresh flowers is so much prettier?

I generally opt for unsprayed (always unsprayed!) elegant flowers such as roses, orchids, tiger lilies, dendrobium orchids, freesia, and snapdragons. Delphiniums and sweet peas are lovely as well, although they do not last more than a couple of hours. Statice, baby's breath, and any frilly or lacy flower and the like can cover stems and create texture between flowers and greens such as various ferns, fica leaves, palm spears, and ivy. The greens provide accent and structure to the bouquet. Look for variety in color, texture, and shape when you're choosing your flowers and avoid lilies of the valley and the berries on holly leaves because of their toxicity. In fact, it's always a good idea to ask your florist if the flowers that interest you are poisonous or harmful in any way.

Fresh Fruit

Fruits in season (and, for some varieties, out of season) add decoration, taste, and extra freshness to your baking. Try strawberries or raspberries arranged around the top of a frosted cake (I'm partial to berries with chocolate), or intersperse flowers with fruit. For a special touch, you can dip the strawberry peaks in melted bittersweet chocolate, allow the chocolate to harden, and then arrange the strawberries point side up on top of the cake.

You can cut thin slices of citrus fruits and press them along the sides of a frosted cake or at the base of a Bundt cake. Or you can slit the slices up the center, twist them and place them on top of the cake to give it height. Put the fruit on the cake just before serving so it won't dry out.

Chocolate Shavings

Chocolate shavings are a perfect final touch for any cake with chocolate in it. Use an ounce of unsweetened or dark chocolate. Using the fine side of a standard kitchen grater, first dust the top of the cake with shavings, then accent it with coarser gratings. For a dramatic effect, shave larger flakes onto the cake using a sharp, thin knife. Press hard as you shave to form more shardlike pieces. Allow the flakes to fall randomly over the top or around the outer edge of the cake.

Salvaging

Even the best of cooks goof on occasion; layers can come out overcooked and cakes sometimes crumble as you transfer them to a plate. That's when you revert to a salvage operation. You can slice a layer horizontally through the middle so that you have two thinner layers, and then smother each half with frozen berries in juice and whipped cream. If that won't work, cut the layers into chunks, toss them with wet fruit—raspberries, strawberries, ripe peach cubes—maybe mix in some vanilla pudding or custard, and put the whole thing in custard cups, crowning it with a piece of fruit and a dollop of whipped cream. Because you need the liquid to moisten the cake, pour the fruit's juice over the chunks as early before serving as possible.

SERVING

Presentation doesn't stop with what's on the cake but includes what the cake is presented on as well. I swear by decorative plates, which I pick up everywhere from china shops to garage sales. I'm partial to lacy paper doilies, but since cutting a frosted cake on a paper doily can be a messy business, I avoid the problem by putting the doily under the *plate* instead of under the cake.

Make sure that your doilies are crisp and clean, your flowers, berries, and nuts are fresh, and all your toppings are perched lightly on the cake, not imbedded in the frosting and looking like ships foundering at sea.

If it's theatricality you want, present your cake on a pedestal cake server and maybe add the circular straw or cloth place mat or a crocheted doily underneath. When you're serving several cakes at once, create tiers by putting one or two on a pedestal and others on flat plates or baskets turned upside down.

Consider serving a Bundt cake or a loaf cake in slices, or with half of it whole and the other half in overlapping slices like felled dominoes. If you're serving part of a Bundt or tube cake, cut thin slices and arrange them in concentric circles on a round plate. Then dress them up by sprinkling confectioners' sugar over the top and strewing strawberries or flowers over all.

Cut frosted cakes with a long, sharp, thin knife. To make each slice come out neatly, dip the knife in hot water and wipe it dry before you make each cut. But if this means bringing a bowl of water to the table, just wipe the knife well after each cut.

Pound cakes, chiffon cakes, sponge cakes, and unfrosted Bundt cakes, which are somewhat fragile, are best cut with a serrated knife, which puts less pressure on them. I find cake servers—slightly wedged-shaped spatulas—useful, especially for removing the first slice or when I'm serving frosted rectangular or square cakes from the pan.

STORING

To keep a frosted cake that has been sliced, pat plastic wrap against the cut surfaces. The wrap will stick to the cake interior and help keep the exposed part of the cake moist. If you plan to finish the cake in a day or two, keep it at room temperature, preferably under a cake dome. Longer than that, a cake needs to be refrigerated, but bring it to room temperature before you serve it again. (Cold cakes usually taste dry and bland.)

Unfrosted cakes don't have a built-in sealer, so they should be kept under a cake dome or covered completely with plastic wrap. Most unfrosted cakes will stay moist for two or three days if they're well covered.

You can freeze any cake (although a cake that's been frozen won't taste as fresh or as flavorful), but you have to seal it from the air. Tupperware dome containers work best placed over cakes wrapped in plastic. But if your generation missed out on Tupperware parties, you can wrap your cake in a layer of plastic wrap, followed by a layer of aluminum foil. Finally, put it in a heavy plastic bag and use one of those twisty things to close it up tight.

RELAXING

All these directions and admonitions—do this, don't do that—may leave you reeling and wondering why anyone in his or her right mind would bother. Bring on the Hostess Twinkies, you say, but the truth is that much of baking becomes second nature quickly.

Perhaps that's why, more than any other class of desserts, cakes seem to bear the individual stamps of their creators. Each has its own style and each has a mystique that I'd be the last to try to analyze. Instead I recommend that you follow these recipes with care, unleash your imagination when the cake comes out of the oven, and then flash a Mona Lisa smile as everyone asks you how you did it.

CHAPTER 3

Layer Cakes

Although I baked my share of cake mixes as a little girl, my most vivid memories of layer cakes were the mile high ones on glass pedestals covered by domes that lined the spotless counters at Hamburg Heaven in Manhattan. These classic American cakes were frosted in velvety buttercreams of different flavors, sometimes covered with coconut. They were irresistible. They looked even better than the ones depicted on the outside of cake mix boxes; almost too good to be real.

What is nice about layer cakes is the many choices that we have for filling and frosting them, and how different those fillings and frostings make the end result. Lemon curd, fresh fruit, chocolate ganache, preserves, and buttercreams are just a few of the many options that create different flavors and textures. These cakes can be decorated with any whimsical doodads that suit the occasion.

From the time we are one year old, most of the special days in our life are celebrated with layer cakes of all sorts—including large sheet pan cakes and single layer squares, also included here. And most of the time, we remember the cakes that made those days even more delicious.

Rosie's Famous Chocolate–Sour Cream Cake Layers

INGREDIENTS

For a two-layer cake:

Vegetable oil or butter for greasing the pans (optional)

4 ounces unsweetened chocolate

2 cups sugar

1½ cups sifted all-purpose flour

¾ teaspoon baking soda

½ teaspoon salt

1 cup hot strong brewed coffee or 5 teaspoons instant coffee powder dissolved in 1 cup hot water

½ cup sour cream, at room temperature

½ cup vegetable oil

2 large eggs, lightly beaten with a fork, at room temperature

* *

I 've read that chocolate contains a chemical similar to the one our bodies produce when we fall in love. This doesn't surprise me because I've never had any doubt that chocolate has transcendent powers. I wish my readers all the love they need, but in a pinch I offer this recipe. Baking the layers a bit below 350°F keeps them moist. In my well-considered opinion, these are the perfect chocolate layers: dark and not too sweet compared to other chocolate cakes, quintessentially American. I have included the measurements for both a two-layer and a three-layer cake. If you're feeling particularly festive, split the layers horizontally for a four-layer or six-layer cake, fill it with the Creamy Dreamy Chocolate Marshmallow Buttercream (page 115), and frost it with the Fudge Frosting (page 112).

The variations that follow match them up with rich fillings and frostings for unbeatably delicious layer cakes.

MAKES 12 TO 16 SERVINGS *when frosted*

1 Place a rack in the center of the oven and preheat to 345°F. Lightly grease two or three 8-inch layer cake pans with vegetable oil or butter or line them with parchment circles or pan inserts.

2 Melt the chocolate in the top of a double boiler placed over simmering water, then turn off the heat.

3   Sift the sugar, flour, baking soda, and salt together into a large mixing bowl.

4   In a separate bowl, blend the hot coffee, sour cream, and vegetable oil with a whisk.

5   With the mixer on low speed, add the coffee mixture in a stream to the dry ingredients and mix until blended, 35 to 45 seconds, depending on how many layers you're making. Stop the mixer several times to scrape the bowl with a rubber spatula.

6   Add the eggs one at a time and mix on medium-low speed after each addition until smooth, about 15 seconds. Scrape the bowl each time. Add the melted chocolate and mix until the batter is uniform in color, 10 to 15 seconds more.

7   Divide the batter evenly among the prepared pans. Bake until the cake springs back to the touch and a tester inserted in the center comes out clean (do not wait for a crust to form), 35 to 38 minutes.

8   Let the layers cool completely in the pans on a rack before frosting.

NOTE: *To make the cake shown in the photo on page 8, follow the measurements for preparing three layers. Don't split the baked layers; leave them whole and frost them with the Creamy Dreamy Chocolate Marshmallow Buttercream (page 115). To frost, follow the directions for frosting a two-layer cake on page 19, making sure to center the middle layer, right side up, on the bottom layer.*

For a three-layer cake:

Vegetable oil or butter for greasing the pan (optional)

6 ounces unsweetened chocolate

3 cups sugar

2¼ cups all-purpose flour

1⅛ teaspoons baking soda

¾ teaspoon salt

1½ cups hot strong brewed coffee or 2 tablespoons plus 2 teaspoons instant coffee powder dissolved in 1½ cups hot water

¾ cup sour cream, at room temperature

¾ cup vegetable oil

3 large eggs, lightly beaten with a fork, at room temperature

* *

Fudge Cake

* *

T wo layers and one terrific frosting stack up to the simplest and dreamiest of chocolate cakes. It's the ultimate at birthday time—copacetic with ice cream—need I say more?

MAKES 12 TO 16 SERVINGS

Follow the directions for filling and frosting a two-layer cake on page 19, using the Fudge Frosting.

INGREDIENTS

Rosie's Famous Chocolate–Sour Cream Cake Layers (opposite)

Fudge Frosting (page 112)

Velvet Underground Cake

* *

A deep dark inside of chocolate cake layered with hot fudge concealed by a velvety buttercream.

MAKES 12 TO 16 SERVINGS

INGREDIENTS

Rosie's Famous Chocolate–Sour Cream Cake Layers (page 26), split into 4 layers (page 18)

Hot Fudge Filling (see page 118)

About 1½ cups Rosie's Buttercream (page 112) or Mocha Buttercream (page 113)

1 ounce bittersweet chocolate, for shaving

1 Following the directions for filling and frosting a four-layer cake on page 20, spread all interior layers with fudge filling, and the outside of the cake with the buttercream.

2 Grate the bittersweet chocolate over the surface of the cake using a fine grater. Then use a sharp knife to shave large thin shards of chocolate over the grated pieces to make darker accents.

* *

Queen Raspberry Cake

* *

An elegant cake that combines chocolate and raspberries with mocha or vanilla buttercream. I decorate it very simply: a dab of raspberry preserves on the center of the top and chocolate shavings around the top edge.

MAKES 12 TO 16 SERVINGS

INGREDIENTS

Rosie's Famous Chocolate–Sour Cream Cake Layers (page 26), split into 4 layers (see page 18)

⅔ cup raspberry preserves, plus 1 teaspoon for garnish

¼ cup Hot Fudge Filling (page 118)

About 1½ cups Rosie's or Mocha Buttercream (page 112 or 113)

1 ounce bittersweet chocolate, for shaving

1 Following the directions for filling and frosting a four-layer cake on page 20, finish the cake as follows: cake layer, ⅓ cup preserves, cake layer, fudge filling, cake layer, ⅓ cup

preserves, cake layer, buttercream on the top and sides.

2   Using a sharp knife, shave a wreath of bittersweet chocolate around the top edge of the cake and place the remaining 1 teaspoon preserves in the center before serving.

* *

Cold Fudge Sundae Cake

* *

I like to serve this cake—a new twist on the classic soda fountain treat—for celebrations, New Year's Eve for instance, accompanied by Champagne. It's particularly festive looking because the sides are not frosted and the whipped cream ruffles out like crinolines between the dark chocolate layers.

MAKES 12 TO 16 SERVINGS

1   Following the directions for filling and frosting a four-layer cake on page 20, finish the cake as follows: cake layer, ¼ cup fudge filling, ½ cup frozen raspberries (leave a ½-inch border of plain fudge to prevent raspberry juice from dripping down the sides of the cake), ½ cup whipped cream (it should extend just beyond the edge of the cake), cake layer, ¼ cup fudge filling, ½ cup frozen raspberries, ½ cup whipped cream, cake layer, remaining ¼ cup fudge filling, remaining frozen raspberries, ½ cup whipped cream, cake layer, and the remaining whipped cream on top. As you stack each layer, press down lightly with your hand so that the whipped cream is squeezed out from between the layers a little.

2   Use a sharp knife to shave the bittersweet chocolate over the surface of the cake and crown it with the fresh raspberries.

INGREDIENTS

Rosie's Famous Chocolate–Sour Cream Cake Layers (page 26), split into 4 layers (see page 18)

Hot Fudge Filling (page 118)

Double recipe Whipped Cream (page 119)

1½ cups frozen raspberries, thawed

1 ounce bittersweet chocolate, for shaving

12 fresh raspberries, for garnish

Texas Ruby Red Cake

* *

L ayers of chocolate cake, raspberry preserves, and fudge frosting make this a very rich choice.

MAKES 12 TO 16 SERVINGS

INGREDIENTS

Rosie's Famous Chocolate–Sour
 Cream Cake Layers
 (page 26), split into
 4 layers (see page 18)

⅔ cup raspberry preserves

Fudge Frosting (page 112)

½ pint fresh raspberries,
 for garnish (optional)

Whipped Cream (page 119),
 for serving

1 Following the directions for filling and frosting a four-layer cake on page 20), finish the cake as follows: cake layer, ⅓ cup preserves, cake layer, ½ cup fudge, cake layer, remaining ⅓ cup preserves, cake layer, remaining fudge on top and sides.

2 Crown the cake with fresh raspberries, if using, and serve each slice with a dollop of whipped cream.

* *

Snowball Cake

* *

R emember those soft fluffy pink and white mounds covered with coconut? Well, this is a more sophisticated version, but at Rosie's we only make it in white!

MAKES 12 TO 16 SERVINGS

INGREDIENTS

Rosie's Famous Chocolate–Sour
 Cream Cake Layers (page 26)

Rosie's Buttercream (page 112)

2 cups sweetened shredded
 coconut

1 Follow the directions for filling and frosting a two-layer cake on page 19, using the buttercream.

2 Pat the coconut gently around the sides of the cake and sprinkle it generously over the top.

Mocha Cake

* *

The wonderful combination of chocolate cake, fudge filling, and mocha buttercream produces one of our all-time favorite cakes at Rosie's.

MAKES 12 TO 16 SERVINGS

1 Following the directions for filling and frosting a four-layer cake on page 20, finish the cake as follows: cake layer, ¼ cup fudge filling, cake layer, ½ cup plus 2 tablespoons buttercream, cake layer, ¼ cup fudge filling, cake layer, remaining buttercream on top and sides.

2 Heat the remaining ¼ cup fudge filling until it's syrupy but not hot and drizzle it over the cake with a spoon or pastry bag fitted with a fine tip.

INGREDIENTS

Rosie's Famous Chocolate–Sour Cream Cake Layers (page 26), split into 4 layers (see page 18)

Hot Fudge Filling (page 118)

Mocha Buttercream (page 113)

* *

Devil's Food Cake

with CREAMY DREAMY CHOCOLATE MARSHMALLOW BUTTERCREAM

* *

Despite its name, this cake is nothing less than heavenly: light and moist with a chocolate frosting that melts in your mouth.

MAKES 12 TO 14 SERVINGS

INGREDIENTS

Vegetable oil or butter for
   greasing the pans (optional)

1 cup cake flour, sifted

¾ cup plus 2 tablespoons
   all-purpose flour

1 cup unsweetened cocoa powder

1¼ teaspoons baking soda

½ teaspoon salt

2 sticks (8 ounces) unsalted
   butter, at room temperature

1¾ cups plus 2 tablespoons sugar

¼ cup vegetable oil

3 large eggs, at room
   temperature

1 large egg yolk

1 cup buttermilk, at room
   temperature

Creamy Dreamy Chocolate
   Marshmallow Buttercream
   (page 115)

1   Place a rack in the center of the oven and preheat to 345°F. Lightly grease two 8-inch layer cake pans with vegetable oil or butter or line them with parchment circles or pan inserts.

2   Sift both flours, the cocoa, baking soda, and salt together into a medium-size bowl and set aside.

3   Cream the butter and sugar together in a medium-size mixing bowl with an electric mixer on medium-high speed until light and fluffy, about 1½ minutes. Stop the mixer once or twice to scrape the bowl with a rubber spatula. Add the oil and beat for 30 seconds more. Scrape the bowl.

4   Add the whole eggs and yolk to the butter mixture one at a time and mix on medium speed until very well blended, about 15 seconds after each addition. Scrape the bowl each time.

5   With the mixer on low speed, add the dry ingredients to the butter mixture in three additions alternating with the buttermilk, and starting and ending with the dry ingredients. Beat for several seconds after each addition, then stop the mixer and scrape the bowl. After the last addition, beat the batter until everything is well blended, about 10 seconds.

6   Divide the batter evenly between the prepared pans. Bake until the cake is set, springs back to the touch, and a tester inserted in the center comes out clean, about 28 minutes.

7   Let the layers cool completely in the pans on a rack before frosting.

8   Split each layer in two following the directions on page 18. Then follow the directions for filling and frosting a four-layer cake on page 20, spreading all interior layers and the outside with the buttercream.

Golden Cake Layers

* *

Rich and buttery tasting, this cake is perfect with any frosting. To make the cake on the cover, bake three layers, split them in half horizontally, spread Creamy Dreamy Chocolate Marshmallow Buttercream (page 115) between the layers, and frost with the Fudge Frosting (page 112).

MAKES 12 TO 16 SERVINGS *when frosted*

1   Place a rack in the center of the oven and preheat to 345°F. Lightly grease two or three 8-inch layer cake pans with vegetable oil or butter or line them with parchment circles or pan inserts.

2   Sift the flour, baking powder, and salt together into a small bowl.

3   Cream the butter, oil, sugar, and vanilla in a medium-size mixing bowl with an electric mixer on medium-high speed until the mixture is light and fluffy, 1½ to 2 minutes, depending on how many layers you're making. Stop the mixer twice to scrape the bowl with a rubber spatula.

4   Add the eggs to the butter mixture one at a time and mix on medium speed after each addition, 5 seconds. Scrape the bowl, then continue to blend on medium speed until very fluffy, 30 to 45 seconds more.

5   Add the cream to the butter mixture, blend on medium-low speed for 10 seconds, and scrape the bowl.

6   Fold one-half of the dry ingredients into the butter mixture with the spatula and mix on low to blend. Add the remaining dry ingredients and continue mixing on low until the batter is smooth and velvety, about 10 to 15 seconds. Stop the mixer twice to scrape the bowl.

7   Divide the batter evenly among the prepared pans. Bake until the layers are golden in color, and a tester inserted in the center comes out clean, about 30 minutes.

8   Let the layers cool completely in the pans on a rack before frosting.

INGREDIENTS

For a two-layer cake:

Vegetable oil or butter for greasing the pans (optional)

2 cups all-purpose flour

2 teaspoons baking powder

¾ teaspoon salt

2 sticks (8 ounces) unsalted butter, at room temperature

2 tablespoons vegetable oil

1¼ cups plus 2 tablespoons sugar

2 teaspoons pure vanilla extract

4 large eggs, at room temperature

½ cup plus 2 tablespoons heavy (whipping) cream

For a three-layer cake:

Vegetable oil or butter for greasing the pans (optional)

3 cups all-purpose flour

1 tablespoon baking powder

1¼ teaspoons salt

3 sticks (12 ounces) unsalted butter, at room temperature

3 tablespoons vegetable oil

2 cups plus 1 tablespoon sugar

1 tablespoon pure vanilla extract

6 large eggs, at room temperature

¾ cup plus 3 tablespoons heavy (whipping) cream

Snow Queen Cake

* *

INGREDIENTS

Golden Cake Layers (page 33),
    split into 4 layers
    (see page 18)

⅔ **cup raspberry preserves**

Rosie's Buttercream (page 112)

This is a golden butter cake layered with raspberry preserves. Probably because I'm getting sentimental in my old age, it tickles me to see that it's the dream cake of both the 10-year-old birthday girl and the bride planning her wedding feast. There will be those with quite different ideas of how to celebrate momentous occasions, I know, but keep in mind that this is the cake those fat little birds were busy festooning in Disney's Sleeping Beauty. *And who am I to argue with Walt Disney?*

MAKES 12 TO 16 SERVINGS

Following the directions for filling and frosting a four-layer cake on page 20, finish the cake as follows: cake layer, ⅓ cup preserves, cake layer, buttercream, cake layer, remaining preserves, cake layer, and the remaining buttercream on the top and sides.

* *

Summertime Cake

* *

INGREDIENTS

Golden Cake Layers (page 33),
    split into 4 layers
    (see page 18)

Lemon Custard Filling (page 120)

About 1½ cups Rosie's
    Buttercream (page 112)

1 lemon, for garnish

This delicately light cake is one of my favorites. It combines the tartness of lemon filling with the sweetness of buttercream icing.

MAKES 12 TO 16 SERVINGS

1 Following the directions for filling and frosting a four-layer cake on page 20, spread the lemon custard over all interior

layers. Frost the outside of the cake with the buttercream. The custard may cause the layers to slip from side to side, so I suggest placing one hand on the top of the cake while you frost the sides with a "base coat" (see page 19).

2 After frosting with the base coat, refrigerate the cake for 1 hour to set the custard. Then complete the frosting.

3 Cut thin slices of lemon and place them on top of the frosted cake as suggested on page 22.

* *

Boston Cream Pie Cake

* *

More Boston than baked beans (which seem to exist mostly in cans around here), this cake creates the taste of Boston cream pie with layers of golden cake layered with a rich vanilla custard and fudge frosting. It's topped with a final layer of dark fudge, and, since Boston is the home of America's first chocolate factory, you can't get more authentic than that.

MAKES 12 TO 16 SERVINGS

1 Following the directions for filling and frosting a four-layer cake on page 20, finish the cake as follows: cake layer, half the custard, cake layer, ½ cup fudge, cake layer, remaining custard, cake layer, remaining fudge on top and sides. The custard may cause the layers to slip from side to side, so I suggest placing one hand on the top of the cake while you frost the sides with a "base coat" (see page 19).

2 After frosting with the base coat, refrigerate the cake for 1 hour to set the custard. Then complete the frosting.

INGREDIENTS

Golden Cake Layers (page 33), split into 4 layers (see page 18)

Fudge Frosting (page 112)

Vanilla Custard Filling (page 119)

Lemon Coconut Layer Cake

with COCONUT BUTTERCREAM

* *

I had my first slice of coconut layer cake at Junior's in Miami Beach; I dreamed about it for years—until I returned to Florida for another slice and then bought an entire cake to carry back with me on the plane. Rather than continue to dream about it, I came up with a recipe that I could bake whenever I got the "coconut cake shakes."

MAKES 10 TO 12 SERVINGS

INGREDIENTS

Vegetable oil or butter for greasing the pans (optional)

Cake

1 cup plus 2 tablespoons cake flour

1 cup all-purpose flour

1 tablespoon baking powder

¾ teaspoon salt

14 tablespoons (1¾ sticks) unsalted butter, at room temperature

1¼ cups sugar

1 tablespoon pure vanilla extract

2 tablespoons grated lemon zest

2 large eggs, at room temperature

3 large egg whites

1 cup light cream or coconut cream

1 Place a rack in the center of the oven and preheat to 350°F. Lightly grease two 8-inch layer cake pans with vegetable oil or butter or line them with parchment circles or pan inserts.

2 Make the cake: Sift both flours with the baking powder and salt into a small bowl and set aside.

3 Cream the butter, sugar, vanilla, and lemon zest in a medium-size mixing bowl with an electric mixer on medium-high speed until light and fluffy, about 1½ minutes. Stop the mixer twice to scrape the bowl with a rubber spatula.

4 Add the whole eggs to the butter mixture one at a time, then add the egg whites, and blend on medium speed, scraping the bowl after each addition. Then beat the mixture until it is light and increases in volume, about 1½ minutes. Scrape the bowl.

5 Add half the dry ingredients to the butter mixture by stirring in lightly with the spatula so that the liquid is absorbed. Then turn the mixer to low to blend partially, 5 seconds. Scrape the bowl.

6 Add half the cream or coconut cream and blend on medium-low speed for 10 seconds. Scrape the bowl, then add the rest of the dry ingredients with the mixer on low.

7   Add the remaining cream in a stream and blend until the batter is velvety in texture, about 10 seconds. Use the spatula to give the batter a few more turns.

8   Divide the batter evenly between the prepared pans. Bake until the cake is lightly golden in color, springs back to the touch, and a tester inserted in the center comes out clean, 28 to 30 minutes.

9   Let the layers cool completely in the pans on a rack before frosting.

10   Meanwhile, make the lemon curd: Sprinkle the gelatin over the lemon juice in a small bowl.

11   Using a whisk, stir the egg yolks and sugar together in a small bowl until blended.

12   Combine the lemon juice mixture and the egg mixture in a small heavy saucepan and stir with the whisk to blend. Place the pan over medium-low heat, and, stirring constantly with the whisk, bring the mixture just to the boiling point.

13   Remove from the heat, strain the mixture into a small metal bowl, and stir in the butter. Place a piece of plastic wrap over the surface of the curd and refrigerate until fully cooled.

14   Make the buttercream: Place the egg whites and sugar in the top of a double boiler placed over simmering water. Stir with the whisk until the mixture is opaque and warm to the touch and the sugar is dissolved, 4 to 5 minutes.

15   Place the egg-white mixture in a medium-size mixing bowl and mix on medium-high speed with the whisk attachment until it is tepid, 5 to 7 minutes.

16   With the mixer still on medium-high, add the butter to the egg-white mixture, 2 to 3 pieces at a time, to incorporate. Stop the mixer frequently to scrape down the bowl. Add the coconut extract and continue to beat until light and fluffy, 1 to 2 minutes more. Use the frosting immediately or it will have to be rewhipped.

17   Following the directions for filling and frosting a four-layer cake on page 20, finish the cake as follows: cake layer, half the lemon curd, cake layer, buttercream, cake layer, remaining lemon curd, cake layer, and the remaining buttercream on the top and sides. Generously sprinkle the coconut on top of the frosted cake and pat it around the sides. Refrigerate the cake for several hours before serving.

Lemon Curd

¼ teaspoon unflavored gelatin powder

⅓ cup plus 1 tablespoon fresh lemon juice

4 large egg yolks

½ cup sugar

1½ teaspoons unsalted butter

Buttercream Frosting

3 large egg whites

1 cup sugar

3 sticks (12 ounces) unsalted butter, at room temperature, cut into 10 pieces

1 tablespoon coconut extract

Harvard Mocha Cake

* *

P eople who like their chocolate in moderation love this cake, which gives them four layers of golden cake layered with mocha buttercream and frosted all over with fudge. I'm not sure why I named it after Harvard.

MAKES 12 TO 16 SERVINGS

INGREDIENTS

**Golden Cake Layers (page 33),
    split into 4 layers
    (see page 18)**

**2 cups Mocha Buttercream
    (page 113)**

Fudge Frosting (page 112)

Following the directions for filling and frosting a four-layer cake on page 20, spread ½ cup buttercream over each interior layer. Frost the top and sides of the cake with fudge frosting and crown the cake with mocha buttercream rosettes (see page 21).

* *

Fresh Berry Sponge Cake

* *

W henever I make this dessert for Passover, people are surprised that a cake made with matzoh cake flour can taste so wonderful. Oftentimes cakes made with matzoh cake meal (also called matzoh cake flour) can have a grainy texture and slightly strange aftertaste. This lemony sponge cake has a fine texture and a lovely flavor, and is a great alternative to the usual berry shortcake.

MAKES 12 TO 14 SERVINGS

1   Place a rack in the center of the oven and preheat to 350°F. Line two 8-inch layer cake pans with parchment circles or pan inserts.

2   Sift the matzoh flour, potato starch, and salt together into a small bowl.

3   Beat the egg yolks, water, 1 cup plus 1 tablespoon of the sugar, the lemon juice and zest, and the vanilla in a medium-size mixing bowl with an electric mixer on medium speed until blended, about 10 seconds. Scrape the bowl with a rubber spatula.

4   Blend the dry ingredients into the egg-yolk mixture on low speed until incorporated, about 10 seconds. Scrape the bowl.

5   In another mixing bowl, with clean, dry beaters, beat the egg whites on medium-high speed until frothy, about 30 seconds. Gradually add the remaining ¼ cup sugar and continue beating the whites to firm peaks, about 90 seconds more.

6   Stir one-third of the egg whites into the batter to loosen it, then gently fold the remaining egg whites into the batter.

7   Divide the batter evenly between the prepared pans. Shake the pans gently to level off the batter. Bake until the cake is a rich golden color, springs back to

the touch, and a tester inserted in the center comes out clean, about 25 minutes.

8   Let the layers cool completely in the pans on a rack.

9   Remove the layers from the pans and remove the paper liners. Place one layer right side up on a cake plate. Slice it horizontally through the middle so that you have 2 layers. Spread ½ cup of the berries over the bottom layer, leaving a ½-inch border at the edge.

10   Put one-third of the whipped cream around this outer edge, like a wreath, and gently spread the cream toward the center of the layer with a frosting spatula. (This keeps the berries and the juice from dripping down the sides of the layer as you spread the cream.) Slice the other cake into two layers as well. Place 1 layer over the cream and continue layering the cake with the remaining berries and another one-third of the cream.

11   Place the remaining layer on top of the cake. Before frosting the top, press down lightly on the top layer with your hand to make the whipped cream between each layer ooze out a little and form a ruffle. Then frost the top layer with the rest of the whipped cream. Stud the top of the cake decoratively with the 12 fresh strawberries or 24 fresh raspberries.

INGREDIENTS

10 tablespoons matzoh cake meal

6 tablespoons potato starch

½ teaspoon salt

6 large eggs, separated, at room temperature

2 tablespoons water

1¼ cups plus 1 tablespoon sugar

2 tablespoons fresh lemon juice

1 tablespoon grated lemon zest

2 teaspoons pure vanilla extract

1½ cups fresh or frozen sliced strawberries or raspberries, thawed if frozen

Double recipe Whipped Cream (page 119)

12 whole fresh strawberries or 24 fresh raspberries, for garnish

Carrot-Pineapple Layer Cake

* *

INGREDIENTS

Vegetable oil or butter for greasing the pans (optional)

2 cups all-purpose flour

2 teaspoons baking powder

1½ teaspoons baking soda

1 teaspoon salt

2 teaspoons ground cinnamon

½ teaspoon ground cloves

½ teaspoon ground allspice

½ teaspoon ground mace

1 cup drained crushed pineapple

2 cups grated carrots (about 4 carrots)

½ cup chopped walnuts

1¾ cups sugar

1½ cups vegetable oil

1 teaspoon pure vanilla extract

4 large eggs, at room temperature

Cream Cheese Frosting (optional; page 116)

This is a wonderfully moist, fruity cake, delicious plain or frosted with Cream Cheese Frosting.

MAKES 8 TO 12 SERVINGS

1 Place a rack in the center of the oven and preheat to 350°F. Lightly grease two 9-inch layer cake pans with butter or vegetable oil or line them with parchment circles or pan inserts.

2 Sift the flour, baking powder, baking soda, salt, and spices together into a small bowl and set aside.

3 Pat the pineapple dry with paper towels and place in a medium-size bowl. Stir in the carrots and walnuts.

4 Mix the sugar, oil, and vanilla together in a medium-size mixing bowl using an electric mixer on medium speed until completely blended, 20 seconds. Stop the mixer to scrape the bowl twice with a rubber spatula.

5 Add the eggs to the sugar mixture one at a time and mix on medium speed after each addition until blended, 10 seconds. Scrape the bowl each time.

6 Add the dry ingredients to the sugar mixture and beat on low speed for 5 seconds. Scrape the bowl, then mix the batter by hand until the dry ingredients are incorporated.

7 Blend in the pineapple mixture with several turns of the mixer at low speed.

8 Divide the batter between the prepared pans. Bake until the cake is golden, springs back to the touch, and a tester inserted in the center comes out clean, about 45 minutes.

9 Let the layers cool in the pan on a rack.

10 Follow the directions for filling and frosting a two-layer cake page 19, using the Cream Cheese Frosting.

Banana Cake

* *

B*anana cake par excellence: a sheet cake that's perfect in flavor, delicate and moist in texture, and another one that doesn't need a frosting. However, it is extra good slathered with Cream Cheese Frosting.*

MAKES 12 TO 18 SERVINGS

1 Place a rack in the center of the oven and preheat to 350°F. Lightly grease a 13 × 9-inch baking pan with vegetable oil or butter.

2 Sift both flours, the baking soda, and salt together into a small bowl and set aside.

3 In a second small bowl, stir the buttermilk into the mashed banana and set aside.

4 Cream the butter, oil, both sugars, and the vanilla in a medium-size mixing bowl with an electric mixer on medium speed until light and fluffy, about 2 minutes. Scrape the bowl with a rubber spatula.

5 Add the eggs to the butter mixture one at a time and mix on medium speed after each addition until blended, about 10 seconds. Scrape the bowl each time.

6 Add one-third of the dry ingredients to the butter mixture with the mixer on low speed, and mix for 8 seconds. Scrape the bowl. Add half the banana mixture, mix 10 seconds, and scrape the bowl. Add the rest of the dry ingredients and the rest of the banana mixture and mix for 10 seconds. Scrape the bowl and stir the batter several times by hand to mix thoroughly.

7 Pour the batter into the prepared pan. Bake until the cake is golden, springs back to the touch, and a tester inserted in the center comes out clean, 30 to 35 minutes. Let the cake cool completely in the pan on a rack.

8 Eat as is or frost with Cream Cheese Frosting.

INGREDIENTS

Vegetable oil or butter for greasing the pan

2¼ cups sifted cake flour

5 tablespoons all-purpose flour

1½ teaspoons baking soda

½ teaspoon salt

1 cup plus 2 tablespoons buttermilk, at room temperature

¾ cup mashed banana (about 2 very ripe bananas, skin should be brown)

10 tablespoons (1¼ sticks) unsalted butter, at room temperature

6 tablespoons vegetable oil

¾ cup (lightly packed) light brown sugar

¾ cup granulated sugar

1 teaspoon pure vanilla extract

3 large eggs, at room temperature

Cream Cheese Frosting (optional; page 116)

Coconut-Pecan Oatmeal Cake

* *

This is a hearty cake, almost more of a fall or winter snack than a dessert. Be careful not to let the oatmeal stand or it will coagulate. Serve this cake soon after it has baked—it's great warm.

MAKES 12 SERVINGS

INGREDIENTS

Vegetable oil or butter for greasing the pan

Cake

1⅓ cups all-purpose flour

1 teaspoon baking soda

½ teaspoon baking powder

1 teaspoon salt

½ teaspoon ground cinnamon

1 cup quick-cooking oats

8 tablespoons (1 stick) unsalted butter, at room temperature

1 cup plus 3 tablespoons sugar

2 teaspoons pure vanilla extract

2 large eggs, at room temperature

1⅓ cups boiling water

Topping

6 tablespoons (¾ stick) unsalted butter, at room temperature

1 cup (lightly packed) light brown sugar

¼ cup light cream, half-and-half, or whole milk

1 teaspoon pure vanilla extract

½ cup chopped pecans

½ cup sweetened shredded coconut

1   Place a rack in the center of the oven and preheat to 350°F. Lightly grease an 11 × 7-inch broilerproof baking pan with vegetable oil or butter.

2   For the cake, sift the flour, baking soda, baking powder, salt, and cinnamon together into a small bowl. Place the oats in a medium-size bowl.

3   Cream the butter, sugar, and vanilla together in a second medium-size mixing bowl with an electric mixer on medium speed until light and fluffy, about 2 minutes. Stop the mixer twice to scrape the bowl with a rubber spatula.

4   Add the eggs to the butter mixture one at a time and mix on medium speed after each addition until blended, 10 seconds. Scrape the bowl each time.

5   Pour the boiling water over the oatmeal and stir several times with a wooden spoon. Add the oatmeal to the egg mixture and mix on medium speed until blended, 6 to 7 seconds.

6   Partially fold in the dry ingredients by hand with the spatula, using several broad strokes. Then mix on medium speed until all the ingredients are blended, about 10 seconds. Scrape the bowl.

7   Pour the batter into the prepared pan. Bake until the cake is golden and springs back to the touch, 25 to 30 minutes. Remove the cake from the oven and allow it to cool for 15 minutes.

8   Meanwhile, make the topping: Put all the ingredients in a medium-size mixing bowl and stir vigorously with a whisk until they are blended.

9 Preheat the broiler.

10 Spread the topping over the cake with a frosting spatula, then place the cake on a baking sheet (to catch any drips). If your broiler is part of your oven, place the cake on the center rack of the oven. If you have a separate broiler unit, place the cake as far as possible from the heat. With the oven or broiler door open, broil, rotating the pan several times, until the topping bubbles to a deep golden color, 5 to 6 minutes. Watch it carefully. Let cool for 10 minutes, then serve warm.

* *

Fresh Blueberry-Muffin Breakfast Cake

* *

T his is really a blueberry muffin masquerading as a cake, which makes it perfect for brunch or snacking—anytime you want something to accompany a cup of tea or coffee or a glass of milk. The cake should be served quite warm, soon after it comes out of the oven, and I especially like my piece with a thin veneer of sweet butter. Cranberries can be substituted for blueberries when they are in season.

MAKES 9 TO 12 SERVINGS

INGREDIENTS

Vegetable oil or butter for greasing the pan

Cake

2 cups all-purpose flour

2 teaspoons baking powder

¾ teaspoon salt

10 tablespoons (1¼ sticks) unsalted butter, at room temperature

1½ cups granulated sugar

1½ teaspoons pure vanilla extract

2 large eggs, at room temperature

¾ cup whole milk, at room temperature

1¾ cups blueberries

Topping

8 tablespoons (1 stick) unsalted butter, cut into 8 pieces, at room temperature

⅓ cup all-purpose flour

½ cup granulated sugar

½ cup (lightly packed) light brown sugar

2 teaspoons ground cinnamon

Pinch of salt

1   Place a rack in the center of the oven and preheat to 350°F. Lightly grease a 9-inch square baking pan with vegetable oil or butter.

2   Make the cake: Sift the flour, baking powder, and salt together into a small bowl.

3   Cream the butter, sugar, and vanilla in a medium-size mixing bowl with an electric mixer on medium speed until the mixture is light and fluffy, about 2 minutes. Stop the mixer once or twice to scrape the bowl with a rubber spatula.

4   Add the eggs to the butter mixture one at a time and mix on medium speed after each addition until blended, 8 to 10 seconds. Scrape the bowl each time.

5   Fold one-third of the dry ingredients into the butter mixture by hand, just until they have absorbed the liquid but are not thoroughly blended. Fold in half the milk by hand with several strokes, then the rest of the dry ingredients, folding just until they are absorbed. Add the rest of the milk and fold it in just until the batter is smooth.

6   Gently fold in the blueberries.

7   Pour the batter into the prepared pan. Bake until the top is just set but not golden, 25 to 30 minutes.

8   Meanwhile, make the topping: Place all the ingredients in a food processor and pulse until blended, about 10 pulses. Or mix all the dry ingredients in a small bowl and rub the butter into the mixture with your fingers.

9   When the top of the cake is set, cover the surface with spoonfuls of topping and return the cake to the oven until the topping spreads and begins to get crunchy, 15 to 20 minutes.

10   Remove the cake from the oven and serve it hot. It is good eaten plain or buttered like a muffin.

Lemon Pudding Cake

* *

A layer of light lemon cake sitting atop a layer of tart lemon pudding, this dessert is wonderful served warm right out of the oven or at room temperature. But it is just as delicious cold on Day Two when its texture has become like that of a cheesecake.

MAKES 9 SERVINGS

1 Place a rack in the center of the oven and preheat to 350°F. Have ready an 8-inch square baking pan and a larger baking pan in which the smaller pan fits comfortably.

2 Whisk ½ cup plus 1 tablespoon of the sugar, the flour, and salt together in a medium-size mixing bowl. Add the butter, lemon zest, and lemon juice to the flour mixture.

3 Whisk the egg yolks and cream in a small bowl until blended.

4 Add the egg-yolk mixture to the flour mixture and blend with an electric mixer on medium-low speed until the batter is velvety, about 15 seconds. Set aside.

5 With a clean, dry whisk attachment, whisk the egg whites in a medium-size mixing bowl using an electric mixer at medium-high speed until frothy, about 30 seconds. Gradually add the remaining 3 tablespoons sugar and continue beating the egg whites to firm peaks, 45 seconds more. Gently fold the whites into the flour mixture.

6 Pour the batter into the 8-inch square baking pan. Place the pan in the larger baking pan. Pour water into the larger pan to come about halfway up the sides of the smaller pan. Bake until the top is golden and springs back to the touch, 35 to 40 minutes.

7 Spoon the cake immediately onto individual dessert plates or allow to cool to room temperature before serving.

INGREDIENTS

½ cup plus 4 tablespoons sugar

¼ cup all-purpose flour

⅛ teaspoon salt

3 tablespoons unsalted butter, melted

1 tablespoon plus 2 teaspoons grated lemon zest

6 tablespoons fresh lemon juice

3 large eggs, separated, at room temperature

1½ cups heavy (whipping) cream, at room temperature

INGREDIENTS

Vegetable oil for greasing the pan

1½ cups all-purpose flour

½ cup sugar

1½ teaspoons baking soda

2 tablespoons ground ginger

¼ teaspoon ground cloves

¼ teaspoon salt

¼ teaspoon ground black pepper

½ cup vegetable oil

½ cup molasses

½ cup plus 1 tablespoon strong brewed coffee

1 large egg, at room temperature

Perfect Gingerbread

for ANY OCCASION

* *

Regardless of the season, I have always been a fan of a dark, moist gingerbread served hot with vanilla ice cream, and this one is perfect! I use a lot of ground ginger and a touch of ground black pepper to give it an extra kick. It may sink slightly in the center, but that is just the nature of the beast and, actually, the center is my favorite part.

MAKES 9 TO 12 SERVINGS

1 Place a rack in the center of the oven and preheat to 350°F. Lightly grease an 8-inch square pan with vegetable oil.

2 Place the flour, sugar, baking soda, ginger, cloves, salt, and pepper in a medium-size mixing bowl and stir with a whisk.

3 Place the oil, molasses, coffee, and egg in a large measuring cup or a small bowl and whisk vigorously to blend.

4 Make a hole in the center of the dry ingredients. Pour in the liquid ingredients and use a rubber spatula to lightly toss the dry ingredients into the liquid until the liquid is absorbed. Use the whisk to stir the mixture just until it appears smooth. Do not overmix.

5 Pour the batter into the prepared pan. Bake until the cake springs back to the touch and a tester inserted in the center comes out clean or with a few moist crumbs, 28 to 30 minutes.

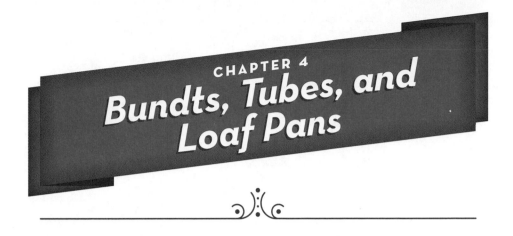

CHAPTER 4
Bundts, Tubes, and Loaf Pans

The cakes in this chapter are fuss free, and the results are fantastic! Some of my first creations were baked in Bundt and tube pans, and I have always delighted in how these cakes present. Besides being voluptuous, they're very versatile, and lend themselves beautifully to being crowned with frosting, drizzled with glaze, or dusted with confectioners' sugar. They stand tall, are easy to transport, and are easy to cut. You can actually take pretty much any batter and create a good-looking cake in a Bundt or tube pan and if you add chips, nuts, raisins, berries, or chopped fruit, you hardly need more than a light glaze or dusting of confectioners' sugar to make it special.

Cakes and sweet breads baked in loaf pans are wonderfully transportable, making them great for picnics and casual events, or just to keep around the house for snacks, especially in mid afternoon. A thick slice, maybe slightly warm, with a cup of freshly brewed coffee or tea, or even a mug of hot chocolate, takes the edge off a winter day. In summer, that slice makes a lovely accompaniment to a glass of lemonade or iced tea. Loaves can be eaten as is, or frosted, glazed or dusted with confectioners' sugar.

Bundt cakes, tube cakes, and loaves are the cakes you'll want to bake over and over again—to have on hand for everyday family desserts and for when friends drop by.

Poppy-Seed Chocolate-Chip Cake

* *

T*he name is complicated, but the cake is a straightforward butter cake embroidered with chocolate and poppy seeds, a surprisingly complementary combination.*

MAKES 12 TO 16 SERVINGS

INGREDIENTS

Vegetable oil or butter for greasing the pan

2½ cups all-purpose flour, plus flour for dusting the pan

2 teaspoons baking powder

1 teaspoon baking soda

¼ teaspoon salt

2 sticks (8 ounces) unsalted butter, at room temperature

1 cup plus 4 tablespoons sugar

2 teaspoons pure vanilla extract

1 teaspoon ground cinnamon

4 large eggs, separated, at room temperature

1 cup buttermilk, at room temperature

1 cup (6 ounces) semisweet chocolate chips, coarsely chopped by hand

1½ ounces unsweetened chocolate, grated

¼ cup poppy seeds

Confectioners' sugar, for garnish

1   Place a rack in the center of the oven and preheat to 350°F. Lightly grease a 10-inch Bundt pan with vegetable oil or butter, then dust with flour.

2   Sift the flour, baking powder, baking soda, and salt together into a small bowl.

3   Beat the butter, 1 cup plus 1 tablespoon of the sugar, the vanilla, and cinnamon together in a medium-size mixing bowl with an electric mixer on medium speed until blended, about 2 minutes. Stop the mixer once or twice to scrape the bowl with a rubber spatula.

4   Add the egg yolks to the butter mixture one at a time and mix on medium speed after each addition until blended, 10 seconds. Scrape the bowl once during the mixing and again at the end. The batter will not be smooth at this point.

5   Fold one-third of the dry ingredients into the butter mixture with the spatula. Then fold in half the buttermilk, another one-third of the dry ingredients, the remaining buttermilk, and the remaining dry ingredients. Do not fully blend in the ingredients after each addition until the end.

6   With clean, dry beaters, beat the egg whites in another medium-size mixing bowl with an electric mixer on medium-high speed until frothy, about 30 seconds. Gradually add the remaining 3 tablespoons sugar and beat the whites to soft peaks, about 30 seconds more. Stir one-third of the whites into the batter to loosen it, then fold in the rest of the whites with the spatula. Fold in the chocolate chips, grated chocolate, and poppy seeds.

7 Scoop the batter into the prepared pan and distribute it evenly. Bake until the cake is golden and a tester inserted in the center comes out clean, about 1 hour.

8 Let the cake cool completely in the pan on a rack. Then remove it from the pan, sift confectioners' sugar over the top, and serve.

From Pan to Plate

Getting a cake out of a tube pan is much easier if your pan has a removable bottom. After the cake has cooled, simply run a spatula around the side of the pan to loosen the cake, then lift the cake out by pushing up on the bottom insert. Once the cake is free of the pan side, use a spatula to loosen the base of the cake from the pan bottom and invert it onto a plate so it's right side up.

Bundt pans come in wonderful shapes, but they don't have a removable bottom, making getting the cake out somewhat trickier. They must be greased generously and floured, which will help release the cake. Once the cake is baked, turn the pan upside down and tap its edge gently on a work surface as you rotate it so as to loosen the cake. This is best done when the cake is still slightly warm, perhaps an hour after it is removed from the oven. Then with the pan still upside down, carefully slide the cake out onto a plate. If some cake sticks to the bottom of the pan, don't panic; try to remove it in one piece, and place it back where it came from. You can always dust it with powdered sugar or cover it with glaze or frosting and no one will know! No matter what, it will still taste good.

INGREDIENTS

Vegetable oil or butter for greasing the pan

Flour for dusting the pan

Cake

2 cups all-purpose flour

1½ teaspoons baking soda

½ teaspoon salt

8 tablespoons (1 stick) unsalted butter, at room temperature

1 cup granulated sugar

½ cup (lightly packed) light brown sugar

1½ teaspoons ground cinnamon

1½ teaspoons ground nutmeg

1 teaspoon ground cloves

½ teaspoon ground ginger

½ teaspoon ground allspice

3 tablespoons unsweetened cocoa powder

2 large eggs, at room temperature

1½ cups unsweetened applesauce, at room temperature

¾ cup raisins

¾ cups chopped walnuts

Glaze

1½ cups sifted confectioners' sugar

1 tablespoon ground allspice

2 teaspoons ground ginger

1 teaspoon ground cinnamon

6 tablespoons (¾ stick) unsalted butter

3 tablespoons heavy (whipping) cream

¼ cup chopped walnuts

Applesauce-Raisin Cake

* *

D*ark and hearty, this cake is a great fall and winter treat. I like to use unsweetened applesauce because the cake doesn't need the extra sweetness.*

MAKES 12 TO 16 SERVINGS

1 Place a rack in the center of the oven and preheat to 350°F. Generously grease a 10-inch Bundt pan with vegetable oil or butter, then dust with flour.

2 Make the cake: Sift the flour, baking soda, and salt together into a small bowl.

3 Cream the butter, both sugars, the spices, and the cocoa together in a medium-size mixing bowl with an electric mixer on medium-high speed until light and fluffy, about 2 minutes. Stop the mixer once or twice to scrape the bowl with a rubber spatula.

4 Add the eggs to the butter mixture one at a time and mix on medium-low speed after each addition until blended, 8 to 10 seconds. Scrape the bowl after each addition. After the final scraping mix again on medium speed, about 10 seconds.

5 Blend the applesauce into the butter mixture with the spatula. Then mix on medium speed for 5 seconds.

6 Fold the dry ingredients in with the spatula until they are almost incorporated. Then turn the mixer to medium speed and blend the ingredients until the batter is well mixed, about 8 seconds.

7 Fold the raisins and ¾ cup walnuts in with the spatula.

8 Pour the batter into the prepared pan. Bake until the top is firm to the touch and a tester inserted in the center comes out clean, about 1 hour 10 minutes.

9 Let the cake cool completely in the pan.

10 Meanwhile, make the glaze: Sift the confectioners' sugar and spices together into a small bowl.

11   Melt the butter in a small saucepan over low heat, add the cream when the butter has melted, and cook just until the cream is hot. Stir the butter mixture vigorously into the sugar mixture with a whisk until they are absorbed. There will be lumps.

12   Pour the glaze into a blender and blend on medium speed until smooth, about 20 seconds.

13   Remove the cake from the pan and place it on a cake plate. Pour the glaze over the top of the cake, allowing it to run down the outer sides and down the center hole. Allow the glaze to set for 1 hour and sprinkle the remaining ¼ cup walnuts on top before cutting the cake.

* *

Lemon-Glazed
Orange Chiffon Cake

* *

*T*his cake is light and spongy with an orange flavor and a refreshing lemon glaze. In order to enjoy it at its peak of flavor, serve it on the day it's baked. I like to accompany it with fresh or frozen strawberries.

MAKES 12 TO 14 SERVINGS

1   Place a rack in the center of the oven and preheat to 325°F. Have ready a 10-inch tube pan with a removable bottom. Do not grease it.

2   Make the cake: Sift the flour, 1½ cups of the sugar, the baking powder, and salt together into a large bowl.

3   In a small bowl, whisk together the egg yolks, orange zest, orange juice, and oil until blended.

4   Add the egg-yolk mixture to the dry ingredients and mix with an electric mixer on low speed

INGREDIENTS

Cake

2¼ cups cake flour

2 cups granulated sugar

1 tablespoon baking powder

½ teaspoon salt

6 large eggs, separated, at room temperature

1 tablespoon grated orange zest

¾ cup orange juice

½ cup vegetable oil

Glaze

9 tablespoons (1 stick plus 1 tablespoon) unsalted butter

2¼ cups confectioners' sugar

4½ tablespoons hot water

5½ tablespoons fresh lemon juice (1½ to 2 lemons)

Frozen strawberries, thawed, or fresh strawberries, hulled, sliced, and lightly sugared to make a juice, for serving (optional)

until the batter is smooth, 1½ to 2 minutes. Stop the mixer once to scrape the bowl with a rubber spatula. Do not overmix.

5   With clean, dry beaters, beat the egg whites in a medium-size bowl with an electric mixer on medium-high speed until frothy, about 30 seconds. Gradually add the remaining ½ cup sugar and beat the whites to firm peaks, about 1 minute more. Stir one-third of the egg whites into the batter, then fold in the remaining whites with the spatula.

6   Pour the batter into the tube pan. Bake until the top of the cake is golden and springs back to the touch, 1 hour.

7   Cool the cake upside down on a funnel or bottle (see page 12).

8   Meanwhile, make the glaze: Melt the butter in a small saucepan over low heat and transfer it to a small bowl. Add the confectioners' sugar and hot water and whisk until blended. Add the lemon juice and whisk again. Pour the mixture through a strainer into a second small bowl.

9   When the cake has completely cooled, remove it from the pan and place it upside down on a cake plate. Pour half the glaze over the top of the cake so that it drips down the outside and down the inside of the hole. Allow this to set for 30 minutes.

10   Whisk the remaining glaze in the bowl and pour it over the cake for a second coating. Eat the cake that day, accompanied by strawberries, if desired.

Bittersweet Orange Cake

with a LEMON GLAZE

* *

If a cake can contradict itself, this one does: It combines the bite of the citrus fruits with the sweetness of the raisins, the crunch of the nuts with a moist texture. To me, though, that's what makes this cake special. Try it with a cappuccino alongside.

MAKES 12 TO 16 SERVINGS

1 Place a rack in the center of the oven and preheat to 350°F. Generously grease a 10-inch Bundt pan with vegetable oil or butter, then dust with flour.

2 Make the cake: Sift the flour, baking soda, baking powder, and salt together into a small bowl.

3 Put the oranges and raisins in a food processor and process with short pulses until the ingredients are chopped but not pureed, about 30 pulses. Add the nuts and pulse 6 more times.

4 Cream the butter, sugar, and lemon zest together in a medium-size mixing bowl with an electric mixer on medium speed until light and fluffy, about 1½ minutes. Stop the mixer once or twice to scrape the bowl with a rubber spatula.

5 Add the eggs to the butter mixture one at a time and mix on medium speed after each addition until blended, 10 seconds. Scrape the bowl after each addition.

6 Fold the orange mixture in by hand. The batter will appear curdled.

7 Fold in the dry ingredients by hand alternating with the buttermilk as follows (to prevent overmixing, do not completely blend each addition): one-third of the dry ingredients, half the buttermilk, one-third of the dry ingredients, remaining buttermilk, and final one-third of the dry ingredients. Mix on low speed just until blended, several seconds.

8 Pour the batter into the prepared pan. Bake until the top is a deep golden color and

INGREDIENTS

Vegetable oil or butter for greasing the pan

Flour for dusting the pan

Cake

3 cups all-purpose flour

1½ teaspoons baking soda

1½ teaspoons baking powder

¾ teaspoon salt

1½ oranges, unpeeled, cut into chunks and seeds removed

1½ cups raisins

¾ cup walnut pieces

12 tablespoons (1½ sticks) unsalted butter, at room temperature

1½ cups sugar

1 tablespoon grated lemon zest

3 large eggs, at room temperature

1½ cups buttermilk, at room temperature

Glaze

½ cup fresh lemon juice

¼ cup fresh orange juice

5 tablespoons sugar

53

a tester inserted in the center comes out clean, about 1¼ hours.

9   Let the cake cool completely in the pan on a wire rack.

10   Meanwhile, make the glaze: Whisk both juices and the sugar together in a small bowl until blended.

11   When the cake has cooled, remove it from the pan, put it on a plate, and poke holes over the entire surface with a fork. Use a pastry brush to brush the glaze repeatedly over the surface of the cake until all the glaze has been absorbed. Then, slice and serve.

INGREDIENTS

Vegetable oil or butter for greasing the pan

3 cups cake flour

3 sticks (12 ounces) unsalted butter, at room temperature

8 ounces cream cheese, at room temperature or warmed lightly in a microwave

3 cups sugar

1 tablespoon pure vanilla extract

6 large eggs, at room temperature

* *

Cream Cheese Pound Cake

* *

I *dedicate this dessert to my sister-in-law Laura, who is such a fan that when she first tasted it, she devoured nearly the entire cake. The cream cheese combines with the other ingredients to make it velvety and moist, but it doesn't overpower the flavor of the butter.*

MAKES 12 TO 16 SERVINGS

1   Place a rack in the center of the oven and preheat to 325°F. Lightly grease a 10-inch tube pan with vegetable oil or butter.

2   Sift the cake flour into a small bowl and set aside.

3   Cream the butter, cream cheese, sugar, and vanilla in a medium-size mixing bowl with an electric mixer on medium-high speed until light and fluffy, about 2 minutes. Stop the mixer once or twice to scrape the bowl with a rubber spatula.

4   Add the eggs to the butter mixture one at a time and mix on medium speed after each addition until blended, about 10 seconds. Scrape the bowl after

each addition. When all the eggs are added, mix 30 seconds more.

5   Stir the flour gently into the batter with the spatula. Then mix on low speed for 5 seconds, scrape the bowl, and blend until the batter is smooth and even, 5 to 10 seconds.

6   Pour the batter into the prepared pan. Bake until the cake is golden and firm to the touch and a tester inserted in the center comes out clean, about 1 hour 35 minutes.

7   Let the cake cool completely in the pan on a rack before removing it and serving.

* *

Poppy-Seed Pound Cake

* *

P*ound cakes got their name because originally they were made with a pound of each ingredient. For this recipe, I kept the name but changed the weight to come up with a remarkably versatile cake. It's ideal sliced as a tea cake or an after-school snack, served with fresh fruit as dessert, or dunked into coffee in place of a breakfast doughnut. That probably accounts for its popularity, although the crunchiness of the whole poppy seeds also has something to do with it. You can also substitute 1¼ cups blueberries, cranberries, chocolate chips, or nuts for the poppy seeds and have an equally scrumptious cake.*

MAKES 12 TO 16 SERVINGS

INGREDIENTS

Vegetable oil or butter for greasing the pan

4 cups all-purpose flour

1 tablespoon baking powder

2 teaspoons baking soda

½ teaspoon salt

2 sticks (8 ounces) unsalted butter, at room temperature

2 cups sugar

1 tablespoon pure vanilla extract

4 large eggs, at room temperature

2 cups sour cream, at room temperature

½ cup plus 1½ tablespoons poppy seeds

55

1 Place a rack in the center of the oven and preheat to 350°F. Lightly grease a 10-inch tube pan with vegetable oil or butter.

2 Sift the flour, baking powder, baking soda, and salt together into a medium-size bowl.

3 Cream the butter, sugar, and vanilla in a large mixing bowl with an electric mixer on medium speed until light and fluffy, about 2 minutes. Stop the mixer once or twice to scrape the bowl with a rubber spatula.

4 Add the eggs to the butter mixture one at a time and mix on medium-low speed after each addition until blended, 5 seconds. Scrape the bowl each time. When all the eggs are added, beat the mixture for 10 seconds. The batter will not be smooth at this point.

5 Add one-third of the dry ingredients to the egg mixture and fold them in lightly with the spatula so that the liquid is absorbed. Mix on low speed for 5 seconds until partially blended. Scrape the bowl. Add half the sour cream and mix on low speed until partially blended, 5 seconds. Mix the batter with several broad strokes of the spatula and scrape the bowl. Add another one-third of the dry ingredients, the remaining sour cream, and then the remaining dry ingredients using this same procedure. Mix the batter on low speed until it is velvety, about 15 seconds.

6 Add ½ cup of the poppy seeds on low speed and mix just until blended, about 15 seconds.

7 Pour the batter into the prepared pan. Sprinkle the remaining poppy seeds over the top. Bake until the cake is high and golden and a tester inserted at the highest point comes out clean, about 1 hour 10 minutes.

8 Let the cake cool in the pan on a rack for several hours before removing it and serving.

Apple Cake

* *

Since apples taste best in fall or winter, this cake is a seasonal treat and one that can be stored nearly forever—if it makes it as far as the fridge.

MAKES 12 TO 16 SERVINGS

1 Place a rack in the center of the oven and preheat to 350°F. Lightly grease a 10-inch tube pan with a removable bottom with vegetable oil or butter.

2 Sift the flour, cinnamon, baking soda, and salt together into a small bowl.

3 Cream the butter, oil, sugar, and vanilla in a medium-size mixing bowl with an electric mixer on medium speed until the ingredients are blended, about 2 minutes. Stop to scrape the bowl twice with a rubber spatula.

4 Add the eggs to the butter mixture one at a time and mix on medium-low speed after each addition until blended, 10 seconds. Scrape the bowl after each addition. Once the eggs are added, mix again for 10 seconds.

5 Add half the dry ingredients to the butter mixture and blend on low speed for 15 seconds. Scrape the bowl, add the rest of the dry ingredients, and mix on low speed until blended, about 5 seconds more.

6 Add the apples with a few turns of the mixer or by folding them in by hand with a wooden spoon.

7 Spoon the batter into the prepared pan. Sprinkle the top with the cinnamon-sugar. Bake until the cake is golden, the top is firm, and a tester inserted at the cake's highest point comes out clean, about 1 hour 5 minutes. Let the cake cool completely in the pan on a rack. Then release the side of the pan and serve.

INGREDIENTS

Vegetable oil or butter for greasing the pan

3 cups all-purpose flour

2 teaspoons ground cinnamon

1 teaspoon baking soda

1 teaspoon salt

2 sticks (8 ounces) unsalted butter, at room temperature

¼ cup vegetable oil

2 cups sugar

2 teaspoons pure vanilla extract

3 large eggs, at room temperature

4 cups peeled Granny Smith apple cubes (½ inch; 3 to 4 large apples)

1 teaspoon cinnamon mixed with 1 tablespoon sugar for topping

Parisian
Brownie Walnut Pound Cake

INGREDIENTS

Vegetable oil or butter for greasing the pan

6 ounces bittersweet chocolate

2 ounces unsweetened chocolate

¾ cup plus 1 tablespoon all-purpose flour

⅛ teaspoon baking soda

2 sticks (8 ounces) unsalted butter, at room temperature

1¼ cups plus 2 tablespoons sugar

3 large eggs, at room temperature

¼ cup buttermilk

1 cup walnut pieces

* *

W hen I traveled to France in the late 1980s, I discovered a then well-known bakery that sold a brownie walnut pound cake by the pound. What I loved about the cake was that it did indeed have a texture that was halfway between a brownie and a pound cake. I went back every day and had a big hunk for brunch, ignoring all the classic pastries that were found in every corner French bakery. I tried for years to re-create the recipe but finally gave up. Just this year, I decided to try again and I have come up with a version that is pretty close.

MAKES 8 TO 10 SERVINGS

1 Place a rack in the center of the oven and preheat to 325°F. Lightly grease a 9 × 5 × 3-inch loaf pan with vegetable oil or butter.

2 Melt both chocolates in the top of a double boiler placed over simmering water. Let cool to room temperature.

3 Sift the flour and baking soda together into a small bowl.

4 Cream the butter and sugar in a medium-size mixing bowl with an electric mixer on medium speed until light and fluffy, about 1½ minutes. Stop the mixer once or twice to scrape the bowl with a rubber spatula.

5 Add the eggs to the butter mixture one at a time and beat on medium speed until fully blended, about 30 seconds.

6 Add the cooled chocolate to the butter mixture and mix on medium speed until blended, about 30 seconds. Stop the mixer once to scrape the bowl. Scrape it again after the chocolate is blended.

7 Add half the dry ingredients to the butter mixture and mix on low speed for 10 seconds. Add the buttermilk and mix for 5 seconds. Add the remaining dry ingredients and mix until blended, 5 seconds. Stop the mixer and scrape the bowl, then mix for 5 seconds more. Add ¾ cup of the nuts and blend on low for several seconds.

8 Spoon the batter into the prepared pan. Top with the remaining walnuts and bake until the top is set and a tester inserted in the center comes out with a few moist crumbs, about 1½ hours. Let the cake cool completely in the pan on a rack. Then remove it from the pan, slice, and serve.

* *

Kathy's Lemon Vanilla Pound Cake

* *

My good friend and neighbor, Kathy, likes to make this classic butter pound cake on a weekly basis for her son Jonathon. It just so happens that she makes it on the night the two of us watch our favorite weekly drama, Damages. *Needless to say, we tend to consume the bulk of the cake while Jonathon is upstairs doing homework.*

MAKES 8 TO 10 SERVINGS

1 Place a rack in the center of the oven and preheat to 350°F. Lightly grease a 9 × 5 × 3-inch loaf pan with vegetable oil or butter.

2 Sift both flours, the baking powder, and salt together into a small bowl and set aside.

INGREDIENTS

Vegetable oil or butter for greasing the pan

1 cup plus 3 tablespoons all-purpose flour

1 cup plus 2 tablespoons cake flour

1½ teaspoons baking powder

½ teaspoon salt

2 sticks (8 ounces) unsalted butter, at room temperature

1¼ cups sugar

1½ tablespoons grated lemon zest

1 tablespoon pure vanilla extract

4 large eggs, at room temperature

½ cup sour cream

3 tablespoons whole milk

3   Cream the butter, sugar, lemon zest, and vanilla in a medium-size mixing bowl with an electric mixer on medium speed, until light and fluffy, about 1½ minutes. Stop the mixer twice to scrape the bowl with a rubber spatula.

4   Add the eggs to the butter mixture one at a time and mix on medium speed after each addition until blended, 10 seconds, scraping the bowl after each addition. Then beat on medium speed until the mixture grows in volume slightly, about 2 minutes.

5   Place the sour cream in a small bowl and whisk in the milk. Add one-third of the dry ingredients to the egg mixture and mix on low speed for 5 seconds. Scrape the bowl. Then turn the mixer to low again, add half the sour cream mixture, blend for a few seconds, and scrape the bowl. Add another one-third of the dry ingredients and blend for 3 seconds, scrape the bowl, and add the rest of the sour cream mixture. Add the remaining dry ingredients and mix on high speed for 2 seconds. Scrape the bowl.

6   Pour the batter into the prepared pan. Bake until the cake is golden in color and firm and spongy in texture and a tester inserted in the center comes out clean, 1 to 1¼ hours.

7   Let the cake cool in the pan on a rack for several hours. Then remove it from the pan, slice, and serve—any time of day.

Lift Out

Generally, it's not difficult removing a loaf cake from a pan that's well greased. Simply sliding a table knife between the sides of the pan and the cake loosens it enough for it to easily tip out. But if the loaves give you trouble, here's a tip you might want to try next time. Cut a piece of parchment paper that's as long as the length of the pan plus enough extra to generously overhang the ends of the pan. Place the parchment in the pan, add the butter, and bake. Then when your loaf has baked and cooled, you just loosen the sides that don't have the parchment and use the parchment overhangs to lift the cake out of the pan. It works beautifully when the cake has cooled completely or is still slightly warm.

Almond Pound Cake

* *

H*ere is a simple butter pound cake with a distinctive almond taste. I top it with an almond glaze and crushed almonds.*

MAKES 8 TO 12 SERVINGS

1   Place a rack in the center of the oven and preheat to 350°F. Lightly grease a 9 × 5 × 3-inch loaf pan with vegetable oil or butter.

2   Make the cake: Sift the cake flour, baking powder, baking soda, and salt together into a small bowl.

3   Cream the butter, sugar, and both **extracts** in a medium-size mixing bowl with an electric mixer on medium speed until light and fluffy, about 2 minutes. Stop the mixer once or twice to scrape the bowl with a rubber spatula.

4   Add the eggs to the butter mixture one at a time and mix on medium speed after each addition until blended, 10 seconds. Scrape the bowl each time. The eggs will not be fully mixed into the batter at this point.

5   Add half the dry ingredients to the butter mixture and mix on low speed for 10 seconds. Add half the sour cream and mix for 5 seconds. Scrape the bowl. Add the remaining dry ingredients and mix 5 seconds, then add the remaining sour cream and mix another 5 seconds. Scrape the bowl. The batter should be velvety.

6   Pour the batter into the prepared pan. Bake until the top is firm and golden and a tester inserted in the center comes out clean, about 50 minutes. The top will crack slightly. Let the cake cool completely in the pan on a rack.

7   Make the glaze: Stir the confectioners' sugar, almond extract, and water together in a small bowl with a small whisk until the sugar is completely dissolved.

8   Remove the cake from the pan and place it on a baking sheet covered by a sheet of waxed paper. Pour the glaze over the

INGREDIENTS

Vegetable oil or butter for greasing the pan

Cake

1½ cups plus 3 tablespoons cake flour

¾ teaspoon baking powder

½ teaspoon baking soda

¼ teaspoon salt

10 tablespoons (1¼ sticks) unsalted butter, at room temperature

¾ cup granulated sugar

2 teaspoons pure almond extract

1 teaspoon pure vanilla extract

3 large eggs, at room temperature

½ cup plus 1 tablespoon sour cream

Glaze

1 cup confectioners' sugar, sifted

2¼ teaspoons pure almond extract

2 tablespoons hot water

¼ cup chopped slivered almonds

cake slowly so that it covers the top and drips down the sides. Sprinkle the almonds over the

top immediately. When the glaze hardens, transfer the cake to a pretty serving plate.

* *

Banana Chocolate Chip Cake

* *

W*e make this cake into muffins at Rosie's and they have a cult following. There is tremendous excitement whenever they appear warm from the oven. Imagine a hearty banana bread with warm, melty chocolate chips . . . what a way to start off the day.*

MAKES 8 TO 10 SERVINGS

INGREDIENTS

Vegetable oil or butter for greasing the pan

1½ cups plus 1 tablespoon all-purpose flour

¾ teaspoon baking soda

¾ teaspoon salt

¼ cup sour cream

¾ cup plus 2 tablespoons mashed ripe banana (3 bananas)

4 tablespoons (½ stick) unsalted butter, at room temperature

¼ cup vegetable oil

½ cup granulated sugar

¼ cup plus 1 tablespoon (lightly packed) light brown sugar

1 teaspoon pure vanilla extract

2 large eggs, at room temperature

½ to ¾ cup (your choice) plus 2 tablespoons chocolate chips

1   Place a rack in the center of the oven and preheat to 350°F. Lightly grease a 9 × 5 × 3-inch loaf pan with vegetable oil or butter.

2   Sift the flour, baking soda, and salt together into a small bowl and set aside.

3   Stir the sour cream into the mashed bananas in a second small bowl, and set aside.

4   Cream the butter, oil, both sugars, and the vanilla in a medium-size mixing bowl with an electric mixer on medium speed until light and fluffy, about 1 minute. Stop the mixer twice to scrape the bowl with a rubber spatula.

5   Add the eggs to the butter mixture one at a time and after each addition mix on medium speed until blended, 10 seconds. Scrape the bowl after mixing in each addition. Then mix for an additional 20 seconds.

6 Add half of the banana mixture to the butter mixture and mix on medium speed until blended, 10 seconds. Scrape the bowl. Add half the flour mixture and mix on low speed until almost blended, 8 seconds. Scrape the bowl. Add the remainder of the banana mixture and mix on low for a few seconds. Scrape the bowl. Add the rest of the flour mixture and mix on low until almost blended, 10 seconds. Scrape the bowl.

7 Fold in ½ to ¾ cup of the chocolate chips (depending on how much chocolate you want)

with the rubber spatula and continue to stir the batter by hand to mix thoroughly.

8 Pour the batter into the prepared loaf pan. Jiggle the pan from side to side to distribute the batter evenly. Sprinkle the remaining 2 tablespoons chips over the loaf and bake until the cake is golden, springs back to the touch, and a tester inserted in the center comes out clean or with a few moist crumbs, about 1¼ hours. Let the cake cool slightly in the pan on a rack. Then remove it from the pan, slice, and serve.

* *

Carrot Pudding Cake

* *

O*ne of the first carrot cakes that I baked when I started my business in the seventies was this adaptation of my friend Richard's mom's recipe. It is actually made with little jars of pureed baby carrots like the kind so many of us ate as kids. It gives both moisture and flavor to this cake when combined with the spices and other ingredients. You can frost it with Cream Cheese Frosting (page 116), but I like it just fine the way it is with a nice cup of tea.*

MAKES 8 SERVINGS

INGREDIENTS

¾ cup golden raisins

Vegetable oil or butter for greasing the pan

1½ cups all-purpose flour

¾ teaspoon baking powder

¾ teaspoon baking soda

1 teaspoon ground cinnamon

½ teaspoon ground nutmeg

½ teaspoon salt

8 tablespoons (1 stick) unsalted butter, at room temperature

1 cup sugar

½ cup vegetable oil

2 large eggs, at room temperature

3 jars (4 ounces each) pureed carrot baby food

½ cup walnut pieces

1 Place the raisins in a small heatproof bowl. Bring a small amount of water to a boil and pour it over the raisins to cover. Set aside.

2 Place the rack in the center of the oven and preheat to 350°F. Generously grease a 9 × 5 × 3-inch loaf pan with vegetable oil or butter.

3 Sift the flour, baking powder, baking soda, cinnamon, nutmeg, and salt together into a small bowl.

4 Cream the butter, sugar, and oil together in a medium-size mixing bowl with an electric mixer on medium-high speed until light and fluffy, about 1 minute. Stop the mixer once or twice to scrape the bowl with a rubber spatula.

5 With the mixer running at medium speed, add the eggs to the butter mixture one at a time and mix until fluffy, about 30 seconds.

6 Add ¼ cup of the dry ingredients to the butter mixture with the mixer on low and mix until blended, 5 seconds. Scrape the bowl.

7 Add the pureed carrots and blend on medium speed until incorporated, 5 seconds. Scrape the bowl.

8 Add the remaining dry ingredients with the mixer on low, then turn the mixer to medium speed and blend until the dry ingredients are incorporated, about 10 seconds. Stop the mixer once to scrape the bowl.

9 Drain the golden raisins and pat dry. Fold the nuts and raisins into the batter with the spatula.

10 Pour the batter into the prepared pan. Bake the cake for 1 hour, then turn the temperature down to 325°F and continue to bake until the top is firm to the touch and a tester inserted in the center comes out clean, an additional 25 minutes.

11 Let the cake cool slightly in the pan on a rack. Then remove it from the pan, slice, and serve.

CHAPTER 5
Rolled Cakes, Cheesecakes, and More

Quite a disparate grouping, I think, but I find that these are the cakes that are beloved by eaters but are baked by them less often than the cakes in the previous two chapters. I'm not sure why that is. Perhaps, fear of rolling? Fear of falling (when it comes to the mousse cake I've included here)? Fear of anything baked in a springform pan?

Believe me, these cakes are worth overcoming any fears. Chocolate rolls filled with mocha cream, butter cakes and fudge cakes topped with raspberry sauce or a rich ganache, cheesecakes galore—even one in the style of old-time New York restaurant favorite, Reuben's. I've even included a skillet-baked Pineapple Upside-Down Cake. Wait till you try them. You are going to be so glad you did—and so will your family and friends!

Tom's Birthday Roll

* *

INGREDIENTS

Vegetable oil or butter for
   greasing the pan and waxed
   paper

Cake

4 ounces semisweet chocolate

2 ounces unsweetened chocolate

3 tablespoons strong brewed
   coffee

5 large eggs, separated, at room
   temperature

½ cup plus 2 tablespoons sugar

Filling and Garnish

5 teaspoons instant coffee
   powder

1 tablespoon water

1 tablespoon sugar

1 cup heavy (whipping) cream,
   chilled

2 tablespoons unsweetened
   cocoa powder, for sprinkling

Strawberries or raspberries,
   for garnish (optional)

While I was testing recipes for the book, my neighbor Tom could always be counted on to stop by and sample the results. So he's tasted my desserts in every stage from batter and scraps to pièce de résistance. I made this cake especially for his birthday, and it seems only appropriate that after all the leftovers he's consumed, he should get something special named for him. Made without flour, this moist chocolate cake is rolled into a log with a coffee whipped cream filling.

MAKES 12 TO 16 SERVINGS

1   Place a rack in the center of the oven and preheat to 350°F. Lightly grease a jelly-roll pan (15 × 10 inches) with vegetable oil or butter, line it with waxed paper, and grease the paper.

2   Make the cake: Melt both chocolates in the coffee in the top of a double boiler placed over simmering water. Cool until tepid.

3   Beat the egg yolks with ½ cup of the sugar in a medium-size mixing bowl with an electric mixer on medium speed until thick and yellow in color, 3 to 4 minutes. Add the chocolate mixture and blend thoroughly, about 10 seconds, stopping the mixer to scrape the bowl with a rubber spatula.

4   In a deep mixing bowl, with clean, dry beaters, beat the egg whites on medium-high to soft peaks, about 30 seconds. Add the remaining 2 tablespoons sugar and continue beating until the whites are stiff but not dry, about 30 seconds more. Carefully fold the egg whites into the chocolate mixture with the spatula.

5   Pour the batter into the prepared pan and spread it evenly. Bake until the surface is spongy and the cake springs back to the touch, about 15 minutes. Remove the pan from the oven. Cover the cake with a damp kitchen towel and let sit for 1 hour.

6   Ten minutes before the hour is up, make the filling: In a medium-size mixing bowl, dissolve the instant coffee in the water. Add the sugar and cream and beat with an electric mixer on medium speed until firm peaks form, about 1¼ minutes.

7   Sprinkle the cocoa over a sheet of waxed paper or a damp kitchen towel (not terry cloth) that is 4 inches longer than the cake.

8   Remove the covering from the cake pan. Run a thin knife around the edge of the cake to loosen it. Carefully flip the pan upside down onto the prepared waxed paper. Carefully peel off the waxed paper lining from the bottom of the cake.

9   Spread the whipped cream filling over the cake, leaving a ½-inch border uncovered along one long side.

10   Starting from the long side with filling all the way to the edge, roll up the cake, using the waxed paper to help. There will be cracks in the cake, but they give the surface an interesting texture. Twist the ends of the waxed paper like a hard-candy wrapper and refrigerate the cake a minimum of 3 hours.

11   When ready to serve, remove the cake from the refrigerator and unwrap it. Trim the edges if they appear irregular or unattractive (they're delicious, by the way). Place the cake on an oval or rectangular platter that has been covered with a white lace doily, and garnish with fresh strawberries or raspberries, if desired.

Chocolate Custard Sponge Roll

* *

This is a moist chocolate sponge cake rolled with chocolate custard and finished with whipped cream, which you can spread over its surface like icing or serve as a garnish with each slice.

MAKES 16 SERVINGS

INGREDIENTS

Vegetable oil for greasing the pan and waxed paper

Cake

3 tablespoons cake flour

2 tablespoons all-purpose flour

¼ cup unsweetened cocoa powder

¾ teaspoon baking soda

¼ teaspoon salt

4 large eggs, separated, at room temperature

¼ cup plus 5 tablespoons sugar

1 teaspoon instant espresso powder

1 teaspoon water

1 Place a rack in the center of the oven and preheat to 400°F. Lightly grease a jelly-roll pan (15 × 10 inches) with vegetable oil, line it with waxed paper, and grease the paper.

2 Make the cake: Sift both flours, the cocoa, baking soda, and salt together in a medium-size bowl.

3 Beat the egg yolks with ¼ cup of the sugar in a medium-size mixing bowl with an electric mixer on medium-high speed until light in color, 3 to 4 minutes.

4 Dissolve the espresso powder in the water and add it to the egg-yolk mixture with the mixer on medium speed. Beat until it is incorporated, about 10 seconds.

5 With clean, dry beaters, beat the egg whites in another mixing bowl on medium-high speed until frothy, about 30 seconds. Gradually add 3 tablespoons of the sugar and continue beating to medium-firm peaks, about 1 minute more. Fold the whites gently into the egg yolks with a rubber spatula. Do not overmix!

6 Sift the dry ingredients (again) over the egg mixture and fold them in gently until the batter is uniform in color.

7 Pour the batter into the prepared pan and tip the pan gently back and forth so that the batter is evenly distributed. Bake until the cake springs back to the touch but has not formed a crust, about 12 minutes.

8 Allow the cake to cool for 10 minutes.

9 Sprinkle the remaining 2 tablespoons sugar over a sheet of waxed paper or a damp kitchen towel (not terry cloth) that is 4 inches longer than the cake. Run a thin knife around the edge of the cake to loosen it. Carefully flip the pan upside down onto the waxed paper. Carefully peel off the waxed paper lining from the bottom of the cake.

10 Starting from one long side, roll up the cake in the waxed paper, using the paper to help. The cake should never roll onto itself (the cake will stick to itself). Twist the ends of the waxed paper like a hard-candy wrapper and refrigerate the cake a minimum of 3 hours.

11 Meanwhile, make the filling: Dissolve the cornstarch in ¼ cup of the milk and set aside.

12 Heat the remaining ¾ cup milk with the chopped chocolate in a small saucepan over medium-low heat until the chocolate is completely melted, about 5 minutes. Stir the mixture vigorously with a whisk for the last few minutes to ensure that it is uniform in color and all specks of chocolate are gone.

13 Vigorously whisk the sugar and the dissolved cornstarch into the chocolate, then whisk in the egg yolk.

14 Heat, stirring or whisking constantly, over low heat until the mixture begins to boil, 3 to 4 minutes. Remove it from the heat, stir it several times in the pan and pour it into a small bowl. Allow it to sit for 20 minutes, stirring it gently several times to release steam. Then cover the surface directly with plastic wrap and refrigerate until it is cool.

15 When you're ready to fill the cake, remove it from the refrigerator and unroll it on a counter so that it is lying on the waxed paper in which it was rolled.

16 Spread the filling over the cake, leaving a ½-inch border uncovered along one long side. Starting from the long side with filling all the way to the edge, roll up the cake, peeling off the waxed paper as you roll (this time don't roll the paper into the cake!). The roll should end up resting on its seam.

17 Rewrap the roll in the waxed paper and refrigerate it for several hours.

18 Just before serving, unwrap the cake and place it on an oval or rectangular serving platter. Frost the cake with the whipped cream and grate chocolate shavings over the top or use the whipped cream as a side garnish with fresh raspberries.

Filling

2 tablespoons cornstarch

1 cup whole milk

2 ounces unsweetened chocolate, chopped

½ cup sugar

1 large egg yolk

Topping and Garnish

Whipped Cream (page 119)

Fresh raspberries for garnish (optional)

1 ounce unsweetened chocolate (for shaving) or 12 raspberries

INGREDIENTS

Vegetable oil for greasing the
pan and waxed paper

Cake

6 large eggs, at room
temperature

¾ cup plus 3 tablespoons
granulated sugar

2 teaspoons grated lemon zest

1½ teaspoons pure vanilla extract

2 tablespoons fresh lemon juice

¾ cup plus 3 tablespoons all-
purpose flour

1 rounded tablespoon sifted
confectioners' sugar, for
sprinkling

Filling

4 large egg yolks

⅓ cup plus 1½ tablespoons sugar

¼ cup plus 3 tablespoons fresh
lemon juice

¼ teaspoon unflavored gelatin
powder

4 tablespoons (½ stick) unsalted
butter, cut into small chunks

8 to 10 strawberries, cut into
¼-inch-thick slices

Topping

Whipped Cream (page 119)

6 whole strawberries

Lemon-Strawberry Sponge Roll

* *

I don't know any blues singers paying tribute to my sweet
lemon jelly roll, but maybe that's because they haven't
tasted this one yet. It's a springy roll, with tart lemon custard
and strawberries substituted for the jelly inside. Then it's
frosted with whipped cream. Try it in the spring or summer.

MAKES 16 SERVINGS

1 Place a rack in the center of
the oven and preheat to 350°F.
Lightly grease a jelly-roll pan
(15 × 10 inches) with vegetable oil,
line it with waxed paper, and grease
the paper with vegetable oil.

2 Make the cake: Separate 3 of
the eggs. Place the egg whites in
a mixing bowl and set aside. Beat
the 3 egg yolks and the 3 whole
eggs in a medium-size mixing
bowl with an electric mixer on
medium-high speed until blended.

3 Add ½ cup plus 3 tablespoons
of the sugar and the lemon zest
and beat the mixture on high
speed until it is pale and thick,
about 3½ minutes. (It may be
necessary to hold a dish towel
around the bowl to contain
splatters until the mixture
thickens.) Stop the mixer several

times to scrape the bowl with a
rubber spatula. Beat in the vanilla
and lemon juice.

4 Fold in the flour with the
spatula until it is incorporated.

5 With clean, dry beaters, beat
the egg whites with the mixer on
medium-high speed until frothy,
about 30 seconds. Gradually
add the remaining ¼ cup sugar
and continue beating just to soft
peaks, about 30 seconds more.
Fold the whites into the batter.

6 Pour the batter into the
prepared pan and tip the pan
gently back and forth so that the
batter is evenly distributed. Bake
until the cake is light golden and
spongy and springs back to the
touch, about 16 minutes.

7   Allow the cake to cool for 10 minutes.

8   Sprinkle the confectioners' sugar over a sheet of waxed paper or a damp kitchen towel (not terry cloth) that is 4 inches longer than the cake. Run a thin knife around the edge of the cake to loosen it. Carefully flip the pan upside down onto the waxed paper. Carefully peel off the waxed paper lining from the bottom of the cake.

9   Starting from one long side, roll up the cake in the waxed paper, using the paper to help. The cake should never roll onto itself (the cake will stick to itself). Twist the ends of the paper like a hard-candy wrapper and refrigerate the cake a minimum of 3 hours.

10   Meanwhile, make the filling: In a small saucepan, mix the egg yolks and the sugar with a whisk until they are blended. Warm the lemon juice slightly in another small saucepan. Add the gelatin to the lemon juice and stir to blend.

11   Add the gelatin mixture to the egg-yolk mixture and cook over medium heat, stirring constantly with a wooden spoon, until the mixture thickens, about 3 minutes. When you run your finger across the spoon, it should leave a path in the mixture.

12   Remove the lemon curd from the stove and strain into a small bowl. Add the butter and stir until blended. Let the lemon curd cool for 20 minutes, stirring occasionally. Puncture a piece of plastic wrap in several places and use it to cover the surface of the lemon curd. Allow the lemon curd to set at room temperature until it is of spreading consistency, 30 to 40 minutes.

13   When the lemon curd is set, remove the cake roll from the refrigerator and unroll it.

14   Spread the lemon curd evenly over the cake, leaving a 1-inch border uncovered along one long side. Distribute the sliced strawberries evenly over the lemon curd. Starting at a long end with filling all the way to the edge, roll up the cake, peeling off the waxed paper as you roll (this time don't roll the paper into the cake!). Put the roll in a fresh piece of waxed paper or plastic wrap and refrigerate it for several hours.

15   Just before serving, trim the ends, transfer the cake to a long serving tray and frost it with the Whipped Cream. Place the whole strawberries, points up, on top of the log.

Sour Cherry Fudge Cake

* *

An odd combination of tastes, you say? Not once you try it. The tartness of the cherries contrasts wonderfully with the sweetness of the chocolate, and all together it makes a dense and substantial cake. You can make it for Passover by substituting matzoh cake flour for the all-purpose flour in the recipe.

MAKES 12 TO 16 SERVINGS

INGREDIENTS

Vegetable oil or butter for greasing the pan

1½ cups (8 ounces) semisweet chocolate chips

4 ounces unsweetened chocolate

¼ cup water

2 sticks (8 ounces) unsalted butter, at room temperature

2 cups sugar

2 teaspoons pure vanilla extract

6 large eggs, separated, at room temperature

1 cup all-purpose flour, sifted

2 cups canned or frozen sour red cherries, drained well and patted dry with a paper towel

1   Place a rack in the center of the oven and preheat to 300°F. Lightly grease the bottom of a 9-inch springform pan with vegetable oil or butter.

2   Melt both chocolates in the water in the top of a double boiler placed over simmering water. Set aside to cool to room temperature.

3   Cream the butter, 1½ cups of the sugar, and the vanilla in a medium-size mixing bowl with an electric mixer on medium speed until light and fluffy, about 2 minutes. Stop to scrape the bowl several times with a rubber spatula.

4   Using a whisk, stir the egg yolks into the chocolate and add this mixture to the butter mixture. Beat on medium speed until smooth, about 2 minutes, stopping to scrape the bowl once or twice.

5   With the mixer on low speed, add the flour to the butter mixture and mix until incorporated, about 20 seconds.

6   With clean, dry beaters, beat the egg whites in another mixing bowl until frothy, about 30 seconds. Gradually add the remaining ½ cup sugar and continue beating until the whites form soft peaks, about 45 seconds more.

7   Whisk one-third of the whites into the batter to loosen it, then fold the remaining egg whites into the batter with the spatula. Place the cherries evenly over the surface of the batter and fold them in very gently with several slow strokes of the spatula.

8   Pour the batter into the prepared pan. Bake until the cake has risen and set and a tester inserted in the center comes out

with some moist crumbs, about 2 hours 10 minutes. Let cool completely in the pan on a rack before removing the side and serving.

NOTE: *The cake will form a crust on top while baking; when the cake cools it will drop and the crust will crack. If you are bothered by its appearance, spread a layer of whipped cream on top and sprinkle chocolate shavings over the whipped cream or just sprinkle confectioners' sugar over the cake and eat it plain.*

* *

Chocolate Mousse Cake

* *

After indulging in my first piece of chocolate mousse cake on a visit to New York years ago, I decided that Rosie's could go no longer without our own version. By definition, the cake is rich and a little piece goes a long way, so I aimed to balance its richness with a deep semisweet chocolate flavor. A thin base of flourless cake supports a thick layer of mousse, which I accent with rum (though brandy or framboise will work, too), then it's topped off with a veneer of whipped cream. The result looks very fancy, making this a perfect dessert for a dinner party or any celebration. Because this cake is made with uncooked eggs, be sure to prepare the mousse quickly and to refrigerate it while the base is baking. For some reason, the mousse doesn't turn out well if you omit the alcohol, so it's important that you include it.

MAKES 16 SERVINGS

INGREDIENTS

8 ounces semisweet chocolate, lightly chopped

8 ounces unsweetened chocolate, lightly chopped

2 sticks (8 ounces) unsalted butter

5 large eggs, separated

¼ cup rum

1 teaspoon pure vanilla extract

⅓ cup plus 1 teaspoon sugar

1¾ cups heavy (whipping) cream, chilled

1 ounce dark chocolate, for shaving

The Bottom of the Springform

Removing a cake from a springform pan is easy; you simply release the side. But what about the bottom? Certainly you can place the cake, bottom and all, on a serving plate and cut slices without further ado. But if the bottom must come off, see step 10 on page 79. You can also remove the cake from the pan bottom by loosening it with a metal spatula and then placing both the spatula and your hand under the cake and carefully transferring it to a plate.

1   Place a rack in the center of the oven and preheat to 350°F. Line the bottom of a 9-inch springform pan with a parchment circle or pan insert.

2   Melt both chocolates and the butter in the top of a double boiler placed over simmering water. Transfer the chocolate mixture to a large mixing bowl and allow it to cool to room temperature.

3   Add the egg yolks, rum, and vanilla to the chocolate mixture and whisk briskly until blended, 5 seconds.

4   With clean, dry beaters, beat the egg whites in a medium-size mixing bowl with an electric mixer on medium-high speed until frothy, about 30 seconds. Gradually add ⅓ cup of the sugar and continue beating just until the peaks are stiff but not dry, about 1 minute more.

5   Add one-third of the egg whites to the chocolate mixture and whisk gently to lighten the batter. Add the rest of the egg whites and whisk until blended.

6   To form the cake base, spread one-third of the chocolate mixture evenly in the prepared pan with a rubber spatula. Refrigerate the rest immediately.

7   Bake the base until it rises and then drops, 18 to 20 minutes. Cool it in the pan in the refrigerator, 15 minutes.

8   Meanwhile, whip 1 cup of the cream in a medium-size mixing bowl with an electric mixer on medium-high speed until stiff peaks form, 1½ minutes. Fold the cream into the remaining chocolate mixture using the rubber spatula.

9   Scoop the chocolate mixture onto the cooled base and smooth the surface with the spatula. Stretch a piece of plastic wrap over the top of the pan and place the cake in the freezer overnight.

10 The next morning, run a frosting spatula around the sides of the springform pan and remove the side. Place a large plate upside down on the top of the cake and flip the cake onto the plate. Remove the bottom of the pan and the paper. Then flip the cake right side up onto a second large plate.

11 Beat the remaining ¾ cup cream and 1 teaspoon sugar in a mixing bowl with an electric mixer on medium-high speed until stiff peaks form, about 1 minute. Spread half the whipped

cream gently over the top of the mousse cake.

12 Place the remaining whipped cream in a pastry bag fitted with a decorative tip. Pipe rosettes of whipped cream around the top edge of the cake. Using the large holes of a grater, shave the dark chocolate over the top of the cake and refrigerate it for 8 hours.

13 Remove the cake from the refrigerator 1 hour before serving.

* *

Chocolate Nut Torte

* *

T his is a luxuriously rich cake that I often garnish with whipped cream, although dark, moist, and chocolate-glazed cake is fine on its own. As I suggest for the Sour Cherry Fudge Cake on page 72, you can substitute matzoh cake flour for the all-purpose flour in the recipe and have an elegant Passover cake. Have all the ingredients prepared before starting because the chocolate starts to harden immediately when added to the egg yolks.

MAKES 12 TO 16 SERVINGS

INGREDIENTS

Vegetable oil or butter for
   greasing the pan

Cake

8 ounces semisweet chocolate

4 ounces unsweetened chocolate

3 sticks (12 ounces) unsalted
   butter

1 cup ground almonds
   (about 1⅓ cups slivered
   almonds ground in a food
   processor)

¼ cup slivered almonds,
   for garnish

9 large eggs, separated,
   at room temperature

1½ cups sugar

½ cup sifted all-purpose flour

Glaze

6 ounces semisweet chocolate

3 ounces unsweetened chocolate

4 tablespoons (½ stick) unsalted
   butter

1½ tablespoons light corn syrup

3 teaspoons boiling water

1   Place a rack in the center of the oven and preheat to 300°F. Lightly grease a 10-inch springform pan with vegetable oil or butter.

2   Make the cake: Melt both chocolates and the butter in the top of a double boiler placed over simmering water. Let cool slightly.

3   Place the ground almonds on half of a baking sheet and place the slivered almonds on the other half. Toast them in the oven until they are golden, about 10 minutes. Leave the oven on.

4   Beat the egg yolks and 1 cup of the sugar with an electric mixer on medium-high speed until they are thick and lemon colored, 4 minutes.

5   With clean, dry beaters, beat the egg whites in another mixing bowl on medium-high speed until frothy, 45 seconds to 1 minute. Gradually add the remaining ½ cup sugar and continue beating until soft peaks form, about 45 seconds more. Set them aside.

6   Add the chocolate mixture to the egg-yolk mixture and mix on low speed until blended, 5 to 8 seconds. Scrape the bowl with a rubber spatula and mix on low speed again until blended, about 5 seconds more. Transfer the mixture to a large bowl.

7   Combine the ground almonds and the flour and sprinkle them on top of the chocolate mixture.

8   Place the whites on top of the nuts and flour and with gentle strokes of the spatula, fold everything together.

9   Pour the batter into the prepared pan. Bake until a tester inserted in the center comes out with very moist crumbs, 1¼ hours. Let the cake cool in the pan on a rack.

10   When the cake has cooled, make the glaze: Melt both chocolates and the butter in the top of the double boiler placed over simmering water.

11   Dissolve the corn syrup in the boiling water and stir this into the chocolate mixture.

12   Release the side of the pan and turn the cake upside down onto a plate. Remove the pan bottom. Place a second rack over a large piece of aluminum foil. Flip the cake right side up onto the rack. Pour the glaze over the top of the cake. Use a frosting spatula to spread the glaze to the edge of the top so it can drip down the sides of the cake.

13   Crush the toasted slivered almonds in your hand and sprinkle them around the top edge of the cake. Allow the glaze to set before slicing the cake.

Chocolate Delirium

* *

H*ere's a melt-in-your mouth, not-too-sweet, flourless chocolate cake that makes a welcome dessert for all chocolate lovers, including those who are gluten intolerant. I like to serve this cake with whipped cream or coffee ice cream, and occasionally I will throw some toasted chopped almonds or walnuts on top. If you don't want to bother with the Chocolate Ganache, just dust the cake with cocoa powder and you still have a winner. After the guests have gone, I have been known to crawl into bed with a small piece that I have heated in the microwave and topped off with a little more ice cream.*

MAKES 12 TO 16 SERVINGS

1 Place a rack in the center of the oven and preheat to 325°F. Lightly grease a 10-inch springform pan with butter. Line the bottom of the pan with a parchment circle or pan insert.

2 Melt the butter with the sugar and coffee in a large saucepan over medium-low heat.

3 Add the chopped chocolate to the butter mixture and stir. Turn the heat off, cover, and let sit until the chocolate has melted, about 10 minutes. Transfer to a large mixing bowl and stir with a whisk until smooth. Set aside.

4 Whisk together the whole eggs and egg yolks in a small mixing bowl. Pour this mixture in a stream into the chocolate mixture while stirring vigorously with the whisk until blended.

5 Whip the cream in a small mixing bowl with an electric mixer until firm peaks form, about 40 seconds. Stir the whipped cream into the chocolate mixture until fully incorporated.

6 Pour the batter into the prepared pan. Bake until the center is set but still slightly spongy in texture and a tester inserted in the center comes out with moist crumbs, about 1½ hours.

INGREDIENTS

Butter for greasing the pan

1 pound (4 sticks) unsalted butter

1 cup sugar

1 cup strong brewed coffee or espresso

1 pound bittersweet chocolate (or a combination of 8 ounces unsweetened chocolate and 8 ounces semisweet), chopped into small pieces

6 large eggs, at room temperature

6 large egg yolks

¼ cup plus 2 tablespoons heavy (whipping) cream, chilled

Chocolate Ganache (page 116)

Whipped Cream (page 119) or ice cream of your choice, for serving

7   Cool the cake in the pan on a rack for several hours.

8   Remove the side of the pan and flip the cake onto the rack. Remove the pan bottom and the paper. Place a second rack over a large piece of aluminum foil. Flip the cake right side up onto the rack.

9   Pour the Chocolate Ganache over the top of the cake and use a frosting spatula to spread it evenly over the top so that it drips down the sides. Then use the spatula to lightly spread it around the sides of the cake. When the glaze sets, carefully lift the cake off the rack with a metal spatula and place it on a cake plate.

10   Serve with Whipped Cream or the ice cream of your choice.

* *

Deep Dark
Raspberry Fudge Cake

* *

This dense cake is layered with a mixture of raspberry preserves and raspberries that permeate the cake to create a sensational texture and flavor. I like to garnish the top of the cake with a halo of fresh berries before the ganache covering has set.

MAKES 12 TO 16 SERVINGS

1   Place a rack in the center of the oven and preheat to 300°F. Line the bottom of a 9-inch springform pan with a parchment circle or pan insert. Lightly grease the sides of the pan with vegetable oil or butter.

INGREDIENTS

Vegetable oil or butter for greasing the pan

Cake

1 pound semisweet chocolate, chopped

6 ounces unsweetened chocolate, chopped

¼ cup water

7 large eggs, separated

2 sticks (8 ounces) unsalted butter, at room temperature

2 cups sugar

1½ teaspoons pure vanilla extract

1 cup all-purpose flour, sifted

2   Melt the two chocolates in the water in the top of a double boiler placed over simmering water. Allow to cool for 5 minutes.

3   Stir the egg yolks into the cooled chocolate mixture.

4   Beat the butter, 1½ cups of the sugar, and the vanilla in a medium-size mixing bowl with an electric mixer on medium speed until blended, 1 to 1½ minutes. Stop the mixer once or twice to scrape the bowl with a rubber spatula. Add the chocolate mixture and continue beating until just smooth.

5   Reduce the speed to low and add the flour. Mix just until blended, about 10 seconds, stopping the mixer once to scrape the bowl. Turn the mixer to high and beat for a few seconds to blend.

6   With clean, dry beaters, beat the whites in another mixing bowl with an electric mixer on medium-high speed until frothy, 30 to 40 seconds. Gradually add the remaining ½ cup sugar and continue beating until soft peaks form, about 1½ minutes more.

7   Stir one-third of the egg whites into the chocolate batter. Mix on low speed for several seconds to blend and loosen the batter. Transfer this mixture to a larger, shallower bowl, then fold the remaining whites gently into the batter.

8   Pour the batter into the prepared pan. Use the spatula to gently spread the batter evenly in the pan. Bake until set and a tester inserted in the center comes out clean, about 1½ hours.

9   Cool the cake in the pan on a rack. As it cools, the cake will drop a bit and break away from the top crust; this is to be expected.

10   When the cake has completely cooled, remove any pieces of top crust. Run a frosting spatula around the sides of the cake and release the side of the pan. Invert the cake onto a large plate or cutting board and carefully pull off the pan bottom and the paper. Use your hands to press any rough pieces into the cake, molding it as if it were made of clay. Place the cake in the refrigerator for 1 hour.

11   Using a long serrated knife that has been dipped in very hot water, cut the cake (still upside down) horizontally to form two layers. Carefully slide two metal spatulas or a flat plate between the layers and remove the top layer.

12   Make the filling: Stir the raspberries and juice into the preserves and spread this mixture on the bottom layer. Slide the top layer back onto the cake.

Filling and Glaze

4 ounces frozen raspberries, completely thawed, juice reserved

3 tablespoons raspberry preserves

½ cup heavy (whipping) cream

4 ounces semisweet chocolate, chopped, or ¾ cup chocolate chips

Garnish and Serving

Fresh raspberries

Whipped Cream (page 119)

13   Make the glaze: Heat the cream in a small saucepan over medium-low heat just to the boiling point. Remove from the heat, add the chocolate, cover, and set aside so the chocolate can melt. After 1 minute, whisk the chocolate mixture until it is velvety smooth. Remove ½ cup of the glaze and put it in the freezer until it stiffens, about 10 minutes.

14   Use the ½ cup stiff glaze to make a base coat. Smooth it over the sides and top of the cake. Pour the looser glaze over the cake and use a frosting spatula to spread it evenly over the top, allowing it to drip down the sides in a random fashion. Or pour it on top of the cake and tilt the plate in a rotating manner to allow the glaze to cover the top and drip down the sides. Run the frosting spatula around the sides to smooth them out.

15   When the glaze has set, use a metal spatula to transfer the cake to a clean flat plate and garnish with fresh raspberries. Serve at room temperature with Whipped Cream.

* *

Sunken Chocolate Cake

* *

R*ich and chocolaty, this flourless cake has an incredible texture and a wonderful bittersweet flavor. You will be amazed at how simple a procedure can produce such amazing results. I am also constantly astonished that a cake that tastes so good has no butter in it. And no flour. It will crack on top and sink in the middle; that's just part of its charm—it has nothing to do with anything you have done! Any flavor ice cream goes well with this cake.*

MAKES 12 TO 14 SERVINGS

1   Place a rack in the center of the oven and preheat to 300°F. Lightly grease a 10-inch springform pan with butter.

2   Melt both chocolates in the coffee and water in the top of a double boiler placed over simmering water. Transfer the chocolate mixture to a large mixing bowl and whisk until smooth.

3   Whip the cream in a small mixing bowl with an electric mixer on medium-high speed until soft peaks form, about 1½ minutes. Place in the refrigerator.

4   Beat the eggs and sugar in a medium-size mixing bowl with a whisk attachment on medium-high speed until pale and yellow and tripled in volume, about 6 minutes.

5   Using a whisk, stir one-third of the egg mixture into the chocolate mixture. Fold the remaining egg mixture and the whipped cream alternately into the chocolate mixture with a rubber spatula, folding in each addition before the previous one is fully incorporated. Fold gently until the three mixtures are blended completely.

6   Pour the batter into the prepared pan. Bake until firm to the touch and a tester inserted in the center comes out with moist crumbs, about 1 hour 20 minutes.

7   Let the cake cool completely on a rack. The cake will sink in the center and crack as it cools, but that is just the nature of this cake. Refrigerate the cake overnight.

8   The next day, remove the side of the pan. If pieces of the crust fall off, just press them back into place. Place the cake on a plate (no need to flip it to remove the pan bottom) and, using a small strainer, dust the top with cocoa powder.

INGREDIENTS

Butter for greasing the pan

1 pound semisweet chocolate, chopped

2 ounces unsweetened chocolate, chopped

¼ cup strong brewed coffee

¼ cup water

1½ cups heavy (whipping) cream, chilled

6 large eggs, at room temperature

½ cup plus 1 tablespoon sugar

Unsweetened cocoa powder, for dusting

Desert Island Butter Cake

* *

T*his cake got its name because it would be my choice if I were stranded on a desert island and could have only one sweet. (How come no one ever gets stranded on a "desserts" island?) This cake is unbelievably easy and quick to make with a flavor and texture halfway between a sponge and a pound cake. You can gussy it up with strawberries or cut off a chunk to eat plain with an occasional dunk in your coffee.*

MAKES 12 TO 16 SERVINGS

INGREDIENTS

Vegetable oil or butter for greasing the pan

2 sticks (8 ounces) unsalted butter

3 large eggs, at room temperature

1 cup sugar

1 cup sifted all-purpose flour

Frozen strawberries, thawed, or fresh strawberries, hulled, sliced, and lightly sugared to make a juice, for serving (optional)

1   Place a rack in the center of the oven and preheat to 350°F. Lightly grease an 8-inch springform pan with vegetable oil or butter.

2   Melt the butter in a saucepan over low heat.

3   Beat the eggs and sugar in a medium-size mixing bowl with an electric mixer on high speed until the mixture is thick and pale, about 4 minutes.

4   Sift the flour (again) over the egg mixture and fold it in gently with a rubber spatula. When the flour is almost but not completely incorporated, slowly fold in the melted butter with gentle strokes.

5   Pour the batter into the prepared pan. Bake until the center puffs up and then falls level with the outer edges, 35 to 40 minutes.

6   Let the cake cool in the pan on a rack. The center will drop slightly as the cake cools to room temperature.

7   For the best flavor, refrigerate the cake overnight, covered, in the pan. Remove it from the refrigerator several hours before serving. Remove the side of the pan (no need to flip the cake to remove the bottom). Place on a plate and serve with the strawberries, if desired.

Breakfast Coffeecake

* *

A classic sour-cream coffeecake layered and topped with a sweet, crunchy pecan mixture.

MAKES 12 TO 16 SERVINGS

1 Place one rack in the center of the oven and a second rack at the lowest position. Place a piece of aluminum foil or a baking sheet on the bottom oven rack just in case the pan leaks or overflows. Preheat the oven to 350°F. Lightly grease a 9-inch springform pan with vegetable oil or butter.

2 Make the topping: Combine the brown sugar, cinnamon, and pecans in a medium-size bowl and rub the butter into this mixture with your fingertips until it is incorporated. Set aside.

3 Make the cake: Sift the flour, baking powder, baking soda, and salt together into a small bowl.

4 Cream the butter, granulated sugar, and vanilla in a medium-size mixing bowl with an electric mixer on medium speed until light and fluffy, about 2 minutes. Stop the mixer twice to scrape the bowl with a rubber spatula.

5 Add the eggs to the butter mixture one at a time and mix on medium-low speed after each addition until blended, 5 seconds. Scrape the bowl after each addition. Then mix on medium for 20 seconds more.

6 By hand, add the dry ingredients to the butter mixture in four additions alternately with the sour cream in three additions, beginning and ending with the dry ingredients. Do not blend each addition in fully before adding the next. When everything has been added, scrape the bowl, then turn the mixer on low and blend until smooth, 5 seconds.

7 Spread half of the batter in the prepared pan and distribute half the topping over it. Spoon the remaining batter on top, smooth it out evenly, and distribute the remaining topping over the top.

8 Place the cake on the center rack and bake until the top turns golden, about 40 minutes.

INGREDIENTS

Vegetable oil or butter for greasing the pan

Topping

1⅓ cups (lightly packed) light brown sugar

1 tablespoon ground cinnamon

1½ cups chopped pecans

8 tablespoons (1 stick) unsalted butter, cool but not cold

Cake

2⅔ cups all-purpose flour

1¼ teaspoons baking powder

1 teaspoon baking soda

½ teaspoon salt

12 tablespoons (1½ sticks) unsalted butter, at room temperature

1 cup plus 2 tablespoons granulated sugar

2 teaspoons pure vanilla extract

4 large eggs, at room temperature

1⅓ cups sour cream, at room temperature

9   Gently place a piece of foil over the top of the cake (do not mold it) and continue to bake until a tester inserted in the center comes out clean, about 40 minutes more.

10   Cool the cake in the pan on a rack for 15 minutes. Remove the side of the pan (no need to flip the cake to remove the pan bottom). Place on a plate and serve warm or at room temperature.

* *

Pineapple Upside-Down Cake

* *

I don't believe I've ever met an American who hasn't tasted a pineapple upside-down cake—although it's true that I don't ask everyone I meet. It's such a classic! The cake can be made in a regular baking pan, but it's best to make it in a cast-iron skillet. The skillet can get really hot, which helps to caramelize the butter and brown sugar, adding flavor and texture to the topping—and that is how our forefathers made it in their hearth ovens. This cake is best served warm on day one before the caramel mixture loses its gloss. You can also make this cake with plums or peaches or even apples, but I think the pineapple takes the cake. Because of the way the batter is prepared (see step 6), you'll need a stand mixer to prepare this cake.

MAKES 8 TO 12 SERVINGS

INGREDIENTS

Topping

5½ tablespoons unsalted butter

½ cup plus 1 tablespoon (lightly packed) light brown sugar

¼ cup (lightly packed) dark brown sugar

10 canned, unsweetened pineapple rings, 7 left whole, 3 cut in half

5 to 6 maraschino cherries (optional)

1   Place a rack in the lower third of the oven and preheat to 375°F. Have ready a 10-inch cast-iron skillet. Place a baking sheet large enough to support the skillet on the rack in the oven.

2   Make the topping: Melt the butter in the cast-iron skillet over low heat. Add both brown sugars and stir with a wooden spoon until all the lumps are gone. Increase the heat to medium-high

and bring just to a simmer. Cook, sliding the pan gently back and forth so that the mixture cooks evenly and does not burn, 2 minutes. Turn off the burner and immediately place the whole pineapple rings in the hot syrup and place a maraschino cherry (if using) in the center of each ring. Place the pineapple halves around the side of the pan.

3   Make the cake: Sift the flour, baking soda, baking powder, and salt together into a small bowl.

4   Cream the butter, ¾ cup granulated sugar, and vanilla together in a stand mixer on medium speed until light and fluffy, 1½ minutes. Stop the mixer twice to scrape the bowl with a rubber spatula.

5   Add the egg yolks to the butter mixture and beat on low speed until they are incorporated, 30 seconds.

6   With the mixer on low speed, add half the dry ingredients to the butter mixture and blend until just incorporated. Add the buttermilk and mix on low for about 8 seconds. Scrape the bowl. Fold in the rest of the dry ingredients by hand, then turn the mixer on low for a few seconds. Scrape the bowl.

7   In another medium-size mixing bowl and with the whisk attachment, whisk the egg whites on medium-high speed until frothy, about 15 seconds. Gradually add the remaining ¼ cup sugar and continue beating the whites to soft peaks, about 15 seconds more.

8   Stir one-third of the whites into the batter with a wooden spoon to loosen the mixture. Fold in the remaining whites with the spatula.

9   Pour the batter over the pineapple and gently spread to distribute. Place the skillet on the sheet pan in the oven. Bake until the cake is golden, springs back to the touch, and a tester inserted in the center comes out clean, about 45 minutes.

10   Let the cake sit for a few minutes, then run a frosting spatula around the sides. Invert a plate that is slightly larger than the skillet over the cake and, using oven mitts or pot holders, hold the pan and plate together and flip them over so that the cake falls out onto the plate. Lift off the pan.

Cake

1 cup all-purpose flour

½ teaspoon baking soda

½ teaspoon baking powder

¼ teaspoon salt

6 tablespoons (¾ stick) unsalted butter, at room temperature

1 cup granulated sugar

1½ teaspoons pure vanilla extract

2 large eggs, separated, at room temperature

½ cup buttermilk, at room temperature

INGREDIENTS

Crust

1¼ cups vanilla wafer crumbs (about 35 wafers)

1 tablespoon sugar

6 tablespoons (¾ stick) unsalted butter, melted

½ cup ground almonds, walnuts, or pecans (optional)

Filling

3 pounds cream cheese, at room temperature or warmed slightly in the microwave

1½ cups sugar

2 teaspoons pure vanilla extract

3 large eggs, at room temperature

2 large egg yolks, at room temperature

1 tablespoon fresh lemon juice

Traditional Cheesecake

à la REUBEN'S

* *

When I was a kid in New York City, a Sunday treat was lunch at Reuben's (a one-time landmark restaurant and deli): a to-die-for corned beef sandwich topped off with a fat slice of cheesecake. Their cake was so creamy, it stuck to the roof of my mouth until I washed it down with several gulps of milk. Frankly, I think Reuben's broke the mold when they created their cheesecake, but I've tried with this recipe to re-create both the cheesecake and my childhood memory.

MAKES 12 TO 16 SERVINGS

1 Place a rack in the center of the oven and a second one at the lowest position. Preheat the oven to 350°F.

2 Make the crust: Place the cookie crumbs, sugar, melted butter, and nuts (if using) in a small bowl and toss them lightly with a fork until they are well blended.

3 Press this mixture firmly over the bottom of a 10-inch springform pan. Bake it on the bottom oven rack until crisp and golden, about 15 minutes. Let cool.

4 Reduce the oven temperature to 300°F and place a roasting pan or baking dish filled with hot water on the bottom rack of the oven to create moisture.

5 Make the filling: Beat the cream cheese, sugar, and vanilla in a medium-size mixing bowl with an electric mixer on medium speed until light and fluffy, 30 to 60 seconds, depending on the temperature of the cream cheese. Scrape the bowl with a rubber spatula, then beat 45 seconds more.

6 Lightly whisk the whole eggs and egg yolks together in a small bowl, then add them to the cream cheese mixture with the lemon juice. Mix on low speed until they are incorporated and the batter is velvety, about 30 seconds. Scrape the bowl, then mix at medium-high speed for 10 seconds more.

7 Pour the filling mixture evenly over the crust. Bake until the cake appears golden and set and a tester inserted in the center comes out clean, about 1 hour 15 minutes.

8 Cool the cake in the pan on a rack. When cool, refrigerate it overnight in the pan. The next day, release the side of the pan (no need to remove the pan bottom). Place on a plate and serve.

* *

Caramel-Topped Pecan Cheesecake

* *

Y*ou might call this the Southern cousin of traditional New York cheesecake, its creaminess interrupted by a generous helping of nuts.*

MAKES 12 TO 16 SERVINGS

1 Place a rack in the center of the oven and a second at the lowest position. Preheat the oven to 375°F.

2 Make the crust: Place the cracker crumbs, butter, and sugar in a small bowl and toss them together with a fork.

3 Press the crust mixture firmly over the bottom of a 9-inch springform pan. Bake the crust on the bottom rack until it is crisp and golden, about 10 minutes. Let cool.

4 Reduce the oven temperature to 300°F. Place a roasting pan or baking dish filled with hot water on the bottom rack to create moisture.

5 Make the filling: Cream the cream cheese in a medium-size mixing bowl with an electric mixer on medium speed for 1 minute. Scrape the bowl with a rubber spatula. Add the brown sugar and beat on medium-high

INGREDIENTS

Crust

1¼ cups graham cracker crumbs (7 to 8 whole graham crackers)

6 tablespoons (¾ stick) unsalted butter, melted

3 tablespoons granulated sugar

Filling

1½ pounds cream cheese, at room temperature

1¼ cups (lightly packed) light brown sugar

3 large eggs, at room temperature

1½ teaspoons pure vanilla extract

2 tablespoons all-purpose flour

1 cup chopped toasted pecans

Topping

½ cup (lightly packed) light brown sugar

¼ cup heavy (whipping) cream

¾ teaspoon unsalted butter, melted

speed until the cream cheese is fluffy, about 1 minute. Scrape the bowl.

6   Add the eggs and vanilla and beat the mixture on medium-low speed until smooth, about 45 seconds. Scrape the bowl.

7   Add the flour and mix on low speed for 4 seconds. Add the pecans and mix to blend, 15 to 20 seconds.

8   Pour the filling mixture evenly over the crust. Bake the cake on the center rack until the top is set and a tester inserted in the center comes out clean, about 1 hour 45 minutes.

9   Cool the cake in the pan on a rack. When cool, refrigerate it in the pan overnight.

10   Two hours before serving the cake, make the topping: Stir the brown sugar, cream, and butter in a small saucepan over medium heat until the sugar is dissolved. Bring the mixture to a boil and continue to boil for 1½ minutes, stirring occasionally. The mixture will look like a thick golden syrup. Pour the topping into a small heatproof bowl to stop the cooking process. When it stops bubbling, pour it over the cheesecake. Tip the springform pan from side to side so that the topping coats the cake evenly.

11   Keep the cake at room temperature until ready to serve. Then, release the side of the pan (no need to remove the pan bottom), place the cake on a plate, and serve.

Pumpkin Cheesecake

* *

I was weaned on Reuben's cheesecake, and, as a result, I remained an uncompromising purist when it came to variations on the theme. Let them keep their Kahlúa, amaretto, Grand Marnier variations, I scoffed; real cheesecake is dense and creamy and unadulterated. Then I tasted Pam Ososky's (a former Rosie's baker) pumpkin cheesecake and relented. I bid farewell to pumpkin pie at Thanksgiving and replaced it with this rich and flavorful concoction, which I top with sour cream and pecans. I serve it on a large round cake plate or platter lined with a white paper lace doily, garnished with bits of holly or evergreen and topped with whole cranberries for a festive holiday look.

MAKES 14 TO 16 SERVINGS

1 Place a rack in the center of the oven and a second at the lowest position. Preheat the oven to 375°F.

2 Make the crust: Place the gingersnap crumbs, sugar, butter, and nuts in a small bowl and toss lightly with a fork until well blended.

3 Press the crust mixture firmly over the bottom of a 10-inch springform pan. Bake it on the bottom oven rack until golden, 5 to 7 minutes. Set it aside to cool.

4 Reduce the oven temperature to 300°F and place a roasting pan or baking dish filled with hot water on the bottom rack of the oven to create moisture.

5 Make the filling: Lightly whisk together the pumpkin puree and spices in a small bowl until blended. Set aside.

6 Beat the cream cheese, sugar, and vanilla in a medium-size mixing bowl with an electric mixer on medium speed until light and fluffy, about 30 seconds. Scrape the bowl with a rubber spatula, then beat 30 seconds more.

7 Add the whole eggs and egg yolks, one at a time, to the cream cheese mixture with the mixer on

INGREDIENTS

Crust

2 cups gingersnap crumbs (35 Nabisco gingersnaps)

3 tablespoons sugar

6 tablespoons (¾ stick) unsalted butter, melted

¼ cup pecan halves, finely chopped

Filling

1½ cups canned unsweetened pumpkin puree

1 tablespoon plus 1½ teaspoons ground cinnamon

1 tablespoon ground ginger

2½ teaspoons ground cloves

2½ teaspoons ground nutmeg

1 teaspoon ground allspice

2½ pounds cream cheese, at room temperature

1⅓ cups sugar

1 teaspoon pure vanilla extract

5 large eggs, at room temperature

2 large egg yolks, at room temperature

Topping

1 cup sour cream, at room temperature

3 tablespoons sugar

¼ cup pecan halves, finely chopped, plus 14 pecan halves left whole

low speed. Blend each egg until incorporated, about 30 seconds. Scrape the bowl after each addition.

8   Add the pumpkin mixture to the cream cheese batter and blend on medium speed until the mixture is velvety, about 1 minute. Scrape the bowl and beat another minute.

9   Pour the filling mixture evenly over the crust. Bake the cake on the center rack until the top is set and a tester inserted in the center comes out clean, about 1 hour 40 minutes. Turn off the oven, partially open the oven door, and allow the cake to cool in the oven for 1 hour. Remove to a rack to cool completely.

10   While the cheesecake is cooling, make the topping: Mix the sour cream and sugar together in a small bowl.

11   Preheat the oven to 350°F.

12   Spread the sour cream mixture evenly over the surface of the cake with a frosting spatula and sprinkle the chopped pecans on top. Evenly space the pecan halves around the edge of the cake.

13   Bake the cheesecake to set the topping, 5 to 7 minutes. Cool the cake in the pan on a rack. Refrigerate, covered, overnight before releasing the side of the pan (no need to remove the pan bottom) and transferring to a plate to serve.

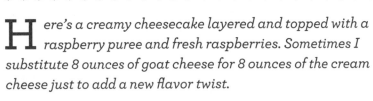

Raspberry Cheesecake

* *

H ere's a creamy cheesecake layered and topped with a raspberry puree and fresh raspberries. Sometimes I substitute 8 ounces of goat cheese for 8 ounces of the cream cheese just to add a new flavor twist.

MAKES 12 TO 14 SERVINGS

1 Place a rack in the center of the oven and a second at the lowest position. Preheat the oven to 375°F.

2 Place the cranberry juice, raspberry preserves, and cornstarch in a small saucepan and whisk vigorously to dissolve the cornstarch. Place over medium-low heat and continue to whisk until the mixture comes to a boil, about 1½ minutes.

3 Add the lemon juice and continue to whisk until the mixture is thick and shiny, about 1 minute. It should not be "powdery" in texture. Transfer to a small heatproof bowl and refrigerate until completely cool.

4 Meanwhile, make the crust: Place the cracker crumbs, butter, and sugar in a small mixing bowl and toss them together with a fork. Press this mixture firmly into the bottom of a 9-inch springform pan. Bake the crust on the center rack until it is crisp and golden, about 10 minutes. Let cool.

5 Reduce the oven temperature to 300°F. Place a roasting pan or baking dish filled with hot water on the bottom rack of the oven to create moisture.

6 Make the filling: Beat the cream cheese, sugar, eggs, vanilla, sour cream, and heavy cream in a medium-size mixing bowl with an electric mixer on medium speed until smooth, 1 to 1½ minutes. Scrape the bowl with a rubber spatula, then beat for 1½ minutes more.

7 Pour half the filling mixture evenly over the crust, then drizzle with ½ cup of the raspberry filling. Dot ¼ cup of the fresh raspberries over the raspberry filling, then pour in the rest of the cheese filling.

8 Bake until the cheesecake appears lightly golden and set, and a tester inserted in the center comes out clean, about 1 hour 20 minutes. Turn off the oven, partially open the oven door, and allow the cake to cool in the oven for 1 hour. Remove to a rack to cool completely.

9 When the cake has cooled completely, pour the remaining raspberry filling over the cake and tip from side to side to cover completely.

10 Refrigerate the cake overnight. Then, release the side of the pan (no need to remove the pan bottom) and place the cake on a plate. Crown with the remaining ¼ cup fresh raspberries before serving.

INGREDIENTS

Raspberry Filling

10 tablespoons cranberry or pomegranate juice

¾ cup seedless raspberry preserves

1 tablespoon plus 1 teaspoon cornstarch

¼ cup fresh lemon juice

Crust

1¼ cups graham cracker crumbs (7 to 8 whole graham crackers)

5 tablespoons unsalted butter, melted

¼ cup sugar

Cheese Filling

2 pounds cream cheese (at room temperature)

1 cup sugar

3 large eggs, at room temperature

2 teaspoons pure vanilla extract

6 tablespoons sour cream

¼ cup heavy (whipping) cream

½ cup fresh raspberries

Passover Apple Rustica

* *

This is a Passover dessert that you can eat any time during the year because it is so delicious. A creamy cheesecake batter chock-full of apples and white raisins and topped with cinnamon and sugar and walnuts is housed in a sweet hand-patted crust made with matzoh cake meal (sometimes called matzoh cake flour).

MAKES 10 TO 12 SERVINGS

INGREDIENTS

Crust

6 tablespoons sugar

1½ cups matzoh cake meal

6 ounces unsalted butter, melted

Filling

⅔ cup sugar

1 tablespoon plus ¼ teaspoon
   ground cinnamon

2 cups peeled Granny Smith
   apple cubes (⅓ inch; about
   2 large apples)

1¼ pounds cream cheese,
   at room temperature

3 tablespoons heavy (whipping)
   cream

2 tablespoons sour cream

2 teaspoons pure vanilla extract

2 large eggs

1 large egg yolk

1 tablespoon fresh lemon juice

2 teaspoons grated lemon zest

Topping

2 tablespoons sugar

½ teaspoon ground cinnamon

⅓ to ½ cup golden raisins

½ cup chopped walnuts

1   Place a rack in the center of the oven and preheat to 375°F. Have ready a 9-inch springform pan.

2   Make the crust: Mix the sugar and matzoh cake meal together in a medium-size bowl. Add the melted butter, tossing gently with a fork to incorporate fully.

3   Press the dough firmly into the bottom and three-quarters of the way up the sides of the pan. Bake the crust until lightly golden, about 18 minutes. Set it aside to cool and reduce the oven temperature to 350°F.

4   Meanwhile, make the filling: Mix the sugar and cinnamon together in a small bowl. Place the apple cubes in a medium-size bowl and toss with the cinnamon-sugar mix.

5   Blend the cream cheese, heavy cream, sour cream, vanilla, whole egg, egg yolk, lemon juice, and lemon zest in a medium-size mixing bowl with an electric mixer on medium-high speed until smooth, 1½ to 2 minutes. Stop the mixer several times to scrape the bowl with a rubber spatula. Then add all but 3 tablespoons of the apple cubes.

6   Make the topping: Mix the sugar and cinnamon together in a small bowl. Fold in the raisins, adding ⅓ cup at first. If that doesn't seem like enough, add more.

7   Pour the filling mixture evenly over the crust. Toss the walnuts and the remaining apple cubes on top. Sprinkle the raisin mixture evenly over the surface.

8 Bake for 50 minutes. Lower the oven temperature to 325°F and continue baking until the filling is set but still jiggly and a tester inserted in the center comes out with moist crumbs, 25 minutes. Open the oven door, turn off the oven, pull out the oven rack, and let the cake sit for about 15 minutes before transferring it to a rack to cool.

9 Refrigerate, covered, overnight, then the next day remove the side (no need to remove the pan bottom) and serve. This cake can be served cold or at room temperature.

* *

Baby Cheesecakes

* *

These little cheesecakes with prebaked graham cracker crusts are made on top of the stove, then put in the refrigerator to set—which means they are a lot easier and quicker to make than the full-grown version. When you trim them with fresh berries, they look as stunning as they taste: the perfect ending to a dinner party.

MAKES 24 MINI CHEESECAKES

1 Place a rack in the center of the oven and preheat to 375°F. Line 24 mini muffin cups with paper liners.

2 Make the crust: Place the graham cracker crumbs, sugar, and melted butter in a small bowl and toss together with a fork. The crumbs should be moistened with the butter.

INGREDIENTS

Crust

1 cup minus 2 tablespoons graham cracker crumbs (about 6 whole graham crackers)

2 tablespoons sugar

4 tablespoons (½ stick) unsalted butter, melted

Filling

8 ounces cream cheese, at room temperature

¼ cup sugar

2 tablespoons sour cream

½ teaspoon pure vanilla extract

2 teaspoons fresh lemon juice

1 teaspoon unflavored gelatin powder

6 tablespoons whole milk

1 large egg yolk

Garnish

24 fresh berries, such as strawberries, raspberries, blueberries, blackberries, or a combination

3   Spoon 1 teaspoon of this mixture into each paper liner and press it down with a finger (the mixture will naturally come a bit up the sides when you do this). Bake until the shells are crisp and golden, about 8 minutes. Remove from the oven and refrigerate.

4   Make the filling: Place the cream cheese, sugar, sour cream, vanilla, and lemon juice in a food processor and process until smooth, 10 seconds. Scrape the sides of the bowl with a rubber spatula.

5   Sprinkle the gelatin over the milk in a small saucepan and allow to soften for 3 to 4 minutes. Stir with a whisk and heat over medium heat, stirring constantly with the whisk, until it comes to a boil, about 2 minutes.

6   Add the egg yolk, break it with the whisk, and bring the mixture to a boil again, continuing to stir constantly. Remove the mixture from the heat and pour it through a small strainer into the cream cheese mixture. Process to blend for 5 seconds.

7   Scoop a generous tablespoon of the cream cheese mixture into each crust-lined cup, and refrigerate until set, about 4 hours.

8   Remove the cheesecakes from the muffin tins. If serving right away, garnish each with a fresh berry (see Note).

NOTE: *To store the baby cheesecakes, refrigerate them (without garnish) in an airtight container with plastic wrap, parchment paper, or waxed paper between the layers, if stacked, for up to 2 days. For longer storage, they can be frozen for up to 2 weeks. Bring them to room temperature before garnishing and serving.*

CHAPTER 6
Cupcakes, Mostly

Okay, why the sudden craze? Cupcake shops popping up everywhere. TV shows devoted only to cupcakes. Haven't these frosted fun little cakes always been an uncontested childhood favorite? So why are they now front-page news? Maybe because as grown-ups we've realized that cupcakes don't have to be relegated to first-grade birthday parties but are perfect for all kinds of black-tie events . . . even weddings. In other words, we never outgrow cupcake love—there's no need to hide it.

Any cake batter can be baked up as cupcakes. And any filling can be used to fill them, and any frosting can be used to top them. Even sophisticated flourless chocolate cakes can present as elegant cupcakes. In this chapter, there's a selection of traditional cupcakes, some unusual cupcakes, and a couple of cupcake wannabes (a favorite muffin of mine and a delicious mini éclair). At Rosie's we delight both kids and adults by decorating these individual portion cakes with colorful sprinkles and fun ornaments like brightly colored sugar peace signs, soccer balls, dinosaurs, ballerinas. Rejoice! The world is your cupcake.

Cupcake Storage Times
Unless the recipe indicates otherwise, all the cupcakes in this chapter can be stored at room temperature if you plan to eat them on the first or second day (cover them with plastic wrap if you're holding them over for Day Two). Otherwise refrigerate them (without frosting) in an airtight container with plastic wrap, parchment, or waxed paper between the layers, for up to 4 days. For longer storage, they can be frozen for up to 3 weeks.

Chocolate Cupcakes

* *

It's always good to have a basic chocolate cake recipe for cupcakes. Not that any other chocolate cake recipe in the book won't work, but just for the ease of it, this one won't take any experimenting on your part; the details are all laid out for you. These cupcakes have the texture of a classic cupcake— not too heavy, just right. They are delicious with an array of buttercreams and fillings, so what are you waiting for!

MAKES 12 CUPCAKES

INGREDIENTS

1 cup plus 2 tablespoons
    all-purpose flour

½ cup unsweetened cocoa
    powder

¾ teaspoon baking soda

¼ teaspoon salt

6 tablespoons (¾ stick) unsalted
    butter

1 cup sugar

¼ cup vegetable oil

2 large eggs, at room
    temperature

1 cup buttermilk,
    at room temperature

Frosting of your choice
    (see Frostings and Fillings,
    page 111)

1   Place a rack in the center of the oven and preheat to 350°F. Line 12 standard-size muffin cups with paper liners.

2   Sift the flour, cocoa, baking soda, and salt together into a medium-size bowl.

3   Cream the butter, sugar, and oil together in a medium-size mixing bowl with an electric mixer on medium-high speed until light and fluffy, about 1½ minutes. Stop the mixer twice to scrape the bowl with a rubber spatula.

4   Add the eggs to the butter mixture one at a time and mix on medium speed after each addition until very well blended, about 20 seconds. Scrape the bowl after each addition.

5   With the mixer on low speed, add the dry ingredients to the butter mixture in three additions alternating with the buttermilk, starting and ending with the dry ingredients. Beat for several seconds after each addition, then stop the mixer and scrape the sides of the bowl with the rubber spatula. After the last addition, beat the batter until everything is well blended, about 10 seconds.

6   Scoop the batter into the muffin cups so that it comes almost to the top of the liner.

7   Bake until the cupcakes have risen and are set, about 20 minutes. Allow them to cool completely in the pan on a rack before frosting.

PRESTO CHANGE-O, CAKES BECOME CUPCAKES

Turn any of the cake batters in the previous chapters into cupcakes and be as creative as you like. They can be made in all sizes, depending on the event and the age group. I advise boosting the oven temperature suggested in the cake recipe by about 25°F; each cupcake uses a small amount of batter which can tolerate a higher heat. This will help give the little cake a nice rounded top.

To fill the cupcakes, I use a pastry bag fitted with a half-inch tip which I insert into the center of the top of the cupcake before frosting it. Cupcakes are small and don't need a lot of filling, so go slowly. Once you've done a few, you'll get the hang of it.

Here are some suggested batter, filling, and frosting combos that would make delicious cupcakes.

Chocolate-Sour Cream Cake Layers or Devil's Food Cake filled with:

• raspberry preserves, and topped with Fudge Frosting

• Chocolate Ganache, and topped with Creamy Dreamy Vanilla Marshmallow Buttercream

• Chocolate Ganache and topped with Rosie's Buttercream or Mocha Buttercream

Deep Dark Raspberry Fudge Cake filled with:

• raspberry preserves and topped with Chocolate Ganache

Golden Cake Layers filled with:

• raspberry preserves and topped with Rosie's Buttercream

• Vanilla Custard and topped with Chocolate Ganache

• Chocolate Ganache and topped with Creamy Dreamy Chocolate Marshmallow Buttercream

• Lemon Curd and topped with Rosie's Buttercream and sweetened shredded coconut

Lemon Coconut Layer Cake filled with:

• Lemon Curd and topped with Creamy Dreamy Vanilla Marshmallow Buttercream

Banana Cake filled with:

• Cream Cheese Frosting

Perfect Gingerbread filled with:

• Creamy Dreamy Vanilla Marshmallow Buttercream

Blackbottoms

* *

Hrow could you not love a cupcake called a blackbottom? Especially when you find out that it's deeply chocolate cake with cream cheese filling and chocolate chips. Blackbottoms are delicious when cooled just to room temperature and the chips are still soft enough to burst in your mouth.

MAKES 24 MINI CUPCAKES

INGREDIENTS

Filling

8 ounces cream cheese,
    at room temperature,
    cut into 8 pieces

¼ cup sugar

⅛ teaspoon salt

1 large egg, at room temperature

1 tablespoon all-purpose flour

1 cup (6 ounces) semisweet
    chocolate chips

Cake

½ cup warm water

½ teaspoon distilled white
    vinegar

¾ cup all-purpose flour

3 tablespoons unsweetened
    cocoa powder

¼ teaspoon plus ⅛ teaspoon
    baking soda

⅛ teaspoon salt

4½ tablespoons unsalted butter,
    at room temperature

½ cup plus 1 tablespoon sugar

½ teaspoon pure vanilla extract

1 Place a rack in the center of the oven and preheat to 350°F. Line 24 mini muffin cups with paper liners.

2 Make the filling: Place the cream cheese, sugar, salt, egg, and flour in a food processor and process until completely smooth and blended, 30 seconds. Stop the processor once during the mixing to scrape the bowl with a rubber spatula.

3 Fold in the chocolate chips with the rubber spatula or a wooden spoon.

4 Make the cake: Stir the warm water and the vinegar together in a cup.

5 Sift the flour, cocoa, baking soda, and salt together into a small bowl.

6 Cream the butter, sugar, and vanilla together in a medium-size bowl with an electric mixer on medium speed until light and fluffy, 1 minute. Scrape the bowl.

7 Add half the flour mixture to the butter mixture and mix on medium speed until blended, 25 seconds, stopping the mixer once to scrape the bowl. Continue mixing, then scrape the bowl, and when blended, scrape the bowl again. With the mixer on low speed, add the water mixture in a stream and mix just until blended, 20 seconds, stopping the mixer once to scrape the bowl. Add the remaining flour mixture and mix on low speed just until blended, 20 seconds. Stop the mixer once during the process to scrape the bowl.

8   Drop a slightly rounded teaspoon of the batter into each paper cup. Then top each with a rounded teaspoon of the cream cheese filling (the filling should be mounded, not level).

9   Bake the blackbottoms until the tops are set and a tester inserted in the center of one comes out clean, 22 to 25 minutes. Let cool in the pans on a rack.

NOTE: *Leave the blackbottoms at room temperature if you plan to eat them the day you bake them. After that, they can be stored in an airtight container in the refrigerator for a day or two (with plastic wrap, parchment paper, or waxed paper between the layers), or you can freeze them for up to 2 weeks. Bring the blackbottoms to room temperature before serving.*

* *

Chocolate Babycakes

* *

Because they're practically flourless, these miniature chocolate sensations resemble a soufflé as much as a cupcake. Their taste is bittersweet and their appearance lustrous, with a shiny chocolate glaze. I top each with a fresh raspberry in season and arrange them on an antique platter.

MAKES ABOUT 24 BABYCAKES

1   Place a rack in the center of the oven and preheat to 325°F. Lightly grease 24 mini muffin cups with butter.

2   Make the cake: Melt the chocolate in the top of a double boiler placed over simmering water. Remove it from the heat and let it cool to room temperature.

INGREDIENTS

Butter for greasing the muffin cups

Cake

4 ounces unsweetened chocolate

6 tablespoons (¾ stick) unsalted butter, at room temperature

9 tablespoons sugar

½ teaspoon pure vanilla extract

3 large eggs, separated

2 tablespoons all-purpose flour

2 to 3 tablespoons raspberry preserves

Glaze and Garnish

6 tablespoons heavy (whipping) cream

3 ounces bittersweet chocolate

24 fresh raspberries

3   Cream the butter, 5 tablespoons of the sugar, and the vanilla in a medium-size mixing bowl with an electric mixer on medium-high speed until light and fluffy, 30 seconds. Scrape the bowl with a rubber spatula.

4   Add the egg yolks and beat on medium speed until blended, 30 seconds, stopping the mixer once to scrape the bowl.

5   Add the flour on medium-low speed and blend for 15 seconds, stopping the mixer once to scrape the bowl. Then add the melted chocolate on medium speed and blend for 15 seconds, stopping the mixer once to scrape the bowl.

6   With clean, dry beaters, beat the egg whites in a separate bowl on medium speed until foamy, 20 seconds. Increase the speed to medium-high and gradually add the remaining 4 tablespoons sugar, beating until the whites form firm but not dry peaks, about 45 seconds.

7   Using the rubber spatula, stir one-third of the whites into the batter to loosen it. Then gently fold in the remaining whites.

8   Fill each muffin cup two-thirds full with batter. Then place a generous ¼ teaspoon of the preserves in the center of the batter, and spoon enough batter over the preserves to just fill the muffin cup.

9   Bake the babycakes until set, about 15 minutes. Let cool completely in the pan on a rack.

10   If serving the babycakes the day they are baked, make the glaze now (or see Note): Heat the cream in a small saucepan to the boiling point. Remove the pan from the heat, add the chocolate, cover, and set aside for 5 minutes. When the chocolate is melted, stir with a whisk until shiny and smooth, about 5 seconds. Transfer the glaze to a small deep bowl.

11   Dip the top of each babycake into the glaze so it is well covered. Place the cakes on racks, and garnish the top of each one with a raspberry. Allow to set for 3 hours before serving, or place them in the refrigerator for 1½ hours to speed the process.

NOTE: *Serve the babycakes that day or store them overnight, uncovered, on a plate in the refrigerator. If you are making them more than 2 days ahead of time, do not frost them; freeze the unfrosted cakes in an airtight container with plastic wrap, parchment paper, or waxed paper between the layers, for up to 2 weeks. Bring them to room temperature for glazing on serving day or the day before.*

Brownie Mint Mini Cupcakes

* *

What's better . . . eating an entire box of Junior Mints or snacking on one—okay, maybe two—of these? It is highly unlikely you'll need more because they are so rich and decadent and utterly satisfying.

MAKES 24 MINI CUPCAKES

1   Place a rack in the center of the oven and preheat to 345°F. Line 24 mini muffin cups with paper liners.

2   Melt the chocolate and the butter together in the top of a double boiler placed over simmering water. Let the mixture cool for 5 minutes.

3   Place the sugar in a medium-size mixing bowl and pour in the chocolate mixture. Mix until blended with an electric mixer on medium speed, about 25 seconds. Scrape the bowl with a rubber spatula.

4   Beat in the vanilla on medium-low speed. Add the eggs one at a time, blending well after each addition, about 10 seconds. Then scrape the bowl and blend until the mixture is velvety, about 15 seconds more. Scrape the bowl.

5   Add the flour on low speed and mix for 20 seconds, stopping the mixer once to scrape the bowl. Finish the mixing by hand, taking care to incorporate any flour at the bottom of the bowl.

6   Fill each muffin cup almost to the top of the liner with the batter. Then embed a Junior Mints in each cupcake. Bake until the cupcakes are set, about 15 minutes. Let cool in the pan on a rack.

7   Meanwhile, make the glaze: Heat the cream in a small saucepan just to the boiling point. Remove the pan from the heat, add the chocolate, cover, and set aside for 5 minutes. When the chocolate has melted, stir with a whisk until shiny and smooth, about 15 seconds. Place the mixture in a small deep bowl.

INGREDIENTS

Cake

6 ounces unsweetened chocolate

2 sticks (8 ounces) unsalted butter

2 cups sugar

1 teaspoon pure vanilla extract

4 large eggs, at room temperature

1¾ cups all-purpose flour

24 Junior Mints candies

Glaze

6 tablespoons heavy (whipping) cream

3 ounces bittersweet or semisweet chocolate

8 When the cupcakes have cooled, dip the top of each one into the glaze. Place right side up on a plate or rack. Allow the topping to set for 15 minutes before eating.

NOTE: *Store the cupcakes in an airtight container with plastic wrap, parchment paper, or waxed paper between the layers. They'll keep at room temperature or in the refrigerator for 3 days.*

* *

Almond Raspberry Gems

* *

The dazzle of these moist mini cupcakes earned them their name. They're made with lots of almond paste, filled with raspberry preserves, and crowned with an almond-flavored confectioners' sugar glaze. If you want to really gild the lily, garnish them with almond halves and raspberries.

MAKES 36 MINI CUPCAKES

INGREDIENTS

Cake

¾ cup all-purpose flour

½ teaspoon baking powder

⅛ teaspoon salt

1 package (7 ounces) almond paste (not marzipan), cut into 8 pieces

½ cup plus 6 tablespoons sugar

1½ teaspoons grated lemon zest

12 tablespoons (1½ sticks) unsalted butter, at room temperature, cut into 12 pieces

½ teaspoon pure vanilla extract

½ teaspoon pure almond extract

4 large eggs, at room temperature

About 2 tablespoons raspberry preserves

1 Place a rack in the center of the oven and preheat to 350°F. Line 36 mini muffin cups with paper liners.

2 Make the cake: Sift the flour, baking powder, and salt together into a small bowl.

3 Combine the almond paste and ½ cup of the sugar in a food processor. Process until the mixture looks like coarse sand, 25 seconds. Add the lemon zest and pulse 5 times.

4 Scatter the butter pieces over the almond mixture and process until creamy, 40 seconds. Scrape the bowl with a rubber spatula. Then add the vanilla and almond extracts and process for 10 seconds.

5 Beat the eggs and the remaining 6 tablespoons sugar in a medium-size mixing bowl with an electric mixer on high speed until thick and pale, 5 to 6 minutes.

6 Sift the flour mixture (again) over the almond paste mixture. Then pour in the egg mixture and incorporate with 25 quick pulses. Scrape the bowl, and then pulse 5 more times to blend. Do not overmix.

7 Place a slightly rounded teaspoon of batter in each cupcake liner. Dot ⅛ teaspoon raspberry preserves into the center and cover that with another slightly rounded teaspoon of batter. (The batter should reach almost to the top of the liner.)

8 Bake until the cupcakes have risen and are set, 20 to 25 minutes. Let them cool in the pans on a rack before glazing.

9 Meanwhile, make the glaze: Place the confectioners' sugar, almond extract, and hot water in a small bowl and whisk vigorously until smooth.

10 Dip the tops of 18 cupcakes into the glaze and stand an almond half, if using, pointed end up, in the center of the top.

11 For the remaining cupcakes, use a fork or spoon to drizzle the glaze back and forth over the top. Top each of these with a fresh raspberry, if using. Allow the glaze to set for 2 to 3 hours.

Glaze

10 tablespoons confectioners' sugar

1 teaspoon pure almond extract

1 tablespoon hot or boiling water

Garnish (optional)

18 almond halves

18 fresh raspberries

* *

Maya's Little Butter Cupcakes

* *

I named these for my daughter because they're as petite, adorable, and perfect as she is. They are light and fluffy in texture and can be devoured in one bite.

MAKES 24 MINI CUPCAKES

103

INGREDIENTS

Cake

1 cup plus 3 tablespoons cake
    flour

¾ teaspoon baking powder

¼ teaspoon baking soda

¼ teaspoon salt

6 tablespoons buttermilk,
    at room temperature

¼ cup whole milk, at room
    temperature

7 tablespoons unsalted butter,
    at room temperature

¾ cup plus 2 tablespoons sugar

1½ teaspoons pure vanilla extract

1 large egg, at room temperature

Frosting

½ cup heavy (whipping) cream

5 ounces bittersweet chocolate,
    broken into small chunks

6 tablespoons (¾ stick) unsalted
    butter, at room temperature

1   Place a rack in the center of the oven and preheat to 350°F. Line 24 mini muffin cups with paper liners.

2   Sift the flour, baking powder, baking soda, and salt together into a small bowl.

3   Stir the buttermilk and milk together in a cup.

4   Cream the butter, sugar, and vanilla together in a medium-size bowl with an electric mixer on medium speed until light and fluffy, 1 to 1½ minutes. Stop the mixer once during the process to scrape the bowl with a rubber spatula. Then scrape the bowl once again after mixing.

5   Add the egg to the butter mixture and mix on medium speed until fluffy, 40 seconds. Scrape the bowl.

6   Add half the flour mixture to the butter mixture and mix on low speed until partially blended, 10 seconds. Scrape the bowl. Then add half the buttermilk mixture in a stream while the mixer is running on low speed, and mix just until the flour is absorbed, 5 to 10 seconds. Add the remaining flour with the mixer on low speed, and blend just until the flour begins to be absorbed. Scrape the bowl. With the mixer on low speed again, add the rest of the buttermilk mixture in a stream. Mix until

smooth and velvety, about 10 seconds, stopping the mixer once to scrape the bowl.

7   Spoon rounded tablespoons of the batter into the prepared muffin cups. Bake until the cakes have risen and are set, 22 to 25 minutes. Let cool in the pans on a rack.

8   If you are planning to serve the cupcakes the day you bake them, make the frosting now (or see Note): Heat the cream in a small saucepan to the boiling point. Remove from the heat, stir in the chocolate, cover, and set aside for 5 minutes. Transfer the chocolate mixture to a small mixing bowl and refrigerate until set, 30 to 40 minutes.

9   Add the butter to the chocolate mixture and beat with an electric mixer until the mixture is light and fluffy, 2 to 3 minutes. Stop the mixer three times during the process to scrape the bowl.

10   When the cupcakes are cool, use a butter knife or a small frosting spatula to frost the tops (use about 1½ teaspoons per cupcake); or pipe the frosting onto the cupcakes with a pastry bag fitted with a ½-inch tip. Leave the cupcakes at room temperature until serving.

NOTE: *If you do not plan to eat the cupcakes the day they are made, do not frost them. Place them on a baking sheet and cover them tightly with plastic wrap; then frost the next day. If you want to bake them farther ahead of time, freeze the unfrosted cupcakes in an airtight container with plastic wrap, parchment paper, or waxed paper between the layers, for up to 2 weeks. Defrost them overnight before frosting and serving, so they'll be soft.*

* *

Coconut Fluff Babycakes

* *

When I was applying to colleges, I attended a tea for prospective Wellesley students at a stunning town house in New York City. I remember the house, I remember being nervous, and I remember what we were served: white cake with white frosting and coconut. I didn't get into Wellesley, but no matter—that kind of cake is still my weakness. I've transformed it here into cupcakes, which I'm sure will raise all SAT scores by at least 100 points.

MAKES 24 MINI CUPCAKES

1 Place a rack in the center of the oven and preheat to 350°F. Line 24 mini muffin cups with paper liners.

2 Make the cake: Sift the flour, baking powder, and salt into a small bowl.

3 Cream the butter, oil, ½ cup of the sugar, and the vanilla in a medium-size bowl with an electric mixer on medium-high speed until light in color, 10 seconds. Stop the mixer once during the process to scrape the bowl with a rubber spatula. Clean the mixer beaters.

4 Lightly stir one-third of the dry ingredients into the butter mixture with the spatula. Then

INGREDIENTS

Cake

1 cup plus 2 tablespoons cake flour

1½ teaspoons baking powder

½ teaspoon salt

2 tablespoons unsalted butter, at room temperature

2 tablespoons plus 1 teaspoon vegetable oil

¾ cup sugar

1½ teaspoons pure vanilla extract

½ cup whole milk

2 large egg whites

3 to 4 teaspoons fruit preserves

Frosting

2 large egg whites, at room temperature

6 tablespoons sugar

3 tablespoons light corn syrup

½ teaspoon pure vanilla extract

⅓ cup shredded sweetened coconut

turn the mixer to low speed and blend partially, 5 seconds. Scrape the bowl. Add half of the milk, and blend it in with several broad strokes of the spatula. Then fold in the remaining dry ingredients by hand, followed by the remaining milk. Turn the mixer to low speed and blend until the batter is velvety, 5 to 10 seconds.

5   Beat the egg whites in another bowl with the electric mixer on medium-high speed until frothy, 20 seconds. Gradually add the remaining ¼ cup sugar and continue beating until soft peaks form, 20 to 30 seconds.

6   Using the rubber spatula, gently fold the whites into the batter.

7   Fill each cupcake liner half full with batter. Then place ⅛ teaspoon of the preserves in the center of the batter, and fill the liner with more batter so that it reaches almost to the top of the liner.

8   Bake until risen and set, 15 minutes. Cool in the pan on a rack for 20 minutes. Then remove them from the pan and set them on racks to cool completely, about 40 minutes.

9   If you're serving the cupcakes the day you bake them, make the frosting now (or see

Note): Place the egg whites, sugar, and corn syrup in the top of a double boiler placed over rapidly boiling water and beat with a handheld mixer (electric or rotary) until soft peaks form, about 4 minutes.

10   Transfer the mixture to a medium-size mixing bowl. Add the vanilla and beat with an electric mixer (whisk attachment if possible) on medium-high speed until soft peaks form again, about 30 seconds.

11   Scoop 1 tablespoon of the frosting onto each cupcake, and using a small spatula or a butter knife, spread it over the top of the cupcake.

12   Place the coconut in a small bowl, and dip the top of each cupcake lightly into the coconut. Leave the cupcakes at room temperature until serving.

NOTE: *If you do not plan to eat the cupcakes the day they are made, do not frost them. Place them on a baking sheet and cover them tightly with plastic wrap; then frost the next day. If you want to bake them farther ahead of time, freeze the unfrosted cupcakes in an airtight container, with plastic wrap, parchment paper, or waxed paper between the layers, for up to 2 weeks. Defrost them overnight before frosting and serving, so they'll be soft.*

Rosie's Blueberry Muffins

* *

These mini versions of Rosie's popular blueberry muffins are chock-full of fresh berries and accented with lemon zest—a perfect little snack any time of day and a lovely teatime treat. The substitution of some of the all-purpose flour with the cake flour just makes them a bit lighter in texture than most muffins.

MAKES 20 MINI MUFFINS

1   Make the topping: Place the flour, oats, brown sugar, and cinnamon in a small bowl and stir to mix with a whisk or fork. Add the butter, and using a small knife, cut it repeatedly into the dry ingredients until the mixture forms coarse crumbs. Refrigerate while you prepare the muffin batter.

2   Place a rack in the center of the oven and preheat to 375°F. Line 20 mini muffin cups with paper liners or grease them generously with vegetable oil or butter.

3   Make the muffins: Sift both flours, the baking powder, and salt together into a medium-size bowl.

4   Cream the butter, granulated sugar, vanilla, and lemon zest together in a medium-size bowl with an electric mixer on medium speed until light and fluffy, 45 to 60 seconds. Add the egg and beat for 10 seconds. Scrape the bowl with a rubber spatula. The mixture should be fairly smooth at this point.

5   Add half the flour mixture to the butter mixture. With the mixer running on medium-low speed, add half the milk in a stream and beat for 10 seconds. Scrape the bowl. Repeat with the remaining flour and milk. Scrape the bowl, then turn the mixer to medium-high speed and beat until smooth, 10 seconds. Scrape the bowl again.

6   Gently fold in the blueberries with the rubber spatula. Then scoop the batter by generously rounded tablespoons into the muffin cups. Pour a little water into each of the unfilled cups in the pan to prevent burning during baking.

INGREDIENTS

Topping

1 tablespoon all-purpose flour

1 teaspoon quick-cooking oats

1½ teaspoons (lightly packed) light brown sugar

⅛ teaspoon ground cinnamon

2 teaspoons cold unsalted butter

Vegetable oil or butter for greasing the muffin cups

Muffin

½ cup plus 2 tablespoons all-purpose flour

½ cup plus 3½ tablespoons cake flour, or another ½ cup plus 2 tablespoons all-purpose flour

1½ teaspoons baking powder

¼ teaspoon salt

4 tablespoons (½ stick) unsalted butter, at room temperature

5 tablespoons granulated sugar

1¼ teaspoons pure vanilla extract

¼ teaspoon grated lemon zest

1 large or extra-large egg, at room temperature

5 tablespoons whole milk

¾ cup blueberries

7 Sprinkle the topping over the muffins. Bake until the muffins are firm and lightly golden, about 17 minutes. Cool the muffins in the pan.

NOTE: *Leave the muffins at room temperature for the first day. To hold them for the following day,* *simply cover them with plastic wrap. To store them longer, place them in an airtight container in the freezer for up to 2 weeks. Before eating, bring them to room temperature or wrap them in foil and heat them in a 275°F oven for 15 to 20 minutes.*

* *

Best-Ever Bake Sale
Peanut Butter Cups

* *

Sort of a cross between a cookie and a cupcake, my friend Wendy O'Brien made these for a school bake sale. There were many things to choose from at the sale, but these sold out way before anything else. I assumed they were a kid thing, but to my amazement, when I made them, I found that grown-ups loved them just as much.

MAKES ABOUT 22 CUPS

INGREDIENTS

½ recipe Rosie's Classic Chocolate Chip Cookies dough (page 134)

1 tablespoon all-purpose flour

22 mini Reese's Peanut Butter Cups

1 Prepare a half batch of the chocolate chip cookie dough, then blend in the additional flour.

2 Place a rack in the center of the oven and preheat to 375°F. Line 22 mini muffin cups with paper liners.

3 Fill each muffin cup three-fourths full with the cookie dough. Place the peanut butter cup in the center of the batter and press down gently so that the dough rises up on the sides of the cup. Bake until lightly golden, about 13 minutes.

4 Let the peanut butter cups cool in the pan on a rack, then serve.

Mini Eclairs

* *

V*oilà! Here's the solution to the problem of how to eat éclairs so that the filling doesn't spurt out the other end: You make them bite-size and put the whole thing in your mouth at once. These miniatures have all the goodness of full-size éclairs: They're filled with custard and coated with either a bittersweet chocolate glaze or a coffee glaze.*

MAKES 30 ECLAIRS

1 Make the custard: Place the whole egg, egg yolk, sugar, flour, cornstarch, and salt in a blender and blend for 30 seconds.

2 With the motor running, add the scalded milk through the lid hole, and blend for 5 seconds.

3 Pour this mixture into a 1-quart saucepan and bring to a boil over medium heat, stirring constantly with a wooden spoon. Let boil, continuing to stir, until the mixture thickens, 1 minute.

4 Then, pour the custard mixture into a medium-size bowl. Add the butter and vanilla and stir with the spoon until the butter has completely melted. Place a piece of plastic wrap directly over the surface of the custard and refrigerate until it is cold, about 3 hours.

5 When the custard has chilled, make the éclairs: Place a rack in the center of the oven and preheat to 375°F. Line 2 baking sheets with parchment paper, and fit a pastry bag with a ½-inch plain tip.

6 Sift the flour, salt, sugar, and baking powder together into a small bowl.

7 Bring the water to a boil in a medium-size saucepan over medium-high heat. Add the butter and bring to a second rolling boil. Boil until the butter is fully melted, 2 to 3 minutes.

8 Remove the pan from the heat and add the flour mixture, stirring vigorously with a wooden spoon.

9 Return the pan to the stove and cook over medium heat, stirring constantly, until the mixture leaves the sides of the pan and forms a ball, 1 to 2 minutes. Cook until a slight film

INGREDIENTS

Custard

1 large egg

1 large egg yolk

⅓ cup sugar

2 tablespoons all-purpose flour

2 tablespoons cornstarch

Pinch of salt

1¼ cups whole milk, scalded

1 tablespoon unsalted butter

½ teaspoon pure vanilla extract

Eclairs

½ cup plus 1 tablespoon all-purpose flour

½ teaspoon salt

1½ teaspoons sugar

Pinch of baking powder

½ cup water

4 tablespoons (½ stick) unsalted butter

2 large eggs, at room temperature

Chocolate Glaze

¼ cup heavy (whipping) cream

1½ teaspoons sugar

1½ teaspoons unsalted butter

4 ounces bittersweet chocolate, finely chopped

Coffee Glaze

1¾ cups confectioners' sugar

1½ teaspoons instant coffee powder

2 tablespoons boiling water

1 tablespoon light corn syrup

¼ teaspoon pure vanilla extract

forms on the bottom of the pan, 30 to 60 seconds more.

10   Let the mixture cool for 1 minute, then transfer it to a medium-size mixing bowl and beat the dough with an electric mixer on medium speed until the steam stops rising, 1 to 1½ minutes.

11   Add the eggs one at a time, beating until glossy after each addition, about 1 minute per egg.

12   Transfer the dough to the pastry bag and pipe 2-inch fingers onto the prepared baking sheets, leaving 1½ inches between éclairs.

13   Bake the éclairs until they are puffed and nicely browned, about 20 minutes. Then open the oven door, pull out the oven rack, and puncture each éclair once with the tip of a knife to allow the steam to escape (to prevent soggy éclairs). Return the éclairs to the oven for another 3 minutes. Allow them to cool completely on the baking sheets before filling, about 30 minutes.

14   Meanwhile, prepare your choice of glaze: For the chocolate glaze, place the cream, sugar, and butter in a small saucepan and bring to a boil over medium heat, stirring with a wooden spoon, 3 to 4 minutes. Remove from the heat.

Add the chocolate, and stir until it has melted and the mixture is smooth and shiny.

15   To make the coffee glaze, sift the confectioners' sugar into a medium-size bowl. Dissolve the coffee powder in the boiling water in a small bowl. Then mix in the corn syrup and vanilla. Pour this mixture into the center of the confectioners' sugar and whisk vigorously until smooth. If the glaze seems too thick, add additional teaspoons of hot water, one at a time, until the mixture is a good spreading consistency.

16   Finish the éclairs: Spread sheets of parchment or waxed paper on a work surface. Using a sharp serrated knife, cut off the top third of each éclair. Dip these tops in the glaze (see Note) and set them aside on the parchment paper to dry.

17   Fill a pastry bag fitted with a ½-inch tip with custard and pipe a line of custard down the middle of each éclair bottom. Set the dry tops gently on top of the filling. Serve immediately or within several hours for the best results.

NOTE: *The glaze should be warm when you dip the éclair tops into it. If it has cooled, place the bowl of glaze into a larger bowl of hot water and stir to loosen it.*

CHAPTER 7
Frostings and Fillings

The handful of frostings and fillings in this short chapter are the belles of the ball. They give true meaning to the term "the icing on the cake"—both literally and figuratively. They are the final touches, the glorious creations that will dress up any chocolate or yellow layers, any sheet cake or cupcake. They can be spread on in big swooping swirls or in thin smears for just a bit of extra flair.

You'll see that throughout the book, each recipe that calls for a frosting or filling suggests one or more that will fill the bill, but they're only suggestions. By all means, get creative and mix and match those that best appeal to you.

And of course there are plenty of recipes throughout this book that come with their own glazes and fillings attached. They can be used on other recipes as well. You simply can't go wrong!

Fudge Frosting

* *

If Rosie's house is built on chocolate, this frosting is the foundation—or is it the roof? Whatever the metaphor, it's the perfect frosting: dark and glossy and it looks as good as it tastes on any layer cake or brownie.

MAKES 1¾ CUPS, *enough to frost a six-layer cake and to fill and frost a two-layer cake*

INGREDIENTS

6 ounces unsweetened chocolate

1 cup plus 2 tablespoons evaporated milk

1½ cups sugar

1   Melt the chocolate in the top of a double boiler placed over simmering water. Let cool slightly.

2   Place the evaporated milk first, then the sugar in a blender (see Note) and blend on medium speed for 2 seconds.

3   Add the chocolate to the sugar mixture in the blender and blend on high speed until the frosting is thick and shiny, 1 to 1½ minutes.

4   Spoon the frosting into a bowl and allow it to set at room temperature for 30 minutes. Then cover the bowl with plastic wrap and allow the frosting to set until firm, anywhere from several hours to overnight, depending on the weather. Do not refrigerate the frosting, even if you don't plan to use it for a few days. Store it in an airtight container at room temperature for up to 3 days.

NOTE: *This frosting can be made only in a blender.*

* *

Rosie's Buttercream

* *

A fluffy white frosting that's not overly sugary, this recipe is one you'll use often. It lasts for several days out of the refrigerator, but will require rewhipping to restore its fluffy texture after it sits for a while.

MAKES 2 TO 2¼ CUPS, *enough to fill and frost a two- or four-layer cake*

1 Place the butter, sugar, and cream in a food processor and process until smooth. The mixture will go through a curdling stage before it gets to the desired velvety texture, about 5 minutes. Stop the machine several times to scrape down the sides of the bowl with a rubber spatula.

2 Transfer the buttercream to a medium-size mixing bowl and, using the paddle attachment of an electric mixer, continue to beat on medium-high speed until the buttercream is white and fluffy, 15 to 20 minutes (yes, really that long). Stop the mixer to scrape the bowl several times. (If you do not have a paddle attachment, you can use the whisk attachment.) Use the buttercream for frosting within an hour or it will need rewhipping. If not using the day it is made, store the buttercream in an airtight container at room temperature for up to 3 days. Rewhip right before using.

INGREDIENTS

8 tablespoons (1 stick) unsalted butter, at room temperature

1¼ cups confectioners' sugar

¾ cup plus 2 tablespoons heavy (whipping) cream, cold

* *

Mocha Buttercream

* *

F*lavored lightly with coffee, this variation on Rosie's Buttercream has a lovely café au lait color.*

MAKES 2 TO 2¼ CUPS, *enough to fill and frost a two- or four-layer cake*

Dissolve the coffee in the water and place the butter, sugar, and cream in a food processor.

Proceed as directed for Rosie's Buttercream (opposite).

INGREDIENTS

¼ cup instant coffee powder

4½ teaspoons hot water

8 tablespoons (1 stick) unsalted butter, at room temperature

1¼ cups confectioners' sugar

¾ cup plus 2 tablespoons heavy (whipping) cream, cold

Creamy Dreamy
Vanilla Marshmallow Buttercream

* *

Like its chocolate counterpart, this is a light, fluffy buttercream by virtue of the fact that it incorporates the butter into an Italian meringue, creating an especially smooth and creamy texture.

MAKES ABOUT 2¼ CUPS, *enough to frost a two- or four-layer cake*

INGREDIENTS

3 large egg whites

1 cup sugar

3 sticks (12 ounces) unsalted butter, each stick cut into 10 pieces, at room temperature

1 tablespoon pure vanilla extract

1 Place the egg whites and sugar in the top of a double boiler placed over simmering water. Stir with a whisk until the mixture is opaque and warm to the touch and the sugar has dissolved, 4 to 5 minutes.

2 Transfer the egg-white mixture to a medium-size mixing bowl. Using an electric mixer with a whisk attachment, beat on medium-high speed until the mixture is tepid, 5 to 7 minutes.

3 With the mixer still on medium-high, add the butter to the egg-white mixture 2 to 3 pieces at a time, beating until incorporated. Stop the mixer frequently to scrape down the sides of the bowl with a rubber spatula. Add the vanilla and continue to beat until light and fluffy, an additional 1 to 2 minutes. Use the frosting within an hour or it will have to be rewhipped. If not using the day it is made, store the buttercream in an airtight container in the refrigerator for up to 3 days. Rewhip right before using.

Creamy Dreamy Chocolate Marshmallow Buttercream

* *

This buttercream is a bit lighter than the Rosie's Buttercream because it incorporates a syrup that has been made by cooking egg whites and sugar to create an Italian meringue when whipped. To this is added a lot of butter and vanilla ... so how can you go wrong?

MAKES ABOUT 2¼ CUPS, *enough to fill a six-layer cake and to fill and frost a two- or four-layer cake*

1 Melt the chocolate in the top of a double boiler placed over simmering water. Let cool.

2 Place the egg whites and granulated sugar in the top of a double boiler over simmering water. Stir with a whisk until the mixture is opaque and warm to the touch and the sugar has dissolved, 4 to 5 minutes.

3 Transfer the egg-white mixture to a medium-size mixing bowl. Beat with an electric mixer with the whisk attachment on medium-high speed until the mixture is tepid and looks like marshmallow fluff, 5 to 7 minutes.

4 With the mixer still on medium-high, add the butter to the egg-white mixture 2 to 3 pieces at a time, and beat until incorporated. Stop the mixer frequently to scrape down the sides of the bowl with a rubber spatula. Once all the butter has been added, add the melted chocolate and continue to beat on medium-high for an additional 1½ minutes, stopping the mixer several times to scrape the bowl. Use the buttercream within an hour or it will have to be rewhipped. If not using the day it is made, store the buttercream in an airtight container in the refrigerator for up to 3 days. Rewhip right before using.

INGREDIENTS

4 ounces unsweetened chocolate, melted and cooled

3 large egg whites, at room temperature

1 cup sugar

3 sticks (12 ounces) unsalted butter, each stick cut into 10 pieces, at room temperature

Cream Cheese Frosting

* *

A fluffy white frosting that's sweet yet slightly tart. The butter gives it richness and helps to give it that fluffy texture.

MAKES 2 CUPS, *enough to fill and frost a two- or four-layer cake*

INGREDIENTS

8 ounces cream cheese, at room temperature

1 cup confectioners' sugar

8 tablespoons (1 stick) unsalted butter, at room temperature, cut into pieces

1 teaspoon pure vanilla extract

⅛ teaspoon fresh lemon zest

1   Cream the cream cheese, sugar, butter, vanilla, and lemon zest in a medium-size mixing bowl with an electric mixer on medium speed until light and fluffy, 5 to 6 minutes. Stop the mixer several times to scrape the bottom and sides of the bowl with a rubber spatula.

2   Keep the frosting refrigerated until you are ready to frost the cake. For best results, frost as soon as possible after whipping. If using later in the day, leave the frosting in the mixing bowl and rewhip right before frosting.

* *

Chocolate Ganache

* *

E asy and delicious, this ganache makes an elegantly sleek icing or filling for your favorite layers.

MAKES 1⅓ CUPS, *enough to fill or ice a two- or four-layer cake*

1   Heat the cream in a small saucepan over medium-low heat just to the boiling point.

2   Remove the pan from the heat, add the chocolate, cover, and set aside for 5 minutes.

3   When the chocolate has melted, stir with a whisk until shiny and smooth. Use immediately.

INGREDIENTS

¾ cup heavy (whipping) cream

6 ounces bittersweet chocolate, chopped into small pieces

* *

Butterscotch-Coconut Topping

* *

My friends Susan and Stanley were visiting from Seattle when I was working on this German Chocolate Cake topping, and they were so enamored of it that they insisted that it accompany every dessert I served them. An extreme reaction, perhaps, but not wholly improbable. This topping is creamy, strong on butterscotch, and full of coconut and walnuts. In addition to keeping Susan and Stanley happy, I use it to frost Rosie's Famous Chocolate–Sour Cream Cake Layers (page 26).

MAKES ABOUT 2 CUPS, *enough to fill and frost a two-layer cake (not including the sides)*

1   Dissolve the cornstarch in the milk.

2   Place the milk mixture, both sugars, the egg yolks, butter, and salt in a medium-size saucepan.

Cook over medium-low heat, stirring constantly, until the mixture thickens and just starts to bubble, about 7 minutes.

3   Transfer the mixture to a

INGREDIENTS

1 tablespoon plus 1 teaspoon cornstarch

1 cup evaporated milk

½ cup granulated sugar

½ cup (lightly packed) light brown sugar

6 large egg yolks, at room temperature

4 tablespoons (½ stick) unsalted butter

⅛ teaspoon salt

¾ teaspoon pure vanilla extract

⅓ cup chopped walnuts

1 cup shredded sweetened coconut

blender and blend on medium-low speed for 7 seconds. Scrape the sides of the blender with a rubber spatula and blend until nicely thick, several more seconds.

4 Transfer the mixture to a medium-size bowl and stir in the vanilla. Put a piece of plastic wrap directly over the surface and allow it to cool to room temperature or refrigerate it. When the mixture is cool, stir in the nuts and coconut. If not using the day it is made, store the topping in an airtight container in the refrigerator for up to 1 day.

* *

Hot Fudge Filling

* *

Tradition has it that the hot fudge sundae was invented in Boston at Bailey's, which puts this recipe in honored company. It's a wonderful bittersweet filling for layer cakes, and it's great ladled warm over ice cream.

MAKES ¾ CUP, *enough to fill a four-layer cake*

INGREDIENTS

2 ounces unsweetened chocolate

2 tablespoons unsalted butter

5 ½ tablespoons sugar

6 tablespoons hot water

½ teaspoon pure vanilla extract

1 Place the chocolate, butter, sugar, and hot water in the top of a double boiler placed over simmering water and cook uncovered, stirring occasionally with a wooden spoon, until the chocolate is melted and the sugar has dissolved, 30 minutes. The mixture will be smooth and velvety.

2 Pour the fudge into a small bowl, stir in the vanilla, and refrigerate until the mixture is thick and of spreading consistency, about 2 hours.

NOTE: *This filling can be kept, covered, at room temperature for 2 days, although it will need to be rewhipped before using. It can also be refrigerated for the same amount of time, but needs to be brought to room temperature before using. That will take 4 to 5 hours.*

Whipped Cream

* *

Whipped cream may be rich, but it's not too sweet and is the perfect accent to so many desserts. Be sure not to overwhip the cream—you want it to have a fluffy texture.

MAKES JUST OVER 2 CUPS

Place the cream and the sugar in a medium-size bowl and using the whisk attachment (if possible) of an electric mixer, beat on high speed to soft peaks (1 minute) or firm peaks (1¼ minutes). This will vary depending on the recipe. Use immediately.

INGREDIENTS

1 cup heavy (whipping) cream, cold

1 to 2 tablespoons granulated or confectioners' sugar

* *

Vanilla Custard Filling

* *

A thick, creamy filling for layer cakes and tarts, this is also delicious spooned over a bowl of fresh berries.

MAKES 1½ CUPS, *enough to fill a four-layer cake*

1 Bring the cream, 4 tablespoons of the milk, and the sugar almost to a boil in a medium-size saucepan over medium-low heat.

2 Dissolve the cornstarch in the remaining 6 tablespoons milk.

3 Add the egg yolk to the cornstarch mixture and stir it rapidly with a fork or whisk. Add this mixture to the scalded cream mixture and whisk over medium-low heat constantly until it thickens, 1½ to 2 minutes, and then for 30 seconds more.

INGREDIENTS

¾ cup heavy (whipping) cream

10 tablespoons whole milk

6 tablespoons sugar

3 tablespoons cornstarch

4 large egg yolks

1 teaspoon pure vanilla extract

4   Remove the custard from the heat, stir in the vanilla, and pour it into a nonmetal bowl. Allow it to cool for 10 minutes, stirring it gently several times.

5   Put a piece of plastic wrap that has been punctured several times directly over the surface of the custard to prevent a skin from forming, and refrigerate until completely chilled, at least 6 hours or as long as overnight. Use when chilled.

* *

Lemon Custard Filling

* *

I put this thick custard filling between layers of cakes because I like the way its tartness contrasts with a sweet buttercream frosting.

MAKES ABOUT 1½ CUPS, *enough to fill a four-layer cake*

INGREDIENTS

3 tablespoons cornstarch

¾ cup plus 3 tablespoons water

2 large eggs, at room temperature

½ cup sugar

⅛ teaspoon salt

½ cup fresh lemon juice

1   Dissolve the cornstarch in 3 tablespoons of the water in a small bowl. Add the eggs and whisk until blended.

2   Heat the remaining ¾ cup water, the sugar, and salt in a medium-size saucepan over medium-low heat until the sugar dissolves and the mixture is hot, about 2 minutes.

3   Add the cornstarch mixture to the hot liquid, whisking constantly. Add the lemon juice and continue to cook, whisking constantly until the mixture thickens, 3 to 4 minutes.

4   Push the custard through a strainer into a small bowl. Allow it to cool for 10 minutes, stirring it gently several times.

5 Put a piece of plastic wrap that has been punctured several times directly over the surface of the custard to prevent a skin from forming, and refrigerate until completely chilled, at least 6 hours or as long as overnight. Use when chilled.

Cookies

2

CHAPTER 8
Baking Cookies

There's no getting around it: I love cookies. We go back a long way—cookies and me—ever since I first made their acquaintance by way of a zwieback that my mother stuck in my eager hands around the time I got my first tooth. I like to think it was more than mere instinct that led me to insert it directly into my mouth and gum away to my heart's content, knowing with baby certainty that here was a thing of glory.

Call it a knowledge bred in the bone, or maybe an omen, that one day I would switch from living *for* cookies to making my living *from* cookies. It's a big burden to put on a little cookie, I know, but the memory of zwieback's combination of crunch and light sweetness came flooding back when I became a professional baker years later, and it stayed with me as I opened each Rosie's Bakery, reminding me that there are few things in this world more deeply satisfying than a really good cookie.

Armed with that first taste of happiness, I became a toddler with a mission. It was

cookies I craved, and cookies I demanded. As soon as my first tooth was joined by a few others, I moved on to arrowroots. Now *there* was a cookie: crisp, buttery, dainty, decidedly more big-girl than zwieback. I sucked on the arrowroots, too, but when I was ready to take real bites, I graduated to Lorna Doones, which even grown-ups ate.

HOT ON THE COOKIE TRAIL
After that, whole worlds opened up to me, and with those limitless possibilities, nothing would do but to try them all. From the store: Oreos, Vienna Fingers, Nutter

Butters, gingersnaps, the wafers (sugar and vanilla), Fig Newtons, animal crackers, windmills, and chocolate chips. And then there were the bar cookies: the brownies and butterscotch bars and dream bars and lemon bars and congo bars. I reveled in them all, Nabisco's best and those homemade blue-ribbon winners.

Obviously, I didn't arrive home from school each day to batches of cookies freshly pulled from the oven. My mother wasn't exactly the Norman Rockwell type, but that didn't matter. She knew a good cookie when she met one, and since cookies carved out a place for themselves in my pantheon of essential foods, I made sure I got my fix in lots of other places.

In my childhood, midtown Manhattan wasn't what you'd call Girl Scout country, but some enterprising little girl always made her way up to our apartment each spring, bearing boxes of mint chocolate wafers and peanut butter sandwiches, which I urged my parents to buy in bulk and squirrel away for emergencies. (My kids did the same with me, thinking that they were urging me, too, but the truth is that I'd never skip a year of doing my part for Girl Scout cookie sales.)

Then there were the cookies you could buy by the pound at William Greenberg, a New York bakery that's still going strong. There were bite-size, many-shaped, and just sweet enough to please—a classier version of the bakery cookies that were standard fare at every bar mitzvah and wedding reception throughout the 1950s (although I confess to a lingering fondness for the pink and green checkered ones that were part of that mix).

Come high school, I made a daily stop at a bakery on my way home to get a half moon, those chubby cakelike rounds iced half with chocolate, and half with vanilla. And on weekends there were all those favorites on the grocery store shelves. I could spend a half-hour, easy, deciding which kind to buy.

Any time was cookie time, but it was mostly at night that I indulged. You know—a little milk, a few cookies to soak it up, the perfect ending to a day. I could still go through a bag in a sitting today, if I hadn't reached this age of stunning self-restraint. Now, at the end of a meal I crave just a taste of something sweet, and I'm glad to see restaurants offering a cookie or two as an alternative to elaborate desserts. Hold the tiramisù, the kumquat–passion fruit coulis, the chocolate mocha devil's food mud pie. Just give me a couple of cookies on a plate, stately and elegant in their simplicity.

As kids, we nosh on them, then we learn to bake by making them when Mom or our teacher lets us add the chocolate chips and, in time, crack the eggs and mix the batter. Later on, we binge on them while we pull all-nighters at college, whip up a batch to impress our lovers, sell them at bake sales to raise money for worthy causes. Eventually we come full circle to teach our children how to make them, and finally we offer them joyfully to our beloved grandchildren.

Given all that, it's clear that cookies aren't just for kids. There's the occasional ambivalence: We tsk-tsk over those caught with their hand in the cookie jar or imply that we must tuck cookies away with our ballerina and firefighter dreams in order to be serious adults. But over thirty years of chocolate chip cookies on Rosie's bestseller list have convinced me that the craving for cookies doesn't lessen with age. Cookies, it seems, are something we can all agree on.

The cookie recipes in this book fall into five categories: Each type has different characteristics, so each has its own requirements. But cookies are democratic creatures, and on some levels, they're all created equal. Hence, before we specialize, here are a few general principles.

PREPARING BAKING SHEETS

Baking parchment is a wonderful invention that saves you time and the bother of greasing your baking sheets. On top of that—or on bottom, to be accurate—lining the sheets with the paper protects the bottoms of the cookies from overbaking. If you don't have parchment, grease your baking sheets lightly with butter or oil. Some very buttery cookies like shortbread are the exception; their sheets don't need any greasing.

When you drop or place your dough on the baking sheets, rest the sheets on a counter or table, not on a hot stove. If the dough melts before it goes into the oven, it can affect the baking time and the texture.

OVEN TEMPERATURE

Although the oven temperature varies from cookie to cookie, a few simple rules apply in most cases. First, it's always a good idea to have your oven preheating for at least 15 minutes before you put your cookies in, if it does not automatically register when ready.

Second, if you have any question about your oven's dependability, test its temperature against the one recommended in the recipe by baking a couple of cookies for the time called for before you do the whole batch. If the suggested temperature is off, you can adjust it for the remainder before it's too late.

Third, baking time will vary depending on the size of the cookies, large cookies (in most cases) obviously taking more time than small ones. If you choose to make your cookies a different size from the one suggested in the recipe, remember to adjust the baking time accordingly.

Finally, I never bake more than one baking sheet at a time because the center rack is the only place that bakes evenly in a domestic oven. It takes longer, but it's worth it. If you'd rather bake two sheets at a time, you'll have to set the oven racks in the upper third and lower third of the oven. Halfway through the baking time, rotate the baking sheets from one rack to the other and turn the sheets back to front. This way you'll ensure even baking.

HANDLING THE DOUGH

Generally, cookie doughs are hardier than batters for cakes or pastries, so, in most cases, mixing them requires much less caution. The less moisture a dough has, the longer you can beat it without having to worry about your cookies coming out tough or dry, especially when the recipe doesn't use eggs. Rosie's Raspberry Thumbprints and Pecan Crunchies, for example, can be beaten for a long time.

Classic cookies like chocolate chip or oatmeal, which contain eggs and a bit more liquid, need more delicate beating. But the cookies that require the greatest caution are cakelike cookies because they use a substantial amount of liquid and come out tough and rubbery, just like cake, if they're beaten for a long time.

FREEZING DOUGH

With the exception of cakelike cookies, most cookie doughs freeze well for up to three weeks, and some stay fresh in the refrigerator for three or four days. Doughs for drop cookies, shortbreads, rolled cookies, and brownies that don't contain leavening all do well in the refrigerator. The reason that cakelike cookies don't last in the fridge, however, is that the leavening and liquid in the dough become active over time and affect that cookie's flavor and texture. Doughs containing oats or oatmeal can be frozen, but they become a little drier because the oatmeal soaks up the liquid. To compensate,

I sometimes add a bit of water to the dough before baking, or I flatten the mounds after I drop them onto the baking sheet so they will spread better.

STORING COOKIES

All cookies should be stored in airtight containers—plastic if you have them, but any container with a tight-fitting lid should do. If you plan to eat them within two days, you can leave them at room temperature. Otherwise, they should be refrigerated.

To keep chewy cookies moist, I have a great trick. I place the cookies in the container, spreading parchment paper or waxed paper between the layers. Then I moisten a sponge or crumpled-up paper towel and place it on a piece of plastic wrap in the container with the cookies, but not lying directly on them, and snap on the lid.

When you want to restore the crunch in crisp cookies that have gone soggy, place them in a 275°F to 300°F oven for 10 to 15 minutes. This works especially well for shortbread cookies.

Freezing works very well with all cookies, but frozen cookies need to be kept at room temperature for several hours before eating to allow their flavor to come out. If you don't have that much time, pop them into a 200°F oven until they're warm, or microwave them lightly.

THE COOKIE'S IN THE MAIL

When people talk about e-mail, they leave me bored, but I perk up when it comes to b-mail. For the uninitiated, that's bakery mail. I speak from experience when I say that the best way to ship baked goods is in a sturdy tin lined with plain or decorative cellophane. For gifts, line the tin with a doily, then fit a piece of cellophane over the bottom and up the sides, leaving several inches extra to tuck over the top. Put your firmest, sturdiest, least gooey things on the bottom, cover them with cellophane, arrange another layer of goodies, follow with more cellophane, and continue until the tin is full but not too tightly packed.

When I send something moist, like a brownie, I usually wrap it in plastic before I put it in the tin to keep it from sticking to anything else. If there's a gap somewhere, fill it with a crinkled piece of cellophane or tissue paper to keep things from shifting around. When all the pieces are fitted in securely, fold the excess cellophane over them to keep them snug. Close the tin and freeze it overnight.

Just before shipping, pack the tin in a heavy cardboard box that is large enough for the tin to be surrounded by packing peanuts. Popcorn (the real thing) works too as a cushion, should you happen to have some sitting around the house. Or swathe the tin in bubble wrap and pack it securely enough to keep it from moving around. If you still have extra room, wad up newspaper or parchment paper to stuff the shipping box.

Overnight mail is best, of course, but that can get expensive; two-day mail is usually fine.

COOKIE TYPES

Beyond these general rules, it's every cookie for itself. So before you begin baking, the best thing to do is read through the sections. They are specific to the types of cookie featured in this book.

Drop Cookies (can include Chewy Crunchy, Crispy Chompy, Cakey, Formed, Shortbread)

Drop cookies form the bedrock of cookiedom: chocolate chip, oatmeal raisin, peanut butter, gingersnaps. You make them by dropping dollops of dough (usually made from the standard butter, sugar, egg, leavening, flour mixture) onto the baking sheet. In some recipes like Chocolate Peanut Butter Volcanoes and Coconut Dainties, the cookies are formed into balls or other shapes with your hands and so they are called "formed" cookies. For the most part, drop cookies are easy and quick to whip up. Texture can vary from thin and crispy like the Oatmeal Lace Cookies to thick and chewy in the center like some of the chocolate chip cookies.

OVEN TEMPERATURES:
- Chewy Crunchy cookies are chewy in the center and crunchy around the edges. Baking the dough at a higher temperature—

anywhere from 375°F to 400°F—allows the edges to turn golden and set quickly, thereby preventing the dough from spreading. Since the center is the last to bake, when the cookies are removed from the oven, it is still high and light in color.

- Crispy Chompy cookies can be baked at a lower temperature—between 325°F and 375°F—which will result in a more consistent texture.
- Cakey cookies are best baked at 400°F because here, too, the high heat prevents the dough from spreading, while giving the center of the cookie the boost it needs to rise and thus form a nice cakey texture.

PAN PREPARATION: Lightly grease the baking sheets with vegetable oil or butter or line them with parchment paper.

SHAPING: Most often dropped in heaping tablespoons onto the baking sheet, drop cookies are sometimes formed before being baked.

TESTING FOR DONENESS:

- Chewy Crunchy cookies are done when their edges are golden and crunchy and their centers are still puffy and lighter in color.
- Crispy Chompy cookies are done when they are even in color and baked through.
- Cakey cookies are done when they have risen and set just like a cake.

COOLING:

- Chewy Crunchy cookies and Crispy Chompy cookies can cool on the baking sheets.
- Cakey cookies should cool on the sheet for 2 to 3 minutes, then slide the cookies still on their parchment paper onto a counter so the bottoms don't continue to bake. If you didn't use parchment, transfer the cookies to a sheet of aluminum foil or waxed paper to continue cooling.

EATING:

- Chewy Crunchy cookies are great to eat warm.
- Crispy Chompy cookies and Cakey cookies taste best when completely cooled.

STORING:

- Chewy Crunchy cookies are best eaten within a day or two of baking. If you're keeping them longer than that, store them in an airtight container in the freezer for up to 2 weeks.
- Crispy Chompy cookies can go straight into the cookie jar, where they'll stay fresh for a week.
- Cakey cookies, like Chewy Crunchy cookies, should be eaten within a day or two of baking or stored in the freezer in an airtight container for up to 2 weeks. If the cookies are glazed, wait until the glaze is hardened, then separate layers of cookies with parchment paper before freezing them.

Refrigerator Cookies

Refrigerator cookies, such as Pecan Crunchies, are made of a stiff shortbread-like dough that is rolled into a log, chilled, sliced, and then baked. They hold their shape well during baking and come out of the oven nice and crunchy.

OVEN TEMPERATURE: Refrigerator cookies usually call for a low temperature (between 275°F and 325°F) so the cookies bake evenly and get crisp.

PAN PREPARATION: Lightly grease the baking sheets with butter or oil or line them with baking parchment paper.

SHAPING: When the dough is mixed, form it into logs about 2 inches in diameter. (You may want to dip your hands in flour before molding so that the dough doesn't stick to them.) Place a log near the edge of a piece of waxed paper that has been cut slightly longer than the log. Roll the log inside the waxed paper and twist the paper ends like a hard-candy wrapper.

Chill the log for 2 hours, then while it is still in its waxed paper wrapping, roll it gently back and forth on a counter with the palms and fingers of your hands until it forms a smooth cylinder. Return the log to the fridge for several hours more. Finally, cut the log into slices ¼ to ⅜ inch thick and place them about 1½ inches apart on a baking sheet.

TESTING FOR DONENESS: Refrigerator cookies are done when they are lightly golden and crisp to the touch. When done, they should be completely baked.

COOLING: These cookies can cool on the baking sheet or a wire rack since they are sturdy and can be transferred easily.

EATING: Let the cookies cool completely before you eat them or, better yet, wait until the next day. They can taste a little doughy when they're warm, but that disappears soon.

STORING: Log cookies stored in an airtight container remain fresh and can be stacked on top of each other if they're not frosted or adorned with jam. If they get soggy, simply put them in a preheated 275°F oven for 10 minutes to restore their crispness. These cookies freeze well, too, but taste best at room temperature. The unbaked logs can be stored for 4 to 5 days in the refrigerator, or they can be frozen for up to several weeks.

Shortbread Cookies

This category includes cookies such as Very Short Shortbread Cookies and Noah Bedoahs. Their doughs contain very little if any liquid, so they can be beaten without worry.

OVEN TEMPERATURE: I like to bake these cookies at a low temperature (300°F to 325°F) for a long time to ensure crunchiness throughout. As a rule of thumb, the bigger the cookie, the lower the oven temperature.

PAN PREPARATION: Line baking sheets with parchment paper or place the batter directly on the baking sheets. Because of the cookies' high butter content and the absence of liquid, the sheets do not need greasing.

SHAPING: These cookies can be molded by hand or dropped from a spoon onto the baking sheets.

TESTING FOR DONENESS: The cookies should be lightly golden and baked throughout, so I test for doneness by cutting one in half to ensure that there is no doughy strip.

COOLING AND EATING: These cookies taste best when they're well cooled or even the next day when the flavors have settled.

STORING: Stored in an airtight container in or out of the refrigerator, these cookies last for weeks. If they *do* get soggy, you can crisp them again by warming them in a preheated 275°F oven for 10 minutes.

Rolled Cookies (can include Sugar Cookies, Shortbread Cookies, and Filled-Pastry Cookies)

Rolled sugar cookies, such as Ruby Gems, are made from a stiff dough that has been chilled before it is rolled out and cut. You can mix the dough in a food processor, with an electric mixer, or by hand.

OVEN TEMPERATURE: This varies between 350°F and 400°F depending on the recipe.

PAN PREPARATION: Line baking sheets with parchment paper or grease them lightly with butter or oil. Use an ungreased sheet for cookies that contain a lot of butter.

SHAPING: Chill the dough in disks and then roll it out ⅛ to ¼ inch thick; the thickness will vary with the recipe. Use cookie cutters to make special shapes or the top of a glass dipped in flour for round cookies. Cut the cookies as close together as possible to minimize the dough scraps. I use a metal spatula to lift the cut-out cookies onto the baking sheets.

TESTING FOR DONENESS: Rolled cookies are ready when they have just begun to turn golden around the edges.

COOLING: These cookies cool best directly on the baking sheet. They're delicate and may break if you try to move them while they're hot.

EATING: Let the rolled cookies cool before you eat them to allow the floury taste to settle down.

STORING: Use your trusty airtight container for storing these cookies in the freezer or refrigerator. The dough also stores well for 4 to 5 days in the refrigerator, or it can be frozen.

Rolled Filled Cookies

Rolled filled pastry cookies, which include such delicacies as rugalah, are made from a rich dough filled with fruit, jam, nuts, cheese, or whatever, and rolled into distinctive shapes.

OVEN TEMPERATURE: Use a hot oven, 370°F to 400°F. The dough must be chilled before baking and baked quickly so that the considerable amount of butter doesn't melt out of the dough and cause the pastries to lose their shape.

PAN PREPARATION: Lightly grease the baking sheets with vegetable oil or butter or line them with parchment paper.

SHAPING: This varies depending on the cookie.

TESTING FOR DONENESS: The dough should be lightly golden in color.

COOLING: Remove filled pastry cookies from the baking sheet immediately; use a metal spatula to place them on a plate or cooling rack. If they sit on the sheet, their filling may harden and stick to the pan or parchment paper.

EATING: The texture of some pastry cookies is better on the second day (rugalah is an example). Crisp pastries, such as Maya's Pocketbooks, taste best the day they're made.

STORING: Store pastry cookies in an airtight container. You can freeze or refrigerate them with no problem. The dough, too, can be stored for 4 to 5 days in the fridge and can be frozen for up to several weeks.

SERVING

Whatever the taste or shape of cookie, I encourage you to think creatively when it comes to serving them because, contrary to conventional wisdom, cookies can provide an elegant closing to a dinner party as well as a casual snack after school. Even hearty cookies like Soho Globs, chocolate chips, or oatmeal raisin work well as a dessert if you make them small and dainty, and most cookies complement sorbet or ice cream perfectly.

In fact, the well-dressed cookie can go anywhere. Cover a platter with a doily and build a cookie mosaic using a variety of sizes, shapes, and colors or go for an Ali Baba's cave effect and pile them high on a plate in an embarrassment of riches.

But you don't need entertaining as an excuse to whip up a batch of your favorite cookies. It's easy to keep a batch on hand and ready for when you crave a little something sweet.

CHAPTER 9
Chewy Crunchy

I usually get into trouble when I make sweeping pronouncements, but I'll go out on a limb and proclaim this category of cookie America's sweetheart. It includes such basics as chocolate chip cookies, oatmeal and peanut butter cookies, snickerdoodles, and macaroons.

While I've raided other cultures and climates for some of the ingredients, most of these cookies are quintessentially American—a fistful of good taste straight out of a Norman Rockwell kitchen—and so is what goes into them. Our southern states give the world its pecans, oatmeal probably came over with the pilgrims, great New England fortunes were founded on molasses and rum (hermit cookies were created by Cape Cod bakers to last the long sea voyages of American clipper ships), and what else but American ingenuity would come up with something like peanut butter?

A large part of the widespread appeal of these cookies comes, I think, from their texture. There's something so reinforcing, so comforting and rewarding, about biting through a crunchy edge and encountering a moist, chewy center and often a further prize of raisins or nuts. There's a word used in Louisiana, *lagniappe,* which means an unexpected extra something. That's how I think of my chewy crunchy cookies.

Baking Reminder

As I discussed in my general cookie baking instructions, I like to home-bake cookies one baking sheet at a time, usually in the center of the oven. If you'd rather bake two sheets at a time, set the oven racks in the upper third and lower third of the oven before preheating it. Halfway through the baking time, rotate the baking sheets from one rack to the other and turn the sheets back to front. This way you'll ensure even baking.

These cookies are baked large and generous and tend to keep well, so when we imagine the perfect cookie jar filler, these chewies often come to mind. Even the names are straightforward, telling us that what we see is what we get. (I know, there's "snickerdoodles," and where that name came from is anybody's guess. But it's fun to say, so who cares?)

Most of the cookies in this chapter are made from sturdy doughs, so carefully regulated mixing isn't as important as in other baking. If you're the type of baker who needs to be anxious about something, concentrate on finding the right baking time and temperature to create the texture you want. Chewier cookies are dropped in mounds on the baking sheet and removed from the oven when their centers are less done than their edges. Crunchier cookies can be pressed flatter on the baking sheet and baked until their centers and edges are the same doneness. Play around to get precisely the chew and crunch that your heart desires.

* *

Rosie's Classic
Chocolate Chip Cookies

* *

There is little doubt that the chocolate chip or Toll House cookie is America's favorite; so much so that it may qualify as one of the basic food groups. This adaptation is crisp around the edges and chewy in the middle. To achieve that consistency it's crucial that you take the cookies out of the oven when the centers are light colored and puffy and the edges are golden. The slightly underdone centers will drop when they cool and become chewy. With these cookies, I always figure on ending up with fewer than the stated recipe yield because everyone who wanders into the kitchen can't seem to resist sticking a fingerful of the dough into their mouths. But then, neither can I.

MAKES 24 LARGE COOKIES

1 Preheat the oven to 385°F. Line several baking sheets with parchment paper or lightly grease them with vegetable oil or butter.

2 Sift the flour, baking soda, and salt together into a small bowl and set aside.

3 Cream the butter, both sugars, and the vanilla together in a medium-size bowl with an electric mixer on medium speed until light and fluffy, 1½ to 2 minutes. Stop the mixer twice to scrape the bowl with a rubber spatula.

4 Add the eggs to the butter mixture and beat on medium speed until they are blended, about 30 seconds. Scrape the bowl.

5 Add the dry ingredients and mix on low speed for 15 seconds. Scrape the bowl.

6 Add the chocolate chips and blend until they are mixed in, 5 to 8 seconds.

7 Drop the dough by heaping tablespoons 2 inches apart onto the prepared baking sheets.

8 Bake the cookies until the edges are dark golden and the center is light and slightly puffed up, 11 to 12 minutes. Remove the cookies from the oven and allow them to cool on the baking sheets. These are best eaten the same day they are baked.

NOTE: *This dough also works beautifully when it's refrigerated a minimum of 4 hours; it tends to produce a thicker, chewier cookie that is crisp around the edges.*

INGREDIENTS

Vegetable oil or butter for greasing the baking sheets (optional)

2 cups plus 1 tablespoon all-purpose flour

1 teaspoon baking soda

¾ teaspoon salt

2 sticks (8 ounces) unsalted butter, at room temperature

1 cup plus 1 tablespoon (lightly packed) light brown sugar

½ cup plus 2 tablespoons granulated sugar

1 teaspoon pure vanilla extract

2 large eggs, at room temperature

1½ cups (9 ounces) semisweet chocolate chips

Soho Globs

* *

INGREDIENTS

Vegetable oil or butter for greasing the baking sheets (optional)

5 ounces semisweet chocolate

3 ounces unsweetened chocolate

6 tablespoons (¾ stick) unsalted butter, at room temperature

⅓ cup all-purpose flour

1 teaspoon baking powder

¼ teaspoon salt

2 large eggs, at room temperature

2 teaspoons pure vanilla extract

1 tablespoon instant espresso powder

¾ cup sugar

¾ cup (4 ounces) semisweet chocolate chips

⅓ cup chopped pecans

⅓ cup chopped walnuts

*T*he first time I was introduced to a glob at the Soho Charcuterie (a popular American restaurant in the 1980s) in New York, I was outraged at the price. Two dollars indeed, I fumed—until I bit into one and immediately went back for two more. Globs are the ideal combination of a bittersweet chocolate flavor and a chewy consistency, all studded with pecans and chocolate chips—kind of cookiedom's answer to the brownie. And then there's the name. No wonder I became a believer.

MAKES 20 COOKIES

1 Preheat the oven to 325°F. Line several baking sheets with parchment paper or lightly grease them with vegetable oil or butter.

2 Melt the semisweet and unsweetened chocolate and the butter in the top of a double boiler placed over simmering water. Let cool slightly.

3 Sift the flour, baking powder, and salt together into a small bowl and set aside.

4 With an electric mixer on medium speed, beat the eggs, vanilla, and espresso powder in a medium-size mixing bowl until they are mixed together, about 10 seconds.

How Heaping Is Heaping?

I like to measure my drop cookie dough by heaping tablespoons. But, what exactly does that mean? Because size affects baking time, I did a careful measure and it turns out that my heaping tablespoon is the equivalent of 3 level tablespoons. Quite a heap.

5   Add the sugar to the egg mixture and blend it all until thick, about 1 minute. Scrape the bowl with a rubber spatula.

6   Add the melted chocolate and blend 1 minute more. Scrape the bowl.

7   Add the flour mixture on low speed and mix until blended, 10 seconds. Fold in the chocolate chips and nuts by hand or with the mixer on low speed.

8   Drop the dough by heaping tablespoons about 2 inches apart onto the prepared baking sheets. Bake the cookies until they rise slightly and form a thin crust, about 13 minutes. Immediately transfer the cookies from the baking sheets to a rack to cool.

* *

Big Jakes

* *

I named this dark moist cookie studded with white chocolate after my son Jake because when he was little, his face would light up with joy and get coated with chocolate as he ate it.

MAKES 20 COOKIES

Prepare the recipe as directed in Soho Globs, substituting the white chocolate for the chips and nuts in step 7.

INGREDIENTS

Soho Globs (opposite), omitting the chocolate chips and nuts

¾ cup (4 ounces) good quality chopped white chocolate

Peanut Butter Chocolate Chunk Cookies

* *

Baked with generous amounts of all-natural peanut butter and chocolate chunks, these cookies are particular favorites of kids. The amount of dough doesn't result in a large batch, so they'll go pretty quickly.

MAKES 18 LARGE COOKIES

INGREDIENTS

1⅓ cups all-purpose flour

½ teaspoon baking soda

½ teaspoon salt

10 tablespoons (1¼ sticks) unsalted butter, at room temperature

⅔ cup plus 1 tablespoon crunchy all-natural peanut butter

1 teaspoon pure vanilla extract

10 tablespoons (lightly packed) light brown sugar

½ cup granulated sugar

1 large egg, at room temperature

6 ounces bittersweet chocolate, broken into good-size pieces

Vegetable oil or butter for greasing the baking sheets (optional)

1   Sift the flour, baking soda, and salt into a small bowl and set aside.

2   Cream the butter, peanut butter, vanilla, and both sugars together in a medium-size mixing bowl with an electric mixer on medium speed until light and fluffy, about 1½ minutes. Stop the mixer twice to scrape the bowl with a rubber spatula.

3   Add the egg to the peanut butter mixture and beat on medium speed until blended, about 1 minute. Scrape the bowl.

4   Add the flour mixture and the chocolate pieces and mix on low speed until blended, about 15 seconds. Scrape the bowl and mix several seconds more.

5   Measure out heaping tablespoons of the dough and roll them into balls with your hands. Use a fork or a potato masher to press down on the balls to create an imprint. Place the cookies on a baking sheet, cover with plastic wrap, and refrigerate for several hours or overnight or place in the freezer for 1 to 2 hours.

6   Fifteen minutes before baking, preheat the oven to 375°F. Line several baking sheets with parchment paper or lightly grease them with vegetable oil or butter.

7   Place the balls 2 inches apart on the prepared baking sheets. Bake the cookies until they are dark gold around the edges and slightly puffy and light in the center, about 12 minutes. Let them cool on the baking sheets.

Fudgie Wudgies

* *

Named by my son Jake, this extra-fudgy, almost flourless, abounding-in-nuts-and-chips cookie is a dark—as dark can be—sensation. It's a chocoholic's dream, and not bad for the casual indulger, too.

MAKES 20 LARGE COOKIES

1 Preheat the oven to 325°F. Line several baking sheets with parchment paper or lightly grease them with vegetable oil or butter.

2 Melt the 1 cup of chocolate chips and the butter in the top of a double boiler placed over simmering water. Then remove the pan from the heat and let cool slightly.

3 Sift the flour, baking powder, cocoa, and salt together into a small bowl and set aside.

4 Beat the eggs and vanilla in a medium-size mixing bowl with an electric mixer on medium speed until they are blended, about 10 seconds.

5 Add the sugar to the egg mixture and blend on medium speed until the mixture is thick, about 1 minute. Scrape the bowl with a rubber spatula.

6 Add the melted chocolate to the egg mixture and blend on medium 1 minute more. Scrape the bowl.

INGREDIENTS

Vegetable oil or butter for greasing the baking sheets (optional)

1¾ cups (10 ounces) semisweet chocolate chips

10 tablespoons (1¼ sticks) unsalted butter

6 tablespoons all-purpose flour

1 teaspoon baking powder

3 tablespoons unsweetened cocoa powder

⅛ teaspoon salt

2 large eggs, at room temperature

2 teaspoons pure vanilla extract

¾ cup sugar

½ cup chopped pecans or walnuts

Storing Cookies

Although storing cookies is discussed in the Baking Cookies chapter, I think it's worth repeating the general instructions. They are good for most cookies, but if a cookie has a specific instruction, I'll mention it in the recipe.

The cookies in this chapter are best eaten on the day they're baked, but if there are leftovers, store them in an airtight container overnight at room temperature using parchment paper, plastic wrap, or waxed paper between the layers. At the end of the second day, place the container in the refrigerator for up to 2 days more. For longer storage, it's best to freeze the cookies. Most will stay fresh for up to 2 weeks in an airtight container in the freezer. Before serving, leave yourself plenty of time for the cookies to come to room temperature.

7   Add the flour mixture on low speed and mix until blended, 10 seconds. Scrape the bowl.

8   Add the remaining ¾ cup chocolate chips and the nuts, and blend on low speed until they are mixed in, 5 to 8 seconds.

9   Drop the dough by heaping tablespoons about 2 inches apart onto the prepared baking sheets. Bake the cookies until they rise slightly and form a thin crust, 14 to 16 minutes. Immediately transfer the cookies from the baking sheets to racks to cool.

* *

Pecan Chocolate Chips

* *

*I*n the baking biz, the big debate is nuts versus no nuts. *Nearly everyone under age twelve falls firmly in the no-nuts camp, but those of us who have made it through adolescence are less predictable and depend more on mood. I, for one, consider the nutted chocolate chip cookie to be a valuable variation on the classic, and this is one of the best of its breed. It's chewy in the center, crunchy around the edges, and enhanced by the chomp of chopped pecans.*

MAKES 40 COOKIES

INGREDIENTS

Vegetable oil or butter for greasing the baking sheets (optional)

2¼ cups plus 2 tablespoons all-purpose flour

2 teaspoons baking soda

1 teaspoon salt

2 sticks (8 ounces) unsalted butter, at room temperature

1 cup (lightly packed) light brown sugar

7 tablespoons granulated sugar

1 tablespoon pure vanilla extract

2 tablespoons light corn syrup

2 teaspoons water

2 large eggs, at room temperature

2 cups (12 ounces) semisweet chocolate chips

1½ cups chopped pecans

1   Preheat the oven to 400°F. Line several baking sheets with parchment paper or lightly grease them with vegetable oil or butter.

2   Sift the flour, baking soda, and salt together into a small bowl and set aside.

3   Cream the butter, both sugars, and the vanilla together in a medium-size bowl with an electric mixer on medium speed until light and fluffy, 1½ to 2 minutes. Stop the mixer twice to scrape the bowl with a rubber spatula. Add the corn syrup and the water and mix on medium for several seconds more.

4   Add the eggs to the butter mixture and beat on medium speed until they are blended, about 30 seconds. Scrape the bowl.

5   Add the flour mixture and mix on low speed for 15 seconds. Scrape the bowl.

6   Add the chocolate chips and the nuts and blend on low speed until they are mixed in, 5 to 8 seconds.

7   Drop the dough by heaping tablespoons 2 inches apart onto the prepared baking sheets. Bake the cookies until the edges are dark golden and the centers are light and slightly puffed up, 11 to 12 minutes. Let the cookies cool on the baking sheets.

A Happy Solution

If you were to ask any group of people anywhere in this country what their favorite cookie was, the answer, hands down, would be chocolate chip. I know this for a fact because pollsters have asked people everywhere just that—though I'm always a little perplexed about what we're supposed to do with the information.

The chocolate chip—or Toll House cookie, as it was first known—has topped the American hit parade almost since the fateful day eighty years ago when Ruth Wakefield, proprietor of the Toll House Inn in Whitman, Massachusetts, stumbled onto the perfect ménage à trois of butter, sugar, and chocolate. That story has been told often: How Mrs. Wakefield set out to make an old colonial recipe called the Butter Drop Do. How she didn't have the nuts the recipe called for, so cut up a bar of semisweet chocolate, expecting it to melt evenly. How it didn't, but instead studded the cookies with luscious bits of soft chocolate. How a guest sampled the cookies and told a journalist friend in Boston about them. And how Nestlé bought out Mrs. Wakefield, created the chocolate chip, and put her recipe on the package for posterity.

Which goes to show that many an empire has been founded on a goof.

I'm grateful to Ruth Wakefield—who would want to live in a world devoid of chocolate chip cookies?—and also to Nestlé, who, I think, still makes the best chocolate chips. I use no other for my cookies. You may decide otherwise, but whatever brand you use, make sure that they're real chocolate, not chocolate-flavored.

Chocolate Chunkers

* *

R emember Chunky, the candy? Well, meet Chocolate Chunkers, the cookie. It's a craggy mountain stuffed full of chocolate chips, raisins, and pecans, then coated with a velvety chocolate ganache. For the kid in all of us.

MAKES 24 COOKIES

INGREDIENTS

Vegetable oil or butter for greasing the baking sheets (optional)

Cookies

3½ ounces unsweetened chocolate

8 tablespoons (1 stick) unsalted butter

1 cup plus 2 tablespoons all-purpose flour

⅛ teaspoon baking powder

1¼ cups sugar

2 large eggs, at room temperature

1 large egg yolk

1 cup raisins

¾ cup chopped pecans

¾ cup (4 ounces) semisweet chocolate chips

Glaze

½ cup heavy (whipping) cream

2 tablespoons sugar

8 ounces bittersweet chocolate, chopped small

1 tablespoon unsalted butter

1 Preheat the oven to 325°F. Line several baking sheets with parchment paper or lightly grease them with vegetable oil or butter.

2 Make the cookies: Melt the unsweetened chocolate and the butter in the top of a double boiler placed over simmering water. Remove the pan from the heat and let cool slightly.

3 Sift the flour and baking powder together into a small bowl and set aside.

4 Place the sugar in a medium-size mixing bowl. Add the melted chocolate mixture and blend with an electric mixer on low speed for 10 seconds. Scrape the bowl with a rubber spatula.

5 Add the eggs and the yolk to the chocolate mixture and mix on low until blended, 10 seconds, stopping the mixer once to scrape the bowl.

6 Add the flour mixture on low speed and mix until blended, 10 seconds, stopping the mixer once to scrape the bowl.

7 Add the raisins and blend on low speed for 5 seconds. Then add the nuts and chocolate chips, and blend several seconds more. Finish the mixing by hand.

8 Scoop heaping tablespoons of dough and form them into mounds with your hands. Arrange them 2 inches apart on the prepared baking sheets. Bake the cookies until they form a thin crust, 20 to 25 minutes. Let them cool on the baking sheets.

9 Meanwhile, make the glaze: Place the cream and sugar in a small saucepan and bring to a boil, whisking occasionally. Remove from the heat immediately. Add the chocolate and butter to the pan, cover, and let sit about 5 minutes until the chocolate melts. Stir the mixture with a whisk until it is shiny and velvety, 15 seconds.

10   Dip each cookie, upside down, in the glaze, coating the entire top. Place right side up on racks or on a sheet of parchment paper to set for several hours.

* *

Whole-Grain Earthy Chocolate Chips

* *

G*o on, sneak in a little healthiness. Your kids will never know. These cookies contain bran, wheat germ, and whole wheat flour, and they still taste good. Or should I say that's why they taste good!*

MAKES 26 COOKIES

1   Preheat the oven to 400°F. Line several baking sheets with parchment paper or lightly grease them with vegetable oil or butter.

2   Sift the flour, baking soda, and salt together into a small bowl and set aside.

3   Mix the oats, wheat bran, and wheat germ together in another small bowl and set aside.

4   Cream the butter, both sugars, and the vanilla together in a medium-size bowl with an electric mixer on medium speed until light and fluffy, 1½ to 2 minutes. Stop the mixer twice to scrape the bowl with a rubber spatula.

5   Add the eggs to the butter mixture and beat on medium speed until they are blended, about 30 seconds. Scrape the bowl.

6   Add the flour mixture and mix on low speed for 10 seconds. Scrape the bowl.

INGREDIENTS

Vegetable oil or butter for greasing the baking sheets (optional)

2¼ cups plus 2 tablespoons whole wheat flour

1 teaspoon baking soda

1 teaspoon salt

¾ cup plus 2 tablespoons quick-cooking oats

2 tablespoons wheat bran (coarse or fine)

2 tablespoons toasted wheat germ

2 sticks (8 ounces) unsalted butter, at room temperature

1 cup (lightly packed) light brown sugar

½ cup granulated sugar

1½ teaspoons pure vanilla extract

2 large eggs, at room temperature

1½ cups (9 ounces) semisweet chocolate chips

143

7   Add the oat mixture and mix on low speed for several seconds to blend.

8   Add the chocolate chips and blend until they are mixed in, 5 to 8 seconds.

9   Drop the dough by heaping tablespoons 2 inches apart onto the prepared baking sheets. Bake the cookies until the edges are dark golden and the centers are light and slightly puffed up, 11 to 12 minutes. Let them cool on the baking sheets.

* *

INGREDIENTS

Vegetable oil or butter for greasing the baking sheets (optional)

¾ cup all-purpose flour

¾ teaspoon baking soda

¾ teaspoon ground cinnamon

½ teaspoon salt

8½ tablespoons (1 stick plus 1½ teaspoons) unsalted butter, at room temperature

⅓ cup plus 2 tablespoons (lightly packed) light brown sugar

7 tablespoons granulated sugar

1 tablespoon plus 1 teaspoon molasses

2¼ teaspoons water

½ teaspoon pure vanilla extract

1 large egg, at room temperature

2 cups plus 1 tablespoon old-fashioned rolled oats

½ cup shredded sweetened coconut

½ cup plus 2 tablespoons golden raisins

Rosie's Oatmeal Cookies

with COCONUT *and* GOLDEN RAISINS

* *

Moist, chewy, and replete with golden raisins, this cookie is a staple at Rosie's. So, I had to adapt the recipe for home use. Here it is: the perfect choice for easy baking, moist in the center and crunchy around the edges. Bake them longer if you like your oatmeal cookies crunchier—they are good both ways.

MAKES 20 COOKIES

1   Preheat the oven to 375°F. Line several baking sheets with parchment paper or lightly grease them with vegetable oil or butter.

2   Sift the flour, baking soda, cinnamon, and salt together into a small bowl and set aside.

3   Cream the butter, both sugars, the molasses, water, and vanilla together in a medium-size bowl with an electric mixer on medium speed until light and fluffy, about 1½ minutes. Stop the mixer twice to scrape the bowl with a rubber spatula.

4   Add the egg to the butter mixture and mix on medium-low speed to incorporate it, about 20 seconds.

5   Add the flour mixture and mix on medium-low speed for 10 seconds. Scrape the bowl, then mix until blended, about 5 seconds more. Scrape the bowl.

6   Add the oats and mix for several seconds on low speed to blend them in. Add the coconut and raisins and mix until blended.

7   Drop the dough by heaping tablespoons about 2 inches apart onto the prepared baking sheets. Bake the cookies until they are golden around the edges and lighter in the center, 12 to 14 minutes. Let them cool on the baking sheets.

* *

Pecan Oatmeal Chips

* *

I adapted these cookies from what was purportedly an original Neiman Marcus creation, and I must say that they're a good argument for department stores branching out into everything under the sun. The oats are ground into flour before you add them to the batter. Neither chic nor expensive, like the source of this recipe, these cookies are downright earthy.

MAKES 20 COOKIES

1   Preheat the oven to 375°F. Line several baking sheets with parchment paper or lightly grease them with vegetable oil or butter.

2   Process the oats in a food processor until they have the consistency of coarse flour. Set aside.

INGREDIENTS

Vegetable oil or butter for greasing the baking sheets (optional)

1¼ cups old-fashioned rolled oats

1 cup all-purpose flour

¾ teaspoon baking soda

½ teaspoon salt

12 tablespoons (1½ sticks) unsalted butter, at room temperature

½ cup (lightly packed) light brown sugar

½ cup granulated sugar

1½ teaspoons pure vanilla extract

1 large egg, at room temperature

1 cup (6 ounces) semisweet chocolate chips

½ cup chopped pecans

3   Sift the flour, baking soda, and salt together into a small bowl and set aside.

4   Cream the butter, both sugars, and the vanilla together in a medium-size bowl with an electric mixer on medium speed until light and fluffy, 1 to 1½ minutes. Stop the mixer twice to scrape the bowl with a rubber spatula.

5   Add the egg to the butter mixture and beat on medium speed until blended, about 15 seconds. Scrape the bowl.

6   Add the flour mixture and mix on low speed for 15 seconds. Scrape the bowl. Add the oats and blend for 8 to 10 seconds.

7   Add the chocolate chips and pecans and blend on low speed until they are mixed in, 5 to 8 seconds.

8   Drop the dough by heaping tablespoons 2 inches apart onto the prepared baking sheets. Bake the cookies until the edges are dark golden and the centers are light and slightly puffed up, 12 to 14 minutes. Let them cool on the baking sheets.

* *

Chocolate Peanut Butter Volcanoes

* *

With all due credit to George Washington Carver, I'm sure it was a kid who invented the peanut butter–chocolate combination. It certainly is a perfect one. The next time your kids (or you) are in the mood for a Reese's Peanut Butter Cup, bake a batch of these cookies instead. They're little peanut butter volcanoes erupting in soft chocolate lava.

MAKES 30 COOKIES

1 Preheat the oven to 350°F. Line several baking sheets with parchment paper or lightly grease them with vegetable oil or butter.

2 Make the lava: Melt both chocolates together in the top of a double boiler placed over simmering water.

3 Combine the condensed milk and the vanilla in a medium-size bowl.

4 Using a whisk, stir the melted chocolate vigorously into the milk until the mixture is smooth and well blended. Set it aside.

5 Make the cookie dough: Sift the flour, baking soda, and salt together into a small bowl and set aside.

6 Cream the butter, peanut butter, both sugars, and the vanilla together in a medium-size mixing bowl with an electric mixer on medium speed until light and fluffy, about 1½ minutes. Stop the mixer twice to scrape the bowl with a rubber spatula.

7 Add the egg to the peanut butter mixture and beat on medium speed until blended, about 1 minute. Scrape the bowl.

8 Add the flour mixture and mix on low speed until blended, about 15 seconds. Scrape the bowl and mix several seconds more.

9 Measure out heaping tablespoons of the dough and roll them into balls with your hands. Using your thumb, press a deep hole into the center of each ball, and plop a heaping teaspoon of the lava mixture into the hole. Pinch the opening together just a little bit so the lava will not overflow, but so that it is still visible.

10 Place the balls 2 inches apart on the prepared baking sheets. Bake the cookies until they are lightly golden, 16 to 18 minutes. Let the cookies cool on the baking sheets or eat them while they're still warm for an extra-special treat.

NOTE: *Store these cookies in an airtight container in the refrigerator for 1 day. After that, store them in the freezer for up to 2 weeks. Bring them to room temperature before eating.*

INGREDIENTS

Vegetable oil or butter for greasing the baking sheets (optional)

Lava

½ cup (3 ounces) semisweet chocolate chips

½ ounce unsweetened chocolate

½ cup sweetened condensed milk

1½ teaspoons pure vanilla extract

Cookie Dough

1¾ cups all-purpose flour

¼ teaspoon plus ⅛ teaspoon baking soda

¼ teaspoon salt

11 tablespoons (1 stick plus 3 tablespoons) unsalted butter, at room temperature

¾ cup smooth peanut butter

½ cup plus 1 tablespoon (lightly packed) light brown sugar

6 tablespoons granulated sugar

¾ teaspoon pure vanilla extract

1 large egg, at room temperature

Chocolate-Dipped Almond Macaroons

* *

My father was a sucker for these cookies, which he would pick up in one of New York's Jewish bakeries. I grew to love them and wanted to make sure I included my version in this book in honor of my dad.

MAKES 12 COOKIES

INGREDIENTS

Cookies

½ cup all-purpose flour

½ teaspoon plus ⅛ teaspoon baking powder

6 ounces (slightly rounded ¾ cup) almond paste (not marzipan)

½ cup plus 2 tablespoons sugar

1 teaspoon pure vanilla extract

2 large egg whites

Vegetable oil or butter for greasing the baking sheet (optional)

Glaze

5 ounces bittersweet chocolate, chopped

1   Make the cookies: Sift the flour and baking powder together into a small bowl and set aside.

2   Cut the almond paste into 8 pieces and distribute them in the bowl of a food processor. Add the sugar and vanilla, and process until the mixture resembles coarse meal, about 15 seconds. Distribute the flour mixture evenly over the almond mixture, and pulse 3 times to blend.

3   Pour the egg whites evenly over the almond mixture and pulse 4 or 5 times to incorporate. Scrape the bowl with a rubber spatula. Then pulse several more times, until the mixture just starts to form a sticky pastelike dough.

4   Scrape the contents of the processor bowl into a small bowl, cover with plastic wrap, and refrigerate for 2 to 3 hours (or freeze for 1 to 1½ hours).

5   When ready to bake, place a rack in the center of the oven and preheat to 350°F. Line a baking sheet with parchment paper or lightly grease it with vegetable oil or butter.

6   Remove the dough from the refrigerator or freezer, and scoop out heaping tablespoons. Using your hands, roll them into balls and place them 2 inches apart on the prepared sheet. Press them down slightly with the palm of your hand. Bake the cookies for 15 minutes, then lower the heat to 300°F and bake until they are risen, slightly cracked, and lightly golden, 5 minutes

more. Let the cookies cool on the baking sheet for 1 hour.

7   Make the glaze: Melt the bittersweet chocolate in the top of a double boiler placed over simmering water. Using a metal spatula, remove the cookies from the baking sheet. Dip half of each cookie in the chocolate.

8   Place the cookies back on the sheet and allow to set for 4 hours before eating (or place the sheet in the refrigerator for about 1 hour).

* *

Chocolate Macaroons

* *

*T*he recipe for these cookies comes from the archives of Leah Winograd, erstwhile caterer of bar mitzvahs, baker extraordinaire, and mother of my partner, Eliot. Bored with the usual Passover fare, she served these for the occasion, though I like to make them year-round. They have a thin outer crust and a chewy inside.

MAKES 12 COOKIES

1   Preheat the oven to 375°F. Line a baking sheet with parchment paper or lightly grease it with vegetable oil or butter.

2   Melt both chocolates in the top of a double boiler placed over simmering water, then let the chocolate cool to tepid.

3   Beat the egg whites in a medium-size mixing bowl with an electric mixer on medium-high speed until frothy, about 30 seconds.

4   Gradually add the sugar and continue beating until the mixture is the consistency of marshmallow fluff, about 30 seconds more. Blend in the

INGREDIENTS

Vegetable oil or butter for greasing the baking sheet (optional)

4 ounces semisweet chocolate

2 ounces unsweetened chocolate

2 large egg whites, at room temperature

½ cup sugar

1 teaspoon pure vanilla extract

2 cups shredded sweetened coconut

vanilla with a rubber spatula, then fold in the melted chocolate, then the coconut.

5   Drop heaping tablespoons of the dough about 1½ inches apart onto the prepared baking sheet. Bake the cookies until a light crust forms on the outside, about 13 minutes. Let them cool on the baking sheet or transfer the cookies to a rack.

* *

Baker's Best
Snickerdoodles

* *

W*hen my family tasted these classics at a street fair, they went wild. Those chewy centers, those crispy edges! I tracked down Michael Baker, proprietor of Baker's Best in Newton Highland, Massachusetts, and he was kind enough to share his recipe with me. You can play with the baking time to get the chewy-crisp combo just the way you want.*

MAKES 30 COOKIES

1   Preheat the oven to 375°F. Line several baking sheets with parchment paper or lightly grease them with vegetable oil or butter.

2   Sift the flour, baking powder, and salt together into a small bowl and set aside.

3   Combine the cinnamon with the 2 tablespoons sugar in a small bowl. Stir together thoroughly, and pour into a plastic bag.

4   Cream the butter, the 1½ cups sugar, and the vanilla together in a medium-size mixing bowl with an electric mixer on

INGREDIENTS

Vegetable oil or butter for greasing the baking sheets (optional)

3 cups all-purpose flour

1 tablespoon plus 1 teaspoon baking powder

½ teaspoon salt

2 teaspoons ground cinnamon

1½ cups plus 2 tablespoons sugar

2 sticks (8 ounces) unsalted butter, at room temperature

1 teaspoon pure vanilla extract

2 large eggs, at room temperature

medium speed until light and fluffy, 1 minute. Stop the mixer once to scrape the bowl with a rubber spatula, and scrape the bowl again at the end.

5   Add the eggs to the butter mixture and beat on medium speed until they are blended, about 30 seconds. Scrape the bowl.

6   Add half of the flour mixture, and mix on low speed for 10 seconds. Scrape the bowl. Add the remaining flour mixture and blend on low for 25 seconds, stopping the mixer twice to scrape the bowl.

7   Measure out generously rounded tablespoons of the dough, and roll them into balls with your hands. Place 2 cookies at a time in the cinnamon-sugar mix and shake the bag to coat, then place the balls 2 inches apart on the prepared baking sheets. Bake until the centers are risen and slightly cracked and the edges are crisp, 16 to 18 minutes. Let the cookies cool on the baking sheets.

CHAPTER 10

Crispy Chompy

This chapter encompasses the wonderful world of shortbreads, crisps, florentines, ground-nut cookies, and spritzes. Sounds a little like something from Jane Austen: Under the watchful eye of a Shortbread, that guardian of standards, a sophisticated Florentine gossips behind her lace fan to a demure Spritz, who blushes prettily, while a gingery Crisp thumbs her nose at convention and marries well anyway.

Though "crisp" and "chomp" are shared by all the cookies in this chapter, the texture is arrived at by different means for different cookies. Pecan cookies take their texture from their fleshy nuts, for instance; biscotti and mandelbrot are double-baked for crispness; and cookies like classic sugar cookies are rolled thin to achieve their crispy nature.

Shortbread, of course, depends on butter to give these cookies their distinctive sandy texture. That butter flavor also makes them seem to melt in your mouth—a mixed blessing, since they may disappear almost too quickly. That's just as well because some of them may lose their crispness when left at room temperature for more than two days. Crispy cookies freeze beautifully, though, so you don't have to eat them all at once.

The crispier of these cookies can be fragile, so handle them carefully when removing them from the baking sheet, arranging them on a plate, and most especially, sending them through the mail.

Crunchy Chocolate Chips

* *

T his cookie is for those of you who think that a good chocolate chip cookie should be crunchy.

MAKES 48 COOKIES

1 Preheat the oven to 400°F. Line several baking sheets with parchment paper or lightly grease them with vegetable oil or butter.

2 Sift the flour, baking soda, baking powder, and salt together into a small bowl and set aside.

3 Cream the butter, both sugars, and the vanilla together in a medium-size bowl with an electric mixer on medium speed until light and fluffy, 1 minute. Stop the mixer once to scrape the bowl with a rubber spatula.

4 Add the egg and yolk to the butter mixture and beat on medium speed until they are blended, about 30 seconds. Scrape the bowl.

5 Add the flour mixture and mix on low speed for 15 seconds. Scrape the bowl.

6 Add the chocolate chips and blend on low until they are mixed in, 5 to 8 seconds.

7 Drop the dough by heaping teaspoons 2 inches apart on the prepared baking sheets. Bake the cookies until they are firm and very light golden with darker golden edges, 15 minutes. Let them cool on the baking sheets.

INGREDIENTS

Vegetable oil or butter for greasing the baking sheets (optional)

1¾ cups all-purpose flour

¼ teaspoon baking soda

¼ teaspoon baking powder

½ teaspoon salt

13 tablespoons (1 stick plus 5 tablespoons) unsalted butter, at room temperature

½ cup plus 2½ tablespoons (lightly packed) light brown sugar

5 tablespoons granulated sugar

1½ teaspoons pure vanilla extract

1 large egg, at room temperature

½ large egg yolk, at room temperature

¾ cup (4 ounces) semisweet chocolate chips

Baking Reminder

To bake two sheets of cookies at a time, set the oven racks in the upper third and lower third of the oven before preheating it. Halfway through the baking time, rotate the baking sheets from one rack to the other and turn the sheets back to front. This way you'll ensure even baking.

Thin Crisp Chocochips

* *

Despite their dainty and elegant appearance, these waferlike cookies completely satisfy your chocolate chip cravings! They're lovely served as an accent with fruit, sorbet, or ice cream, or with a cup of tea in the afternoon.

MAKES 75 COOKIES

INGREDIENTS

Vegetable oil or butter for greasing the baking sheets (optional)

1½ cups all-purpose flour

¼ teaspoon baking powder

½ teaspoon salt

14 tablespoons (1¾ sticks) unsalted butter, at room temperature

1 cup (lightly packed) light brown sugar

½ cup granulated sugar

1½ teaspoons pure vanilla extract

1 large egg, at room temperature

1 cup (6 ounces) semisweet chocolate chips

1   Preheat the oven to 400°F. Line several baking sheets with parchment paper or lightly grease them with vegetable oil or butter.

2   Sift the flour, baking powder, and salt together into a small bowl and set aside.

3   Cream the butter, both sugars, and the vanilla together in a medium-size bowl with an electric mixer on medium speed until light and fluffy, 1 minute. Stop the mixer once to scrape the bowl with a rubber spatula. Scrape the bowl again at the end.

4   Add the egg to the butter mixture and beat on medium speed until blended, about 10 seconds. Scrape the bowl.

5   Add the flour mixture and mix on low speed for 15 seconds. Scrape the bowl.

6   Add the chocolate chips and blend until they are mixed in, 5 to 8 seconds.

7   Drop the cookies by heaping teaspoons 2 inches apart on the prepared baking sheets. Flatten each cookie to ¼-inch thickness. Bake the cookies until they are firm and light golden with deep golden edges, about 12 minutes. Let them cool on the baking sheets.

Storage Reminder

The cookies in this chapter bake up into pretty big batches. If you're not serving them at a party, you're likely to have leftovers (delicious as they are, I don't think it's a good idea to down 75 cookies in one sitting!). Take a look at page 127 for some storage tips.

Noah Bedoahs—
Rosie's Chocolate Chip Shortbread

* *

One of my favorites, these are mounds of shortbread with chocolate chips and walnuts. They bake low and long to achieve a wonderfully crunchy texture.

MAKES 15 COOKIES

1 Preheat the oven to 275°F. Line 2 baking sheets with parchment paper.

2 Sift the flour, baking powder, and salt together into a small bowl and set aside.

3 Cream the butter and sugar together in a medium-size mixing bowl with an electric mixer on medium speed until light and fluffy, about 1½ minutes. Stop the mixer to scrape the bowl several times with a rubber spatula.

4 Add the dry ingredients to the butter mixture on low speed and continue to blend for 10 seconds. Increase the speed to medium-high and beat until fluffy, 2 to 2½ minutes. Scrape the bowl.

5 Add the chocolate chips and nuts with several turns of the mixer, then complete the mixing by hand with a wooden spoon.

6 Measure out heaping tablespoons of dough and roll them into balls with your hands. Place the balls 1½ inches apart on the baking sheets, and press them down lightly to form a flat bottom. Bake the cookies until they are crunchy and golden, about 1 hour. To test for doneness, remove one cookie from the sheet and cut it in half. There should be no doughy strip in the center. Transfer the cookies to a rack to cool.

INGREDIENTS

1¾ cups plus 2 tablespoons all-purpose flour

½ teaspoon baking powder

¼ teaspoon salt

2 sticks (8 ounces) unsalted butter, at room temperature

½ cup sugar

¾ cup (4 ounces) semisweet chocolate chips

½ cup chopped walnuts or pecans

Chocolate Chip Pecan Mounds

* *

This sturdy chocolate chip cookie is made with both whole wheat and white flour, which gives it a somewhat earthy texture. The recipe comes from Amy Nastasi, architect par excellence, designer of Rosie's stores, and like me, the mother of twins.

MAKES 20 COOKIES

INGREDIENTS

Vegetable oil or butter for greasing the baking sheets (optional)

1 cup whole wheat flour

2 cups all-purpose flour

1 teaspoon baking soda

1 teaspoon salt

2 sticks (8 ounces) unsalted butter, at room temperature

½ cup granulated sugar

1 cup (lightly packed) light brown sugar

1 teaspoon pure vanilla extract

2 extra-large eggs, at room temperature

1½ cups (9 ounces) semisweet chocolate chips

1 cup chopped pecans (optional)

1   Preheat the oven to 375°F. Line several baking sheets with parchment paper or lightly grease them with vegetable oil or butter.

2   Sift both flours, the baking soda, and the salt together into a small bowl and set aside.

3   Cream the butter, both sugars, and the vanilla together in a medium-size bowl with an electric mixer on medium speed until light and fluffy, about 1 minute.

4   Add the eggs to the butter mixture and beat on medium speed until they are blended, about 30 seconds. Scrape the bowl.

5   Add the flour mixture and mix on low speed for 15 seconds. Scrape the bowl.

6   Add the chocolate chips and blend until they are mixed in, 5 to 8 seconds. Add the nuts, if using, and blend until smooth, 5 seconds more.

7   Drop the dough in ¼-cup mounds, spaced 2 inches apart, onto the prepared baking sheets. Bake the cookies until the edges are a rich golden color and the top is lightly golden, risen, and slightly tender, 14 to 18 minutes, depending on desired chewiness. Let the cookies cool on the baking sheets.

Hazelnut White Chocolate Chunk Cookies

* *

Imagine peanut butter cookies with chunks of chocolate. Then imagine substituting hazelnuts for the peanuts and white chocolate for the chunks. Finally, imagine a delicious cookie like none you've ever tasted, and now we're talking Hazelnut White Chocolate Chunks.

MAKES 54 COOKIES

1 Preheat the oven to 350°F. Line several baking sheets with parchment paper or lightly grease them with vegetable oil or butter.

2 Sift the flour, baking soda, and salt together into a small bowl and set aside.

3 Coarsely chop ½ cup of the hazelnuts and set aside.

4 Place the remaining ¾ cup hazelnuts and the 2 tablespoons melted butter in a food processor and process until the mixture forms a crumbly paste, 30 seconds.

5 Cream the butter, both sugars, and the vanilla together in a medium-size mixing bowl with an electric mixer on medium speed until blended, 30 seconds. Stop once to scrape the bowl with a rubber spatula.

INGREDIENTS

Vegetable oil or butter for greasing the baking sheets (optional)

1½ cups all-purpose flour

½ teaspoon baking soda

½ teaspoon salt

1¼ cups skinned toasted whole hazelnuts (see box, below)

2 tablespoons unsalted butter, melted

7 tablespoons unsalted butter, at room temperature

½ cup (lightly packed) light brown sugar

½ cup granulated sugar

1 teaspoon pure vanilla extract

1 large egg, at room temperature

1 cup (6 ounces) coarsely chopped white chocolate or whole white chocolate chips

Skinning and Toasting Hazelnuts

To remove the skin from hazelnuts, toast the nuts on a baking sheet in a preheated 350°F oven for 5 minutes. Then immediately transfer the nuts (about a cupful at a time) onto a clean kitchen towel and lift all four corners to make a bundle. Using one hand to keep the bundle closed, use the other hand to massage the hazelnuts to loosen the skin, about 30 seconds. Then open the towel and place the nuts in a small bowl, making sure not to transfer the skins. (It will be impossible to remove all the skins from the nuts, but a good portion should come off.)

6   Add the hazelnut mixture to the butter mixture and beat on medium speed for 10 seconds to blend. Scrape the bowl.

7   Add the egg and continue to beat on medium speed until blended, 10 seconds. Scrape the bowl.

8   Add the flour mixture and mix on low speed until almost blended, 20 seconds. Scrape the bowl. Then add the reserved chopped nuts and the white chocolate and mix for 3 seconds. Finish the mixing by hand.

9   Drop the dough by heaping teaspoons about 2 inches apart onto the prepared baking sheets. Using the tines of a fork, press each cookie down lightly, making a crisscross pattern. Bake the cookies until they are firm and lightly golden, 16 to 18 minutes. Let them cool on the baking sheets.

INGREDIENTS

2¼ cups all-purpose flour

¼ teaspoon baking powder

¼ teaspoon salt

2 sticks (8 ounces) unsalted butter, at room temperature

½ cup sugar

½ cup raspberry preserves with seeds

* *

Rosie's Raspberry Thumbprints

* *

T his butter cookie with its dollop of jam in the middle echoes something in nearly everyone's past: a grandmother or aunt who served them when you visited, a neighborhood bakery that sold them by the pound, or a roommate's relative who sent them during exam week, bless all their hearts. With this classic recipe, you can carry on the tradition. Do not devour these cookies when they're hot (hard as it may be to resist) because the jam can burn the roof of your mouth.

MAKES 48 COOKIES

1   Sift the flour, baking powder, and salt together into a small bowl.

2   Cream the butter and sugar together in a medium-size mixing bowl with an electric mixer on medium-high speed until light and fluffy, about 2 minutes. Stop the mixer twice to scrape the bowl with a rubber spatula.

3   Add the dry ingredients and mix on low speed for several seconds. Scrape the bowl, then turn the mixer to high speed and beat until the batter is light and fluffy, about 1 minute.

4   Refrigerate the batter in plastic wrap or a covered container for 3 hours.

5   Fifteen minutes before baking, preheat the oven to 275°F. Line several baking sheets with parchment paper.

6   Measure out rounded teaspoonfuls of dough and roll them into balls with your hands. Place the balls about 1½ inches apart on the prepared baking sheets. Then make a firm indentation in the center of each cookie with your thumb or index finger. Bake the cookies until lightly golden, 25 to 30 minutes. Remove the sheet from the oven and increase the heat to 325°F.

7   Place ½ teaspoon jam in the center of each cookie and return the sheet to the oven. Bake the cookies just until the jam melts and spreads, about 10 minutes. Let them cool on the baking sheets before eating.

* *

Classic Sablés

* *

There is something so simple and delicious about these traditional buttery French cookies, which are named for their "sandy" texture (sablé means "sand"). There is not a bakery in all of France that does not make them.

MAKES 34 TO 40 COOKIES

INGREDIENTS

3 large egg yolks, at room
   temperature, separated

1½ teaspoons pure vanilla extract

2 cups all-purpose flour

⅔ cup sugar

¼ teaspoon salt

12 tablespoons (1½ sticks)
   unsalted butter, cold,
   cut into tablespoons

1   Stir 2 of the egg yolks and the vanilla together in a small cup using a fork. Set aside the third yolk.

2   Process the flour, sugar, and salt in a food processor for 10 seconds.

3   Add the butter to the flour mixture and process until it resembles coarse meal, 20 to 30 seconds.

4   With the machine running, add the yolk mixture and process for 5 seconds. Scrape the bowl, then pulse just until the liquid is evenly absorbed, about 10 times.

5   Remove the dough and place it on a work surface. Work the dough with your hands just until you can form it into a mass. Divide the dough in half and shape it into 2 thick disks. Wrap each one in plastic wrap. Refrigerate the dough until chilled, 2 hours.

6   When you are ready to prepare the cookies, preheat the oven to 350°F. Line several baking sheets with parchment paper or lightly grease them with vegetable oil or butter.

7   Remove the dough from the refrigerator and allow it to soften slightly, then place each piece of dough between 2 pieces of plastic wrap and roll it a generous ½ inch thick.

8   Remove the top piece of plastic wrap and using a 1¼-inch round cookie cutter, cut about 17 rounds from each half. Place the rounds ¾ inch apart on the prepared baking sheets. Gather up the dough scraps and reroll the dough to make as many cookies as possible.

9   Add a drop of water to the reserved yolk and stir with a fork. Using a pastry brush, glaze the top of each cookie with the glaze. Bake until the cookies are firm and golden, about 11 minutes. Let them cool on the baking sheets.

NOTE: *You can store these cookies for days in an airtight container at room temperature; they seem to get better with age.*

Crunchy Sugar Drop Cookies

* *

We call these snickerdoodles at Rosie's but, in fact, they are just classic vanilla drop cookies with cinnamon and sugar on top. They can be baked crunchy or soft-centered if you underbake them. They are the perfect cookie to down with a glass of milk or a cup of coffee.

MAKES 20 COOKIES

1 Preheat the oven to 350°F. Line several baking sheets with parchment paper or lightly grease them with vegetable oil or butter.

2 Sift the flour, baking soda, cream of tartar, and salt together in a small bowl and set aside.

3 Cream the butter, ½ cup of the granulated sugar, the confectioners' sugar, oil, and the vanilla together in a medium-size mixing bowl with an electric mixer on medium-high speed until light and fluffy, about 1 minute. Stop the mixer once to scrape the bowl with a rubber spatula.

4 Add the ½ egg to the butter mixture, mixing at medium speed until incorporated, about 30 seconds. Scrape the bowl.

5 Add the flour mixture on low speed and mix until blended, 15 to 20 seconds. Scrape the bowl and blend for 10 seconds more.

6 Stir the cinnamon and remaining ¼ cup granulated sugar together in a small bowl. Measure out heaping tablespoons of the dough and roll them into balls with your hands. Dip each ball in the mixture and place dipped side up on the prepared sheets. Use the palm of your hand to press down very lightly to form thick slabs. Bake the cookies until they are firm, 16 to 18 minutes depending on how soft you want your centers. Let them cool on the baking sheets.

INGREDIENTS

Vegetable oil or butter for greasing the baking sheets (optional)

2 cups plus 3 tablespoons all-purpose flour

¾ teaspoon baking soda

¾ teaspoon cream of tartar

¼ teaspoon salt

8 tablespoons (1 stick) unsalted butter, at room temperature

¾ cup granulated sugar

½ cup plus 1 tablespoon confectioners' sugar

¼ cup plus 3 tablespoons vegetable oil

1½ teaspoons pure vanilla extract

½ large egg (see Note, page 347)

¾ teaspoon ground cinnamon

Coconut Dainties

* *

Melt-in-your-mouth coconut wafers—crisp, delicate, coated with confectioners' sugar. They came to me from Susan Allison of Healdsburg, California—they're an Allison family heirloom.

MAKES 50 COOKIES

INGREDIENTS

2 cups plus 2 tablespoons cake flour

5 tablespoons granulated sugar

½ teaspoon salt

2 sticks (8 ounces) unsalted butter, cold, cut into 16 pieces

½ teaspoon pure vanilla extract

1 teaspoon pure almond extract

2 cups shredded sweetened coconut

2 cups sifted confectioners' sugar, for coating

1 Preheat the oven to 350°F. Line several baking sheets with parchment paper.

2 Place the flour, sugar, and salt in a food processor and process to blend, 5 seconds.

3 Scatter the butter over the flour mixture and dribble the extracts over that. Process until the butter is blended and the dough is beginning to come together, 35 seconds. Scrape the sides and bottom of the bowl with a rubber spatula.

4 Add the coconut and pulse 7 or 8 times to blend.

5 Scoop out rounded teaspoonfuls of the dough and use your hands to form them into 2-inch-long logs about ¼ inch thick. Place the logs 2 inches apart on the prepared baking sheets and flatten them with your hands so that they form an oval shape.

6 Bake the cookies until they are firm and golden around the edges, 15 to 18 minutes. Let them cool on the baking sheets.

7 Place the confectioners' sugar in a plastic bag or a bowl, and one by one drop the cookies in, tossing lightly to coat.

Pecan Crunchies

* *

These crunchy, melt-in-your-mouth cookies—an all-time favorite at Rosie's—are perfect for any occasion.

MAKES 48 COOKIES

INGREDIENTS

- 2 cups all-purpose flour
- ¾ teaspoon salt
- 1 cup pecan pieces
- 2 sticks (8 ounces) plus 2 tablespoons unsalted butter, at room temperature
- ⅓ cup (lightly packed) light brown sugar
- ¾ cup plus 3 tablespoons granulated sugar

1   Sift the flour and salt together into a small bowl and set aside.

2   Grind the pecans in a food processor until they are finely chopped but not powdery, about 30 seconds. Set them aside.

3   Cream the butter, brown sugar, and ¼ cup plus 3 tablespoons of the granulated sugar in a medium-size mixing bowl with an electric mixer on medium speed until the ingredients are light and fluffy, about 2 minutes. Scrape the bowl with a rubber spatula.

4   Add the flour mixture and the pecans to the butter mixture and beat on medium-low speed for 20 seconds. Scrape the bowl, then beat until the flour and nuts are completely incorporated, about 15 seconds.

5   Spread a 2-foot length of waxed paper on a work surface. With floured fingers, shape the dough into a rough log 18 to 20 inches in length and 2 inches in diameter, and place it along one long side of the paper. Roll the log up in the waxed paper and twist the ends like a hard-candy wrapper. Refrigerate the dough for 2 hours. (If necessary, cut the log in half and wrap each half separately in order to fit it in the refrigerator.)

6   Remove the log from the refrigerator and, with the dough still in the waxed paper, gently roll it back and forth on the work surface to round the log. Place the log back in the refrigerator for several more hours.

7   Preheat the oven to 300°F. Line several baking sheets with parchment paper.

8   Place the log on the counter, unwrap it, and cut the log into ⅓-inch-thick slices. Dip one side of each cookie in the remaining ½ cup granulated sugar and place them sugar side up 1 inch apart on the baking sheets.

9   Bake the cookies until they are firm to the touch and slightly golden, about 25 minutes. Be careful not to underbake

these cookies, which alters the texture significantly. To test for doneness, remove a cookie from the sheet and cut it in half. There should be no doughy strip in the center. Let the cookies cool on the baking sheets.

* *

Fresh Ginger Crisps

* *

I *'m willing to bet that these are the gingeriest cookies you'll ever taste—so gingery that you can see the strands of fresh ginger in each cookie, so gingery that the taste lingers on your tongue for minutes after you've eaten your last bite.*

MAKES 40 COOKIES

INGREDIENTS

1 cup plus 5 tablespoons all-purpose flour

¼ teaspoon baking soda

¼ teaspoon salt

10 tablespoons (1¼ sticks) unsalted butter, at room temperature

½ cup (lightly packed) light brown sugar

¼ teaspoon ground cinnamon

¼ teaspoon ground allspice

2 teaspoons grated lemon zest

¼ cup grated fresh ginger (use the finest holes on a hand grater)

¼ cup molasses

1   Sift the flour, baking soda, and salt together into a small bowl and set aside.

2   Cream the butter, brown sugar, cinnamon, allspice, lemon zest, and ginger together in a medium-size bowl with an electric mixer on medium speed until light and fluffy, 2½ to 3 minutes. Stop the mixer once or twice to scrape the bowl with a rubber spatula.

3   Add the molasses to the butter mixture and mix on low speed for several seconds. Scrape the bowl.

4   Add the flour mixture and mix on low speed until the mixture is fluffy again, about 45 seconds. Scrape the bowl. Divide the dough in half.

5   Place a 15-inch length of waxed paper or plastic wrap on a work surface. Shape one portion of the dough into a rough log 10 to 11 inches long and 2 inches in diameter, and place it along one long side of the paper. Roll the dough up in the paper, and twist the ends like a hard-candy wrapper. Repeat with the second portion of dough. Refrigerate the dough to chill, 2 hours.

6   Remove the logs from the refrigerator. Using your hands, gently roll the wrapped dough back and forth on the

work surface to smooth out the cylinder. Refrigerate for 4 to 6 hours or as long as overnight.

7 Fifteen minutes before baking, preheat the oven to 350°F. Line several baking sheets with parchment paper.

8 Remove the logs from the refrigerator, unwrap them, and cut them into ¼-inch-thick slices. Place the cookies 1 inch apart on the prepared baking sheets. Bake until they are crisp and firm, golden in color with brown edges, 14 to 16 minutes. Let them cool on the baking sheets.

* *

Hazelnut Crisps

* *

*L*acy ladylike cookies with a strong hazelnut flavor and enough crisp to keep them interesting.

MAKES 50 COOKIES

1 Preheat the oven to 375°F. Line several baking sheets with parchment paper or lightly grease them with vegetable oil or butter.

2 Place the flour, baking powder, salt, cinnamon, and both sugars in a food processor and process for 5 seconds.

3 Distribute the butter over the flour mixture and process until blended, 10 to 15 seconds. Scrape the bowl with a rubber spatula.

4 With the machine running, add the egg white through the feed tube and process to blend, several seconds. Scrape the bowl.

5 Add the hazelnuts and process until they are ground, 90 seconds. (The grind will be somewhat irregular.) Stop the processor once to scrape the bowl.

6 Drop the dough by rounded teaspoons 2 inches apart on the prepared baking sheets. Press them down lightly with the tip of a finger. Bake the cookies until they have spread and are a rich golden color with deep golden edges, 12 to 14 minutes. Let them cool completely on the baking sheets.

INGREDIENTS

Vegetable oil or butter for greasing the baking sheets (optional)

6 tablespoons all-purpose flour

½ teaspoon baking powder

¼ teaspoon salt

⅛ teaspoon ground cinnamon

½ cup granulated sugar

½ cup (lightly packed) light brown sugar

7 tablespoons unsalted butter, at room temperature, cut into 7 pieces

1 large egg white

1¼ cups skinned toasted whole hazelnuts (see box on page 157)

Oatmeal Lace Cookies

* *

T hese cookies are very sweet, like those caramels orthodontists outlawed because they stuck in your braces but that you snuck anyway because who could resist. Delicate and crisp, they're particularly good as an accent to ice cream.

MAKES 24 COOKIES

INGREDIENTS

Vegetable oil or butter for greasing the baking sheets (optional)

2 tablespoons all-purpose flour

1 cup old-fashioned rolled oats

1 teaspoon ground cinnamon

8 tablespoons (1 stick) butter, cut into 8 pieces

¾ cup (lightly packed) light brown sugar

2 tablespoons water

1 large egg, at room temperature

1 teaspoon pure vanilla extract

¼ cup finely chopped walnuts

1 Preheat the oven to 350°F. Line several baking sheets with parchment paper or lightly grease them with vegetable oil or butter. Have ready a large bowl of ice water.

2 Combine the flour, oats, and cinnamon in a small bowl and set aside.

3 Heat the butter, brown sugar, and water in a medium-size saucepan over low heat until the butter is melted, about 2 minutes. Increase the heat to medium-high and allow the mixture to come to a full boil. Boil for 1 minute.

4 Dip the bottom of the saucepan in the bowl of ice water and whisk constantly for about 3 minutes to cool the mixture.

5 Transfer the mixture to a medium-size mixing bowl and rapidly whisk in the egg and vanilla. Stir in the flour mixture and the nuts with a wooden spoon.

6 Dip the bottom of the mixing bowl in the ice water and allow the dough to cool and thicken slightly (don't stir), about 4 minutes.

7 Drop the dough by level teaspoons about 2 inches apart onto the prepared baking sheets. Bake until the cookies are golden with darker edges, 10 to 12 minutes. Let them cool on the baking sheets for 30 to 40 minutes, then carefully transfer them with a metal spatula to a plate.

NOTE: *These cookies are best eaten the day they're baked because they tend to lose their crispness.*

* *

Glazed Lemon Cookies

* *

I *love the pure citrus taste of these cookies. They're strongly flavored with lemon and topped with a tart lemon glaze. They make a lovely dessert served with fresh berries. Or offer them as part of a platter along with Thin Crisp Chocochips (page 154) and Orange Pecan Crisps (page 170).*

MAKES 44 COOKIES

1 Make the cookies: Combine the flour, baking powder, salt, lemon zest, and both sugars in a food processor and process for 10 seconds.

2 Scatter the butter over the flour mixture and process until the dough just comes together, about 45 seconds. During this time, while the machine is running, add the vanilla and lemon juice through the feed tube.

3 Spread a 24-inch length of waxed paper on a work surface. With floured fingers, shape the dough into a rough log about 18 inches long and 2 inches in diameter, and place it along one long side of the paper. Roll the log up in the waxed paper and twist the ends like a hard-candy

INGREDIENTS

Cookies

2 cups plus 2 tablespoons cake flour

¼ teaspoon baking powder

½ teaspoon salt

1 tablespoon plus 1 teaspoon grated lemon zest

¾ cup confectioners' sugar

¼ cup granulated sugar

12 tablespoons (1½ sticks) unsalted butter, cold, cut into 12 pieces

1 teaspoon pure vanilla extract

2 tablespoons fresh lemon juice

Glaze

6 tablespoons confectioners' sugar

2½ teaspoons heavy (whipping) cream

2 teaspoons fresh lemon juice

wrapper. Refrigerate the dough for 2 hours. (If necessary, cut the log in half and wrap each half separately in order to fit in the refrigerator.)

4   Remove the dough from the refrigerator and, using your hands, gently roll the wrapped dough back and forth on the work surface to smooth out the log. Return the log to the refrigerator and chill it for 2 to 3 more hours.

5   Preheat the oven to 325°F. Line 2 baking sheets with parchment paper.

6   Unwrap the log and cut it into ⅜-inch-thick slices. Place the cookies 2 inches apart on the prepared baking sheets. Bake until the centers are set and the edges are golden, 25 to 30 minutes. Transfer the cookies to racks set over waxed paper, and let them cool completely.

7   Meanwhile, make the glaze: Combine the confectioners' sugar, cream, and lemon juice in a small bowl and stir vigorously with a whisk until smooth.

8   When the cookies are completely cool, drizzle the glaze randomly over the tops. If possible, place the racks in the refrigerator for the glaze to set, or leave them out for 2 to 3 hours so the glaze can harden.

NOTE: *If you plan to eat them the first day, place the cookies on a plate. After that, layer the cookies in an airtight container, using plastic wrap, parchment paper, or waxed paper between the layers, and store the container in the refrigerator for 2 days or in the freezer for up to 2 weeks. Bring the cookies to room temperature before eating.*

Lovely Lemon Crisps

* *

A s a child I was always fond of thin, crisp lemon wafers, delicate in texture yet pungent in flavor—like these. I like to dunk them in milk, but they're also lovely served with tea or as an accompaniment to sherbet.

MAKES 72 COOKIES

1 Sift the flour, baking powder, baking soda, and salt together into a small bowl and set aside.

2 Cream the butter, sugar, vanilla, and lemon zest together in a medium-size mixing bowl with an electric mixer on medium speed until light and fluffy, 45 seconds. Stop the mixer once to scrape the bowl with a rubber spatula.

3 Add the lemon juice to the butter mixture and mix on medium speed for 15 seconds.

4 Add the flour mixture and mix on low speed until the mixture is fluffy again, about 30 seconds. Scrape the bowl.

5 Place a 20-inch length of waxed paper or plastic wrap on a work surface. Shape the dough into a rough log about 18 inches long and 2 inches in diameter, and place it along one long side of the paper. Roll the log up in the paper and twist the ends like a hard-candy wrapper. Refrigerate the dough for 2 hours. (If necessary, cut the log in half and wrap each half separately in order to fit in the refrigerator.)

6 Remove the dough from the refrigerator and, using your hands, gently roll the wrapped dough back and forth on a work surface to smooth out the log. Refrigerate it for 4 to 6 hours or as long as 2 days.

7 Fifteen minutes before baking, preheat the oven to 350°F. Line several baking sheets with parchment paper.

8 Unwrap the log and cut it into ¼-inch-thick slices. Place the cookies 1 inch apart on the baking sheets. Bake the cookies until they are golden around the edges, 10 or 11 minutes. Let them cool on the baking sheets.

INGREDIENTS

1½ cups all-purpose flour

½ teaspoon baking powder

¼ teaspoon baking soda

¼ teaspoon salt

10 tablespoons (1¼ sticks) unsalted butter, at room temperature

½ cup plus 3 tablespoons sugar

1 teaspoon pure vanilla extract

1 tablespoon plus 1 teaspoon grated lemon zest

¼ cup fresh lemon juice

169

Orange Pecan Crisps

* *

A wonderful waferlike cookie bursting with the flavor of oranges and loaded with pecans. Adjust the amount of pecans in either direction according to your taste.

MAKES 90 COOKIES

INGREDIENTS

2¼ cups all-purpose flour

¼ teaspoon baking soda

½ teaspoon salt

2 sticks (8 ounces) unsalted butter, at room temperature

½ cup (lightly packed) light brown sugar

½ cup granulated sugar

¼ cup grated orange zest

1 large egg, at room temperature

2 tablespoons frozen orange juice concentrate, thawed

1 cup chopped pecans

1   Sift the flour, baking soda, and salt together into a medium-size bowl and set aside.

2   Cream the butter, both sugars, and the orange zest together in a medium-size mixing bowl with an electric mixer on medium speed until light and fluffy, about 1 minute. Scrape the bowl with a rubber spatula.

3   Add the egg and orange juice concentrate to the butter mixture, and beat on medium speed until blended, 20 seconds. Scrape the bowl.

4   Add the flour mixture and beat on medium-low speed for 20 seconds. Scrape the bowl. Then add the nuts and beat until they are completely incorporated, about 15 seconds.

5   Spread a 13-inch length of waxed paper on a work surface. With floured fingers, shape the dough into a rough log about 12 inches long and place it along one long side of the paper. Roll the log in the waxed paper and twist the ends like a hard-candy wrapper. Refrigerate the dough for 2 hours.

6   Remove the dough from the refrigerator and, using your hands, gently roll the dough back and forth on the work surface to smooth out the log. Refrigerate the dough for 4 hours, or up to 2 days.

7   Fifteen minutes before baking, preheat the oven to 400°F. Line several baking sheets with parchment paper.

8   Unwrap the dough and cut it into ⅛-inch-thick slices. Place the slices 2 inches apart on the baking sheets. Bake the cookies until they are firm to the touch and golden around the edges, 7 to 8 minutes. (They should be crisp through and through when cooled.) Let them cool on the baking sheets.

Pecan Fingers

* *

T his is a taste memory that's bred in the bone: Biting into these thin crispy cookies and being greeted with a browned-butter-pecan flavor brings back my childhood in the form of a Danish butter cookie that my mother used to buy at a sensational gourmet store called the Danish Bowl. I was always thrilled when she went there because it meant a dinner of lobster salad finished off with pecan cookies.

MAKES 40 SMALL FINGERS

1 Make the cookies: Sift the 1¼ cups flour, baking powder, and salt together into a small bowl and set aside.

2 Cream the butter, both sugars, and the vanilla in a medium-size mixing bowl with an electric mixer on medium speed until light and fluffy, 1 minute. Stop the mixer twice to scrape the bowl with a rubber spatula.

3 Add the egg to the butter mixture, and mix at medium-high speed until blended, 15 seconds. Scrape the bowl.

4 Add the flour mixture and beat on medium-low speed until blended, 20 seconds, stopping the mixer once to scrape the bowl. Then scrape the bowl again at the end.

5 Divide the dough in half, wrap each half in plastic wrap, and refrigerate for 4 hours or as long as 2 days.

6 Fifteen minutes before baking, preheat the oven to 300°F. Line 2 baking sheets with parchment paper or lightly grease them with vegetable oil or butter.

7 Using a frosting spatula or your fingertips repeatedly dipped in flour, spread each portion of the dough out on one of the baking sheets to form a rough rectangle ⅛ inch thick (the shape is not important).

8 Glaze the dough: Using a pastry brush, lightly brush each portion of dough with the milk. Then sprinkle each with the sugar and the chopped pecans.

INGREDIENTS

Cookies

1¼ cups all-purpose flour, plus extra for forming the dough

¼ teaspoon baking powder

¼ teaspoon salt

12 tablespoons (1½ sticks) unsalted butter, at room temperature

5 tablespoons (lightly packed) light brown sugar

5 tablespoons granulated sugar

2½ teaspoons pure vanilla extract

1 large egg, at room temperature (optional)

Vegetable oil or butter for greasing the baking sheets (optional)

Glaze

2 teaspoons milk

2 tablespoons granulated sugar

6 pecans, finely chopped

9   Bake for 30 minutes. Then remove the baking sheets from the oven and cut the shortbreads into strips, about 20 pieces each. Move the pieces ½ inch apart, and return the sheets to the oven. Bake until the cookies are a deep golden color, 15 to 20 minutes. Let the cookies cool completely on the baking sheets before eating.

* *

Chinese Almond Cornmeal Wafers

* *

W hen I was younger, Chinese restaurants offered up lovely round cookies with an almond in the center, along with the inevitable fortune cookies. Maybe some still do. Although this sweet and buttery almond cookie is considerably different, it was created in honor of my childhood memory.

MAKES 48 COOKIES

INGREDIENTS

Cookies

1¼ cups all-purpose flour

1 cup yellow cornmeal

½ teaspoon salt

2 sticks (8 ounces) unsalted butter, at room temperature

½ cup (lightly packed) light brown sugar

¾ cup confectioners' sugar

½ teaspoon pure vanilla extract

1 cup finely chopped almonds

Glaze and Topping

1 large egg, at room temperature

1 tablespoon water

1 cup sliced almonds

1   Make the cookies: Place the flour, cornmeal, and salt in a small bowl and stir with a whisk.

2   Cream the butter, both sugars, and the vanilla together in a medium-size mixing bowl with an electric mixer on medium speed until light and fluffy, 2 minutes. Stop the mixer three times to scrape the bowl with a rubber spatula.

3   With the mixer on low, add the flour mixture and beat just until blended, 20 seconds. Scrape the bowl.

4   Add the almonds and blend on low speed for 5 seconds. Divide the dough in half. (If the dough is sticky, wrap each portion in plastic wrap and refrigerate for 1 hour before rolling.)

5   Preheat the oven to 350°F. Line several baking sheets with parchment paper.

6   Place one portion of the dough between two pieces of plastic wrap and roll it out ⅛ inch thick (see page 330 for rolling technique). Remove the top piece of plastic wrap, and using a 2¼- or 2½-inch round cookie cutter, cut out about 20 cookies. Place the cookies about ¾ inch apart on the prepared baking sheets. Gather up the dough scraps and reroll the dough to make as many cookies as possible. Repeat with the second portion of dough.

7   Make the glaze: Stir the egg and water together in a small cup with a small whisk or fork to blend. Brush the glaze over each cookie with a pastry brush. Then arrange the almond slices in a circle around the edges of each cookie, and gently glaze once again to set the almonds.

8   Bake the cookies until they are a rich golden brown, about 16 minutes. Let them cool on the baking sheets.

* *

Très French Palmiers

* *

I confess that these elegant cookies look more like elephant ears than palm leaves to me, but I know better than to argue with French chefs. After all, who would want to eat an elephant's ear? These palmiers are made of a very buttery puff pastry that's swirled into concentric circles and baked to crunchy perfection. Magnifique! And just the right thing to accompany a tisane.

MAKES 54 PALMIERS

1   Make the dough: Melt 4 tablespoons (½ stick) of the butter in a microwave oven or in a small saucepan over low heat. Remove from the heat.

2   Cut the remaining 1½ sticks butter into 12 pieces, and cut the 12 pieces in half. Place these chunks in the freezer for 5 minutes.

INGREDIENTS

Dough

2 sticks (8 ounces) unsalted butter, cold

2 cups all-purpose flour

¼ teaspoon salt

½ cup heavy (whipping) cream, cold, plus 2 tablespoons if needed

Filling

⅓ cup plus ¾ cup sugar

1½ teaspoons ground cinnamon

3   Place the flour and salt in a food processor and process for 5 seconds.

4   Distribute the butter over the flour mixture and pulse 5 or 6 times, just to break up the pieces.

5   Pour the ½ cup cream evenly over the flour-butter mixture. Pulse several times, until the crumbs appear to be evenly moist (the size of the butter chunks will stay fairly large and inconsistent, ranging from a grain of rice to a pea). Test for moistness: Pinch some crumbs together. If the mixture holds together like pie dough, there is enough cream. If it doesn't, add 1 tablespoon of cream and pulse twice. Retest. If the dough is still not moist enough, add 1 more tablespoon of cream and pulse twice.

6   Place the (crumbly) dough on a work surface covered with a large piece of plastic wrap and gently mold it into a 4 × 12-inch rectangle.

7   Cover the dough with another large piece of plastic wrap and roll it out to form a 10 × 20-inch rectangle (see page 330 for rolling technique). Remove the top piece of plastic wrap.

8   Using a pastry brush, brush the clear yellow part of the melted butter (the milky solids will have sunk to the bottom) over the surface of the dough.

9   With the point of a sharp knife, lightly score the dough lengthwise into thirds. Take the right-hand third of the dough and fold it over the middle third. Then take the left-hand third and fold it over the double thickness. You will have a rectangle measuring about 3½ by 20 inches.

10   Beginning at one short end of the length, and using the plastic wrap to lift it, roll the dough up like a jelly roll, to form one big fat roll.

11   Place a piece of plastic wrap over this roll and, using a rolling pin, roll it out to a 5-inch square. Cut the square in half, forming two rectangles, each 2½ × 5 inches. Wrap each rectangle in plastic wrap, and refrigerate for several hours or as long as overnight (but no more than 48 hours).

12   Make the filling: Mix the ⅓ cup sugar and the cinnamon together in a small bowl and set aside. Remove one rectangle of dough from the refrigerator and unwrap it.

13 Sprinkle 1½ tablespoons of the remaining sugar on a large piece of plastic wrap, and place the dough on the plastic. Sprinkle another 1½ tablespoons sugar on top of the dough, cover it with a second piece of plastic, and roll it out, flipping the dough several times, to form a 6 × 12-inch rectangle.

14 Remove the top piece of plastic, sprinkle half of the cinnamon-sugar mixture over the dough, replace the plastic, and roll it out to form a 9 × 12-inch rectangle.

15 Remove the top plastic. Take the long sides of the rectangle and fold them in toward the center so that the edges just meet. Then fold the rectangle in half the long way, as if closing a book. You should have a 9 × 3-inch rectangle.

16 Sprinkle 1½ tablespoons sugar over the rectangle, then flip it over and sprinkle 1½ tablespoons sugar over the other side.

17 Roll a rolling pin very gently over the length of the rectangle—just to seal it, not

to flatten it. It should be about ⅓ inch thick. Wrap it in plastic wrap and chill for 1 hour.

18 Repeat steps 13 through 17 with the second rectangle.

19 When you are ready to bake the palmiers, preheat the oven to 350°F. Line several baking sheets with parchment paper.

20 Remove the dough from the refrigerator and cut the rectangles into ⅓-inch-thick slices. Place them, cut side down, 1½ inches apart on the prepared baking sheets. Bake until crisp in texture and deep golden in color, 18 to 21 minutes. Let them cool on the baking sheets.

NOTE: *Because of their incredibly flaky nature, these are best if eaten the first day. However, if storing is a must, place them in an airtight container in the freezer for up to 2 weeks.*

Aunt Florence's Anise Biscotti

* *

I can't believe a crunchier, more perfect biscotti exists. I happen to love the anise flavor, but if you are not a fan, you can substitute the same amount of almond, hazelnut, or even orange extract. The beauty of biscotti is that if you store it properly, in an airtight container at room temperature, they'll return the favor and last a long time.

MAKES 48 COOKIES

INGREDIENTS

Vegetable oil or butter for greasing the baking sheets (optional)

2¾ cups plus 2 tablespoons all-purpose flour

1 tablespoon baking powder

¼ teaspoon salt

3 large eggs, at room temperature

¾ cup plus 2 teaspoons sugar

1 teaspoon anise extract

8 tablespoons (1 stick) unsalted butter, melted

1 Preheat the oven to 325°F. Line 2 baking sheets with parchment paper or lightly grease them with vegetable oil or butter.

2 Sift the flour, baking powder, and salt together into a small bowl and set aside.

3 Beat the eggs in a medium-size mixing bowl with an electric mixer on medium speed until foamy, 30 seconds. Add the sugar gradually, continuing to beat on medium speed until mixed, 30 seconds. Add the anise extract and the butter and beat until blended, 10 seconds.

4 With the mixer on low speed, add the flour mixture and mix only until blended, 20 seconds, stopping the mixer once to scrape the bowl with a rubber spatula.

Biscottibrot?

You say biscotti, I say mandelbrot. Time was when biscotti were one thing and mandelbrot another, and never the twain did meet. Nowadays they're acknowledged as essentially the same crunchy cookie, separated only by different names and pedigrees. I've long harbored the belief that Jews and Italians view the world in similar ways, and this congruence is just one more manifestation. Dip your mandelbrot in cappuccino or your biscotti in hot milk. The beauty of multiculturalism is that you don't have to choose.

5   Turn the dough out onto a work surface and divide it in half. Form each portion into a strip about 2½ inches wide and 12 inches long and place on a prepared baking sheet. Bake the dough strips until firm to the touch, 30 minutes. Remove the baking sheets from the oven and lower the oven temperature to 275°F. Let the strips cool for 10 minutes.

6   Using a serrated knife, cut each strip crosswise into ½-inch-thick slices. Arrange the slices, standing up, about ½ inch apart on the baking sheets. Bake until thoroughly crisp and lightly golden, about 30 minutes. Let the biscotti cool on the baking sheets. They can be stored in an airtight container at room temperature for up to 2 weeks.

* *

Amy's Mandelbrot

* *

I received this recipe in the mail from my old friend, Amy Etra, who lives in Los Angeles. Although when it showed up I needed a brief respite from baking, the recipe was just too tempting—I tried it and loved it! The cookies are not too rich and so are great any time of the day. Thanks, Amy.

MAKES 56 COOKIES

1   Preheat the oven to 375°F. Line 2 baking sheets with parchment paper or lightly grease them with vegetable oil or butter.

2   Bring the water to a boil in a small saucepan. Turn off the heat, place the raisins in the pan, cover, and let soak while you prepare the dough.

3   Sift the flour, baking powder, and salt together in a medium-size bowl and set aside.

4   Cream the oil, 1 cup of the sugar, the vanilla, and both zests together in a medium-size bowl with an electric mixer on medium-high speed until light and fluffy, 30 to 45 seconds. Stop the machine once to

INGREDIENTS

Vegetable oil or butter for greasing the baking sheets (optional)

1 cup water

½ cup raisins

3 cups all-purpose flour

2½ teaspoons baking powder

1 teaspoon salt

¾ cup vegetable oil

1 cup plus 1½ tablespoons sugar

2 teaspoons pure vanilla extract

1½ teaspoons grated lemon zest

1½ teaspoons grated orange zest

3 large eggs, at room temperature

½ cup chopped walnuts

1½ teaspoons ground cinnamon

scrape the bowl with a rubber spatula.

5   Add the eggs to the oil mixture one at a time, mixing on medium speed until each egg is partially incorporated, about 5 seconds. Scrape the bowl after each addition.

6   Add half the flour mixture to the egg mixture and blend with the mixer on medium speed for 10 to 15 seconds. Scrape the bowl. Then, add the remaining flour mixture and mix on medium speed until the dough is smooth, about 5 seconds.

7   Drain the raisins and pat dry with paper towels. Add the nuts and the raisins to the dough with a few more turns of the mixer on low.

8   Remove the dough from the bowl and divide it into quarters. Using floured hands, lay one-quarter of the dough lengthwise on a prepared baking sheet, molding it into a strip 2½ inches wide × 7 inches long. Make sure it sits about 2 inches from the edge of the pan. Form the remaining dough quarters into strips and

place them on the pans, 2 inches from the edge and 3 inches from each other (there should be 2 strips on each pan).

9   Mix the remaining 1½ tablespoons sugar with the cinnamon. Sprinkle the cinnamon-sugar generously over each strip. Bake the dough strips until firm to the touch and lightly golden, 25 to 30 minutes.

10   Remove the sheets from the oven and lower the oven temperature to 350°F. Let the strips cool for 10 minutes.

11   Using a serrated knife, cut each strip crosswise into ½-inch-thick slices. Arrange the slices, standing up, about ½ inch apart on the sheets. Bake until crisp and lightly golden, about 15 minutes. Let the cookies cool on the baking sheets. They can be stored in an airtight container at room temperature for up to 2 weeks.

Chocolate Chocolate Chip Mandelbrot

* *

This is a brownielike version of a traditional mandelbrot, noteworthy for its richness, density, and ever-so-chocolaty chocolateness. Bake it for the designated length of time if you like your mandelbrot crunchy. For a fudgier texture, take it out of the oven a little sooner.

MAKES 20 COOKIES

1 Make the cookies: Preheat the oven to 350°F. Line a baking sheet with parchment paper or lightly grease it with vegetable oil or butter.

2 Melt both chocolates in the top of a double boiler placed over simmering water. Let it cool to room temperature.

3 Sift the flour, baking powder, and salt together into a medium-size bowl and set aside.

4 If you are using instant coffee, dissolve it in the vanilla. Cream the butter, both sugars, the vanilla (with or without the coffee), and the orange zest (if not making the coffee version) together in a medium-size mixing bowl with an electric mixer on medium-high speed until light and fluffy, 1 to 1½ minutes.

Stop the machine twice to scrape the bowl with a rubber spatula.

5 Add the whole egg and the egg yolk to the butter mixture and mix on medium speed until blended, 10 seconds.

6 Add the melted chocolate with the mixer on medium-low speed and mix to blend, 10 seconds, stopping the mixer once to scrape the bowl.

7 Add the flour mixture with the mixer on low and blend until almost incorporated, 10 seconds. Then add the chocolate chips and blend to mix, 5 more seconds.

8 Lay the dough on the prepared baking sheet and mold it to form a cylindrical strip about 10 inches long × 3 inches wide.

INGREDIENTS

Cookies

Vegetable oil or butter for greasing the baking sheet (optional)

4 ounces bittersweet chocolate

1 ounce unsweetened chocolate

1¼ cups all-purpose flour

1 teaspoon baking powder

¼ teaspoon salt

2 tablespoons grated orange zest or 1 teaspoon instant espresso or coffee powder

1 teaspoon pure vanilla extract

7 tablespoons unsalted butter, at room temperature

5 tablespoons granulated sugar

¼ cup (lightly packed) light brown sugar

1 large egg, at room temperature

1 large egg yolk

½ cup (3 ounces) semisweet chocolate chips

Glaze

2 ounces bittersweet or semisweet chocolate

2 teaspoons vegetable oil

Bake until firm to the touch, about 50 minutes.

9   Remove the baking sheet from the oven, and lower the oven temperature to 275°F. Let the strip cool for 10 minutes.

10   Using a serrated knife, cut the strip crosswise into ½-inch-thick slices. Arrange the slices, standing up, about ½ inch apart on the baking sheet. Bake until crunchy through and through, 20 minutes. Then turn off the oven and let the cookies sit in the oven for an additional 15 minutes. Remove the baking sheet from the oven and let the cookies cool on it.

11   Meanwhile, make the glaze: Melt the chocolate in the top of a double boiler placed over simmering water. Using a whisk, stir in the oil and mix until smooth.

12   When the cookies have cooled, use a pastry brush to paint one side, or the top, of the cookies with the chocolate glaze. Let the glaze set completely, about 3 hours.

13   When the glaze has completely set, place the cookies in an airtight container, with parchment or waxed paper between the layers, and store it in a cool place or in the refrigerator for 2 to 3 days. (At room temperature, the glaze may discolor after several days.) After that, store the container in the freezer for up to 2 weeks. Bring to room temperature before eating.

* *

Lemon Meringues

* *

B uilt of three parts—a crunchy shortbread cookie, a dollop of tart lemon curd, and a cap of airy meringue—this confection offers a contrast of flavors and textures with each bite. They should be eaten on the day they are baked because the meringue will deflate and get limp by the next day. They'll still taste good, just not be perky.

MAKES 55 COOKIES

1 Make the cookies: Place the flour and both sugars in a food processor and process for 5 seconds.

2 Distribute the butter over the flour mixture and process until the mixture resembles coarse meal, about 20 seconds.

3 With the machine running, add the egg yolk through the feed tube and process for 5 seconds. Stop the machine, scrape the bowl with a rubber spatula, and process until the yolk has been absorbed and the dough is just coming together, 30 seconds.

4 Form the dough into 2 logs, each about 4½ inches long and 1½ inches in diameter. Wrap each log in plastic wrap and refrigerate.

5 Make the curd: In a small cup, stir the gelatin into the lemon juice until dissolved. Place the egg yolks and sugar in a small saucepan and mix to blend. Add the gelatin mixture to the yolk mixture and stir. Cook over low heat, stirring constantly, until it just comes to a boil and starts to thicken, about 5 minutes.

6 Remove the pot from the heat, pour the mixture through a strainer into a small bowl, and stir in the butter. Place plastic wrap directly on the surface, and refrigerate both the curd and the cookie dough for 4 to 6 hours.

7 When you are ready to bake, preheat the oven to 375°F. Line several baking sheets with parchment paper or lightly grease them with vegetable oil or butter. Fit a pastry bag with a ¼-inch plain tip and place the bag, tip-side down, in a tall glass.

8 Unwrap the logs of dough and slice them crosswise into rounds a generous ⅛ inch thick. Place them 1 inch apart on the prepared baking sheets. Bake until the edges are golden, 10 to 11 minutes.

9 While the cookies are baking, make the meringue: Place the egg whites, pinch of salt, and the sugar in the top of a double boiler set over simmering water. Stir with a whisk until the mixture is opaque and the sugar is dissolved, 4 to 5 minutes.

10 Place the egg-white mixture in a medium-size mixer bowl. Add the vanilla and, with the whisk attachment, whisk on medium-high speed until the mixture looks like Marshmallow Fluff, about 5 minutes. Fill the pastry bag with the meringue.

11 When the cookies have finished baking, remove them from the oven (but leave the oven on). Place a generous ½ teaspoon of the lemon curd in the center of each cookie, and then pipe a mound of meringue over the curd. Return the cookies

INGREDIENTS

Cookies

1½ cups sifted all-purpose flour

5 tablespoons confectioners' sugar

3 tablespoons granulated sugar

10 tablespoons (1¼ sticks) unsalted butter, cold, cut into 10 pieces

1 large egg yolk

Curd

¼ teaspoon unflavored gelatin powder

⅓ cup plus 1 tablespoon fresh lemon juice

4 large egg yolks

½ cup plus 1 tablespoon granulated sugar

1 tablespoon unsalted butter

Vegetable oil or butter for greasing the baking sheets (optional)

Meringue

2 large egg whites, at room temperature

Pinch of salt

⅔ cup granulated sugar, sifted

¼ teaspoon pure vanilla extract

181

to the oven and bake until the meringue starts to turn golden, 8 or 9 minutes. Remove the cookies from the oven and let them cool on the baking sheets or on racks for 4 hours. These cookies should be eaten on the same day they are baked.

* *

Very Short Shortbread Cookies

(FOR PEOPLE OF ALL HEIGHTS)

* *

I treasure this recipe, which was introduced into my parents' home by my Swedish nanny, Inga. I loved to watch her rub the butter and flour together with a skill that seemed so innate I doubted I would ever master it. To my pleasure, it turned out to be an easy and quick process, so even though you can use a food processor for this recipe, I like to make it by hand in honor of Inga (who was, by the way, very tall).

MAKES 48 COOKIES

INGREDIENTS

2½ cups all-purpose flour

½ cup sugar

½ teaspoon salt

2 sticks (8 ounces) unsalted butter, cold

1 Preheat the oven to 300°F. Line several baking sheets with parchment paper.

2 Sift the flour, sugar, and salt together into a large bowl.

3 Cut the butter into about 32 pieces and distribute them throughout the flour mixture. Rub the pieces into the mixture with your fingers and continue to work the mixture with your hands until all the ingredients hold together and form a dough, 4 to 5 minutes.

4 Measure out generously rounded teaspoons of the dough and roll them into balls with your hands. Place the balls 1½ inches apart on the prepared baking sheets. Use the tines of a fork to flatten the cookies to ¼ inch thick by making crisscross indentations on the top.

5 Bake the cookies until they are lightly golden in the center and a bit darker around the edges, 30 to 35 minutes. Let them cool on the baking sheets.

* *

Chunky Chocolate Almond Shortbread

* *

W andering the streets of SoHo, NYC, one day, I spotted a big log of almond shortbread studded with chopped chocolate sitting in a bakery window. It called out to me. Here is a mini version of that memory.

MAKES 40 COOKIES

1 Preheat the oven to 325°F. Line several baking sheets with parchment paper.

2 Sift the flour, baking powder, and salt together into a small bowl and set aside.

3 Cream the butter, brown sugar, and vanilla in a medium-size mixing bowl with an electric mixer on medium speed until light and fluffy, about 1 minute. Scrape the sides of the bowl with a rubber spatula.

4 Add the egg white to the butter mixture and mix until blended, 10 seconds.

5 Add the flour mixture and the ground almonds, and beat

INGREDIENTS

1 cup plus 3 tablespoons all-purpose flour

¼ teaspoon baking powder

½ teaspoon salt

8 tablespoons (1 stick) unsalted butter, at room temperature

½ cup (lightly packed) light brown sugar

¾ teaspoon pure vanilla extract

1 large egg white

½ cup ground almonds (from 1 scant cup whole almonds)

4 ounces bittersweet chocolate, coarsely chopped

⅓ cup coarsely chopped almonds

¼ cup granulated sugar

on medium-low speed for 20 seconds. Scrape the bowl.

6 Add the chopped chocolate and chopped almonds, and beat on low speed until incorporated, 10 seconds.

7 Place the granulated sugar in a plastic bag. Measure out rounded teaspoons of the dough and roll them into balls with your hands. Place each ball in the bag of sugar and toss to coat.

Place the balls 2 inches apart on the baking sheets. Using your hands or the bottom of a glass that has been dipped in sugar, flatten each cookie to form a round approximately 1¾ inches in diameter.

8 Bake until the cookies are firm and crunchy through and through, 20 to 22 minutes. Let them cool on the baking sheets.

INGREDIENTS

Vegetable oil or butter for greasing the pan (optional)

Cookies

1 cup all-purpose flour

⅔ cup sugar

⅓ cup unsweetened cocoa powder

8 tablespoons (1 stick) unsalted butter, cold, cut into 8 pieces

Glaze

3 ounces bittersweet chocolate, chopped

1 teaspoon vegetable oil

* *

Chocolate-Glazed Chocolate Shortbread

* *

G*ood chocolate shortbread is hard to come by. This one is very chocolaty, delicious, and really easy to throw together. Cut it into rectangles, diamonds, strips, or squares to complement any cookie platter.*

MAKES 8 COOKIES

1 Place a rack in the center of the oven and preheat to 300°F. Line a 9-inch-square baking pan with parchment paper or lightly grease it with vegetable oil or butter.

2   Make the cookies: Place the flour, sugar, and cocoa in a food processor and process for 10 seconds.

3   Scatter the butter over the flour mixture and pulse 60 times to blend. (The mixture will still be crumbly.)

4   Press the mixture evenly into the baking dish. Bake until the shortbread is firm to the touch, about 30 minutes.

5   Remove the dish from the oven and immediately cut the shortbread into 8 pieces (about 4 × 2 inches each) with a sharp knife. Let it cool completely in the pan on a rack.

6   When the shortbread is cool, make the glaze: Melt the chocolate in the top of a double boiler placed over simmering water. Whisk in the oil, stirring until the mixture is smooth, several seconds. Then pour the mixture into a small deep bowl.

7   Working quickly, dip the tines of a fork into the glaze, and moving your wrist rapidly from side to side, drizzle lines of chocolate over the shortbread. Use the tip of a knife to go over the cut lines. Allow the shortbread to set in the pan for 4 to 6 hours, or place it in the refrigerator or freezer for 1 hour.

* *

Toasted Coconut Macadamia Shortbread

* *

D*elicate, crunchy, and chock-full of two of my favorite ingredients, these tropical cookies are good all year round.*
MAKES 58 COOKIES

INGREDIENTS

2 cups all-purpose flour

¼ teaspoon baking powder

½ teaspoon salt

2 sticks (8 ounces) unsalted butter, at room temperature

7 tablespoons confectioners' sugar

¼ cup granulated sugar

2 teaspoons pure vanilla extract

2½ cups shredded sweetened coconut

¾ cup coarsely chopped macadamia nuts

1 large egg white

1   Preheat the oven to 325°F. Line several baking sheets with parchment paper.

2   Sift the flour, baking powder, and salt together into a small bowl and set aside.

3   Cream the butter, both sugars, and vanilla together in a medium-size mixing bowl with an electric mixer on medium-high speed until light and fluffy, about 1½ minutes. Stop the mixer once to scrape the bowl with a rubber spatula.

4   Add the flour mixture and mix on low speed for 5 seconds. Scrape the bowl. Then increase the speed to medium-high and mix until fluffy, 1 minute. Scrape the bowl again.

5   Add ½ cup of the coconut and mix on low speed for 10 seconds. Scrape the bowl. Then add the nuts and mix on low until blended, 5 seconds.

6   Measure out generously rounded teaspoons of the dough and roll them between your hands to form cylinders about 2 inches long × ½ inch thick. Press each between your palms to form an oval shape about 2½ × 1½ inches.

7   Place the egg white in a small bowl. Place the remaining 2 cups coconut in another small bowl. Dip each cookie into the egg white so that it is completely covered. Lift it up, allowing any excess to slide off, and place in the bowl of coconut. Shake the bowl gently so that the cookie is completely coated with coconut.

8   Place the cookies 1 inch apart on the prepared baking sheets. Bake the cookies until they are a deep golden color, about 20 minutes. Reduce the heat to 300°F and continue to bake for 10 to 15 minutes (to ensure crispness). Let the cookies cool on the baking sheets.

Ginger Shortbread

* *

I nstead of a tea cake, I like to offer this as a tea cookie. I
save it for the true ginger lover because it's loaded both
*with ground and candied ginger. It's a shortbread that packs
a punch.*

MAKES 60 COOKIES

1   Sift the flour, baking powder, and salt together into a small bowl and set aside.

2   Cream the butter, brown sugar, vanilla, and ground ginger together in a medium-size mixing bowl with an electric mixer on medium speed until light and fluffy, about 2 minutes. Stop the mixer once or twice to scrape the bowl with a rubber spatula.

3   Add the flour mixture and mix on low speed until the mixture is fluffy again, about 45 seconds. Scrape the bowl.

4   Remove the dough from the bowl and place it on a work surface. Work the candied ginger into the dough with your hands.

5   Divide the dough in half. Place two 16-inch lengths of waxed paper or plastic wrap on a work surface. Shape each half of the dough into a rough log about 10 inches long and 1½ inches in diameter, and place it along one long side of the paper. Roll the log up in the paper and twist the ends like a hard-candy wrapper. Refrigerate the log for 1 to 2 hours.

6   Remove the dough from the refrigerator. Using your hands, gently roll the wrapped dough back and forth on the work surface to smooth out the logs. Refrigerate again for 4 to 6 hours.

7   Fifteen minutes before baking, preheat the oven to 350°F. Line several baking sheets with parchment paper.

8   Remove the dough from the refrigerator, unwrap the logs, and cut them into slices that are a generous ⅓ inch thick. Place the cookies 1 inch apart on the prepared baking sheets. Bake the cookies until they are golden and firm to the touch, 28 to 30 minutes. Let them cool on the baking sheets.

INGREDIENTS

2 cups plus 2 tablespoons all-purpose flour

¼ teaspoon baking powder

¾ teaspoon salt

2 sticks (8 ounces) unsalted butter, at room temperature

⅔ cup plus 1 tablespoon (lightly packed) light brown sugar

¾ teaspoon pure vanilla extract

3 tablespoons ground ginger

1 cup coarsely chopped candied ginger

Cornmeal Shortbread Cookies

* *

There's a lot to be said for cornmeal. The richness of its history, rooted in Native American culture, and the flavor reminiscent of one of our favorite holiday meals make this a very special ingredient. I have always put cornmeal in my pancakes and my daughter, Maya, to this day still enjoys cornmeal mush for breakfast. With all that, why not cornmeal cookies, too? These have the crunchy buteryness of shortbread plus the texture of the cornmeal—light, delicious, and grainy.

MAKES 44 COOKIES

INGREDIENTS

1 large egg, at room temperature

1 teaspoon pure vanilla extract

1¾ cups plus 2 tablespoons all-purpose flour

1 cup yellow cornmeal

⅛ teaspoon baking powder

½ teaspoon salt

¾ cup sugar

2 sticks (8 ounces) unsalted butter, cold, cut into 16 pieces

1 Using a fork, stir the egg and vanilla together in a small cup and set aside.

2 Place the flour, cornmeal, baking powder, salt, and sugar in a food processor and process to blend, 5 seconds.

3 Distribute the butter over the flour mixture and process until the mixture resembles coarse cornmeal, 20 to 30 seconds.

4 With the machine running, add the egg mixture through the feed tube and process for 30 seconds. Scrape the bowl, then process for 3 seconds more.

Remove the dough and knead it for several seconds on a work surface.

5 Place a 16-inch length of plastic wrap on a work surface. Shape the dough into a rough log 11 inches long and 2 inches in diameter and place it along one long side of the plastic wrap. Roll the log up in the plastic wrap and twist the ends like a hard-candy wrapper. Refrigerate the log for 1 hour.

6 Remove the dough from the refrigerator. Using your hands, roll the wrapped dough gently back and forth on a work surface

to smooth out the log. Refrigerate it again for 4 to 6 hours or as long as overnight.

7 Fifteen minutes before baking, preheat the oven to 350°F. Line several baking sheets with parchment paper.

8 Remove the dough from the refrigerator, unwrap it, and cut it into slices that are a generous ¼ inch thick. Place them 1 inch apart on the baking sheets. Bake the shortbread cookies until they are firm and lightly golden around the edges, 20 minutes. Let them cool on the baking sheets.

Crunchy Cookies

Here's something to keep in mind: A beautiful thing about crunchy cookies is that if after they cool they aren't crisp enough, you can throw them back in the oven and let them bake a little longer. I use this method with certain shortbread cookies that may have gotten soggy after two or three days. I just put them right back on a pan and bake them until they "recrisp."

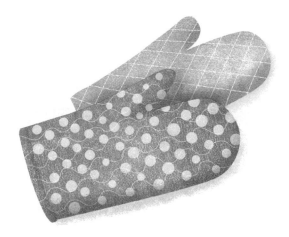

Glazed Molasses Cake Cookies, Banana Cream Cheese Mounds, Lemon-Glazed Hermits. These luscious little heaps of cake, glazed or frosted and passed off as cookies, have a special place in my heart because they allow me to have my cake and eat my cookie, too. It seems I'm not alone in this. When I told a friend I was writing a book of cookie recipes, the first thing he said was, "I certainly hope you plan to include the Maple Softies"—which reaffirmed for me why we're friends.

Cakey cookies make wonderful treats for school birthday parties. They're easier for the teacher to hand out and less messy than cake. They look great, too, especially with a piece of candy or a birthday doodad perched on top. Best of all, they're separate but equal—and as any parent knows, the child who has her own is a happy child.

Because these cookies are essentially miniature cakes, their batters require more delicate mixing than the other types of cookies. They're also fussier about baking time and temperature, and they don't hang around well, so you need to eat them the day of or the day after baking, or you can freeze them for later on. But, once you've made any of these cookies, you'll agree that the effort is certainly worth it.

Baking Reminder
To bake two sheets of cookies at a time, set the oven racks in the upper third and lower third of the oven before preheating it. Halfway through the baking time, rotate the baking sheets from one rack to the other and turn the sheets back to front. This way you'll ensure even baking.

Sacher Tortes

* *

*T*he Sacher torte is a Viennese specialty, a chocolate cake layered with apricot preserves and glazed with more chocolate. I've transformed it into a cookie, keeping all the original ingredients but making it more compact. If you're not a fan of apricots, you can still enjoy the essence of the torte; just leave the preserves out to create a great devil's food cookie with a fudge glaze.

MAKES 30 COOKIES

1 Preheat the oven to 400°F. Line 2 baking sheets with parchment paper or lightly grease them with vegetable oil or butter.

2 Make the cookies: Melt the chocolate in the top of a double boiler placed over simmering water. Remove it from the heat and set aside.

3 Sift both flours, the cocoa powder, baking powder, baking soda, and salt together into a small bowl and set aside.

4 Cream the butter, oil, both sugars, and the vanilla together in a medium-size bowl with an electric mixer on medium-high speed until light and fluffy, 1½ to 2 minutes. Stop the mixer once or twice to scrape the bowl with a rubber spatula.

5 Add the eggs to the butter mixture one at a time, blending on medium speed for 8 seconds after each addition and scraping the bowl each time.

6 Add the sour cream and beat on medium speed until blended, about 5 seconds, then on high speed for 3 seconds.

7 Fold in the melted chocolate with the spatula, mixing until the batter is uniform in color.

8 Fold in the flour mixture with six or seven broad strokes of the spatula. Then mix with the electric mixer on low speed until the batter is velvety, about 10 seconds, stopping once to scrape the bowl.

9 Drop the batter by slightly rounded tablespoons about 2 inches apart on the prepared baking sheets. Bake the cookies

INGREDIENTS

Vegetable oil or butter for greasing the baking sheets (optional)

Cookies

2 ounces unsweetened chocolate

1 cup all-purpose flour

1 cup cake flour

6 tablespoons unsweetened cocoa powder

1 teaspoon baking powder

¼ teaspoon baking soda

½ teaspoon salt

4 tablespoons (½ stick) unsalted butter, at room temperature

¼ cup vegetable oil

1 cup (lightly packed) light brown sugar

3 tablespoons granulated sugar

1½ teaspoons pure vanilla extract

3 large eggs, at room temperature

1 cup sour cream

⅓ cup apricot preserves

Glaze

8 ounces bittersweet chocolate

2 tablespoons light corn syrup

2 tablespoons unsalted butter

2 tablespoons hot water

until they are puffed and just set, about 11 minutes.

10   As soon as the cookies come out of the oven, heat the apricot preserves in a saucepan over low heat just until liquid.

11   Drop a generous ½ teaspoon of the preserves on top of each cookie, and spread it over the surface with a pastry brush. Let the cookies sit for 5 minutes. Then slide the sheet of parchment paper onto the counter (or, using a metal spatula, carefully transfer each cookie to a sheet of aluminum foil or waxed paper on the counter) and let them cool further.

12   While the cookies are cooling, make the glaze: Melt the chocolate in the top of a double boiler placed over simmering water. Remove the pan from the heat and whisk in the corn syrup, butter, and hot water, whisking vigorously until smooth and shiny.

13   Loosen the cookies from the paper with the metal spatula, and dip their tops into the warm glaze (or use a frosting spatula or a butter knife to spread the glaze over the top). Then return the cookies to the paper and allow the glaze to set for 2 hours (or refrigerate for 1 hour to set quickly) before eating.

Cover-Ups

Many of these cookies are topped with a glaze or frosting. I use a liquidy confectioners' sugar glaze, and if the glaze is loose enough, I dip the top of the cookie directly in it. If it's too dense for dipping, I spread the glaze with a small frosting spatula or a butter knife. Frostings are always too thick for dipping, so you have to spread them, using the same utensils.

Banana Cream Cheese Mounds

* *

Soft and moist, these cookies are among my favorites in this book. It has to do with a cherished memory from my childhood: a banana layer cake my mother sometimes brought home as a treat. When I bite into these cookies I'm transported back to our dining room table, with my feet not quite reaching the floor and my fork poised to let the glory begin.

MAKES 13 LARGE COOKIES

1 Preheat the oven to 400°F. Line several baking sheets with parchment paper or lightly grease them with vegetable oil or butter.

2 Make the cookies: Sift the flour, baking powder, baking soda, and salt together into a small bowl and set aside.

3 Cream the butter, both sugars, and the vanilla in a medium-size mixing bowl with an electric mixer on medium speed until light and fluffy, 1 to 1½ minutes. Scrape the bowl with a rubber spatula.

4 Add the egg to the butter mixture, and mix on medium speed until blended, about 15 seconds. Scrape the bowl.

5 Add the banana and mix on medium-low speed until blended, about 10 seconds. Scrape the bowl.

6 Fold in the flour mixture by hand. Then blend with the mixer on low speed for 5 seconds. Scrape the bowl, and mix on low speed until the batter is smooth and velvety, about 10 seconds. Give the batter a stir or two with the spatula.

7 Drop the batter by heaping tablespoons 2 inches apart onto the prepared baking sheets. Bake the cookies until they are puffed and just firm to the touch (but not golden), about 10 minutes. Remove from the oven and let the cookies sit for 2 to 3 minutes. Then slide the sheet of parchment paper onto the counter (or, using

INGREDIENTS

Vegetable oil or butter for greasing the baking sheets (optional)

Cookies

1½ cups plus 1 tablespoon sifted cake flour

1 teaspoon baking powder

⅛ teaspoon baking soda

¼ teaspoon salt

6 tablespoons (¾ stick) unsalted butter, at room temperature

5 tablespoons granulated sugar

¼ cup (lightly packed) light brown sugar

1 teaspoon pure vanilla extract

1 large egg, at room temperature

½ cup plus 2 tablespoons mashed very ripe bananas

Frosting

6 ounces cream cheese, at room temperature

6 tablespoons confectioners' sugar

3 tablespoons unsalted butter, at room temperature

a metal spatula, carefully transfer each cookie to a sheet of aluminum foil or waxed paper on the counter), and let them cool further.

8   Meanwhile, make the frosting: Place the cream cheese, confectioners' sugar, and butter in a food processor and process until smooth, 40 seconds.

9   Using a small frosting spatula or a butter knife, spread a generous tablespoon of the frosting over the top of each cookie.

Storage Reminder

For cookie storage tips, turn to page 127. If the cookies in a specific recipe need storage handling that isn't covered in the general tips, the directions will be in the recipe itself.

Lemon Springtimes

* *

*A*lthough I usually offer these cookies only during the spring and summer at Rosie's, I do on occasion rotate them in during the winter months and have learned that the only thing that makes them more appropriate for the warm season is the name! This cookie is a portable disk of lemon cake topped with a buttery lemon glaze and it is much loved by both me and my customers.

MAKES ABOUT 30 COOKIES

1   Preheat the oven to 375°F and line 2 baking sheets with parchment paper or lightly grease them with vegetable oil or butter.

2   Make the cookies: Sift the flour, baking powder, baking soda, and salt together into a small bowl and set aside.

INGREDIENTS

Vegetable oil or butter for greasing the baking sheets (optional)

Cookies

2 cups plus 3 tablespoons all-purpose flour

¾ teaspoon baking powder

¾ teaspoon baking soda

½ teaspoon salt

8 tablespoons (1 stick) unsalted butter

1½ cups sugar

1 teaspoon pure vanilla extract

2 teaspoons grated lemon zest

3 large eggs

1 large egg yolk

¾ cup plus 2 tablespoons sour cream

3   Cream the butter, sugar, vanilla, and lemon zest together in a medium-size mixing bowl with an electric mixer on medium-high speed until light and fluffy, about 2 minutes. Stop the mixer once or twice to scrape the bowl with a rubber spatula.

4   Add the eggs and the egg yolk to the butter mixture and mix on medium speed until the mixture is light in color and increased in volume about 1½ times, about 2 minutes, stopping the mixer after each addition to scrape the bowl.

5   Gradually add the flour mixture and sour cream in 3 additions with the mixer on low speed, starting with the flour and ending with the cream. Mix each addition for only about 5 seconds, then stop the mixer and scrape the bowl. Finish the final mixing gently by hand with the spatula until the batter appears velvety.

6   Drop the batter by heaping tablespoons 2 inches apart onto the prepared baking sheets. Bake the cookies until they have puffed up, spring back to the touch, and are lightly golden around the edges, about 10 minutes. Carefully transfer the cookies to a cooling rack. Let them cool completely.

7   Meanwhile, prepare the glaze: Place the confectioners' sugar in a medium-size bowl. Add the butter and the lemon juice, and beat vigorously with a whisk until the mixture is smooth and creamy.

8   Once the cookies have cooled, drop heaping ½ teaspoons of the glaze onto each cookie and spread with a small butter knife. Allow them to sit until the glaze hardens, about 2 hours (or pop them in the refrigerator for an hour).

Glaze

1 cup confectioners' sugar

2 tablespoons unsalted butter, melted

1 tablespoon plus 2 teaspoons fresh lemon juice

INGREDIENTS

Vegetable oil or butter for
  greasing the baking sheet
  (optional)

Cookies

2 cups plus 1 tablespoon
  all-purpose flour

2 teaspoons baking soda

¼ teaspoon salt

1¾ teaspoons ground cinnamon

2 teaspoons ground ginger

1¾ teaspoons ground cloves

9 tablespoons (1 stick plus
  1 tablespoon) unsalted butter,
  at room temperature

1 cup (lightly packed) light brown
  sugar

1 large egg, at room temperature

¼ cup molasses

¾ cup raisins

Glaze

1½ cups plus 3 tablespoons
  confectioners' sugar

2 tablespoons plus 2½ teaspoons
  milk

Rosie's Classic Hermit Strips

* *

There's a lot of disagreement about the attributes of a good hermit—the cookie, that is. I'm a strong advocate of something dark, spicy, and chewy, which is what you'll find in this recipe. Although these cookies are basically made from a drop cookie batter, I make them in free-form strips, then cut them after baking. It is important to store these cookies in an airtight container to preserve their chewiness.

MAKES 14 COOKIES

1 Preheat the oven to 375°F. Line a baking sheet with parchment paper or lightly grease it with vegetable oil or butter.

2 Make the cookies: Sift the flour, baking soda, salt, cinnamon, ginger, and cloves together into a small bowl and set aside.

3 Cream the butter and brown sugar together in a medium-size mixing bowl with an electric mixer on medium speed until light and fluffy, about 1½ minutes. Stop the mixer twice to scrape the bowl with a rubber spatula.

4 Add the egg to the butter mixture and mix on medium speed until blended, 20 to 30 seconds. Scrape the bowl.

5 Add the molasses and mix until blended.

6 Add the dry ingredients and the raisins and mix on medium speed until the dough comes together, about 1 minute.

7 Divide the dough in half. Shape each half into a log 1½ inches in diameter × 12 inches long. Arrange the logs on the prepared baking sheet, leaving at least 3 to 4 inches between them.

8 Bake the logs until they are golden but still very soft to the touch and puffy in the center,

17 to 18 minutes. (The dough cracks during baking and it will still seem slightly raw on the inside even when the logs are done.) The logs flatten out and lengthen as they bake. Cool the logs on the baking sheet. Cut into 2-inch-wide slices when cool. Each log makes 7 cookies.

9   Make the glaze: Place the confectioners' sugar and milk in a small bowl and stir them vigorously with a whisk until blended.

10   Drizzle the glaze over the strips or use a pastry brush to paint the surface of the strips with the glaze. Allow the glaze to harden before eating or storing the cookies.

* *

Lemon-Glazed Hermits

* *

Hermits always seem misnamed to me because they're so popular, though it's true that they keep to themselves very well. This version is a moist cakey mound of molasses-and-spice-flavored cookie topped with a white glaze.

MAKES 22 HERMITS

1   Preheat the oven to 400°F. Line several baking sheets with parchment paper or lightly grease them with vegetable oil or butter.

2   Make the cookies: Sift the flour, baking soda, and salt together into a small bowl and set aside.

3   Cream the butter, brown sugar, cinnamon, ginger, cloves, and coffee powder together in a medium-size mixing bowl with an electric mixer on medium-high speed until light and fluffy, about 2 minutes. Stop the mixer twice to scrape the bowl with a rubber spatula, scraping the bowl once again at the end.

INGREDIENTS

Vegetable oil or butter for greasing the baking sheets (optional)

Cookies

2¼ cups all-purpose flour

1 teaspoon baking soda

½ teaspoon salt

14 tablespoons (1¾ sticks) unsalted butter, at room temperature

1 cup plus 2 tablespoons (firmly packed) light brown sugar

1 tablespoon plus 1 teaspoon ground cinnamon

2 tablespoons ground ginger

2 teaspoons ground cloves

1 tablespoon plus 1 teaspoon instant coffee powder

1 large egg, at room temperature

2 large egg yolks, at room temperature

2 tablespoons dark molasses

Glaze

1¼ cups confectioners' sugar

3 tablespoons fresh lemon juice

4 Add the whole egg to the butter mixture and blend on medium speed for about 10 seconds. Scrape the bowl, and then add the egg yolks. Blend on medium speed for 20 seconds. Scrape the bowl.

5 Add the molasses and mix on medium-low speed for about 5 seconds. Scrape the bowl.

6 Fold in the flour mixture by hand. Then mix on low speed for about 5 seconds. Scrape the bowl, and mix on low until the batter is smooth and velvety, 10 seconds. Give the batter a stir or two with the spatula.

7 Drop the batter by generously rounded tablespoons about 2 inches apart onto the prepared baking sheets. Bake the cookies until they are puffed but the tops are not set (they should leave an indentation when touched), about 12 minutes, depending on how chewy you like your hermits. Using a metal spatula, carefully transfer the cookies to racks to cool completely.

8 Meanwhile, make the glaze: Vigorously whisk the confectioners' sugar and lemon juice together in a small bowl until the mixture is smooth and creamy.

9 Drizzle the glaze over the cooled cookies, or spread it over the surface with a frosting spatula or a butter knife. Allow the cookies to sit until the glaze hardens, 2 to 3 hours.

* *

Carrot Cake Cookies

* *

*A*lthough carrot cake is no longer the stuff of "health food" items it was decades ago, it still ranks as a favorite in the repertoire of American desserts. This moist, cakey cookie is topped appropriately with a cream cheese frosting—just like in the old days!

MAKES 20 COOKIES

1 Preheat the oven to 425°F. Line several baking sheets with parchment paper or lightly grease them with vegetable oil or butter.

2 Make the cookies: Sift the flour, baking powder, baking soda, salt, cinnamon, allspice, mace, and ginger together into a medium-size bowl and set aside.

3 Place the grated carrots in a food processor and pulse 8 times to chop the shreds. Set aside.

4 Cream the butter, both sugars, and vanilla in a medium-size mixing bowl with an electric mixer on medium-high speed until light and fluffy, 1 minute. Stop the mixer once to scrape the bowl with a rubber spatula.

5 Add the eggs to the butter mixture one at a time, blending on medium speed for 10 seconds after each addition and scraping the bowl each time.

6 Add the carrots and the pineapple, and mix on medium speed until blended, 10 seconds, stopping the mixer once to scrape the bowl and then scraping it once again at the end.

7 Add the flour mixture and blend on low speed for 8 seconds. Scrape the bowl thoroughly, then turn the mixer to medium-high and blend for 5 more seconds. Scrape the bowl and finish mixing the batter by hand with a few stirs of the spatula.

8 Drop the batter by heaping tablespoons onto the prepared baking sheets. Bake until the centers are puffed, set, and lightly golden, about 13 minutes. Let the cookies cool on the baking sheets, 2 to 3 minutes. Then slide the sheet of parchment paper onto the counter (or, using a metal spatula, carefully transfer each cookie onto a sheet of aluminum foil or waxed paper on the counter) and let them cool further.

9 Meanwhile, make the frosting: Place the cream cheese, confectioners' sugar, and butter in a food processor and process until smooth, 40 seconds.

10 Using a small frosting spatula or a butter knife, spread a generous tablespoon of the frosting over the top of each cookie.

INGREDIENTS

Vegetable oil or butter for greasing the baking sheets (optional)

Cookies

2 cups all-purpose flour

1 teaspoon baking powder

¾ teaspoon baking soda

1 teaspoon salt

1 teaspoon ground cinnamon

½ teaspoon ground allspice

¾ teaspoon ground mace

½ teaspoon ground ginger

2 cups grated carrots (about 4 carrots)

12 tablespoons (1½ sticks) unsalted butter, at room temperature

7 tablespoons (lightly packed) light brown sugar

7 tablespoons granulated sugar

2 teaspoons pure vanilla extract

2 large eggs, at room temperature

1 cup drained crushed pineapple (from one 16-ounce can)

Frosting

8 ounces cream cheese, at room temperature

½ cup confectioners' sugar

4 tablespoons (½ stick) unsalted butter, at room temperature

Sunken Kisses

* *

A great cookie to bake with and for your kids. Put them in charge of unwrapping the Hershey's Chocolate Kisses and placing one carefully in the middle of each cookie and you'll be amazed at their level of concentration. By unanimous decision, though, the making doesn't hold a candle to the eating.

MAKES 48 COOKIES

1   Preheat the oven to 375°F. Line 2 baking sheets with parchment paper or lightly grease them with vegetable oil or butter.

2   Sift the flour, baking soda, and salt together into a small bowl and set aside.

3   Cream the butter, brown sugar, ¼ cup of the granulated sugar, the peanut butter, and vanilla in a medium-size mixing bowl with an electric mixer on medium speed until light and fluffy, 2 to 3 minutes. Stop the mixer twice to scrape the bowl with a rubber spatula.

4   Add the egg to the butter mixture and blend on medium speed until it is almost incorporated, about 10 seconds. Scrape the bowl.

5   Add the dry ingredients on low speed and blend 15 seconds. Stop the mixer to scrape the bowl, then blend until the dough is smooth, about 5 seconds more.

6   Measure out 48 rounded teaspoons of the dough and roll them into balls with your hands. Dip one side of each ball in the remaining ½ cup granulated sugar, if desired, and place them 2 inches apart and sugar-side up on the prepared baking sheets. Bake the cookies until they are just golden, 8 to 10 minutes. Remove the sheets from the oven. Immediately top each cookie with a Chocolate Kiss, wide side down, and press it firmly into the center of the cookie to embed the Kiss.

7   Using a metal spatula, carefully transfer the cookies from the baking sheets and place them on a plate or rack to cool completely.

INGREDIENTS

Vegetable oil or butter for greasing the baking sheets (optional)

1¾ cups all-purpose flour

1 teaspoon baking soda

¼ teaspoon salt

8 tablespoons (1 stick) unsalted butter, at room temperature

¾ cup (lightly packed) light brown sugar

¼ cup granulated sugar, plus ½ cup (optional) for dipping

½ cup peanut butter, smooth or crunchy

1 teaspoon pure vanilla extract

1 large egg, at room temperature

48 Hershey's Chocolate Kisses, removed from their wrappers

Maple Softies

* *

One of my most vivid memories from my college years is my mornings at King Pin Donuts on Telegraph Avenue in Berkeley. I'd go there before classes and inhale a maple bar—a fresh-from-the-oven rectangular doughnut swathed in a maple glaze. This is a tribute to that memory: a tender, cakey drop cookie, finished off with a confectioners' sugar–maple glaze.

MAKES 24 COOKIES

1 Preheat the oven to 400°F. Line several baking sheets with parchment paper or lightly grease them with vegetable oil or butter.

2 Make the cookies: Sift the flour, baking powder, baking soda, and salt together into a small bowl and set aside.

3 Cream the butter, both sugars, and both extracts together in a medium-size mixing bowl with an electric mixer on medium-high speed until light and fluffy, 1 minute. Stop the mixer twice to scrape the bowl with a rubber spatula, scraping it again at the end.

4 Add the eggs one at a time to the butter mixture, blending for about 10 seconds on medium speed after each addition. Scrape the bowl.

5 Add one-third of the flour mixture with the mixer on low speed, and blend for 5 seconds. Scrape the bowl.

6 Add half the sour cream, and blend on low speed for 5 seconds. Scrape the bowl.

7 Repeat steps 5 and 6. Then add the remaining flour mixture and mix on low speed for 5 seconds.

8 Give the batter a few broad strokes with the spatula.

9 Drop the batter by heaping tablespoons 2 inches apart on the prepared baking sheets. Bake the cookies until they are just golden and firm to the touch but not crusty, 11 to 12 minutes. Let the cookies sit for 2 to 3 minutes. Then slide the sheet of parchment paper onto the counter (or, using a metal spatula, carefully transfer each cookie to a sheet of aluminum foil

INGREDIENTS

Vegetable oil or butter for greasing the baking sheets (optional)

Cookies

2 cups plus 6 tablespoons cake flour

½ teaspoon plus ⅛ teaspoon baking powder

½ teaspoon plus ⅛ teaspoon baking soda

½ teaspoon salt

9 tablespoons (1 stick plus 1 tablespoon) unsalted butter, at room temperature

¾ cup granulated sugar

6 tablespoons (lightly packed) light brown sugar

½ teaspoon pure vanilla extract

¾ teaspoon pure maple extract

2 large eggs, at room temperature

¾ cup sour cream

Glaze and Topping

3 cups confectioners' sugar

¼ cup water

3 tablespoons pure maple syrup

1½ tablespoons light corn syrup

1½ tablespoons (lightly packed) light brown sugar

2 teaspoons pure maple extract

About 24 pecan halves

or waxed paper on the counter) and let them cool further.

10 When the cookies have cooled, make the glaze: Place the confectioners' sugar in a medium-size bowl and set aside. In a small saucepan, combine the water, maple syrup, corn syrup, and brown sugar and bring to a boil over medium heat. Remove from the heat and add the maple extract. Immediately add this hot mixture to the confectioners' sugar and beat it vigorously with a whisk until velvety smooth, 20 to 30 seconds.

11 Dip the rounded top of each cooled cookie into the glaze, and place a pecan half on top of the cookie. Return the cookies to the paper or foil, and let them sit until the glaze hardens, 2 to 3 hours (or pop them in the refrigerator for 1 hour to set quickly).

* *

Butter-Glazed Nutmeg Mounds

* *

These are soft, cakelike cookies, flavored with nutmeg and topped with an old-fashioned buttery glaze. I like them even better several hours after they're made when the flavors come into their own and the consistency is softer and moister. Stored in an airtight container, they last a while—assuming you can resist raiding the cookie jar for that long.

MAKES 36 COOKIES

1 Preheat the oven to 375°F. Line several baking sheets with parchment paper or lightly grease them with vegetable oil or butter.

2 Make the cookies: Sift the flour, baking soda, baking powder, nutmeg, and salt together into a small bowl and set aside.

3 Cream the butter, brown sugar, and vanilla together in a medium-size mixing bowl with an electric mixer on medium-high speed until light and fluffy, about 2 minutes. Stop the mixer twice to scrape the bowl with a rubber spatula, scraping the bowl again at the end.

4 Add the egg yolks to the butter mixture and blend on medium speed for about 10 seconds. Scrape the bowl then add the whole egg and mix until blended, about 10 seconds. Scrape the bowl again.

5 Add the sour cream and mix on medium-low speed until well blended, about 10 seconds. Scrape the bowl.

6 Fold in the dry ingredients by hand, then turn the mixer on low speed and mix about 5 seconds. Scrape the bowl and mix on low until the batter is smooth and velvety, 10 seconds. Give the batter a stir or two with the spatula.

7 Drop the batter by heaping tablespoons about 2 inches apart onto the prepared baking sheets. Bake the cookies until they are just golden in color and firm to the touch, but not crusty, about 12 minutes. Using a metal spatula, carefully lift the cookies from the sheet and place them on a rack to cool.

8 While the cookies are cooling, make the glaze: Melt the butter in a small saucepan over medium-low heat until golden in color, about 3 minutes.

9 Place the confectioners' sugar in a small bowl. Add the melted butter, vanilla, and hot water and beat vigorously with a whisk until the mixture is smooth and creamy.

10 When the cookies have cooled, dip the rounded top of each into the glaze. Place the cookies on the baking sheets and let them sit until the glaze hardens, several hours. (If it is a humid day, refrigerate them in order to speed the process.)

NOTE: *Although cake flour gives these cookies a superior texture, you may substitute 2½ cups all-purpose flour for it.*

INGREDIENTS

Vegetable oil or butter for greasing the baking sheets (optional)

Cookies

2¾ cups cake flour (see Note)

¾ teaspoon baking soda

¾ teaspoon baking powder

1 tablespoon plus 1 teaspoon ground nutmeg

½ teaspoon salt

9 tablespoons (1 stick plus 1 tablespoon) unsalted butter, at room temperature

1½ cups (lightly packed) light brown sugar

2 teaspoons pure vanilla extract

2 large egg yolks, at room temperature

1 large egg, at room temperature

1 cup sour cream, at room temperature

Glaze

6 tablespoons (¾ stick) unsalted butter

1½ cups confectioners' sugar

1 teaspoon pure vanilla extract

3 tablespoons hot water

Glazed Molasses Cake Cookies

Vegetable oil or butter for greasing the baking sheets (optional)

Cookies

1½ cups all-purpose flour

1 cup plus 2 tablespoons cake flour

1 teaspoon salt

¾ teaspoon baking soda

1 teaspoon ground ginger

1 teaspoon ground cinnamon

¼ teaspoon ground cloves

13 tablespoons (1½ sticks plus 1 tablespoon) unsalted butter, at room temperature

2 teaspoons grated lemon zest

2 large eggs, at room temperature

2 large egg yolks

1 cup dark molasses

Glaze

1½ cups confectioners' sugar

2 tablespoons plus 2 teaspoons heavy (whipping) cream

1 tablespoon plus 1 teaspoon fresh lemon juice

* *

This moist and flavorful molasses cookie is like a tasty piece of gingerbread in cookie form. Glaze a single cookie or sandwich two cookies together with Creamy Dreamy Vanilla Marshmallow Buttercream (page 114). Either way, they're best on the day they are baked.

MAKES 20 TO 24 COOKIES

1   Preheat the oven to 400°F. Line several baking sheets with parchment paper or lightly grease them with vegetable oil or butter.

2   Make the cookies: Sift both flours, the salt, baking soda, ginger, cinnamon, and cloves together into a small bowl and set aside.

3   Cream the butter and lemon zest together in a medium-size mixing bowl with an electric mixer on medium-high speed until light and fluffy, about 1 minute.

4   Add the whole eggs and the egg yolks to the butter mixture and mix on medium speed until blended, 20 seconds. Stop the mixer once to scrape the bowl with a rubber spatula.

5   Add the molasses and mix on medium to blend, 10 seconds. Scrape the bowl.

6   Add half the flour mixture with the mixer on low speed and blend for 10 seconds. Scrape the bowl. Add the rest of the flour mixture and blend on low for 10 seconds. Finish the mixing by hand, stirring with the spatula until the batter is smooth.

7   Drop the batter by large rounded tablespoons about 2 inches apart on the prepared baking sheets. Bake until the cookies have puffed up and are firm to the touch, about 13 minutes. Let the cookies sit for 2 to 3 minutes. Then slide the sheet of parchment paper onto the counter (or, using a metal spatula, carefully transfer each cookie to a sheet of aluminum foil

or waxed paper on the counter), and let them cool further.

8   While the cookies cool, make the glaze: Vigorously whisk the confectioners' sugar, cream, and lemon juice together in a small bowl until smooth.

9   Using a small frosting spatula or a butter knife, frost the top of each cookie with a generously rounded teaspoon of glaze. Let the cookies set for 2 to 3 hours (or pop them into the refrigerator for 1 hour to set quickly).

* *

Ginger-Snappers

* *

I don't know if the "snap" in gingersnaps refers to the crispness of the cookie or the bite of the ginger, but I do know that Nabisco gingersnaps were a staple in our household when I was growing up. My mother loved to eat two or three at bedtime, dunking them in a glass of milk until they became soft, and giving me a bit of her treat. These ginger cookies don't snap when you break them nor do they need to be dunked—they're cakey soft and chewy—but their ginger taste is distinctive.

MAKES 26 COOKIES

1   Preheat the oven to 350°F. Line several baking sheets with parchment paper or lightly grease them with vegetable oil or butter.

2   Sift the flour, baking soda, salt, cinnamon, and ginger together into a small bowl and set aside.

3   Cream the butter and brown sugar in a medium-size mixing bowl with an electric mixer on medium-high speed until light and fluffy, about 2 minutes. Stop the mixer twice to scrape the bowl with a rubber spatula.

INGREDIENTS

Vegetable oil or butter for greasing the baking sheets (optional)

2½ cups all-purpose flour

2 teaspoons baking soda

½ teaspoon salt

2 teaspoons ground cinnamon

1 tablespoon plus 2 teaspoons ground ginger

12 tablespoons (1½ sticks) unsalted butter, at room temperature

1 cup (firmly packed) dark brown sugar

1 large egg, at room temperature

¼ cup molasses

1 tablespoon grated lemon zest

¼ cup granulated sugar

4   Add the egg to the butter mixture and beat on medium speed until blended, about 10 seconds. Scrape the bowl.

5   Add the molasses and lemon zest and beat on medium until blended, 10 seconds.

6   Fold in half the dry ingredients by hand using several broad strokes of the spatula, then fold in the remaining half. Mix on low speed until blended, about 20 seconds.

7   Measure out rounded tablespoons of the dough and roll them into balls with your hands. Roll the balls in the granulated sugar and place them 2 inches apart on the prepared baking sheets. Bake the cookies just until the edges are lightly golden and the center is puffy, about 12 minutes. Do not overbake them or they will become hard. Remove the cookies carefully from the baking sheets with a metal spatula. Let them cool on a rack.

INGREDIENTS

Vegetable oil or butter for greasing the madeleine forms

6 tablespoons (¾ stick) unsalted butter

½ cup sugar

Pinch of salt

2 large eggs, at room temperature

¾ teaspoon pure vanilla extract

1 teaspoon grated lemon zest

½ cup plus 3 tablespoons cake flour, sifted

* *

M-M-M- Madeleines

* *

S o called because they were the exact sounds uttered by my daughter, Maya, when she tasted these for the first time. I knew she would love them because, like me, she is a lover of basics—in this case a sweet, rich butter flavor accented with vanilla and lemon zest.

MAKES 18 MADELEINES

1   Place a rack in the center of the oven and preheat to 375°F. Thoroughly grease 18 madeleine forms with vegetable oil or butter, using a paper towel or a piece of plastic wrap to spread the butter into all the little grooves.

2   Melt the butter in a small saucepan over medium-low heat.

Remove from the heat and let cool to room temperature, 10 to 15 minutes.

3   Meanwhile, beat the sugar, salt, eggs, vanilla, and lemon zest together in a medium-size mixing bowl using the whisk attachment on an electric mixer until thick and pale, 4 to 5 minutes. Stop the mixer twice to scrape the bowl with a rubber spatula.

4   Resift half of the flour over the egg mixture, and fold it in gently with the spatula so that it is almost, but not completely, incorporated. Repeat with the remaining flour.

5   Pour the melted butter over the batter in a thin stream, folding it in with gentle strokes.

6   Scoop about 2 tablespoons of batter into each madeleine cup, so the batter reaches to about ⅛ inch from the top. Then jiggle the pan slightly to distribute the batter evenly.

7   Place the pans in the oven (if you have two pans, both should fit) and bake until the cookies are puffed and set, with deep golden edges, 12 to 14 minutes. Let the madeleines cool in the pans for 10 minutes. Then use a small frosting spatula or a butter knife to gently loosen them and transfer them to racks to cool, flat-side down.

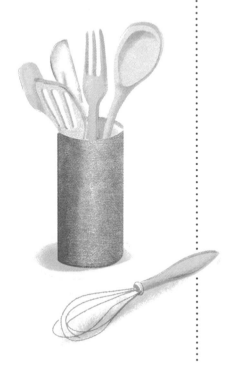

CHAPTER 12
Sandwiched Together

Were there Nobel Prizes in his day, the Earl of Sandwich would surely have been nominated for his culinary contribution to lunch boxes everywhere. The same goes for the unknown genius who translated the Earl's invention into a cookie. I imagine her slaving over a hot Bunsen burner all those long nights in the laboratory, until one red-eyed dawn, just when it seems all has been in vain, she looks up from her calculations, whips off her glasses, and shouts, "Victory is mine! I've got it!"

She had solved the age-old problem of how to keep the filling inside the cookie—and on top of that, she had come up with the added prize of two cookies in one.

Though history cruelly has denied our inventor immortality, it has given us the sandwich cookie to smoosh apart, lick the frosting off, and eat in pieces, or in one piece if we're so inclined. And for that I am grateful.

Sandwich cookies can be made from many types of cookies: cakey, shortbread, and drop, both chewy and crispy. What are they, anyway, but tiny layer cakes in cookie form? Construction of the sandwich isn't hard, but following certain steps helps. Before proceeding, be sure to read the tips in the box on page 210.

Storing Sandwich Cookies

It's best to store all sandwich cookies in a single layer in an airtight container in the refrigerator. If you have to layer them, make sure to put parchment or waxed paper between the layers. They should stay at their peak for 2 days.

Maya Pies

* *

I confess that before my anti-preservative days, I was a fan of Devil Dogs and I recall with fondness their velvety texture and the contrast of those chocolate buns with the sweet cream filling. Even when I gave up eating chemicals, I didn't want to give up Devil Dogs completely, so I came up with a version—named after my daughter, Maya, and made from wholesome ingredients—that I like to think is just as good as the real deal. Their texture improves on the second day, so store them in an airtight container overnight.

MAKES 20 COOKIE SANDWICHES

1 Preheat the oven to 400°F. Line several baking sheets with parchment paper or lightly grease them with vegetable oil or butter.

2 Make the cookies: Sift the cocoa, flour, baking powder, and baking soda together into a small bowl and set aside.

3 Cream the butter, oil, and granulated sugar together in a medium-size mixing bowl with an electric mixer on medium-high speed until light and fluffy, about 2 minutes. Stop the mixer once or twice to scrape the bowl with a rubber spatula.

4 Add the whole eggs and the yolk one at a time to the butter mixture and blend on medium speed for 10 seconds after each addition. Stop the mixer twice to scrape the bowl.

5 Add the sour cream and beat on medium speed until blended, about 5 seconds, then on high speed for 3 seconds more. The mixture may not appear smooth.

6 Fold the dry ingredients in by hand with 6 or 7 broad strokes of the spatula, then mix on low speed until the batter is velvety, about 10 seconds, stopping once to scrape the bowl. Finish mixing by hand.

7 Drop the batter by rounded tablespoons 2 inches apart onto the prepared baking sheets. Bake the cookies until they have risen, spring back to the touch, and a tester inserted in the center of a cookie comes out clean, about 10 minutes.

INGREDIENTS

Vegetable oil or butter for greasing the baking sheets (optional)

Cookies

¾ cup Dutch-process unsweetened cocoa powder, sifted

1 cup plus 2 tablespoons all-purpose flour

1 teaspoon baking powder

½ teaspoon baking soda

12 tablespoons (1½ sticks) unsalted butter, at room temperature

¼ cup vegetable oil

1 cup plus 2 tablespoons granulated sugar

3 large eggs

1 large egg yolk

½ cup sour cream

Filling

1¼ cups marshmallow creme (such as Marshmallow Fluff)

8 tablespoons (1 stick) unsalted butter, at room temperature

1 cup confectioners' sugar

2 tablespoons heavy (whipping) cream

Glaze

Chocolate Ganache (page 116)

8   Carefully lift the cookies from the baking sheets with a metal spatula and place them on a rack to cool.

9   While the cookies are cooling, make the filling: Combine the marshmallow creme, butter, confectioners' sugar, and heavy cream in a medium-size mixing bowl. Using an electric mixer with a paddle attachment, mix on medium-high speed until light and fluffy, about 2 minutes. Stop the mixer twice to scrape the sides of the bowl.

10   When completely cool, turn half the cookies upside down, spread each with a rounded tablespoon of filling, dip the remaining cookies (rounded side down) in the ganache, and then place them on top of the marshmallow-frosted halves.

11   Allow the ganache to set, then store the cookies in an airtight container and eat them the next day. They will continue to soften overnight. Of course, if you can't wait, they will be delicious that day as well.

Filling the Sandwich

For all kinds of sandwiches, let the cookies cool before you fill them. Pair up the cookies, matching them by size, and turn half of them upside down to receive the filling; the other half will be tops.

For cookies that use buttercream, such as Peanut Butter Sandwiches (page 235), dab the right amount of filling in the center of an upside-down cookie and gently press the bottom of its partner down onto it. Let the filling ruffle slightly out the sides to give it a sumptuous look.

Cookies with jam, like Almond Apricot Sandwiches (page 224), look better and are easier to eat when they're neater. Spread the jam sparingly here, so that it doesn't ooze out.

For cookies with melted chocolate fillings, such as Shortbread Sandwiches (page 222), let the chocolate firm up just a bit after it has melted. Spoon the appropriate amount onto the center of the bottom cookie, and using a butter knife or frosting spatula, spread the filling very gently toward the outer edge, stopping just short of it. Then carefully place the top cookie over the chocolate and press ever so lightly until the chocolate comes just to the edge. Allow cookies to set for several hours before eating, though refrigeration will speed up the process.

Birthday Cakes

ON THE GO

* *

I*f your idea of the perfect birthday cake is the same as mine—a yellow cake with raspberry preserves and white frosting—then you'll love these sumptuous cookies. I find them ideal for school birthday treats. For an additional thrill, you can spread colored sprinkles or sugar confetti over the glaze immediately after spreading it.*

MAKES 13 COOKIE SANDWICHES

1   Preheat the oven to 400°F. Line several baking sheets with parchment paper or lightly grease them with vegetable oil or butter.

2   Drop the batter by generous tablespoons onto the prepared baking sheets. Bake until just firm, 10 or 11 minutes. Using a metal spatula, carefully transfer the cookies to racks to cool completely.

3   Make the glaze: Place the confectioners' sugar, butter, and lemon juice in a food processor and process until smooth, about 10 seconds.

4   When the cookies are completely cool, use the metal spatula to turn half of them upside down. Spread each upside-down cookie with a slightly rounded teaspoon of preserves. Top them with the remaining cookies.

5   Using a small frosting spatula or a butter knife, frost the top of each cookie with a generously rounded teaspoon of the glaze. Let the cookies sit until the glaze has set, 2 hours.

INGREDIENTS

Vegetable oil or butter for greasing the baking sheets (optional)

Boston Cream Pies cookie batter (steps 5 through 9, page 212)

1½ cups confectioners' sugar

6 tablespoons (¾ stick) unsalted butter, at room temperature

3 tablespoons fresh lemon juice

About ¾ cup raspberry preserves

Boston Cream Pies

INGREDIENTS

Custard

1 cup milk

6 tablespoons heavy (whipping) cream

6 tablespoons granulated sugar

3 tablespoons cornstarch

¼ teaspoon salt

1 large egg yolk

2 teaspoons pure vanilla extract

Vegetable oil or butter for greasing the baking sheets (optional)

Cookies

1 cup all-purpose flour

1 cup plus 2 tablespoons cake flour

¾ teaspoon baking soda

½ teaspoon salt

9 tablespoons (1 stick plus 1 tablespoon) unsalted butter, at room temperature

1 cup plus 1 tablespoon granulated sugar

2 teaspoons pure vanilla extract

½ teaspoon grated lemon zest

2 large egg yolks, at room temperature

1 large egg, at room temperature

½ cup plus 2 tablespoons buttermilk, at room temperature

* *

B oston cream pie isn't actually a pie—it's a cake. Variations have been floating around for at least a couple of centuries, and Fanny Farmer codified it as a "Favorite Cake" in her 1896 cookbook. For all that history, I remain loyal to my version: two buttery vanilla cake cookies sandwiched together with vanilla custard and topped with a glossy chocolate glaze.

MAKES ABOUT 13 COOKIE SANDWICHES

1   Make the custard: Combine ½ cup plus 2 tablespoons of the milk, all the cream, and the sugar in a medium-size saucepan and bring just to a boil over medium-low heat. Remove from the heat.

2   Dissolve the cornstarch and salt in the remaining 6 tablespoons milk. Whisk in the egg yolk. Add this to the scalded cream mixture and whisk constantly over medium-low heat until it thickens, 2 to 3 minutes. Then cook, stirring, for 30 seconds more.

3   Remove the custard from the heat and stir in the vanilla. Pour it into a ceramic or plastic bowl and let cool for 10 minutes, stirring it gently several times. Puncture a piece of plastic wrap in several places, and place it directly over the surface of the custard. Refrigerate until completely chilled, 2 to 3 hours.

4   Preheat the oven to 400°F. Line several baking sheets with parchment paper or lightly grease them with vegetable oil or butter.

5   Meanwhile, make the cookies: Sift both flours, the baking soda, and salt together into a small bowl and set aside.

6   Cream the butter, granulated sugar, vanilla, and lemon zest together in a medium-size mixing bowl with an electric mixer on medium-high speed until light and fluffy, about 2 minutes. Stop the mixer twice to scrape the bowl with a rubber spatula, scraping the bowl again at the end.

7   Add the egg yolks to the butter mixture and blend on medium speed for about 10 seconds. Scrape the bowl. Then add the whole egg and mix until blended, about 10 seconds. Scrape the bowl again.

8   Add the buttermilk and mix on medium-low speed for about 10 seconds. The mixture will appear curdled. Scrape the bowl.

9   Fold in the flour mixture by hand. Then turn the mixer to low speed and mix for about 5 seconds. Scrape the bowl and mix on low speed until the batter is smooth and velvety, 10 seconds. Give the batter a stir or two with the spatula.

10   Drop the batter by generous tablespoons about 2 inches apart onto the prepared baking sheets. Bake the cookies until they are just firm, yet spongy to the touch (not crusty), 10 to 11 minutes. Using a metal spatula, carefully transfer the cookies to racks to cool.

11   When the custard and the cookies have cooled, use the metal spatula to turn half of them upside down. Spread each upside-down cookie with a heaping tablespoon of custard. Top them with the remaining cookies.

12   Make the glaze: Heat the cream in a small saucepan over medium-low heat just to the boiling point. Transfer the hot cream to a small heatproof bowl and add the chocolate and butter. Cover the bowl with a pot lid or a small plate and leave it for several minutes to melt the chocolate and butter. Then uncover and stir with a small whisk until smooth. Add the confectioners' sugar and stir vigorously until smooth and velvety.

13   Frost each cookie by spreading a scant tablespoon of the chocolate glaze evenly across the top.

Glaze

½ cup heavy (whipping) cream

2 ounces unsweetened chocolate, chopped very fine

1 tablespoon plus 1 teaspoon unsalted butter, at room temperature

6 tablespoons confectioners' sugar

Chocolate Minteos

* *

INGREDIENTS

Vegetable oil or butter for
    greasing the baking sheets
    (optional)

Cookies

2½ cups all-purpose flour

1 teaspoon baking soda

12 tablespoons (1½ sticks)
    unsalted butter, at room
    temperature

1 cup plus 2 tablespoons
    granulated sugar

2 teaspoons pure peppermint
    extract

2 large eggs, at room
    temperature

2 tablespoons water

12 ounces (2 cups) semisweet
    chocolate chips, melted

Filling

8 tablespoons (1 stick) unsalted
    butter, at room temperature

2 cups confectioners' sugar

2 tablespoons plus 2 teaspoons
    half-and-half or light cream

½ teaspoon pure peppermint
    extract

It is my firm belief that no matter how sophisticated our palates become and no matter how we hone our culinary skills, we will never lose the taste memory of Oreos. So here's a tribute to that cookie of our youth. It's thick and crunchy and filled with mint-flavored buttercream, and as my oldest son, Jake, still does, you may eat the inside first. They are especially good when chilled in the fridge—I eat them cold all the time!

MAKES 40 COOKIE SANDWICHES

1   Preheat the oven to 375°F. Line several baking sheets with parchment paper or lightly grease them with vegetable oil or butter.

2   Make the cookies: Sift the flour and baking soda together into a small bowl and set aside.

3   Cream the butter, sugar, and peppermint extract together in a medium-size mixing bowl with an electric mixer on medium speed until light and fluffy, about 1 minute. Scrape the bowl with a rubber spatula.

4   Add the eggs and water to the butter mixture and beat on medium speed until they are blended, about 20 seconds. Scrape the bowl.

5   Add the melted chocolate chips and mix on medium speed until blended, 5 seconds. Scrape the bowl.

6   Add the flour mixture and mix on low speed for 15 seconds. Scrape the bowl.

7   Drop the batter by rounded teaspoons 2 inches apart onto the prepared baking sheets. Using the bottom of a glass that has been dipped in water, press each cookie down so that it forms a round 1½ inches in diameter.

8   Bake the cookies until they are firm to the touch, 17 minutes. Use a metal spatula to transfer them to racks to cool completely.

9   Meanwhile, make the filling: Place the butter, confectioners' sugar, half-and-half, and peppermint extract in a small bowl and whisk until smooth.

10   When the cookies are completely cool, use the metal spatula to turn half of them upside down. Spread a rounded teaspoon of filling on each upside-down cookie. Top them with the remaining cookies. Allow them to set for 2 to 3 hours or pop them in the refrigerator for 1 hour to set quickly.

Chocolate Raspberry Sandwiches

*T*wo delicate, crisp, deeply chocolate wafers sandwiched with raspberry preserves: an elegant addition to a dessert of ice cream or fresh fruit. These cookies are also lovely as the chocolate component on a dessert platter, accompanying Lemon Curd Tartlets (page 377) and Coconut Dainties (page 162).

MAKES 25 TO 30 COOKIE SANDWICHES

1   Sift the flour, cocoa powder, and baking soda together into a small bowl and set aside.

2   Cream the butter, both sugars, and the vanilla together in a medium-size mixing bowl with an electric mixer on medium speed until light and fluffy, 2½ to 3 minutes. Stop the mixer once or twice to scrape the bowl with a rubber spatula.

INGREDIENTS

2 cups plus 2 tablespoons all-purpose flour

½ cup unsweetened cocoa powder

⅛ teaspoon baking soda

2 sticks (8 ounces) unsalted butter, at room temperature

¾ cup confectioners' sugar

½ cup granulated sugar

1 teaspoon pure vanilla extract

Vegetable oil or butter for greasing the baking sheets

1 cup raspberry preserves

12 ounces bittersweet chocolate

3 Add the flour mixture and blend on low speed until the mixture is fluffy again, about 45 seconds. Scrape the bowl.

4 Divide the dough in half and shape it into two thick disks. Wrap each disk in plastic wrap and refrigerate for at least 2 hours or as long as overnight.

5 When you're ready to bake the cookies, preheat the oven to 325°F. Lightly grease several baking sheets with vegetable oil or butter. Remove the dough from the refrigerator, unwrap it, and allow it to soften slightly, about 10 minutes.

6 Place each piece of dough between two fresh pieces of plastic wrap or waxed paper, and roll it out ⅛ inch thick (see page 330 for rolling technique).

7 Remove the top piece of plastic wrap, and using a 2-inch round cookie cutter, cut out about 20 rounds from each half. Place the rounds about ¾ inch apart on the prepared baking sheets. Gather up the scraps and reroll the dough to make as many cookies as possible.

8 Bake the cookies just until they are firm to the touch, 10 to 12 minutes. Let the cookies cool completely on the baking sheets.

9 When the cookies are completely cool, use a metal spatula to turn half of them upside down. Spread each upside-down cookie with a scant teaspoon of preserves. Top them with the remaining cookies.

10 Meanwhile, melt the chocolate in the top of a double boiler placed over simmering water.

11 Pour the melted chocolate into a small deep bowl. Dip half of each sandwich into the chocolate, using the rim of the bowl to scrape any excess chocolate off the bottom of the cookie. Or rotate just the outer edge of the cookie in the chocolate for an alternative design.

12 As they are dipped, place the cookies on a large sheet of waxed or parchment paper and allow them to sit until the chocolate hardens, 2 to 3 hours (or pop them in the refrigerator for 1 hour to set quickly, especially if it is a humid day).

Ruby Gems

* *

These were among my favorite cookies when I was a kid because the jam center seemed like a special reward. The tender texture and butter flavor sent me over the top, and still does.

MAKES ABOUT 22 COOKIE SANDWICHES

1   Using a fork, stir the egg yolk and vanilla together in a small cup.

2   Process the flour, granulated sugar, and salt in a food processor for about 10 seconds.

3   Add the butter and process the mixture until it resembles coarse meal, 20 to 30 seconds.

4   With the machine running, add the yolk mixture through the feed tube and process for 5 seconds. Scrape the bowl with a rubber spatula, then process until the liquid is evenly absorbed, about 10 seconds.

5   Remove the dough and place it on a work surface. Work the dough with your hands just until you can form it into a mass. Divide the dough in half and shape it into two thick disks. Wrap each disk in plastic wrap. Refrigerate the dough several hours or overnight.

6   When you're ready to bake the cookies, preheat the oven to 350°F. Remove the dough from the refrigerator and allow it to soften slightly. Lightly grease several baking sheets with vegetable oil or butter.

7   Place each piece of dough between two fresh pieces of plastic wrap or waxed paper and roll it out ⅛ inch thick (see page 330 for rolling technique).

8   Remove the top piece of plastic wrap and, using a 2-inch round cookie cutter, cut out about 22 rounds from each half. Make small holes in the center of half of the rounds with a smooth bottle cap, a small, sharp knife, or a tiny cookie cutter. Place all the rounds about ¾ inch apart on the prepared baking sheets. Gather up the dough scraps and reroll and cut out the dough as above to make as many more cookies as possible.

INGREDIENTS

1 large egg yolk, at room temperature

1 teaspoon pure vanilla extract

3 cups all-purpose flour

⅔ cup granulated sugar

¼ teaspoon salt

2 sticks (8 ounces) plus 1 tablespoon unsalted butter, very cold, cut into about 16 pieces

Vegetable oil or butter for greasing the baking sheets

¼ cup raspberry or apricot preserves

1 cup confectioners' sugar

9   Bake the cookies until the edges just begin to turn golden, about 15 minutes. Let them cool completely on the baking sheets.

10   When the cookies are completely cool, place ½ teaspoon preserves in the center of each cookie without a hole. Sprinkle confectioners' sugar over the ones with holes and place them on top of the jammed cookies so that the jam forms a perfect little glob in the middle.

* *

Double Crispy Sandwiches

* *

W hen my friend Allen Helschein told me that he had a great cookie recipe using cornflakes, I had my doubts. Well, Allen was right. Nothing besides cornflakes provides the satisfying crunch that contrasts so perfectly with the chocolate filling.

MAKES 46 COOKIE SANDWICHES

1   Preheat the oven to 375°F. Line several baking sheets with parchment paper or lightly grease them with vegetable oil or butter.

2   Make the cookies: Sift the flour, baking soda, and salt together into a medium-size bowl. Stir in the oats and set aside.

3   Cream the butter, both sugars, and the vanilla together in a medium-size mixing bowl with an electric mixer on medium-high speed until light and fluffy, about 1½ minutes. Stop the mixer once to scrape the bowl with a rubber spatula.

4   Add the eggs to the butter mixture one at a time, mixing on medium-low speed for 10 seconds each time, scraping the bowl after each addition and again at the end.

INGREDIENTS

Vegetable oil or butter for greasing the baking sheets (optional)

Cookies

1½ cups all-purpose flour

1 teaspoon baking soda

1 teaspoon salt

1½ cups quick-cooking oats

2½ sticks (10 ounces) unsalted butter, at room temperature

½ cup plus 2 tablespoons granulated sugar

1 cup minus 2 tablespoons (lightly packed) light brown sugar

2 teaspoons pure vanilla extract

2 large eggs, at room temperature

2 cups cornflakes

Filling

9 ounces (1½ cups) semisweet chocolate chips

5   Add the flour mixture and mix on medium-low speed for 10 seconds. Scrape the bowl, then mix until blended, about 5 seconds more. Scrape the bowl.

6   Add the cornflakes and mix on low speed until they're crushed and blended in, 10 seconds. Stop the mixer once to scrape the bowl.

7   Drop the dough by rounded teaspoons about 2 inches apart onto the prepared baking sheets. Bake until the cookies are crisp and lightly golden with darker golden edges, 12 to 14 minutes. Let them cool completely on the baking sheets.

8   While the cookies are cooling, make the filling: Melt the chocolate chips in the top of a double boiler placed over simmering water. Remove from the heat and let cool for 10 minutes.

9   When the cookies are completely cool, use a metal spatula to turn half of them upside down, and spread 1 rounded teaspoon of the chocolate on each upside-down cookie. Place the other cookies over the filling, but don't press down. Let the cookies sit for 2 to 3 hours until the chocolate hardens (or refrigerate them for 1 hour to speed up the process).

* *

Glazed Almond Raspberry Sandwiches

* *

To me, almonds and raspberries are an inspired combination whose taste, texture, and color speak of luxury. They unite here in delicate almond butter cookies, held together with raspberry preserves and accented with a light almond glaze.

MAKES AT LEAST 40 COOKIE SANDWICHES

INGREDIENTS

Cookies

2 large egg yolks

1 teaspoon pure vanilla extract

½ cup granulated sugar

1 package (7 ounces) almond paste (not marzipan)

2 sticks (8 ounces) unsalted butter, cold, cut into 16 pieces

1 cup plus 3 tablespoons all-purpose flour

1 teaspoon salt

1 teaspoon grated lemon zest

Vegetable oil or butter for greasing the baking sheets (optional)

Filling

½ cup raspberry preserves

Glaze

1 cup confectioners' sugar

1½ teaspoons pure almond extract

2 tablespoons hot water

1   Make the cookies: Using a fork, stir the egg yolks and vanilla together in a small cup. Set aside.

2   Process the granulated sugar and almond paste together in a food processor until the mixture looks like coarse sand, 25 seconds. Scatter the butter over the mixture and process for 15 seconds.

3   Add the flour, salt, and lemon zest, and pulse for 40 to 50 seconds to blend.

4   With the machine running, add the yolk mixture through the feed tube and process for 5 seconds. Scrape the bowl with a rubber spatula. Then process just until the liquid is evenly absorbed, 5 to 8 seconds.

5   Remove the dough, place it on a work surface, and form it into two rectangular slabs. Wrap each in plastic wrap and refrigerate for an hour or two.

6   Place each slab of dough between two fresh pieces of plastic wrap, and roll it out ⅛ inch thick (see page 330 for rolling technique). Place the dough, still covered with the plastic wrap, in the freezer or refrigerator and allow it to chill again for 1 to 2 hours.

7   When you are ready to bake the cookies, preheat the oven to 375°F. Line several baking sheets with parchment paper or lightly grease them with vegetable oil or butter.

8   Remove the top piece of plastic wrap, and using a 2-inch round cookie cutter, cut out about 35 rounds from each half. Place the rounds about ¾ inch apart on the prepared baking sheets. Gather up the dough scraps and reroll the dough to make as many more cookies as possible.

9   Bake the cookies until the edges are just beginning to turn golden, about 8 or 9 minutes. Let them cool completely on the baking sheets.

10   When the cookies are completely cool, use a metal spatula to turn half of them upside down. Spread each upside-down cookie with a scant ½ teaspoon of preserves. Top them with the remaining cookies.

11   Make the glaze: Place the confectioners' sugar, almond extract, and hot water in a small bowl and whisk until smooth.

12   Using a spoon, drizzle the glaze over the tops of the cookies. Allow to set for 2 to 3 hours (or place in the refrigerator for 1 hour to speed up the process).

Katz Tongues

* *

There used to be a great place within walking distance of my house called the Bentonwood Bakery and Cafe. Here I discovered homemade Katz Tongues—pastry chef Rick Katz's rendition of the classic French langues de chat, *so named because they resemble a cat's tongue. This version, made of two thin, crispy butter wafers sandwiched together with chocolate, is one of my favorites—particularly because their daintiness belies the ease with which they're made.*

MAKES 24 COOKIE SANDWICHES

1 Preheat the oven to 375°F. Line several baking sheets with parchment paper. If possible, have ready a pastry bag with a #9 tip; flatten the tip with a mallet to form a thin oval so the batter comes out thin.

2 Sift the flour and salt together into a small bowl and set aside.

3 Beat the butter in a medium-size mixing bowl with an electric mixer on medium speed just until fluffy, 15 seconds. Scrape the bowl with a rubber spatula.

4 Turn the mixer to medium-low speed and gradually add the sugar, then the vanilla. Scrape the bowl.

5 Turn the mixer to low speed and gradually add the egg whites. Mix until blended, 30 seconds, stopping the mixer once to scrape the bowl.

6 Add the flour mixture, stirring it in by hand with the spatula. Then blend thoroughly with the mixer on low speed for 10 seconds. Stop the mixer once to scrape the bowl.

7 Place some of the batter in the pastry bag and pipe out strips approximately 2½ inches long onto the parchment paper, leaving 2 inches between cookies. Alternatively, use a spoon to drop the batter onto the baking sheet, and then flatten it to ⅛ inch thickness with a butter knife or frosting spatula.

8 Bake the cookies until they are crisp to the touch in the center and a rich golden color around the edges, 14 to 16 minutes. Watch them carefully as they can

INGREDIENTS

¾ cup all-purpose flour

¾ teaspoon salt

8 tablespoons (1 stick) unsalted butter, at room temperature

1 cup sugar

½ teaspoon pure vanilla extract

½ cup egg whites (from 3 or 4 large eggs), lightly beaten

4 ounces bittersweet chocolate

overbake within seconds. Let them cool completely on the baking sheets. Then carefully loosen them with a frosting spatula.

9   Melt the chocolate in the top of a double boiler placed over simmering water. Remove from the heat and let cool to spreading consistency.

10   When the cookies are completely cool, use a metal spatula to turn half of them upside down. Spread each upside-down cookie with a teaspoon of chocolate, and top with the remaining cookies. Allow to set completely before eating, about 2 hours (or refrigerate to speed up the process).

* *

Shortbread Sandwiches

* *

T his perfect union of shortbread and chocolate offers two thick, not-too-sweet, crunchy cookies with bittersweet chocolate sandwiched between. Eat them as is or do as my son Jake does—pull them apart and devour the filling first.

MAKES 28 COOKIE SANDWICHES

INGREDIENTS

Cookies

2½ cups cake flour

1 cup confectioners' sugar

½ teaspoon baking powder

½ teaspoon salt

2 sticks (8 ounces) unsalted butter, cold, cut into 16 pieces

2 teaspoons pure vanilla extract

Filling

8 ounces bittersweet chocolate

2 tablespoons plus 2 teaspoons vegetable oil

1   Make the cookies: Place the flour, confectioners' sugar, baking powder, and salt in a food processor and process for 10 seconds.

2   Scatter the butter over the flour mixture, add the vanilla, and process until the dough just comes together, 30 to 40 seconds.

3   Place a 2-foot length of waxed paper on a work surface. Shape the dough into a rough log 13 or 14 inches long (or into two logs each 6 to 7 inches long) and 2 inches in diameter, and place them along one long side of the paper. Roll the log up in the waxed paper and twist the ends like a hard-candy wrapper. Refrigerate the log for 2 hours.

4   Remove the log from the refrigerator. Using your hands, roll the wrapped dough gently back and forth on the work surface to smooth out and round the log. Refrigerate for another 3 hours or overnight.

5   Fifteen minutes before baking, preheat the oven to 350°F. Line several baking sheets with parchment paper.

6   Remove the log from the refrigerator, unwrap it, and cut it into slices that are a scant ¼ inch thick. Place the cookies 1 inch apart on the prepared baking sheets, and bake until the edges are golden and the centers are firm, 15 to 17 minutes. Let the cookies cool completely on the baking sheets.

7   While the cookies are cooling, make the filling: Melt the chocolate in the top of a double boiler placed over simmering water. Remove from the heat and whisk in the oil until smooth. Remove the top pot from the bottom one and let the chocolate sit for 15 to 20 minutes to reach spreading consistency.

8   When the cookies are completely cool, use a metal spatula to turn half of them upside down. Spread each upside-down cookie with 1 teaspoon of the chocolate and top them with the remaining cookies. Do not press down. Allow to set for 2 to 3 hours. (They can be chilled in the refrigerator for 1 hour to speed up the process.)

* *

Little Princesses

* *

T *hese rich, buttery vanilla cookies, paired with raspberry preserves and then dusted with powdered sugar, truly live up to their name. Crisp the first day, they tend to soften a bit by the second day no matter how you store them—but either way, they are royally divine.*

MAKES 16 COOKIE SANDWICHES

INGREDIENTS

Vegetable oil or butter for greasing the baking sheets (optional)

6 large egg yolks

¾ teaspoon pure vanilla extract

2 cups all-purpose flour

⅔ cup sugar

½ teaspoon salt

1 tablespoon plus 1 teaspoon grated lemon zest

2 sticks (8 ounces) unsalted butter, cold, cut into 16 pieces

5 to 6 tablespoons raspberry preserves

¼ cup confectioners' sugar

1   Preheat the oven to 375°F. Line several baking sheets with parchment paper or lightly grease them with vegetable oil or butter.

2   Using a fork, stir the egg yolks and vanilla together in a small cup.

3   Place the flour, sugar, salt, and lemon zest in a food processor, and process for 5 seconds.

4   Scatter the butter over the flour mixture and process until the mixture resembles coarse meal, 20 to 30 seconds.

5   With the machine running, add the yolk mixture through the feed tube and process for 5 seconds. Scrape the bowl with a rubber spatula. Then process until the dough comes together, 10 to 15 seconds.

6   Scoop out rounded teaspoons of the dough and roll them into balls with your hands. Place them 2 inches apart on the prepared baking sheets. Using the bottom of a glass that has been lightly dipped in flour, flatten each ball to a generous ⅛-inch thickness, about 2¼ inches in diameter.

7   Bake the cookies until the edges are deep golden, 14 to 16 minutes. Let them cool completely on the baking sheets.

8   When the cookies are completely cool, use a metal spatula to turn half of them upside down. Spread each upside-down cookie with a generous ½ teaspoon of the preserves, and top with the remaining cookies. Sift confectioners' sugar over the tops.

* *

Almond Apricot Sandwiches

* *

A pricot jam holds these rich, nutty cookies together, while a bittersweet chocolate drizzle over the top does double duty as decoration and decadent finishing touch.

MAKES 42 COOKIE SANDWICHES

1   Make the cookies: Using a fork, stir the egg and almond extract together in a small cup and set aside.

2   Place the flour, all but 2 tablespoons of the confectioners' sugar, the granulated sugar, almonds, and salt in a food processor, and process for 5 seconds.

3   Scatter the butter over the flour mixture and process until the mixture resembles coarse crumbs, 30 seconds.

4   With the machine running, add the egg mixture through the feed tube and process just until the dough comes together, 45 seconds.

5   Spread a 2-foot length of waxed paper on a work surface. With floured fingers, shape the dough into a rough log about 20 inches long and 2 inches in diameter, and place it along one long side of the paper. Roll the log up in the waxed paper and twist the ends like a hard-candy wrapper. (Once wrapped, you can cut the log in half in order to fit it in the refrigerator. Make sure to wrap the cut ends.) Refrigerate the dough for 2 hours.

6   Remove the log from the refrigerator, and with the dough still in the waxed paper, gently roll it back and forth on the work surface to smooth out the log. Place the log back in the refrigerator and chill it at least 3 hours more.

7   Fifteen minutes before baking, preheat the oven to 350°F. Line several baking sheets with parchment paper.

8   Place the log on the counter, unwrap it, and cut it into scant ¼-inch-thick slices. Place the cookies 1 inch apart on the prepared baking sheets. Bake until they are firm and lightly golden around the edges, 20 minutes. Let the cookies cool completely on the baking sheets.

9   When the cookies are completely cool, use a metal spatula to turn half of them upside down. Spread 1 scant teaspoon of the preserves over each upside-down cookie. Top them with the remaining cookies. Sift the remaining 2 tablespoons confectioners' sugar over the cookies.

10   Make the glaze: Melt the chocolate in the top of a double boiler placed over simmering water. Remove from the heat and whisk in the oil until smooth.

11   Using a spoon or fork, drizzle the chocolate over the tops of the cookies in a zigzag or crisscross fashion. Allow the glaze to set for 2 to 3 hours (or refrigerate for 1 hour to speed up the process).

INGREDIENTS

Cookies

1 large egg

1 teaspoon pure almond extract

2 cups all-purpose flour

¾ cup confectioners' sugar

6 tablespoons granulated sugar

1½ cups finely ground almonds

¾ teaspoon salt

2 sticks (8 ounces) unsalted butter, cold, cut into 16 pieces

Filling

¾ cup apricot preserves

Glaze

3 ounces bittersweet chocolate

1 tablespoon vegetable oil

Linzer Sandwiches

* *

One of my most vivid food memories comes from the William Greenberg bakery in New York City, where I recall savoring the nutty crunch of a giant linzer cookie, then enjoying a second taste as I licked at the confectioners' sugar mustache it left on my upper lip. I tried to get the recipe from Greenberg's, but without success, so I worked and worked to come as close as I could on my own. I've made my version smaller than the original (a function of age), but other than that, it matches my memory cookie right down to the mustache.

MAKES 20 TO 25 COOKIE SANDWICHES

INGREDIENTS

1 large egg, at room temperature

1 large egg yolk

1 teaspoon pure vanilla extract

1¾ cups all-purpose flour

1¼ cups confectioners' sugar plus 2 to 3 tablespoons for sprinkling

1¼ cups ground almonds

1 tablespoon unsweetened cocoa powder

1 teaspoon ground cinnamon

¼ teaspoon ground cloves

½ teaspoon baking powder

¾ teaspoon salt

2½ tablespoons grated lemon zest

13 tablespoons (1 stick plus 5 tablespoons) unsalted butter, cold, cut into 13 pieces

Vegetable oil or butter for greasing the baking sheets (optional)

½ cup raspberry preserves

1 Using a fork, stir the whole egg, egg yolk, and vanilla together in a small cup. Set aside.

2 Place the flour, 1¼ cups confectioners' sugar, almonds, cocoa, cinnamon, cloves, baking powder, salt, and lemon zest in a food processor and process to blend, 5 seconds.

3 Distribute the butter over the surface of the flour mixture and process until the mixture resembles coarse meal, 20 to 30 seconds.

4 With the machine running, add the egg mixture through the feed tube and process for 3 seconds. Scrape the bowl with a rubber spatula, then process for 3 seconds more.

5 Remove the dough from the machine and shape it into two disks. Wrap each piece of dough in plastic wrap or waxed paper, and refrigerate for 2 hours.

6 When you're ready to bake the cookies, preheat the oven to 350°F. Line several baking sheets with parchment paper or lightly grease them with vegetable oil or butter. Remove the dough from the refrigerator and allow it to soften slightly, about 10 minutes.

7 Place each piece of dough between two fresh pieces of

plastic wrap or waxed paper and roll it out to a generous ⅛-inch thickness (see page 330 for rolling technique). Remove the top piece of plastic wrap and, using a 2-inch round cookie cutter, cut out about 20 rounds from each half. Using a smooth bottle cap, a sharp knife, or a tiny cookie cutter, make small holes in the center of half the rounds. Place all the rounds about ¾ inch apart on the prepared baking sheets. Gather up the dough scraps and reroll the dough to make as many more cookies as possible, again making small holes in the center of half of them.

8   Bake the cookies until they are firm, 14 minutes. Let them cool completely on the baking sheets.

9   When the cookies are completely cool, use a metal spatula to turn the cookies with no holes upside down. Spread each one with a level ½ teaspoon of raspberry preserves, then place another ½ teaspoon of the preserves in a mound in the center of each cookie. Sprinkle the remaining confectioners' sugar over the cookies with holes, and place them on top of the cookie bottoms so that the jam forms a perfect little mound in the middle.

* *

Chocolate Jam Sandwiches

* *

T*wo crunchy, buttery shortbread cookies sandwiched together with a double dose of delectableness: chocolate and raspberry or orange. As an alternative, sandwich the cookies with the preserves or marmalade and use the chocolate as a glaze. You can either dip half the cookie in the glaze or drizzle the glaze over the top.*

MAKES AT LEAST 16 COOKIE SANDWICHES

227

INGREDIENTS

Cookies

1 large egg yolk

½ teaspoon pure vanilla extract

1¼ cups all-purpose flour

5 tablespoons confectioners' sugar

3 tablespoons granulated sugar

2 tablespoons grated orange zest

½ teaspoon salt

8 tablespoons (1 stick) unsalted butter, cold, cut into 8 pieces

Vegetable oil or butter for greasing the baking sheets (optional)

Filling

3 tablespoons heavy (whipping) cream

4 ounces bittersweet chocolate

About 6 tablespoons raspberry preserves or orange marmalade

1 Make the cookies: Using a fork, stir the egg yolk and vanilla together in a small cup. Set aside.

2 Place the flour, both sugars, the orange zest, and salt in a food processor, and process for about 10 seconds.

3 Add the butter to the flour mixture and process until the mixture resembles coarse meal, 20 to 30 seconds.

4 With the machine running, add the yolk mixture though the feed tube and process for 5 seconds. Scrape the bowl with a rubber spatula, then process until the liquid is evenly absorbed, about 10 seconds.

5 Place the dough on a work surface and work it with your hands just until you can form it into a mass. Divide the dough in half and shape it into two thick disks. Wrap each disk in plastic wrap. Refrigerate the dough for at least 1½ hours or overnight.

6 When you're ready to bake the cookies, preheat the oven to 350°F. Line several baking sheets with parchment paper or lightly grease them with vegetable oil or butter. Remove the dough from the refrigerator and allow it to soften slightly, about 10 minutes.

7 Place each piece of dough between two fresh pieces of plastic wrap or waxed paper and roll it out ⅛ inch thick. Slide the dough, still in the plastic wrap, onto a plate and refrigerate it for 15 minutes for easier handling.

8 Remove the top piece of plastic wrap and, using a 2-inch round cookie cutter, cut out about 16 rounds from each half. Place the cookies about ¾ inch apart on the prepared baking sheets. Gather up the scraps and reroll the dough to make as many more cookies as possible.

9 Bake the cookies just until the edges begin to turn golden, 14 to 15 minutes. Let them cool completely on the baking sheets.

10 Meanwhile, make the filling: Heat the cream in a small saucepan over medium heat just to the boiling point. Remove the pan from the heat and stir in the chocolate. Cover and set aside until the chocolate is melted, about 3 minutes. Then stir until smooth, 10 seconds.

11 When the cookies are completely cool, use a metal spatula to turn half of them upside down. Spread ¾ teaspoon of the chocolate filling over each upside-down cookie. Turn the remaining cookies upside down, and spread ½ teaspoon of the preserves over each one.

12 Sandwich the two filled halves together, and allow to set for 3 to 4 hours.

Crispy Fingers

* *

For fans of Pepperidge Farm's Brussels cookie, here's a homemade version. These thin, crispy almond oatmeal wafers sandwiched with bittersweet chocolate make a wonderful teatime cookie or a delicate, elegant garnish for a dish of ice cream at the end of a meal.

MAKES 24 COOKIE SANDWICHES

1 Preheat the oven to 350°F. Line several baking sheets with parchment paper or lightly grease them with vegetable oil or butter. Have ready a pastry bag fitted with a ½-inch plain tip.

2 Make the cookies: Sift the flour, baking soda, and cream of tartar together into a small bowl and set aside.

3 Cream the butter, sugar, both extracts, and the orange zest together in a medium-size mixing bowl with an electric mixer on medium speed until light and fluffy, about 2 minutes. Stop the mixer twice to scrape the bowl with a rubber spatula.

4 Add the egg whites to the butter mixture and beat on medium-high speed until blended, about 1 minute.

5 Add the flour, and mix by hand with the spatula until blended.

6 Add the almonds and oats, and mix by hand until blended.

7 Fill the pastry bag with batter and pipe 2-inch-long fingers 3 inches apart on the prepared baking sheets. Bake until lightly golden with darker golden edges, about 12 minutes. Using a metal spatula, immediately transfer the cookies to racks to cool.

8 Meanwhile, make the filling: Melt the chocolates together in the top of a double boiler placed over simmering water.

9 When the cookies are completely cool, use the metal spatula to turn half of them upside down. Using a small frosting spatula or a butter knife, spread a thin layer of chocolate over each upside-down cookie. Immediately place the remaining cookies on top, pressing down gently.

10 Allow the cookies to set for 2 hours (or refrigerate for 1 hour to speed up the process).

INGREDIENTS

Vegetable oil or butter for greasing the baking sheets (optional)

Cookies

¾ cup all-purpose flour

¼ teaspoon baking soda

¼ teaspoon cream of tartar

8 tablespoons (1 stick) unsalted butter, at room temperature

¾ cup sugar

½ teaspoon pure orange extract

½ teaspoon pure vanilla extract

¼ teaspoon grated orange zest

2 large egg whites, lightly beaten

½ cup finely chopped almonds

¼ cup quick-cooking oats

Filling

1 ounce unsweetened chocolate

4 ounces semisweet chocolate

229

Pumpkin Whoopie Pies

* *

Yes, the day came when I got down from my high horse and used Marshmallow Fluff in a recipe. And you know what? The world didn't end. In fact, it's now all the richer for this yummy filling, which I use here to hold two pumpkin-flavored cakey cookies together. The result is a classic whoopie pie and then some.

MAKES 14 COOKIE SANDWICHES

INGREDIENTS

Vegetable oil or butter for greasing the baking sheets (optional)

Cookies

½ cup plus 1 tablespoon all-purpose flour

¾ cup plus 1 tablespoon cake flour

½ teaspoon baking soda

1 teaspoon baking powder

½ teaspoon salt

9 tablespoons (1 stick plus 1 tablespoon) unsalted butter, at room temperature

½ cup plus 2 tablespoons (lightly packed) light brown sugar

7 tablespoons granulated sugar

2½ teaspoons ground cinnamon

2 teaspoons ground nutmeg

¾ teaspoon ground allspice

½ teaspoon ground cloves

½ teaspoon ground ginger

1 teaspoon pure vanilla extract

2 large eggs, at room temperature

1½ tablespoons molasses

½ cup plus 2 tablespoons canned unsweetened pumpkin puree

¼ cup buttermilk

1   Preheat the oven to 400°F. Line several baking sheets with parchment paper or lightly grease them with vegetable oil or butter.

2   Make the cookies: Sift both flours, the baking soda, baking powder, and salt together into a small bowl and set aside.

3   Cream the butter, both sugars, the cinnamon, nutmeg, allspice, cloves, ginger, and vanilla together in a medium-size mixing bowl with an electric mixer on medium-high speed until light and fluffy, about 1½ minutes. Stop the mixer twice to scrape the bowl with a rubber spatula, and scrape the bowl again at the end.

4   Add the eggs to the butter mixture one at a time, blending on medium speed for about 10 seconds after each addition.

5   Add the molasses and pumpkin, and mix on medium-low speed until well blended, about 10 seconds. Scrape the bowl. Add the buttermilk and blend for 5 seconds.

6   Fold in the flour mixture by hand with the spatula. Then turn the mixer to low speed and mix for about 5 seconds. Scrape the bowl, and mix on low until the batter is smooth and velvety, 10 seconds. Give the batter a stir or two with the spatula.

7   Drop the batter by generously rounded tablespoons about 2 inches apart onto the prepared baking sheets. Bake the cookies until they are risen and firm to the touch, but not crusty, about 12 minutes. Using a metal spatula, carefully transfer the cookies to racks to cool completely.

8 While the cookies are cooling, make the filling: Place the butter, marshmallow creme, confectioners' sugar, and vanilla in a small bowl and beat with an electric mixer on low speed until the sugar is absorbed, 15 to 20 seconds. Scrape the bowl with a rubber spatula, turn the mixer to medium-high, and beat until the mixture is light and fluffy,

3 minutes. Stop the mixer twice to scrape the bowl.

9 When the cookies are completely cool, use a metal spatula to turn half of them upside down. Spread each upside-down cookie with a heaping teaspoon of filling. Top them with the remaining cookies.

Marshmallow Filling

8 tablespoons (1 stick) unsalted butter, at room temperature

5 heaping tablespoons marshmallow creme (such as Marshmallow Fluff)

1 cup confectioners' sugar, sifted

½ teaspoon pure vanilla extract

* *

Summer's Day Sandwiches

* *

L*ittle lemon wafers sandwiched together with white chocolate—perfect with a glass of iced mint tea on a summer's day.*

MAKES 22 COOKIE SANDWICHES

1 Preheat the oven to 375°F. Line several baking sheets with parchment paper or lightly grease them with vegetable oil or butter. Prepare a pastry bag fitted with a ½-inch plain tip.

2 Make the cookies: Place the flour, salt, baking powder, both sugars, and the lemon zest in a food processor and process for 10 seconds.

3 Add the butter and process until partially incorporated, 30 seconds. Scrape the bowl with a rubber spatula.

4 Add the milk and process until the batter comes together, 20 seconds. It will be quite wet.

5 Fill the pastry bag with batter and pipe 1-inch-diameter cookies about ⅜ inch thick,

INGREDIENTS

Vegetable oil or butter for greasing the baking sheets (optional)

Cookies

1 cup all-purpose flour

Generous ¼ teaspoon salt

Pinch of baking powder

7 tablespoons confectioners' sugar

1½ tablespoons granulated sugar

1 tablespoon grated lemon zest

8 tablespoons (1 stick) plus 1 teaspoon unsalted butter, at room temperature

¼ cup whole milk

Filling

3½ ounces good-quality white chocolate, grated or finely chopped (do not use white chocolate chips)

1½ tablespoons vegetable oil

2 inches apart on the prepared baking sheets. Using the bottom of a glass that has been dipped in flour, press each cookie to a diameter of 1½ inches.

6   Bake the cookies until the edges are golden and the centers are firm, 14 minutes. Use a metal spatula to transfer the cookies to racks to cool completely.

7   Meanwhile, make the filling: Bring a pot of water to a boil, and remove it from the heat. Set a small metal bowl inside a larger bowl, and pour the hot water around the small bowl. The water should come about halfway up the sides of the smaller bowl. Make sure the inside of the smaller bowl stays dry. Place the white chocolate in the small bowl, cover the small bowl, and allow the chocolate to sit until it is melted. (You may need to change the water a couple of times to keep it hot.)

8   Stir the oil into the melted chocolate, whisking until the mixture is smooth. Let this set for 30 minutes. It will be fairly loose in texture.

9   When the cookies are completely cool, use the metal spatula to turn half of them upside down. Place a generous ½ teaspoon of the chocolate mixture on each upside-down cookie. Place the remaining cookies on top, pressing just enough for the filling to come to the edge of the sandwich.

10   Allow the cookies to set at room temperature for 2 to 3 hours (or refrigerate for 1 hour to speed up the process).

White Chocolate

You need to take special care when melting white chocolate. It must be heated very slowly or it will seize and separate. So, I don't actually do it over heat. I just chop the white chocolate very fine and let it sit in a dry bowl surrounded by hot water. It takes a little time, but it's worth it.

Triple-Ginger Lemon Sandwiches

* *

H*ere's a triple threat of ground, candied, and fresh ginger, combined to pack a genuine wallop. The lemon buttercream filling adds a wonderful accent. These small, stylish, and sophisticated refrigerator cookies may single-handedly change the perceived wisdom about the appropriateness of cookies as dinner-party fare.*

MAKES 70 COOKIE SANDWICHES

1 Make the cookies: Place the fresh ginger and 2 tablespoons of the granulated sugar in a food processor and process for several seconds to break up the ginger strands.

2 Sift the flour, baking soda, salt, ground ginger, cloves, and cinnamon into a small bowl and set aside.

3 Cream the butter, brown sugar, the remaining 6 tablespoons granulated sugar, and the fresh ginger mixture in a medium-size mixing bowl with an electric mixer on medium speed until light and fluffy, about 1 minute. Stop the mixer once to scrape the bowl with a rubber spatula.

4 Add the molasses to the butter mixture and beat for 10 to 15 seconds on medium speed. Scrape the bowl. Then add the egg and beat to incorporate it, 10 seconds.

5 Add the flour mixture and beat on medium-low speed for 10 seconds. Scrape the bowl, then mix until blended, about 5 seconds more. Scrape the bowl again.

6 Add the oats and candied ginger. Blend for several seconds on low speed.

7 Spread a 13-inch length of waxed paper or plastic wrap on a work surface. Shape one-fourth of the dough into a rough log 9 inches long × 1 inch in diameter along the length of one

INGREDIENTS

Cookies

⅓ cup grated fresh ginger

½ cup granulated sugar

1½ cups all-purpose flour

1½ teaspoons baking soda

½ teaspoon salt

1¼ teaspoons ground ginger

¼ teaspoon ground cloves

1 teaspoon ground cinnamon

13 tablespoons (1 stick plus 5 tablespoons) unsalted butter, at room temperature

½ cup (lightly packed) light brown sugar

¼ cup molasses

1 large egg, at room temperature

1½ cups quick-cooking oats

⅓ cup minced candied ginger or stem ginger

Vegetable oil or butter for greasing the baking sheets (optional)

Filling

2 cups confectioners' sugar

3 tablespoons light corn syrup

3 tablespoons unsalted butter, melted

1½ teaspoons grated lemon zest

2 tablespoons fresh lemon juice

side of the paper. Roll the log up in the waxed paper and twist the ends like a hard-candy wrapper. Make three more logs with the remaining dough, wrap them, and refrigerate for at least 2 hours.

8   Remove the logs from the refrigerator, and with the dough still in the paper, gently roll them back and forth on the work surface to smooth out the log. Return the logs to the refrigerator to chill for 2 to 3 more hours.

9   Fifteen minutes before baking, preheat the oven to 350°F. Line several baking sheets with parchment paper or lightly grease them with vegetable oil or butter.

10   Unwrap the logs and cut them into scant ¼-inch-thick slices. Place the cookies 1 inch apart on the prepared baking sheets. Bake until they are a deep golden color and set but still soft to the touch, 8 to 10 minutes.

11   Let the cookies cool on the baking sheets for 3 or 4 minutes. Then, using a metal spatula, carefully transfer the cookies to racks to cool completely.

12   Meanwhile, make the filling: Place the confectioners' sugar, corn syrup, melted butter, and lemon zest in a small saucepan over low heat, and stir constantly with a whisk until the mixture is of pouring consistency, 4 minutes. Add the lemon juice and stir to mix. Cool for 5 minutes.

13   Using the metal spatula, turn half the cookies upside down. Drop a scant teaspoon of the filling onto the center of each upside-down cookie. Then top them with the remaining cookies, pressing down just enough to bring the filling to the edge of the cookie. Allow the cookies to set at room temperature for about 3 hours (or refrigerate for 1 hour to speed up the process).

Peanut Butter Sandwiches

* *

T*ime may do its work on me, but I'll never outgrow the thrill of a peanut butter cookie—especially this sandwich version, with its thick, crunchy cookies and its layer of peanut butter filling to stick them together (and to the roof of your mouth). A Girl Scout Cookie memory? A triumph for the makers of Skippy? Whatever, these cookies make me sorry I no longer carry a lunch box.*

MAKES 25 COOKIE SANDWICHES

1   Preheat the oven to 350°F. Line several baking sheets with parchment paper or lightly grease them with vegetable oil or butter.

2   Make the cookies: Sift the flour, baking soda, baking powder, and salt together into a small bowl and set aside.

3   Cream the butter, peanut butter, both sugars, and the vanilla together in a medium-size mixing bowl with an electric mixer on medium speed until light and fluffy, about 1½ minutes. Stop the mixer twice to scrape the sides of the bowl with a rubber spatula.

4   Add the egg to the butter mixture and mix on medium-low speed to incorporate it, about 20 seconds.

5   Add the flour mixture and mix on medium-low speed for 10 seconds. Scrape the bowl, then mix until blended, about 5 seconds more. Scrape the bowl again.

6   Add the oats and mix for several seconds on low speed to blend them in.

7   Drop the dough by generously rounded teaspoons about 2 inches apart onto the prepared baking sheets. Using the tines of a fork to create a crosshatch pattern, press the cookies down until they are ¼ inch thick × 2 inches in diameter.

8   Bake the cookies until they are lightly golden with darker golden edges, 10 to 12 minutes. Let them cool completely on the baking sheets.

INGREDIENTS

Vegetable oil or butter for greasing the baking sheets (optional)

Cookies

¾ cup plus 1 tablespoon all-purpose flour

½ teaspoon baking soda

¼ teaspoon baking powder

½ teaspoon salt

8 tablespoons (1 stick) unsalted butter, at room temperature

½ cup creamy or crunchy peanut butter

½ cup granulated sugar

½ cup (lightly packed) light brown sugar

½ teaspoon pure vanilla extract

1 large egg, at room temperature

1 cup minus 2 tablespoons quick-cooking oats

Buttercream Filling

1 cup confectioners' sugar

3 tablespoons unsalted butter, at room temperature

½ cup creamy peanut butter

2 tablespoons plus 1 teaspoon heavy (whipping) cream

Glaze (optional)

2 ounces bittersweet chocolate

2 teaspoons vegetable oil

9   Meanwhile, make the buttercream filling: Cream the confectioners' sugar, butter, and peanut butter together in a medium-size mixing bowl with an electric mixer on low speed for 1 minute, stopping the mixer once to scrape the bowl.

10   Add the cream and mix until fluffy, 40 seconds, stopping the mixer once to scrape the bowl.

11   When the cookies are completely cool, use a metal spatula to turn half of them upside down. Spread each upside-down cookie with a rounded teaspoon of filling and top with the remaining cookies.

12   Make the glaze (if using): Melt the chocolate in the top of a double boiler placed over simmering water. Remove from the heat. Add the oil and stir until smooth.

13   Drizzle the glaze in a pattern over the top of the sandwiches, and allow them to set for 2 to 3 hours at room temperature (or refrigerate for 1 hour to speed up the process).

CHAPTER 13

Holiday Cookies

Of course I'm partial to holiday and special occasion baking. After all, were it not for those heart-shaped Valentine's Day sugar cookies so long ago, Rosie's might never have existed. Any holiday is an excuse for me to bake—although my personal baking doesn't usually begin until the night before the big day, after I'm freed from a week of hustle and bustle at the bakery.

For many people, holidays are the most fun time of the year for pulling out the baking sheets. It's an important part of the family ritual and joins us all together—moms, dads, sisters, brothers, cousins, aunts, uncles, grandparents—in joyous anticipation of the upcoming day.

There is no cookie that cannot be baked for any holiday (other than Passover, when flour is not permitted), but certain cookies have come to symbolize particular holidays. What is Christmas without gingerbread people, Valentine's Day without sugar cookies, Hanukkah without doughnuts? We favor the shapes and flavors that we remember from our childhoods, so it is always important to include those in our holiday fare.

Baking Reminder
To bake two sheets of cookies at a time, set the oven racks in the upper third and lower third of the oven before preheating it. Halfway through the baking time, rotate the baking sheets from one rack to the other and turn the sheets back to front. This way you'll ensure even baking.

Molasses Ginger Cookies

* *

*D*ivinely chewy in the center, crunchy around the edges, dark and gingery with a strong molasses flavor, these are a perfect cookie for the night before Christmas. Just be sure to leave some out for Santa.

MAKES 16 COOKIES

INGREDIENTS

Vegetable oil or butter for greasing the baking sheets (optional)

2 cups all-purpose flour

1 teaspoon baking soda

1 tablespoon ground ginger

2½ teaspoons ground cinnamon

¾ teaspoon ground nutmeg

¾ teaspoon ground cloves

½ teaspoon ground allspice

¾ teaspoon salt

12 tablespoons (1½ sticks) unsalted butter, at room temperature

1 cup granulated sugar

¼ cup (lightly packed) dark brown sugar

¼ cup dark molasses

1 large egg, at room temperature

1 Preheat the oven to 375°F. Line several baking sheets with parchment paper or lightly grease them with vegetable oil or butter.

2 Sift the flour, baking soda, all the spices, and salt together into a small bowl and set aside.

3 Cream the butter and both sugars together in a medium-size mixing bowl with an electric mixer on medium speed until light and fluffy, about 1 minute. Scrape the bowl with a rubber spatula.

4 Add the molasses to the butter mixture and mix on medium speed until blended, 10 seconds. Scrape the bowl. Then add the egg and mix until it is incorporated, 10 seconds.

5 Add the flour mixture and blend on low speed for 15 seconds. Stop the mixer to scrape the bowl, and then blend until the dough is smooth, about 5 seconds more.

6 Drop the dough by heaping tablespoons 2 inches apart onto the prepared baking sheets. Bake the cookies until they are still slightly soft, 15 to 16 minutes. Let them cool completely on the baking sheets.

Storage Reminder
For cookie storage tips, turn to page 127. If the cookies in a specific recipe need storage handling that isn't covered in the general tips, the directions will be in the recipe itself.

Jan Hagels

* *

*T*aste is one of the most evocative senses, and these cookies are among the most evocative I know. They conjure up visions of a wintry Christmas Eve—thin, buttery, and loaded with spices—perfect for snuggling in front of a fire with a mug of hot cider and a plate of these delicacies (and maybe a person to snuggle with, so long as he doesn't eat too many of your cookies).

MAKES 48 COOKIES

1 Sift the flour, cinnamon, cloves, and salt together into a small bowl and set aside.

2 Cream the butter and both sugars together in a medium-size mixing bowl with an electric mixer on medium speed until light and fluffy, about 1 minute. Scrape the bowl with a rubber spatula.

3 Add the flour mixture and mix on low speed for 20 seconds. Scrape the bowl. Then turn the mixer to medium speed and beat just until the dough is blended, about 15 seconds.

4 Turn the dough out onto a work surface and knead it with your hands for several seconds so that it comes together just a bit more. Divide the dough in half, form each half into a disk, and wrap them in plastic wrap. Refrigerate for 2 to 3 hours.

5 Fifteen minutes before baking, preheat the oven to 350°F. Line 2 baking sheets with parchment paper or lightly grease them with vegetable oil or butter.

6 Remove the dough from the refrigerator and roll each disk out between two fresh pieces of plastic wrap to form a rough rectangle approximately 15 × 10 inches and ⅛ inch thick (see page 330 for rolling technique). Remove the plastic wrap and transfer each rectangle to a baking sheet. Using a pastry brush, glaze the rectangles with the egg white, and sprinkle the almonds over the glaze.

7 Bake until golden with darkening edges, about 20 minutes. Remove the baking sheets from the oven, and reduce the oven temperature to 325°F. Cut each rectangle, still

INGREDIENTS

- 2¼ cups plus 3 tablespoons all-purpose flour
- 2¼ teaspoons ground cinnamon
- ¾ teaspoon ground cloves
- ¾ teaspoon salt
- 2 sticks (8 ounces) plus 2 tablespoons unsalted butter, at room temperature
- ½ cup plus 1 tablespoon (lightly packed) light brown sugar
- ½ cup plus 1 tablespoon granulated sugar
- Vegetable oil or butter for greasing the baking sheets (optional)
- 1 large egg white
- ½ cup slivered almonds, coarsely chopped

on the sheets, into 24 pieces (4 lengthwise slices, then 6 crosswise slices) and return them to the oven. Bake until a deeper golden color, about 15 minutes more. Let the cookies cool completely on the baking sheets.

* *

Gingerbread People

* *

I*t's hard to improve on this classic recipe, or on the classic shape of pudgy little people in their three-button uniforms. My kids love them; when they were younger, they were a part of our holiday ritual each winter. Sometimes we'd poke little holes in them before we baked them, so they could be displayed as ornaments on a Christmas tree. Despite their name, this dough can be used to cut out all kinds of shapes, depending on the time of year or simply the mood you're in! Of course, for this cookie, you'll need a 5-inch gingerbread people cookie cutter.*

MAKES FIFTEEN 5-INCH-TALL GINGERBREAD PEOPLE

1 Make the cookies: Using a whisk, vigorously stir the molasses, water, and egg together in a small bowl or cup and set aside.

2 Place the flour, baking soda, salt, brown sugar, orange zest, cinnamon, ginger, cloves, and nutmeg in a food processor and process for 10 seconds.

3 Distribute the butter over the flour mixture and process until the dough resembles coarse meal, about 30 seconds.

4 Pour the molasses mixture over the flour mixture and process just until the dough comes together, about 35 seconds.

5   Remove the dough from the processor, place it on a work surface, and knead it until it's well blended, 10 seconds.

6   Divide the dough into two disks, wrap each in plastic wrap, and refrigerate them for 1 to 2 hours.

7   When you're ready to bake the cookies, preheat the oven to 350°F. Line several baking sheets with parchment paper.

8   Remove one disk of dough from the refrigerator and place it between two fresh pieces of plastic wrap. Roll it out ⅛ inch thick (see page 330 for rolling technique).

9   Remove the top piece of plastic wrap and, using a 5-inch cookie cutter, cut out as many "people" as you can. Using a metal spatula, place the cookies on a prepared baking sheet, leaving about 1 inch between them. Repeat with the second disk. Then reroll the scraps and repeat with that dough.

10   Decorate the cookies: Place currants for the eyes and little cinnamon candies for buttons and the mouth, pressing them down slightly into the dough.

11   Bake the cookies until they are firm, 12 to 14 minutes. Let cool completely on the baking sheet or on racks.

12   While the cookies are cooling, make the icing: Place a writing tip in a pastry bag. Place the bag in a tall glass, tip-side down, and set it aside. Beat the confectioners' sugar and egg whites together in a medium-size mixing bowl using the paddle attachment of an electric mixer on low speed for 30 seconds. Increase the speed to medium-high and beat until smooth, about 3 minutes. The icing should be stiff enough to pipe. If it's not, add up to 2 tablespoons additional confectioners' sugar.

13   Fill the bag with the icing and pipe patterns, as desired, onto the completely cooled cookies. Allow the icing to set for several hours.

NOTE: *Although it's hard to imagine that there would be any gingerbread people left over with kids around, leave the cookies out for a day so the glaze is completely hardened, then store them at room temperature for 1 week in an airtight container with plastic wrap, parchment paper, or waxed paper between the layers. If they are not frosted, the gingerbread people can be stored at room temperature for up to 1 week or frozen for up to 2 weeks.*

INGREDIENTS

Cookies

2 tablespoons dark molasses

1 tablespoon water

1 large egg, at room temperature

3¼ cups all-purpose flour

1 teaspoon baking soda

½ teaspoon salt

1½ cups (lightly packed) light brown sugar

1½ tablespoons grated orange zest

2 teaspoons ground cinnamon

1 tablespoon ground ginger

½ teaspoon ground cloves

¼ teaspoon ground nutmeg

2 sticks (8 ounces) unsalted butter, cold, cut into 16 pieces

Decorations

Dried currants

Red-hot cinnamon candies

Icing

2¾ cups sifted confectioners' sugar, plus 2 tablespoons if needed

2 large egg whites, at room temperature

Orange Pecan Ginger Florentines

* *

INGREDIENTS

⅓ cup chopped candied orange peel (¼-inch pieces)

1 cup plus 1 tablespoon very finely chopped almonds

¼ cup whole almonds, sliced into thirds

⅓ cup chopped crystallized ginger

¼ cup all-purpose flour

3 tablespoons unsalted butter

6 tablespoons plus 2 teaspoons sugar

6 tablespoons plus 2 teaspoons heavy (whipping) cream

3 scant tablespoons honey

¼ cup light corn syrup

6 or 12 ounces bittersweet or semisweet chocolate (see Note)

Most kids loathe Florentines. For starters, they're full of nuts, and then, even if you can pick those out, they still have red and yellow things and bumpy little bits. Luckily, by the time we reach adulthood, most of us have gotten over these childish prejudices. That's a good thing in this case, because these lacelike caramel crunch cookies, full of almonds, candied ginger, and orange peel, are as divine as the city they're named after and a perfect festive treat at Christmas. Glaze them with chocolate, as the recipe suggests, or eat them unadorned. Either way, you'll be a convert.

MAKES 25 COOKIES

1 Preheat the oven to 350°F. Line several baking sheets with parchment paper.

2 Place the candied orange peel, chopped and sliced almonds, and crystallized ginger in a medium-size bowl. Sift the flour over the fruit-nut mixture and toss to coat. Set aside.

3 Combine the butter, sugar, cream, honey, and corn syrup in a medium-size heavy saucepan and place over low heat. Stirring constantly, bring the mixture to a boil and boil for 1 minute. Remove from the heat.

4 Add the fruit-nut mixture to the butter mixture and stir with a wooden spoon just to evenly coat.

5 Drop the batter by heaping teaspoons onto the prepared baking sheets, placing only 5 cookies on each sheet. Dip a fork in water and use it (re-dipping as needed) to flatten each cookie so it is 2 inches in diameter.

6 Bake the cookies until they are bubbling all over and golden in color, 11 to 13 minutes. Let the cookies cool slightly on the baking sheets, then transfer the paper with the cookies still on it to a rack to cool completely.

Carefully remove the cooled cookies from the paper by hand.

7 Meanwhile, melt the chocolate in the top of a double boiler placed over simmering water. Remove from the heat and let the chocolate cool to spreading consistency.

8 Using a frosting spatula, spread the bottom of each cookie with ¾ teaspoon of the melted chocolate, then make a fancy design by running the tines of a fork over the chocolate in a zigzag pattern.

9 Set the cookies aside, chocolate side up, on racks for the glaze to set, about 3 hours; or place them in the refrigerator or freezer to speed up the process, 1 hour.

NOTE: *If you prefer less chocolate on your cookies, use only 6 ounces and, using a spoon, drizzle the chocolate in a crisscross pattern on the bottom of the cookies.*

It's really best to eat these the day they're made in order to enjoy them at the peak of crispness. If this isn't possible, layer them in an airtight container with plastic wrap, parchment paper, or waxed paper between the layers. They will keep this way for 2 days at room temperature and for up to 1 week if frozen.

Almond Chocolate Praline Crisps

* *

T *his is a cookie that should be served to you in a fancy restaurant as an accent to a gourmet dinner—on New Year's Eve, perhaps—and yet these lacelike toffee wafers, studded with almonds and sandwiched with chocolate, are surprisingly easy to make. Just watch them carefully while they're baking, because they burn easily.*

MAKES 18 COOKIE SANDWICHES

INGREDIENTS

8 tablespoons (1 stick) unsalted butter

1¼ cups chopped almonds

½ cup sugar

2 tablespoons all-purpose flour

3 tablespoons milk

¼ teaspoon pure vanilla extract

4 ounces bittersweet chocolate, melted

1   Preheat the oven to 400°F. Line several baking sheets with parchment paper.

2   Melt the butter in a small saucepan over low heat. Add the almonds, sugar, flour, milk, and vanilla. Bring the mixture to a simmer and remove from the heat. Allow it to sit for 5 to 10 minutes.

3   Drop the batter by teaspoons onto the prepared baking sheets, spacing them about 4 inches apart. Bake until the cookies are deeply golden, 7 to 8 minutes (watch carefully—they burn easily).

4   Remove the cookies from the oven and let them cool on the baking sheets for 1 minute. Then use a metal spatula to transfer the cookies to racks to cool completely.

5   Meanwhile, melt the chocolate in the top of a double boiler placed over simmering water. Remove from the heat and let the chocolate cool to spreading consistency.

6   Use the metal spatula to turn half the cookies upside down. Spread ½ teaspoon chocolate over each upside-down cookie. Top them with the remaining cookies. Refrigerate until the chocolate is set, about 2 hours.

NOTE: *It's really best to eat these the day they're made in order to enjoy them at the peak of crispness. If this isn't possible, layer them in an airtight container with plastic wrap, parchment paper, or waxed paper between the layers. They will keep this way for 2 days at room temperature and for up to 1 week if frozen.*

Pecan Crescents

* *

C*rispy. Crunchy. Buttery. These cookies, made with lots of ground pecans, have all the bases covered. They are wonderful choices to pack in holiday tins. And, oh, did I mention that they melt in your mouth?*

MAKES 48 COOKIES

1 Preheat the oven to 325°F. Line several baking sheets with parchment paper or lightly grease them with vegetable oil or butter.

2 Make the cookies: Sift the flour, salt, and cinnamon together into a small bowl and set aside.

3 Cream the butter, sugar, and vanilla in a medium-size mixing bowl with an electric mixer on medium speed until light and fluffy, about 4 minutes. Scrape the bowl with a rubber spatula.

4 Add the flour mixture and the pecans and beat on medium-low speed for 20 seconds. Scrape the bowl. Then beat until the flour and nuts are completely incorporated, about 15 seconds.

5 Make the coating: In a small bowl, stir together the sugar and cinnamon.

6 Break off heaping teaspoons of the dough and form each of them into crescents. Dip the crescents in the coating and place them 2 inches apart on the prepared baking sheets. Bake until lightly golden and firm to the touch, 30 minutes. Let them cool completely on the baking sheets.

INGREDIENTS

Vegetable oil or butter for greasing the baking sheets (optional)

Cookies

2 cups all-purpose flour

½ teaspoon salt

½ teaspoon ground cinnamon

2 sticks (8 ounces) unsalted butter, at room temperature

⅓ cup plus 1 tablespoon sugar

1½ teaspoons pure vanilla extract

1½ cups finely ground pecans

Coating

½ cup sugar

1 teaspoon ground cinnamon

Vanilla Kipfels

* *

When I was a little girl, my mother knew a German dressmaker named Martha, who made the most unbelievable vanilla kipfels—nutty, buttery crescents rolled in vanilla sugar—and presented them to us every Christmas in a decorative tin. I hoped to get the recipe from her, but learned to my regret that she had passed away. So here is my homage to Martha—my attempt to re-create those childhood treats in honor of a fine dressmaker and a fine baker. These make a wonderful gift for the holidays and store beautifully in an airtight tin, the vanilla sugar flavor permeating the cookies more and more each day.

MAKES 36 COOKIES

INGREDIENTS

Vegetable oil or butter for greasing the baking sheets (optional)

6 tablespoons granulated sugar

2 vanilla beans, each about 9 inches long

1½ cups whole unblanched almonds

1¼ cups all-purpose flour

1 teaspoon salt

12 tablespoons (1½ sticks) unsalted butter, cold, cut into 12 pieces

2 large egg yolks, lightly beaten

1½ cups confectioners' sugar or vanilla sugar (see Note), sifted

1 Preheat the oven to 325°F. Line several baking sheets with parchment paper or lightly grease them with vegetable oil or butter.

2 Place the granulated sugar in a small bowl. Split the vanilla beans open lengthwise. Using the point of a knife, gently scrape the seeds into the bowl of sugar.

3 Place the almonds in a food processor and process until fine, 45 seconds; do not overprocess. Add the sugar mixture, flour, and salt, and process, 5 seconds.

4 Scatter the butter pieces over the flour mixture and process until the dough resembles coarse meal, 15 seconds.

5 With the processor running, pour the egg yolks through the feed tube. Stop the processor, then pulse 5 times. Scrape the bowl with a rubber spatula, and then process until the dough comes together, 5 to 10 seconds.

6 Pinch off tablespoons of the dough and form each of them into a crescent. Place the crescents 1½ inches apart on the prepared baking sheets. Bake until lightly golden and firm to the touch, 30 minutes.

7 Let the cookies cool for 5 to 10 minutes on the baking sheets. Then roll them in the confectioners' sugar and place them on racks to cool completely.

NOTE: *To make vanilla sugar, place a split whole vanilla bean in* *3 to 4 cups granulated sugar and let it sit for a minimum of 1 week.*

* *

Classic Spritzes

* *

S*pritzes are great holiday cookies because they can be squeezed into an endless number of festive shapes. You can also sandwich them with chocolate, or sandwich them with jam and then dip half the cookie in melted chocolate. As I worked on this recipe, I discovered that spritzes made with vegetable shortening hold their shape and thickness best, but that spritzes made with butter taste better, even if they spread and flatten out a little more. For the best results, be sure to cream the butter and sugar so the dough is soft enough to squeeze through the press (use whatever decorative tip you like). If you don't have a press, scoop the batter out by the teaspoonful and flatten them slightly before baking.*

MAKES 60 TO 70 COOKIES

INGREDIENTS

Vegetable oil or butter for greasing the baking sheets (optional)

1 large egg, at room temperature

1 large egg yolk

2¼ cups plus 2 tablespoons all-purpose flour

1¼ teaspoons baking powder

¼ teaspoon salt

2 sticks (8 ounces) unsalted butter, at room temperature

1 cup confectioners' sugar

¼ cup granulated sugar

2 teaspoons pure vanilla extract

1 teaspoon grated lemon zest

1   Preheat the oven to 350°F. Line several baking sheets with parchment paper or lightly grease them with vegetable oil or butter.

2   Stir the egg and the yolk together in a small cup and set aside.

3   Sift the flour, baking powder, and salt together in a small bowl and set aside.

4   Cream the butter, both sugars, the vanilla, and lemon zest together in a medium-size mixing bowl with an electric mixer on medium speed until fluffy, 1 to 1½ minutes. Scrape the bowl with a rubber spatula.

5   Add the flour mixture to the butter mixture and continue to mix on medium speed until thoroughly blended, 3 minutes,

stopping the mixer once to scrape the bowl.

6 With the mixer on medium-low speed, add the egg mixture and mix until blended, 30 seconds. Stop the mixer once to scrape the bowl.

7 Feed the dough into a cookie press and press the cookies out, 1 inch apart, onto the prepared baking sheets. Bake the cookies for 10 minutes. Then lower the oven temperature to 325°F and bake until they are firm and lightly golden around the bottom edge. The baking time will vary depending on the shape of the cookies, but the range will probably be 16 to 22 minutes. Let the cookies cool on the baking sheets.

* *

Classic Sugar Cookies

* *

L *et's hear it for the plain old sugar cookie. It has a special place in my heart and on my palate, partly because it tastes great, partly because it played a big part in Rosie's history, and partly because it's so versatile. Sugar cookies are what got me into the baking biz to begin with, and sugar cookies are what keep me creative. You can adorn them with colored sugars and frosting, send them as valentines with endearing messages written on top, throw a decorating party for the kids on your block, deliver them as gifts in satin-lined boxes, or use them as Christmas tree ornaments by forming small holes in them before baking. The sky's the limit!*

MAKES 15 LARGE OR 25 SMALL COOKIES

1 Make the cookies: Place the flour, both sugars, the baking soda, cream of tartar, and salt in a food processor and process for 5 seconds.

2 Distribute the butter over the flour mixture and process until the dough resembles coarse meal, about 30 seconds. Scrape the bowl with a rubber spatula once to make certain the butter is evenly distributed.

3 Stir the egg and vanilla together in a small cup. With the processor running, pour this mixture through the feed tube and process until the dough comes together, about 35 seconds.

4 Remove the dough from the processor, place it on a work surface, and knead it until it's well blended, 10 seconds. Divide the dough into two disks, wrap each in plastic wrap, and refrigerate them for 1 to 2 hours.

5 When you're ready to bake the cookies, preheat the oven to 375°F. Line several baking sheets with parchment paper or grease them lightly with vegetable oil or butter.

6 Remove one disk of dough from the refrigerator and place it between two fresh pieces of plastic wrap. Roll it out ⅛ inch thick (see page 330 for rolling technique).

7 Remove the top piece of plastic wrap and, using the cookie cutter of your choice, cut out as many cookies as you can. Using a metal spatula, place the cookies 1 inch apart on the prepared baking sheets. Gather up the scraps and refrigerate them while you repeat the process with the second disk. Then gather up the scraps from both batches and reroll and cut out more cookies.

8 Bake the cookies until they are firm with lightly golden edges, 15 to 20 minutes, depending on their size. Let them cool on the baking sheets.

9 Meanwhile, make the glaze: Place the confectioners' sugar and the cream in a medium-size bowl and whisk vigorously until smooth and creamy. If you are using food coloring, divide the glaze into separate bowls, one for each color. Whisk in 1 drop of food coloring at a time into each bowl to get the desired color.

10 With the cookies still on the baking sheets, use a spoon to drizzle the glaze, or a small butter knife, or a new, clean paintbrush to spread it on the cookies. Then sprinkle colored sugar, sugar confetti, or candies on the glaze. Place the baking sheets in the refrigerator to speed up the setting of the glaze, or let the cookies set on the baking sheets for 4 to 6 hours at room temperature.

INGREDIENTS

Cookies

2¼ cups all-purpose flour

½ cup granulated sugar

½ cup confectioners' sugar

⅛ teaspoon baking soda

⅛ teaspoon cream of tartar

½ teaspoon salt

12½ tablespoons (1½ sticks plus ½ tablespoon) unsalted butter, cold, cut into 12 pieces

1 large egg, at room temperature

1 tablespoon pure vanilla extract

Vegetable oil or butter for greasing the baking sheets (optional)

Glaze

1 cup minus 2 tablespoons confectioners' sugar

¼ cup heavy (whipping) cream

Food coloring (optional)

Decorations

Colored sugars

Sugar confetti

Tiny candies

NOTE: *Unfrosted sugar cookies should be stored in an airtight container at room temperature for up to 3 days or in the freezer for up to 3 weeks. When glazed or frosted, it's best to store them in the container, with plastic wrap, parchment paper, or waxed paper between the layers.*

* *

Rosie's Award-Winning
Ultra-Rich Rugalah

* *

I first tasted rugalah at Ebinger's Bakery in Queens when I was 10 years old and became an instant convert, so much so that the memory lingered for years after Ebinger's closed. Much later, I came up with my own recipe for this Russian tea pastry. I use the same rich cream-cheese dough filled with preserves and nuts that I remember from my Ebinger's days, and I've yet to meet anyone who doesn't end up feeling the same way I do about it. At Hanukkah time, these pastries look lovely piled high in a basket lined with a crocheted doily. The dough is very moist and difficult to work with, so put on your patience cap and work very slowly and methodically.

MAKES 30 RUGALAH

1 Make the dough: Sift the flour and salt into a small bowl and set aside.

2 Cream the butter and cream cheese together in a medium-size mixing bowl with an electric mixer on medium speed until

light and fluffy, 1½ to 2 minutes. Stop the mixer once or twice to scrape the bowl with a rubber spatula.

3 Add the flour mixture and mix until blended, about 20 seconds, stopping the mixer once to scrape the bowl.

4 Shape the dough into two thick rectangles of equal size, wrap each in plastic wrap, and freeze them for 2 hours.

5 Remove one dough rectangle from the freezer and roll it out between two pieces of plastic wrap into a rectangle about 19 × 8 inches (see page 330 for rolling technique). It may be necessary to refrigerate the dough for 30 minutes during the rolling process because it will become a bit sticky. Once rolled, refrigerate the dough for 30 minutes. While it is resting, remove the second rectangle from the freezer and roll it out the same way you did the first. Place it in the refrigerator for 30 minutes.

6 Spread the filling: Unwrap the first rectangle and place it horizontally on plastic wrap on your work surface. Spread 6 tablespoons of the preserves evenly over the rectangle, leaving a ½-inch strip uncovered along the long side opposite you.

7 Mix the sugar and cinnamon together in a small bowl. Sprinkle half the cinnamon sugar, 2 tablespoons of the nuts, and ¼ cup of the raisins over the preserves.

8 Using a small, sharp knife or a frosting spatula, loosen the side of the dough nearer to you (with jam spread all the way to the edge) and roll it toward the uncovered edge like a jelly roll, peeling off the plastic wrap as you roll. The seam should end up on the underside. Wrap the roll in plastic and refrigerate it. Repeat the process with the other dough rectangle and fillings. Keep the filled rolls refrigerated for 2 hours.

9 Fifteen minutes before baking, preheat the oven to 375°F. Line 2 baking sheets with parchment paper or lightly grease them with vegetable oil or butter.

10 Glaze the rolls: Lightly beat the egg with a fork. Use a pastry brush to apply the glaze to the outside of the rolls. Using a thin, sharp knife, carefully cut the rolls into pieces about 1¼ inches wide and place them about 1 inch apart on the prepared baking sheets.

11 Bake the rugalah until they are golden, about 25 minutes. (Some of the jam will ooze out and start to darken.) Use a frosting spatula to transfer the rugalah immediately to a rack to cool completely.

INGREDIENTS

Dough

1 cup all-purpose flour

½ teaspoon salt

8 tablespoons (1 stick) unsalted butter, at room temperature

9 ounces cream cheese, at room temperature

Vegetable oil or butter for greasing the baking sheets (optional)

Filling

¾ cup apricot preserves

2 tablespoons sugar

1 teaspoon ground cinnamon

¼ cup chopped pecans or walnuts

½ cup golden raisins

Glaze

1 large egg, at room temperature

Sour Cream Rugalah

* *

This recipe is slightly different from the Rosie's Award-Winning Ultra-Rich Rugalah: You form the dough into little crescents rather than long rolls, and you use sour cream to create a light and flaky dough. We like to make them for Hanukkah and Christmas. As my daughter, Maya, would say, "Awesome!"

MAKES 48 RUGALAH

INGREDIENTS

Dough

1 large egg yolk

¾ cup sour cream

2 cups all-purpose flour

½ teaspoon salt

2 sticks (8 ounces) unsalted butter, cold, cut into 12 pieces

Vegetable oil or butter for greasing the baking sheets (optional)

Filling

4½ tablespoons sugar

1½ teaspoons ground cinnamon

1 cup raspberry or apricot preserves

Scant 1 cup golden or dark raisins

Scant 1 cup chopped walnuts or pecans

1   Make the dough: Stir the egg yolk and sour cream together in a small bowl and set aside.

2   Place the flour and salt in a food processor and process for 5 seconds.

3   Distribute the butter over the flour mixture and process until the mixture resembles coarse cornmeal, 15 seconds.

4   With the machine running, pour the sour cream mixture through the feed tube. Stop the processor, then pulse 12 times. Scrape the bowl with a rubber spatula, then pulse another 20 times.

5   Place the dough on a work surface and knead it several times.

6   Divide the dough into four disks, wrap each one in plastic wrap, and refrigerate for 6 to 8 hours or overnight.

7   Remove one disk from the refrigerator and roll it between two fresh pieces of plastic wrap to form a round 9 inches in diameter and approximately ⅛ inch thick (see page 330 for rolling technique). Remove the top piece of plastic and trim the edges of the dough to make a perfect circle. Sandwich the dough in plastic wrap, place it on a plate, and refrigerate it for 1 hour. Repeat with the remaining disks.

8   Line several baking sheets with parchment paper or lightly grease them with vegetable oil or butter.

9   Spread the filling: Mix the sugar and cinnamon together in a small bowl. Remove one round of dough from the refrigerator

and peel off the top piece of plastic wrap. Spread ¼ cup of the preserves over the dough. Then sprinkle it with about 4 teaspoons of the cinnamon sugar, 3 tablespoons of the raisins, and 3 tablespoons of the nuts.

10   Using the point of a sharp, thin knife, cut the disk into 12 wedges. Carefully lift the wide end of each wedge, roll up the triangle toward the tip, and, with the point on the underside, curve in the sides to form a crescent shape. Place the rugalah 1½ inches apart on the prepared baking sheets. Refrigerate for 30 minutes before baking. Repeat with the remaining dough and filling.

11   Fifteen minutes before baking, preheat the oven to 375°F. Bake the rugalah until they are crisp and golden, 18 to 20 minutes. Let the rugalah cool on the baking sheets for several minutes. Then, using a metal spatula, carefully transfer each rugalah to a rack (do this before any jam that has seeped out starts to harden on the baking sheets). Let the rugalah cool completely before eating.

* *

Buttermilk Doughnut Holes

* *

I *bow to no one in my love of old-fashioned doughnutty doughnuts that are crunchy on the outside and soft on the inside—like these doughnut holes. My family devours them in bulk at Hanukkah, when tradition calls for fried food to commemorate the oil that miraculously kept the Temple's sacred light burning for eight days and nights. Even divine intervention wouldn't keep these doughnut holes around my house that long.*

MAKES 20 DOUGHNUT HOLES

INGREDIENTS

1½ quarts vegetable oil

Coatings

1 cup sifted confectioners' sugar
or 1 cup granulated sugar or
both

2 tablespoons ground cinnamon,
if using granulated sugar

Batter

1 cup all-purpose flour

⅔ cup cake flour

1 teaspoon baking powder

½ teaspoon baking soda

½ teaspoon salt

½ teaspoon ground nutmeg

1 large egg, at room temperature

½ cup granulated sugar

1 tablespoon unsalted butter,
melted

½ teaspoon pure vanilla extract

½ cup buttermilk, at room
temperature

1   Attach a candy thermometer to the side of a deep 4- or 5-quart saucepan placed over medium heat. Pour in the oil (it should be 3 to 4 inches deep) and heat until the oil reaches 375°F to 380°F.

2   Prepare one or both coatings: Place the confectioners' sugar in a plastic bag. Place the granulated sugar and cinnamon in another plastic bag and shake (with the bag tightly closed) to mix thoroughly. Set the bags aside.

3   Make the batter: Sift both flours, the baking powder, baking soda, salt, and nutmeg together into a small bowl and set aside.

4   Using a whisk, blend the egg and granulated sugar together in a medium-size bowl. Stir in the melted butter, vanilla, and buttermilk.

5   Resift the flour mixture into the egg mixture and, using a rubber spatula, fold gently until mixed.

6   Using a 1½-inch-diameter ice cream scoop, drop 5 level scoops of the batter, one at a time, into the oil and cook until they are crunchy and deeply golden, 4 to 5 minutes.

7   Using a slotted spoon, remove a doughnut hole from the oil and cut it in half. If the center seems gooey, the doughnut holes need to cook for another minute or two. Remove the doughnuts with the slotted spoon and place them on paper towels to drain. Continue frying the remaining batter in this fashion.

8   To coat the doughnut holes in the cinnamon-sugar mixture: About 1 minute after removing them from the oil, place one doughnut at a time in the bag and toss to coat. Return it to the paper towel to cool.

9   To coat with the confectioners' sugar: Allow the doughnut holes to cool completely. Then place them one by one in the bag and toss to coat.

NOTE: *These doughnut holes should be eaten as soon as possible.*

VARIATION
Cider Doughnut Holes
Substitute ½ cup cider for the buttermilk and add 1 tablespoon ground cinnamon, ¾ teaspoon ground cardamom, and ¾ cup finely chopped peeled apples to the batter.

The Marks's
Matzoh Crunch

* *

A lthough the original recipe appeared in The Boston Globe, *I discovered it in the pages of the self-published* Father-and-Son Cookbook, *a delightful book by the talented father-and-son team of my good friends Roger and Gabriel Marks. The crunch created a sensation at Rosie's and became a staple for Passover, even for those who don't celebrate the holiday. Over the years I have tweaked the recipe so I now consider this my personal version.*

MAKES 6 MATZOH CRUNCH BOARDS

1 Preheat the oven to 350°F. Lightly grease a rimmed baking sheet with butter.

2 Line the baking sheet with the matzoh, breaking the pieces where necessary to fill in all the spaces.

3 Combine the butter and brown sugar in a medium-size saucepan. Stir constantly over medium heat with a wooden spoon until the mixture boils, 5 minutes. Then continue to cook, stirring constantly, for 3 minutes more.

4 Remove the butter mixture from the heat and pour it evenly over the matzoh.

5 Bake until the matzoh is deeply golden in color, 10 to 12 minutes. (After the first 8 minutes, check every 2 minutes to make sure it doesn't burn.)

6 Remove the pan from the oven and sprinkle the chocolate over the matzoh. Allow the chocolate to melt, then use a frosting spatula to spread it over the matzoh. Place the pan in the refrigerator for the chocolate to set, 1 to 2 hours.

7 When the matzoh is completely chilled, break it into pieces.

NOTE: *Whatever does not get eaten can be stored in an airtight container in the freezer. It's actually delicious frozen and my friend Shelley Marcus claims that she keeps hers for months and snacks on a small piece every night.*

INGREDIENTS

Butter for greasing the baking sheet

6 boards plain matzoh

2½ sticks (10 ounces) unsalted butter

1¼ cups (firmly packed) light brown sugar

6 ounces (1 cup) semisweet chocolate chips or chopped semisweet chocolate

The Bar Crowd

3

CHAPTER 14
Brownies

There have been moments in the history of Rosie's when I thought we ought to change our name to "Brownies R Us." Our various brownies are major sellers and recipients of numerous awards, and our Chocolate Orgasms—the fudgy, frosted favorite of family planners and abstention advocates alike—have brought us our share of notoriety. That's not why I created them, though. To me, brownies constitute one of the basic food groups, and these were simply the most luscious to be had.

Line up any ten people and ask them about their ideal brownie and I'm willing to bet that you'll get ten, maybe twelve, different opinions: Cakey, fudgy, dense, packed with nuts, cinnamony, unadulterated . . . So many people think of themselves as connoisseurs that I've considered setting up brownie tastings. I see them as similar to wine tastings, complete with their own esoteric vocabulary and ratings by year—though I'd vote *against* limiting samples to a single bite.

Storing Brownies

Some brownies in this chapter are fine left in the pan and stored, covered with plastic wrap, at room temperature for up to 2 days. After that, it's best to layer the cut pieces in an airtight container with plastic wrap, parchment paper, or waxed paper between the layers and store for another 2 days in the refrigerator or in the freezer for up to 2 weeks. They are delicious cold (defrost if frozen) or at room temperature.

Some brownies in this chapter have creamy toppings. They are best stored in the refrigerator soon after baking. Because you may not be sure what's best for the individual brownies, I've given storing instructions with each recipe.

Rosie's Award-Winning Brownies

* *

G rowing up, there was nothing I craved more than a good brownie. It took me years to come up with my own version—fudgy, but not too sweet. Countless all-nighters slaving over a hot mixing bowl and all those inches on my thighs proved to be worth it, though.

MAKES 9 TO 12 BROWNIES

1 Place a rack in the center of the oven and preheat to 350°F. Lightly grease an 8-inch square pan with vegetable oil or butter, or line the bottom with parchment paper.

2 Melt the chocolate and butter in the top of a double boiler placed over simmering water. Let the mixture cool for 5 minutes.

3 Place the sugar in a medium-size mixing bowl and pour in the chocolate mixture. Using an electric mixer on medium speed, mix until blended, about 25 seconds. Scrape the bowl with a rubber spatula.

4 Add the vanilla. With the mixer on medium-low speed, add the eggs one at a time, blending after each addition until the yolk is broken and dispersed, about 10 seconds. Scrape the bowl after the last egg is added and blend until velvety, about 15 more seconds. Then scrape the bowl again.

5 Add the flour on low speed and mix for 20 seconds, stopping once to scrape the bowl. Finish the mixing by hand, being certain to mix in any flour at the bottom of the bowl. Stir in the nuts, if using.

6 Spread the batter evenly in the prepared pan. Bake just until the center rises to the level of the sides and a tester inserted in the center comes out with moist crumbs, 30 to 35 minutes.

7 Let the brownies cool in the pan on a rack for 1 hour before cutting and serving them. And don't forget the tall glass of milk.

INGREDIENTS

Vegetable oil or butter for greasing the pan (optional)

6 ounces unsweetened chocolate

2 sticks (8 ounces) unsalted butter, at room temperature

2 cups sugar

1 teaspoon pure vanilla extract

4 large eggs, at room temperature

½ cup all-purpose flour

½ cup chopped walnuts (optional)

NOTE: *Leave the brownies in the pan, at room temperature, covered, for up to 2 days. After that, layer them in an airtight container with plastic wrap, parchment paper, or waxed paper between the layers, and store for another 2 days in the refrigerator or in the freezer for up to 2 weeks. They are delicious cold or at room temperature.*

Cutting Brownies

The yield line in this chapter is pretty arbitrary, because a pan of brownies can be cut any number of ways into any number of servings. So, I based my suggestions on how big a piece I feel it takes to enjoy a particular brownie to its fullest. My philosophy: The richer the brownie, the smaller the piece. Of course around your house it could be: The richer the brownie the bigger the piece. I get it. Feel free to cut each pan into as many or as few pieces as suits your mood.

Chocolate Orgasms

* *

O*kay, Daddy, now you can admit you were wrong—this is a great name. After all, it has become Rosie's most famous dessert. Although people of all ages come to my stores and eat big versions of this bar, when I make them at home, I like to cut them into small squares, top each one with a whole walnut or raspberry, and arrange them on a paper lace doily. They are also wonderful served in a small bowl with vanilla, chocolate chip, coffee, or mint ice cream.*

MAKES 36 SMALL BROWNIES

1   Bake the brownies as directed in the recipe and allow them to cool completely in the pan on a rack. Don't cut them yet.

2   To prepare the frosting, melt the chocolate in the top of a double boiler placed over simmering water.

3   Pour the evaporated milk into an electric blender and add the sugar and the melted chocolate. Blend the frosting on medium-low speed until it thickens, about 50 seconds (the sound of the machine will change when this process occurs).

4   Using a frosting spatula, spread the frosting evenly over the surface of the cooled brownies and allow them to sit for 1 hour before cutting them.

NOTE: *When cut, refrigerate the brownies in the pan, covered with plastic wrap, for up to 2 days. After that, layer them in an airtight container with plastic wrap, parchment paper, or waxed paper between the layers, and store for another 2 days in the refrigerator or in the freezer for up to 2 weeks. They are delicious either cold or at room temperature.*

INGREDIENTS

Rosie's Award-Winning Brownies (nuts are optional; page 259)

3½ ounces unsweetened chocolate

½ cup plus 1 tablespoon evaporated milk

¾ cup sugar

Boom Booms

* *

I won't tell you what these were named after—those of us who were around for Rosie's beginnings will guard that secret— but I will tell you that they are a wonderful combination of a dark fudge brownie marbled with a sweet cream cheese mixture. They are beautiful to look at as well.

MAKES 9 TO 12 BROWNIES

INGREDIENTS

Vegetable oil or butter for greasing the pan (optional)

8 ounces cream cheese, cold

1½ teaspoons all-purpose flour

5 tablespoons sugar

1 large egg, at room temperature

¼ teaspoon pure vanilla extract

Rosie's Award-Winning Brownie batter, without nuts (page 259)

1   Place a rack in the center of the oven and preheat to 325°F. Lightly grease an 8-inch square pan with vegetable oil or butter, or line the bottom with parchment paper.

2   Place the cream cheese, flour, sugar, egg, and vanilla in a food processor and process until blended, about 45 seconds. Set aside.

3   Spread about two-thirds of the brownie batter in the prepared pan. Spread the cream cheese filling over the brownie batter. Using a spoon, scoop the remaining brownie batter over the filling in 9 equal mounds arranged in 3 rows so that there is some space between them.

4   Run a chopstick or the handle of a wooden spoon back and forth, alternating directions, for the length of the pan, making parallel lines about 1½ inches apart. Then do the same thing in the other direction as if making a grid. This will marbleize the two mixtures. Shake the pan gently back and forth to level the batter.

5   Bake until a tester inserted in the center comes out clean or with some moist crumbs, about 45 minutes. Let the brownies cool in the pan on a rack for 1 hour before cutting them.

NOTE: *When cut, refrigerate the brownies in the pan, covered with plastic wrap, for up to 2 days. After that, layer them in an airtight container with plastic wrap, parchment paper, or waxed paper between the layers, and store for another 2 days in the refrigerator or in the freezer for up to 2 weeks. They are delicious either cold or at room temperature.*

Peanut Butter Topped Brownies

* *

In homage to the Reese's Peanut Butter Cup, I've combined a layer of peanut butter buttercream with a layer of brownie and then topped all of that with a bittersweet chocolate glaze. Rich enough, do you think? I recommend very small bites.

MAKES 16 BROWNIES

1 Bake the brownies as directed in the recipe and let them cool completely in the pan on a rack (or place the pan in the refrigerator or freezer to speed up the process). Do not cut them.

2 Make the buttercream: Place the peanut butter, confectioners' sugar, butter, and vanilla in a food processor and process until smooth, 60 seconds, stopping the processor once to scrape the bowl with a rubber spatula. (Or place the ingredients in a small mixing bowl and beat with an electric mixer on medium-high speed until smooth.)

3 Using a frosting spatula, spread the buttercream evenly over the cooled brownies and freeze for 1 hour.

4 When the hour is almost up, make the glaze: Melt the chocolate in the top of a double boiler placed over simmering water. Remove the top pan from the bottom one and stir in the corn syrup.

5 Let the glaze cool to the point where it is no longer hot but is still loose and spreadable, 8 to 10 minutes. Using the frosting spatula, spread the glaze over the buttercream. Sprinkle the peanuts (if using) over the glaze. Refrigerate the pan and allow the glaze to harden, about 30 minutes.

6 Cut the brownies into squares with a sharp, thin knife, dipping it in hot water and drying it before each cut.

NOTE: *When cut, refrigerate the brownies in the pan, covered with plastic wrap, for up to 2 days. After that, layer them in an airtight container with plastic wrap, parchment paper, or waxed paper between the layers, and store for another 2 days in the refrigerator or in the freezer for up to 2 weeks. They are delicious either cold or at room temperature.*

INGREDIENTS

Brownies and Buttercream

Rosie's Award-Winning Brownies (page 259)

½ cup plus 2 tablespoons peanut butter, smooth or crunchy

1 cup confectioners' sugar

2½ tablespoons unsalted butter, at room temperature

½ teaspoon pure vanilla extract

Glaze and Topping

5 ounces bittersweet chocolate

2 teaspoons light corn syrup

½ cup chopped unsalted peanuts (optional)

INGREDIENTS

Brownies and Mint Buttercream

Rosie's Award-Winning Brownies, without nuts (page 259)

1½ cups confectioners' sugar

6 tablespoons (¾ stick) unsalted butter, at room temperature

2 teaspoons pure peppermint extract

Glaze

4 ounces bittersweet chocolate

Mint Brownies

* *

The flavor of mint and chocolate combine beautifully in this bar without losing their integrity.

MAKES 16 BROWNIES

1   Bake the brownies as directed in the recipe and let them cool completely in the pan on a rack (or place the pan in the refrigerator or freezer to speed up the process). Do not cut them.

2   Make the buttercream: Cream the confectioners' sugar, butter, and peppermint extract in a medium-size mixing bowl with an electric mixer on high speed until light and fluffy, 2 to 2½ minutes.

3   Spread the buttercream evenly over the cooled brownies and freeze for 1 hour.

4   When the hour is almost up, make the glaze: Melt the chocolate in the top of a double boiler placed over simmering water. Remove the top pan from the bottom one and let the glaze cool.

5   Using a frosting spatula, spread the glaze over the buttercream. Immediately place the pan in the refrigerator and allow the chocolate to harden for about 30 minutes.

6   Cut the brownies into squares with a sharp, thin knife that has been dipped in hot water and dried before each cut.

NOTE: *When cut, refrigerate the brownies in the pan, covered with plastic wrap, for up to 2 days. After that, layer them in an airtight container with plastic wrap, parchment paper, or waxed paper between the layers, and store for another 2 days in the refrigerator or in the freezer for up to 2 weeks. They are delicious either cold or at room temperature.*

Pan Size Alert

Many of the recipes in this chapter call for a 9-inch square baking pan. If you don't have one (they're available online if you're looking to buy), no problem—just bake the brownies in an 8-inch pan, reducing the heat in most cases by 25 degrees and adding 10 to 15 minutes to the cooking time.

Chocolate Raspberry Brownies

* *

The divine combination of chocolate and raspberries is layered in this unforgettable taste experience. For a sophisticated dessert, serve small pieces garnished with whipped cream and fresh raspberries.

MAKES 16 BROWNIES

1 Place a rack in the center of the oven and preheat to 350°F. Lightly grease a 9-inch square baking pan with vegetable oil or butter, or line the bottom with parchment paper.

2 Using a spoon or fork, mash the raspberries and the preserves together in a small bowl until the mixture has a pourable consistency. Set it aside.

3 Scoop half the batter into the prepared pan. Shake the pan gently to distribute the batter evenly. Pour or spoon the raspberry mixture over the batter and spread it out very gently, leaving ¾ inch uncovered around the edges.

4 Spoon or pour the remaining batter in long ribbonlike strips over the filling and spread it gently with a frosting spatula.

(Your goal is for the three layers to remain separate.) Shake the pan gently back and forth to level the batter.

5 Bake until the center rises to the level of the sides and a tester inserted in the center comes out clean or with some moist crumbs, about 45 minutes.

6 Let the brownies cool in the pan on a rack for 1 hour. Cut into squares with a sharp, thin knife.

NOTE: *Leave the brownies in the pan, at room temperature, covered with plastic wrap, for up to 2 days. After that, layer them in an airtight container with plastic wrap, parchment paper, or waxed paper between the layers, and store for another 2 days in the refrigerator or in the freezer for up to 2 weeks. They are delicious either cold or at room temperature.*

INGREDIENTS

Vegetable oil or butter for greasing the pan (optional)

1 cup fresh raspberries or thawed, drained frozen unsweetened raspberries

¼ cup raspberry preserves

Rosie's Award-Winning Brownies batter (page 259), sugar reduced by 1 tablespoon

New York Cheesecake Brownies

* *

W*hat better combo for a gal from New York City who grew up on cheesecake and brownies? A layer of cheesecake and a layer of bittersweet brownie, one creamy, one fudgy, and both utterly divine. Eat at room temperature like a brownie, or chilled just like cheesecake.*

MAKES 16 BROWNIES

INGREDIENTS

Vegetable oil or butter for greasing the pan (optional)

Brownies

3½ ounces unsweetened chocolate

10 tablespoons (1¼ sticks) unsalted butter

1 cup sugar

3 large eggs, at room temperature

½ cup all-purpose flour

Cheesecake Topping

16 ounces cream cheese, cold

½ cup sugar

1 large egg, at room temperature

1 large egg yolk

1½ teaspoons fresh lemon juice

1   Place a rack in the center of the oven and preheat to 300°F. Lightly grease a 9-inch square baking pan with vegetable oil or butter, or line the bottom with parchment paper.

2   Make the brownies: Melt the chocolate and butter together in the top of a double boiler placed over simmering water. Let the mixture cool for 5 minutes.

3   Beat the sugar and eggs together in a medium-size mixing bowl with an electric mixer on medium-high speed until pale yellow, about 2 minutes. Scrape the bowl with a rubber spatula.

4   Add the flour to the sugar mixture on low speed and mix for 5 seconds. Scrape the bowl.

5   Add the cooled chocolate mixture on low speed and blend until mixed, 15 seconds, stopping the mixer once to scrape the bowl.

6   Spread the batter evenly in the prepared pan and place the pan in the freezer for 10 minutes.

7   Meanwhile, make the cheesecake topping: Place the cream cheese, sugar, egg, egg yolk, and lemon juice in a food processor and process until smooth, 1 minute. Stop the machine once to scrape the bowl.

8   Remove the pan from the freezer. Carefully spoon the cheesecake mixture over the brownie layer and,

using the rubber spatula, spread it gently over the brownie so as not to mix the two together.

9   Bake until the top is set and the center is just about level with the sides, 1 hour and 5 to 10 minutes. Let the brownies cool in the pan on a rack for 30 minutes. Using a sharp, thin knife, cut into squares, dipping the knife in hot water and wiping it off after each cut.

NOTE: *When cut, refrigerate the brownies in the pan, covered with plastic wrap, for up to 2 days. After that, layer them in an airtight container with plastic wrap, parchment paper, or waxed paper between the layers, and store for another 2 days in the refrigerator or in the freezer for up to 2 weeks. They are delicious either cold or at room temperature.*

* *

Sour Cherry Cheesecake Brownies

* *

T*he tartness of the sour cherries cuts the sweetness of the chocolate and the cheesecake, sending a rush of contrasting flavors to your tongue. It's unusual to combine all three elements in one brownie, but I figured, why not? I tried it out and found the results to be sensational.*

MAKES 16 BROWNIES

INGREDIENTS

Filling

8 ounces cream cheese,
   at room temperature

¼ cup sugar

1 tablespoon sour cream

2 large egg yolks

Vegetable oil or butter for
   greasing the pan (optional)

Brownies

3½ ounces unsweetened
   chocolate

12 tablespoons (1½ sticks)
   unsalted butter

1½ cups sugar

2 large eggs, at room
   temperature

¾ cup all-purpose flour

¾ cup drained canned pitted sour
   cherries

1   Make the filling: Beat the cream cheese, sugar, and sour cream together in a medium-size mixing bowl with an electric mixer on medium-high speed until blended, 30 seconds. Scrape the bowl with a rubber spatula.

2   Add the egg yolks and mix on medium-low speed until blended, 20 seconds. Set aside.

3   Place a rack in the center of the oven and preheat to 325°F. Lightly grease a 9-inch square baking pan with vegetable oil or butter, or line the bottom with parchment paper.

4   Make the brownies: Melt the chocolate and butter together in the top of a double boiler placed over simmering water. Let the mixture cool for 5 minutes.

5   Place the sugar in a medium-size bowl and pour in the chocolate mixture. Using an electric mixer on medium speed, mix until blended, about 25 seconds. Scrape the bowl with a rubber spatula.

6   With the mixer on medium-low speed, add the eggs one at a time, blending after each addition until the yolk is broken and dispersed, about 10 seconds. Scrape the bowl, then beat until the mixture is velvety, about 15 seconds.

7   Add the flour on low speed and mix for 20 seconds. Finish the mixing with the spatula, being certain to incorporate any flour at the bottom of the bowl.

8   Pour half of the batter into the prepared pan and spread it evenly. Using the spatula, scoop the cream cheese mixture onto the brownie batter and gently spread it evenly over the surface. Distribute the cherries over the filling, and use your fingers to press them down gently into the cream cheese.

9   Drop the rest of the brownie batter over the filling by large spoonfuls. Then, using a frosting spatula, spread it gently over the surface (the cream cheese will show through).

10   Bake until a tester inserted in the center comes out clean or with a few moist crumbs, about 50 minutes. Let the brownies cool in the pan on a rack for 30 minutes. Then cut them into squares with a sharp, thin knife.

NOTE: *When cut, refrigerate the brownies in the pan, covered with plastic wrap, for up to 2 days. After that, layer them in an airtight container, with plastic wrap, parchment paper, or waxed paper between the layers, and store for another 2 days in the refrigerator or in the freezer for up to 2 weeks. They are delicious either cold or at room temperature.*

Chocolate Soufflé Brownies

* *

This fudgy brownie with a thick layer of baked mousse is one of the richest, most luxurious chocolate desserts known to humankind, if I do say so myself. Cut them small or you'll be flying for hours after you eat one. They're delicious cold, at room temperature, or warmed up, topped with vanilla ice cream or whipped cream.

MAKES 36 BROWNIES

1 Place a rack in the center of the oven and preheat to 325°F. Lightly grease a 9-inch square baking pan with vegetable oil or butter, or line the bottom with parchment paper.

2 Make the brownies: Melt the chocolate and butter together in the top of a double boiler placed over simmering water. Let the mixture cool for 5 minutes.

3 Place the sugar in a medium-size mixing bowl and pour in the chocolate mixture. Using an electric mixer on medium speed, mix until blended, about 25 seconds. Scrape the bowl with a rubber spatula.

4 Add the vanilla. With the mixer on medium-low speed, add the eggs one at a time, blending after each addition until the yolk is broken and dispersed, about 10 seconds. Scrape the bowl, then beat until the mixture is velvety, about 15 seconds.

5 Add the flour on low speed and mix for 20 seconds. Finish the mixing by hand, being certain to incorporate any flour at the bottom of the bowl.

6 Spread the batter evenly in the prepared pan and set it aside.

7 Make the topping: Heat the cream in a medium-size saucepan over low heat until hot. Add the unsweetened chocolate and chocolate chips, stir, and remove the pan from the heat. Cover the pan to melt the chocolate. Meanwhile, beat the eggs and sugar together in a medium-size mixing bowl with an electric mixer on medium-high speed

INGREDIENTS

Vegetable oil or butter for greasing the pan (optional)

Brownies

3½ ounces unsweetened chocolate

10 tablespoons (1¼ sticks) unsalted butter

1 cup sugar

½ teaspoon pure vanilla extract

3 large eggs, at room temperature

½ cup all-purpose flour

Topping

¾ cup heavy (whipping) cream

2 ounces unsweetened chocolate

¾ cup (4 ounces) semisweet chocolate chips

3 large eggs

5 tablespoons sugar

until pale and foamy, about 3 minutes.

8   Stir the chocolate mixture with a whisk until smooth. Then add the chocolate mixture to the egg mixture and mix at medium-low speed until well blended, 30 seconds.

9   Pour the topping over the batter and tip the pan gently from side to side so that it spreads evenly.

10   Bake until the top is set, 40 to 45 minutes. (The center of the brownies should never quite rise to the height of the edges.)

11   Let the brownies cool in the pan on a rack for 1 hour before cutting them with a sharp, thin knife.

NOTE: *Leave the brownies in the pan, at room temperature, covered with plastic wrap, for up to 1 day. After that, layer them in an airtight container with plastic wrap, parchment paper, or waxed paper between the layers, and store for another 2 days in the refrigerator or in the freezer for up to 2 weeks. They are delicious either cold or at room temperature.*

* *

Toasted Pecan Orange Brownies

* *

I believe it was Maida Heatter's Mandarin Chocolate Cake that first put me in touch with the wonderful combination of chocolate and orange. This brownie takes that perfect union a couple of steps further by adding candied orange slices and pecans.

MAKES 16 BROWNIES

1 Make the candied orange slices: Place the orange slices and water in a small heavy saucepan over medium heat. Bring to a boil and simmer gently for 3 minutes.

2 Add the sugar and continue stirring until the mixture is slightly thickened and shiny, 5 to 10 minutes. Remove the saucepan from the heat and let cool for 15 to 20 minutes.

3 When the mixture has cooled, drain it, reserving the syrup (there should be about ⅓ cup). Chop the drained orange slices coarsely in a food processor (there will be about ⅔ cup) and set aside.

4 Place a rack in the center of the oven and preheat to 325°F. Lightly grease an 8-inch square baking pan with vegetable oil or butter, or line the bottom with parchment paper.

5 Make the brownies: Melt the chocolate and butter together in the top of a double boiler placed over simmering water. Let the mixture cool slightly.

6 Sift the flour and cocoa powder into a small bowl and set aside.

7 Beat the sugar and eggs together in a medium-size mixing bowl with an electric mixer on medium speed until thick and pale, 2 to 3 minutes. Stop the mixer once to scrape the bowl with a rubber spatula.

8 Add the vanilla to the sugar mixture and mix for several seconds on medium speed.

9 Add the flour mixture and mix on low speed until blended, 15 seconds, stopping the mixer once to scrape the bowl.

10 Turn the mixer to low speed and gradually add the chocolate and butter mixture. Mix until blended, 15 seconds, stopping the mixer once to scrape the bowl.

11 Fold in the nuts and chopped candied orange. Spread the batter evenly in the pan, and bake until a tester inserted in the center comes out with moist crumbs, 35 to 40 minutes. Transfer the pan to a rack.

12 Meanwhile, make the glaze: Melt both chocolates and the butter together in the top of a double boiler placed over simmering water. Using a whisk, vigorously stir in 2 tablespoons of the reserved orange syrup until the glaze is smooth and shiny. If it is too stiff, add more syrup until it reaches glaze consistency.

13 Spread the glaze over the warm brownies. Let the glaze set for 4 to 6 hours in the pan

INGREDIENTS

Candied Orange Slices

1 large orange, thinly sliced

½ cup water

⅔ cup sugar

Vegetable oil or butter for greasing the pan (optional)

Brownies

3 ounces unsweetened chocolate

12 tablespoons (1½ sticks) unsalted butter, at room temperature

¾ cup plus 1 tablespoon all-purpose flour

3 tablespoons unsweetened cocoa powder

1½ cups sugar

3 large eggs, at room temperature

¾ teaspoon pure vanilla extract

2 cups chopped pecans, toasted (see page 272)

Glaze

3 ounces semisweet chocolate

1 ounce unsweetened chocolate

2 tablespoons unsalted butter

(or refrigerate for 1 to 2 hours to speed the process). Cut the squares with a sharp, thin knife.

NOTE: *When cut, refrigerate the brownies in the pan, covered with plastic wrap, for up to 2 days. After that, layer them in an airtight container, with plastic wrap, parchment paper, or waxed paper between the layers, and store for another 2 days in the refrigerator or in the freezer for up to 2 weeks. They are delicious either cold or at room temperature.*

Toasting Nuts

Toasting gives nuts additional flavor. To toast nuts, spread them out on an ungreased baking sheet and place them in a preheated 350°F oven for 5 minutes. Open the oven door and toss the nuts by shaking the pan gently back and forth. Close the door and continue until the nuts give off a toasted aroma and are lightly golden, 3 to 5 minutes more.

* *

Chocolate Hazelnut Brownies

* *

T*his light delicate brownie is made with ground hazelnuts and accented with Frangelico liqueur. The liqueur is optional, but with or without it, these brownies are lovely served in small pieces with a cappuccino.*

MAKES 16 LARGE OR 36 SMALL BROWNIES

1 Place a rack in the center of the oven and preheat to 325°F. Lightly grease a 9-inch square baking pan with vegetable oil or butter, or line the bottom with parchment paper.

2   Melt both chocolates in the top of a double boiler placed over simmering water. Let the mixture cool for 5 minutes.

3   Sift the flour and cornstarch together into a small bowl and set aside.

4   Cream the butter, 11 tablespoons of the sugar, and the vanilla in a medium-size mixing bowl with an electric mixer on medium speed until light and fluffy, 45 seconds. Scrape the bowl with a rubber spatula.

5   Add the egg yolks to the butter mixture and beat on medium speed until blended, 20 seconds. Stop the mixer once to scrape the bowl. Add the chocolate and beat on low speed until blended, 5 seconds. Scrape the bowl again.

6   Dissolve the coffee powder in the Frangelico mixture (or water) and add this to the butter mixture.

7   Add the flour mixture and the ground nuts, and beat on low speed for 10 seconds, stopping the mixer once to scrape the bowl.

8   Beat the egg whites with the salt in a medium-size mixing bowl with an electric mixer on medium-low speed until frothy, about 30 seconds. Increase the speed to medium-high and gradually add the remaining 3 tablespoons sugar. Beat until soft peaks form, about 30 seconds.

9   Using a wooden spoon, stir one-third of the whites into the batter to loosen the mixture. Fold in the remaining whites with the rubber spatula.

10   Spread the batter evenly in the prepared pan. Bake until just set and a tester inserted in the center comes out with moist crumbs, 30 to 35 minutes. Let the brownies cool in the pan on a rack for 1 to 2 hours before cutting them with a sharp, thin knife.

NOTE: *Leave the brownies in the pan, at room temperature, covered with plastic wrap, for up to 2 days. After that, layer them in an airtight container with plastic wrap, parchment paper, or waxed paper between the layers, and store for another 2 days in the refrigerator or in the freezer for up to 2 weeks. They are delicious either cold or at room temperature.*

INGREDIENTS

Vegetable oil or butter for greasing the pan (optional)

2 ounces unsweetened chocolate

5 ounces semisweet chocolate

2 tablespoons all-purpose flour

2 tablespoons cornstarch

10 tablespoons (1¼ sticks) unsalted butter, at room temperature

14 tablespoons sugar

½ teaspoon pure vanilla extract

5 large eggs, separated

1½ teaspoons instant coffee or espresso powder

2 tablespoons Frangelico liqueur plus 2 tablespoons water, or ¼ cup water

½ cup hazelnuts, toasted, skinned (see page 157), and finely ground

¼ teaspoon salt

Bourbon Brownies

* *

A s a rule I like my chocolate unadulterated, but bourbon provides a wonderful accent that complements, rather than disguises, the chocolate taste of these brownies. They're rich and fudgy, so you'll probably want to cut them into small pieces. You may also want to brush the bourbon onto the baked brownie more sparingly than I do; try the recipe once to see.

MAKES 36 BROWNIES

INGREDIENTS

Vegetable oil or butter for greasing the pan (optional)

Brownies

5 ounces unsweetened chocolate

12 tablespoons (1½ sticks) unsalted butter

2 cups sugar

1 teaspoon pure vanilla extract

9 tablespoons bourbon

4 large eggs, at room temperature

1 cup all-purpose flour

Glaze

3 tablespoons heavy (whipping) cream

3 ounces bittersweet chocolate, chopped fine or shaved

1   Place a rack in the center of the oven and preheat to 325°F. Lightly grease an 8-inch square baking pan with vegetable oil or butter, or line the bottom with parchment paper.

2   Make the brownies: Melt the chocolate and butter together in the top of a double boiler placed over simmering water. Let the mixture cool for 5 minutes.

3   Place the sugar in a medium-size mixing bowl and pour in the chocolate mixture. Using an electric mixer on medium speed, mix until blended, about 15 seconds. Scrape the bowl with a rubber spatula.

4   Add the vanilla and 6 tablespoons of the bourbon. With the mixer on medium-low speed, add the eggs one at a time,

blending after each addition until the yolk is broken and dispersed, about 10 seconds. Scrape the bowl, then beat until velvety, about 15 seconds.

5   Add the flour on low speed and mix for 20 seconds. Finish mixing with the rubber spatula, being certain to incorporate any flour at the bottom of the bowl.

6   Spread the batter evenly in the prepared pan. Bake until a thin crust forms on top and a tester inserted in the center comes out with moist crumbs, 45 to 50 minutes.

7   Transfer the pan to a rack. Using a small brush, spread the remaining 3 tablespoons bourbon over the surface of the brownies. Let them cool for at least 1 hour.

8   When the brownies are cool, make the glaze: Heat the cream in a small saucepan over low heat just to the boiling point. Remove the pan from the heat, add the chocolate, and cover the pan for 1 to 2 minutes. Then stir the mixture with a small whisk until smooth and shiny.

9   Using a frosting spatula, spread the glaze evenly over the surface of the brownies. Place the pan in the refrigerator for 1 to 2 hours so the glaze will set. Cut the brownies into squares with a sharp, thin knife.

NOTE: *When cut, refrigerate the brownies in the pan, covered with plastic wrap, for up to 2 days. After that, layer them in an airtight container with plastic wrap, parchment paper, or waxed paper between the layers, and store for another 2 days in the refrigerator or in the freezer for up to 2 weeks. They are delicious either cold or at room temperature.*

* *

Chocolate Almond Amaretto Brownies

* *

T hese almost flourless brownies are so elegant and rich, I recommend serving them in small pieces. You can opt not to add the amaretto and still come out with a superb brownie. They're best made a day ahead so the flavor can settle.

MAKES 16 LARGE OR 36 SMALL BROWNIES

INGREDIENTS

Vegetable oil or butter for greasing the pan (optional)

¾ cup plus 2 tablespoons all-purpose flour

½ teaspoon salt

½ cup (3 ounces) semisweet chocolate chips

3½ ounces unsweetened chocolate

2 sticks (8 ounces) unsalted butter, at room temperature

1½ cups sugar

1 teaspoon pure vanilla extract

1¼ teaspoons pure almond extract

4 large eggs, at room temperature

2 tablespoons amaretto liqueur (optional)

1 cup coarsely chopped almonds, lightly toasted (see page 272)

1   Place a rack in the center of the oven and preheat to 325°F. Lightly grease a 9-inch square baking pan with vegetable oil or butter, or line the bottom with parchment paper.

2   Sift the flour and salt together into a small bowl and set aside.

3   Melt both chocolates and the butter together in the top of a double boiler placed over simmering water. Let the mixture cool for 5 minutes.

4   Place the sugar and the vanilla and almond extracts in a medium-size mixing bowl. Add the chocolate mixture and mix with an electric mixer on medium speed until blended, 30 seconds. Scrape the bowl with a rubber spatula.

5   With the mixer on medium-low speed, add the eggs one at a time, blending after each addition until the yolk is broken and dispersed, about 10 seconds. Scrape the bowl, then beat until velvety, about 15 seconds.

6   Add the flour mixture on low speed and mix for 10 seconds. Scrape the bowl, and complete the blending by hand with several strokes.

7   Spread the batter evenly in the pan and sprinkle the amaretto (if using) over the surface. Tip the pan from side to side to ensure even coverage. Sprinkle the nuts over the surface.

8   Bake until a thin crust forms on top and a tester inserted in the center comes out with moist crumbs, 45 to 50 minutes. Let the brownies cool in the pan on a rack for 1 hour before cutting them with a sharp, thin knife. If possible, serve the brownies the next day.

NOTE: *Leave the brownies in the pan, at room temperature, covered with plastic wrap, for up to 2 days. After that, layer them in an airtight container with plastic wrap, parchment paper, or waxed paper between the layers, and store for another 2 days in the refrigerator or in the freezer for up to 2 weeks. They are delicious eaten either cold or at room temperature.*

Brownie Shortbread

* *

I've added a layer of brownie to the top of a crunchy shortbread for those days when you can't decide which you prefer.

MAKES 12 BROWNIES

1 Place a rack in the center of the oven and preheat to 350°F. Lightly grease an 11 × 7-inch baking pan with vegetable oil or butter, or line the bottom with parchment paper.

2 Make the base: Process the flour and sugar in a food processor, about 15 seconds. Add the butter and process until the dough comes together, 20 to 30 seconds.

3 Pat the dough gently over the bottom of the prepared pan. Bake until it is lightly golden, about 20 minutes. Place the base in the refrigerator for 15 minutes to cool completely. Keep the oven on.

4 Make the topping: Melt the chocolate and butter in the top of a double boiler over simmering water. Let the mixture cool slightly.

5 Beat the eggs, sugar, and baking powder together in a medium-size bowl with a whisk.

Add the chocolate mixture and stir vigorously with the whisk until the batter is blended. Spread the chocolate mixture evenly over the base.

6 Bake until the top rises and forms a very thin crust, about 20 minutes. The center will drop as it cools. A tester inserted in the middle may come out with a fudgy, crumbly batter on it, but it should not be liquidy. Let the brownies cool in the pan on a rack before cutting with a sharp, thin knife.

NOTE: *Leave the brownies in the pan, at room temperature, covered, for up to 2 days. After that, layer them in an airtight container with plastic wrap, parchment paper, or waxed paper between the layers, and store for another 2 days in the refrigerator or in the freezer for up to 2 weeks. They are delicious cold or at room temperature.*

INGREDIENTS

Vegetable oil or butter for greasing the pan (optional)

Shortbread Base

1 cup all-purpose flour

¼ cup sugar

8 tablespoons (1 stick) unsalted butter, at room temperature, cut into 8 pieces

Brownie Topping

3 ounces unsweetened chocolate

8 tablespoons (1 stick) unsalted butter

2 large eggs, at room temperature

¾ cup sugar

½ teaspoon baking powder

Dagwoods

* *

I n my humble opinion, it's texture and thickness that makes this the perfect butterscotch brownie. The recipe came from my mother-in-law, Barbara, who insisted that you had to mix it by hand with a wooden spoon. Old-fashioned superstition, I scoffed, pulling out my KitchenAid and setting to work. Barbara was right, of course. You can make these brownies with a machine, but they come out differently and not nearly as good. So, chastised, I now make them by hand, and I've found that it's just as quick and easy.

MAKES 9 TO 12 BROWNIES

INGREDIENTS

Vegetable oil or butter for greasing the pan (optional)

1¼ cups all-purpose flour

1½ cups (lightly packed) light brown sugar

1½ teaspoons baking powder

⅛ teaspoon salt

2 large eggs, at room temperature

10 tablespoons unsalted butter, melted

2 teaspoons pure vanilla extract

½ cup chopped walnuts

1 Place a rack in the center of the oven and preheat to 350°F. Lightly grease an 8-inch square pan with vegetable oil or butter, or line the bottom with parchment paper.

2 Blend the flour, sugar, baking powder, and salt together in a medium-size bowl with a wooden spoon.

3 In another medium-size bowl, beat the eggs with a whisk until blended. Whisk in the melted butter and the vanilla.

4 Make a well in the center of the flour mixture and pour the egg mixture into the well. Using the wooden spoon, stir until the mixture is blended.

5 Add the nuts with a few broad strokes. Spread the batter evenly in the prepared pan.

6 Bake until golden and a tester inserted in the center comes out clean or with moist crumbs, 35 to 40 minutes. Let the brownies cool in the pan on a rack for 1 hour before cutting them.

NOTE: *Leave the brownies in the pan, at room temperature, covered, for up to 2 days. After that, layer them in an airtight container with plastic wrap, parchment paper, or waxed paper between the layers, and store for another 2 days in the refrigerator or in the freezer for up to 2 weeks. They are delicious cold or at room temperature.*

Congo Bars

* *

The Congo Bar is a chewy butterscotch brownie full of chocolate chips and nuts. I have no idea where the name came from, but regardless of its roots, this was one of Rosie's first products and it remains a perennial favorite.

MAKES 12 BROWNIES

1 Place a rack in the center of the oven and preheat to 350°F. Lightly grease a 13 × 9-inch baking pan with vegetable oil or butter, or line the bottom with parchment paper.

2 Blend the flour, baking soda, and salt in a small bowl with a wooden spoon. Set aside.

3 Cream the butter, sugar, and vanilla in a medium-size mixing bowl with an electric mixer on medium speed until light and fluffy, about 2 minutes. Stop the mixer once or twice to scrape the bowl with a rubber spatula.

4 Add the eggs to the butter mixture and mix on high speed for 3 seconds, then on medium speed until blended, about 5 more seconds.

5 Add the flour mixture and mix on low speed until almost blended, 8 to 10 seconds. Stop the mixer once to scrape the bowl.

6 Add the chocolate chips and nuts and mix on low speed for 5 seconds. Finish the mixing by hand with a wooden spoon. Spread the batter evenly in the prepared pan.

7 Bake until the top has formed a rich golden crust and dropped below the level of the darker golden outer edges, 30 minutes. These bars cannot be tested by inserting a tester because they remain very gooey inside.

8 Let the brownies cool in the pan on a rack for 30 minutes before cutting them. They are best eaten the first day.

INGREDIENTS

Vegetable oil or butter for greasing the pan (optional)

1⅓ cups all-purpose flour

1½ teaspoons baking soda

½ teaspoon salt

9 tablespoons (1 stick plus 1 tablespoon) unsalted butter, at room temperature

1¾ cups (lightly packed) light brown sugar

1¼ teaspoons pure vanilla extract

2 large eggs, at room temperature

1 cup (6 ounces) semisweet chocolate chips

½ cup chopped walnuts

Double Whammies

* *

A pairing of two favorite American classics: chocolate chip cookies and brownies layered to create a bar that has all the tastes and textures that make those favorites so enduring.

MAKES 12 BROWNIES

INGREDIENTS

Vegetable oil or butter for greasing the pan (optional)

Cookie Base

¾ cup plus 2 tablespoons all-purpose flour

½ teaspoon baking soda

½ teaspoon salt

8 tablespoons (1 stick) unsalted butter, at room temperature

½ cup (lightly packed) light brown sugar

¼ cup granulated sugar

1 teaspoon pure vanilla extract

1 large egg, at room temperature

¾ cup (4 ounces) semisweet chocolate chips

Brownie Topping

3 ounces unsweetened chocolate

8 tablespoons (1 stick) unsalted butter, at room temperature

¾ cup plus 2 tablespoons granulated sugar

2 large eggs, at room temperature

2 tablespoons all-purpose flour

1 Place a rack in the center of the oven and preheat to 325°F. Lightly grease an 8-inch square pan with vegetable oil or butter, or line the bottom with parchment paper.

2 Make the base: Sift the flour, baking soda, and salt together into a small bowl and set aside.

3 Cream the butter, both sugars, and the vanilla in a medium-size mixing bowl with an electric mixer on medium speed until light and fluffy, about 1 minute. Stop the mixer twice to scrape the bowl with a rubber spatula.

4 Add the egg to the butter mixture and beat on medium speed until blended, about 10 seconds. Scrape the bowl.

5 Add the flour mixture and mix on low speed for 15 seconds. Scrape the bowl.

6 Add the chocolate chips and blend until they are mixed in, 5 to 8 seconds.

7 Spread the dough evenly over the bottom of the prepared pan with a frosting spatula and set aside.

8 Make the topping: Melt the chocolate and butter in the top of a double boiler placed over simmering water.

9 Meanwhile, place the sugar in a medium-size mixing bowl. When the chocolate mixture has melted, pour it into the sugar. Using an electric mixer on medium speed, mix until blended, about 25 seconds. Scrape the bowl with the rubber spatula.

10 With the mixer on medium-low speed, add the eggs one at a time, blending after each addition. Scrape the bowl, then beat until velvety, about 15 seconds.

11   Add the flour on low speed and mix for several seconds.

12   Pour the brownie batter evenly over the cookie base. Bake until the center has risen and a tester inserted in the center comes out with very moist crumbs. Don't worry if the top looks uneven and higher in some places than others; it will settle as it cools.

13   Let the brownies cool in the pan on a rack for 1 hour before cutting them.

NOTE: *Leave the brownies in the pan, at room temperature, covered with plastic wrap, for up to 2 days, or layer the bars in an airtight container with plastic wrap, parchment paper, or waxed paper between the layers, and store in the refrigerator for 2 to 4 days or in the freezer for up to 2 weeks. Bring the bars to room temperature before eating unless you like your brownies cold.*

* *

White Chocolate Macadamia Brownies

* *

C ustomers at Rosie's clamor for this masterpiece of a bar: a chewy white chocolate base dotted with chunks of white and bittersweet chocolate and toasted macadamia nuts. What a way to gild the lily!

MAKES 16 BROWNIES

1   Place a rack in the center of the oven and preheat to 325°F. Lightly grease a 9-inch square baking pan with vegetable oil or butter, or line the bottom with parchment paper.

INGREDIENTS

Vegetable oil or butter for greasing the pan (optional)

12 ounces white chocolate

4 ounces bittersweet chocolate

1½ cups all-purpose flour

½ teaspoon baking powder

⅛ teaspoon salt

10 tablespoons (1¼ sticks) unsalted butter

¾ cup sugar

3 large eggs, at room temperature

2½ teaspoons pure vanilla extract

¾ cup coarsely chopped macadamia nuts, toasted (see page 272)

2   Very finely chop 6 ounces of the white chocolate and set aside. Coarsely chop the remaining white chocolate and the bittersweet chocolate and set them aside.

3   Sift the flour, baking powder, and salt together into a small bowl and set aside.

4   Melt the butter in a small saucepan over low heat. Do not allow it to bubble. Remove the pan from the heat and add the finely chopped white chocolate, but do not stir. Set it aside.

5   Beat the sugar, eggs, and vanilla in a medium-size mixing bowl with an electric mixer on medium-high speed until thick and pale, about 5 minutes.

6   With the mixer on low speed, add the butter mixture to the sugar mixture and mix to blend, 15 to 20 seconds. Scrape the bowl with a rubber spatula.

7   Add the flour mixture and blend on low speed just to incorporate, 15 seconds. Stop the mixer once to scrape the bowl.

8   Using the spatula, fold in the coarsely chopped white and bittersweet chocolates and the nuts. Spread the batter evenly in the prepared pan.

9   Bake the brownies until just set and a tester inserted in the center comes out with moist crumbs, 30 to 35 minutes. Let the brownies cool in the pan on a rack for 1 hour before cutting them with a sharp, thin knife.

NOTE: *Leave the brownies in the pan, at room temperature, covered with plastic wrap, for up to 2 days. After that, layer them in an airtight container with plastic wrap, parchment paper, or waxed paper between the layers, and store for another 2 days in the refrigerator or in the freezer for up to 2 weeks. They are delicious either cold or at room temperature.*

CHAPTER 15
Linzer, Shortbread, and Crumb Pastry Bars

When I belly up to the bar, it's not to order a cocktail, it's to eat a freshly baked layered concoction. Most often it's created with a luscious shortbread base, spread with a fruit or nut or cheesecake mixture, and finished off with a topping of pastry crumbs or meringue. Now, those are the bars I can go for. So, those are the bars you'll find in this chapter. Rich and dreamy, made with plenty of butter, sugar, and flour, bars are easy to assemble and serve straight from the pan.

I like to bake my shortbreads, pastries, and topping crumbs until they are golden in color and crunchy in texture. Butter, when it is cooked until golden, takes on a deeper, richer flavor. This will also allow the bases and crumbs to remain crunchier when topped or sandwiched with moist mixtures. (To find out more about these crust bases, see the pie chapter beginning on page 328.)

Bars are perfect party fare or to tote to school functions and fund-raisers. They make special afternoon snacks, and when barbecue season rolls around, and there's a crowd of friends enjoying your backyard, nothing ends the meal better than a Chocolate Linzer Bar or Tart Lemon Square.

Cutting Bars

Like brownies, the yield line in this chapter is arbitrary, because the number of folks you'll be serving determines how you divvy up the pan. So, again, I based my suggestions on how big a piece I feel it takes to enjoy a particular bar to its fullest. If you need to go smaller, you'll still have a delicious experience. And if you can go bigger, just consider yourself extra lucky.

INGREDIENTS

Vegetable oil or butter for greasing the pan (optional)

Base

1 cup all-purpose flour

¼ cup confectioners' sugar

8 tablespoons (1 stick) unsalted butter, at room temperature, cut into 8 pieces

1 egg white, for glazing

Topping

4 large eggs, at room temperature

1⅓ cups granulated sugar

2 tablespoons all-purpose flour

¾ cup fresh lemon juice

Confectioners' sugar, for sprinkling

Tart Lemon Squares

* *

I wanted to devise a lemon square recipe, so I decided to research the topic. But all the recipes I found were too sweet. I was looking for something tart enough to make my lips pucker, so I had to come up with a recipe of my own. To contrast with the lemon topping, I added a sweet and crunchy shortbread base.

MAKES 9 TO 12 BARS

1   Place a rack in the center of the oven and preheat to 350°F. Lightly grease an 8-inch square baking pan with vegetable oil or butter, or line the bottom with parchment paper.

2   Make the base: Place the flour and confectioners' sugar in a food processor and process to blend for several seconds. Add the butter and process until the dough comes together, 20 to 30 seconds.

3   Pat the dough gently and evenly over the bottom of the prepared pan. Pour the egg white over the dough and tip the pan from side to side so that the white spreads over the surface to glaze the dough. Pour off the excess.

4   Bake the base until lightly golden, about 25 minutes. Place the base in the refrigerator for 15 minutes to cool completely. Leave the oven on.

5   Meanwhile, make the topping: Gently whisk the eggs in a medium-size bowl until lightly mixed. Add the granulated sugar, flour, and lemon juice and continue to whisk gently until blended.

6   Pour the topping evenly over the base. Bake until the top is set and golden, about 25 minutes. Let cool completely in the pan on a rack. Cracks may form, but they add character.

7   Sprinkle the surface with confectioners' sugar and cut into pieces with a sharp, thin knife that is dipped in hot water and wiped dry before each cut.

NOTE: *Store the bars in the pan in the refrigerator for up to 2 days, then store them in 1 layer in an airtight container in the refrigerator for up to 1 week or in the freezer for up to 2 weeks. The bars are good cold or at room temperature.*

* *

Rhubarb Bars

* *

T*his is one of my all-time favorite desserts; it's fruity, tart, sweet, crunchy, and buttery all in one bar, and that's pretty exciting.*

MAKES 9 TO 12 BARS

1   Place a rack in the center of the oven and preheat to 350°F. Lightly grease an 8-inch square baking pan with vegetable oil or butter, or line the bottom with parchment paper.

2   Make the base: Place the flour and confectioners' sugar in a food processor and process to blend for several seconds. Add the butter and process until the dough comes together, 20 to 30 seconds.

3   Pat the dough gently and evenly over the bottom of the prepared pan. Pour the egg white over the dough and tip the pan from side to side so that the white spreads over the surface to glaze the dough. Pour off the excess.

4   Bake the base until golden, about 25 minutes. Place the base in the refrigerator for 15 minutes to cool completely. Leave the oven on.

INGREDIENTS

Vegetable oil or butter for greasing the pan (optional)

Base

1 cup all-purpose flour

5 tablespoons confectioners' sugar

8 tablespoons (1 stick) unsalted butter, at room temperature, cut into 8 pieces

1 egg white, for glazing

Topping

1 large egg, at room temperature

¾ cup granulated sugar

2½ tablespoons all-purpose flour

¼ teaspoon salt

3 cups sliced (¼ inch thick) rhubarb

5 Meanwhile, make the topping: In a large bowl, stir the egg, granulated sugar, flour, and salt together with a whisk. Add the rhubarb and toss.

6 Spread the rhubarb mixture evenly over the base. Bake until set and lightly golden, about 50 minutes. Let cool completely in the pan on a rack before cutting into pieces.

NOTE: *Store the bars in the pan in the refrigerator for up to 2 days, then store them in 1 layer in an airtight container in the refrigerator for up to 1 week or in the freezer for up to 2 weeks. The bars are good cold or at room temperature.*

* *

Dutch Butter Bars

* *

INGREDIENTS

1¼ cups plus 2 tablespoons all-purpose flour

Pinch of salt

2 sticks (8 ounces) unsalted butter, at room temperature

¾ cup plus 2 teaspoons sugar

2 teaspoons pure vanilla extract

1 large egg, lightly beaten with a fork, at room temperature

¼ teaspoon ground cinnamon

1 egg white, for glazing

When I decided that my kids were old enough to begin collecting taste memories, these bars were among the first treats I offered them. They seemed like a good transitional food since they taste like rich zweiback: not too much sugar but nice and buttery. That makes them appropriate for adults, too, at all hours of the day and night, when they want just a little sweet but a lot of flavor.

MAKES 16 BARS

1 Place a rack in the center of the oven and preheat to 350°F. Have ready an 8-inch square baking pan.

2 Sift the flour and salt together into a medium-size bowl and set aside.

3   Cream the butter, ¾ cup of the sugar, and the vanilla in a medium-size mixing bowl with an electric mixer on medium speed until light and fluffy, about 2 minutes. Stop the mixer once or twice to scrape the bowl with a rubber spatula.

4   Add the whole egg to the butter mixture and beat on medium speed until the egg is incorporated, about 10 seconds. Scrape the bowl.

5   Add the flour mixture and mix on medium-low speed for 10 seconds. Scrape the bowl, then mix until the dough comes together, about 5 seconds. Pat the dough evenly over the bottom of the pan.

6   Mix the remaining 2 teaspoons sugar together with the cinnamon. Pour the egg white over the dough and tip the pan from side to side so that the white spreads over the surface to glaze the dough. Pour off the excess. Sprinkle the cinnamon sugar over the top.

7   Bake until firm to the touch and golden in color, about 30 minutes. Remove the pan from the oven. Leave the oven on and reduce the oven temperature to 250°F.

8   Have ready a baking sheet. Cut the baked dough into 4-inch squares with the tip of a sharp, thin knife. Let the squares sit for 15 minutes, then remove them from the pan with a metal spatula and place them 1 inch apart on the baking sheet.

9   Bake until crisp and golden around the edges, about 1 hour.

10   Transfer the bars to a rack to cool completely before cutting into pieces. Their flavor improves with time so store them overnight in an airtight container before eating.

Jam Sandwiches

* *

These sandwiches are a great after-school treat. They consist of two delicate, buttery bars sandwiched together with strawberry, raspberry, or apricot preserves, kind of a high-class Pop-Tart.

MAKES 16 BARS

INGREDIENTS

1¼ cups all-purpose flour

¼ cup plus 1 tablespoon granulated sugar

10 tablespoons (1¼ sticks) unsalted butter, cold, cut into 8 to 10 pieces

1 egg white, for glazing

½ cup strawberry, raspberry, or apricot preserves

Confectioners' sugar, for sprinkling

1   Place a rack in the center of the oven and preheat to 350°F. Have ready an 8-inch square baking pan.

2   Place the flour and granulated sugar in a food processor and process to blend for 10 seconds. Add the butter and process until the dough comes together, 20 seconds.

3   Divide the dough in half. Cover one half with plastic wrap and place it in the refrigerator. Pat the other half of the dough gently and evenly over the bottom of the pan. Pour the egg white over the dough and tip the pan from side to side so that the white spreads over the surface to glaze the dough. Pour off the excess.

4   Bake the base until golden brown, 15 to 20 minutes. Place the base in the refrigerator for 15 minutes to cool completely. Leave the oven on.

5   Meanwhile, roll out the remaining half of the dough between two pieces of plastic wrap to an 8-inch square.

6   Spread the preserves evenly over the base with a frosting spatula. Peel the top piece of plastic from the rolled-out dough and flip the dough over the jam. Press the dough gently into the sides of the pan to seal the edges. Gently peel the remaining piece of plastic from the dough and remove any excess dough that has climbed up the sides of the pan. Prick the top dough in four or five places with the tip of a sharp knife.

7   Bake until the top turns golden, 30 to 35 minutes. Let cool in the pan on a rack before cutting into pieces. Transfer them to an airtight container and serve the next day, when the flavor has settled, sprinkled over the top with confectioners' sugar.

Whitecaps

* *

These bars look to me like whitecaps on a stormy sea, which is how they got their name. Nothing stormy about their taste, though: They're a sweet, buttery shortbread topped with jam and meringue. Lemon juice added to the jam enhances the contrast of flavors.

MAKES 24 BARS

1   Place a rack in the center of the oven and preheat to 350°F. Lightly grease a 13 × 9-inch baking pan with vegetable oil or butter, or line the bottom with parchment paper.

2   Make the base: Place the flour and confectioners' sugar in a food processor and process to blend for several seconds. Add the butter and process until the dough comes together, 20 to 30 seconds.

3   Pat the dough gently and evenly over the bottom of the prepared pan. Bake until golden in color, 25 to 30 minutes. Place the base in the refrigerator for 15 minutes to cool completely. Leave the oven on.

4   Meanwhile, make the topping: Beat the egg whites in a medium-size mixing bowl with an electric mixer on medium-high speed until frothy, about 50 seconds. Gradually add the granulated sugar and continue beating until the whites resemble Marshmallow Fluff, about 30 seconds.

5   Remove the base from the refrigerator. Stir the preserves and lemon juice together and spread the mixture evenly over the surface.

6   Using a frosting spatula, spread the egg-white mixture over the jam and make small peaks on the surface to form the whitecaps. Sprinkle the coconut over these whitecaps.

7   Bake until the peaks and coconut are golden, 15 to 20 minutes. Rotate the pan after 10 minutes.

8   Let cool in the pan on a rack for 1 hour. Cut into pieces with the tip of a sharp, thin knife that is dipped in hot water and wiped dry before each cut.

NOTE: *Whitecaps taste best on the day they are baked.*

INGREDIENTS

Vegetable oil or butter for greasing the pan (optional)

Base

1½ cups all-purpose flour

¾ cup confectioners' sugar

12 tablespoons (1½ sticks) unsalted butter, at room temperature, cut into 12 pieces

Topping

4 large egg whites, at room temperature

½ cup plus 1 teaspoon granulated sugar

¾ cup raspberry or apricot preserves

2 teaspoons fresh lemon juice

Generous ½ cup sweetened shredded coconut

Honeypots

* *

These sweet, crunchy, buttery bars were part of my original repertoire. My good friend Karen McCarthy—who worked with me back in the day—and I rewarded ourselves for spending endless hours over hot stoves with a Honeypot apiece at the end of the day. It was usually too late for anyone else to be around, which is a good thing because we'd close our eyes and moan loudly from sheer pleasure.

MAKES 16 BARS

INGREDIENTS

Vegetable oil or butter for greasing the pan (optional)

Base

1 cup all-purpose flour

½ cup confectioners' sugar

8 tablespoons (1 stick) unsalted butter, at room temperature, cut into 8 pieces

1 egg white, for glazing

Topping

6 tablespoons (¾ stick) unsalted butter

½ cup (lightly packed) light brown sugar

½ cup honey

1¼ cups chopped walnuts

¼ cup heavy (whipping) cream

1 teaspoon pure vanilla extract

1 Place a rack in the center of the oven and preheat to 350°F. Lightly grease an 8-inch square pan with vegetable oil or butter, or line the bottom with parchment paper.

2 Make the base: Place the flour and confectioners' sugar in a food processor and process to blend for 20 seconds. Add the butter and process until the dough comes together, 20 to 30 seconds.

3 Pat the dough gently and evenly over the bottom of the prepared pan. Pour the egg white over the dough and tip the pan from side to side so that the white spreads over the surface to glaze the dough. Pour off the excess.

4 Bake the base until golden, about 25 minutes. Place the base in the refrigerator for 15 minutes to cool completely. Leave the oven on.

5 Meanwhile, make the topping: Combine the butter, brown sugar, and honey in a medium-size saucepan. Heat, stirring the mixture with a wooden spoon, over medium-low heat until it begins to boil. Boil without stirring for 5 minutes.

6 While the mixture is boiling, put the nuts in a medium-size heatproof bowl; add the cream and the vanilla and stir to combine.

7 Add the boiled honey mixture to the nuts mixture and stir the ingredients together. Pour the topping evenly over the cooled base.

8 Bake until the entire surface is bubbling, about 25 minutes. Let cool in the pan on a rack for 1 hour. Then run a sharp knife around the sides of the pan and let cool completely before cutting into pieces with a cleaver or very strong knife.

NOTE: *Leave the bars in the pan at room temperature, covered with plastic wrap, for a day, or layer them in an airtight container with plastic wrap, parchment paper, or waxed paper between the layers, and store in the refrigerator for up to 1 week or in the freezer for up to 2 weeks. Bring the bars to room temperature before eating.*

* *

Linzer Bars

* *

These bars boast the same unbeatable combination of spice-and-nut base and raspberry jam as a linzertorte, but they're much quicker and easier to make. They can be just as elegantly served cut into small pieces and sprinkled with confectioners' sugar

MAKES 16 TO 20 BARS

1 Cream the butter, confectioners' sugar, cinnamon, and lemon zest together in a medium-size mixing bowl with an electric mixer on low speed until just mixed, about 1 minute. Scrape the bowl with a rubber spatula, then mix on medium speed until smooth, 2 to 3 minutes more. Stop the mixer once or twice to scrape the bowl.

2 Add the whole egg and 1 egg white and mix on medium speed until incorporated, about 10 seconds. Scrape the bowl.

3 Blend in the flour and almonds with the mixer on low speed until they are incorporated and the dough comes together, 5 to 8 seconds.

INGREDIENTS

11 tablespoons (1 stick plus 3 tablespoons) unsalted butter, at room temperature

2 cups confectioners' sugar, sifted

1 teaspoon ground cinnamon

Grated zest of 1 small lemon

1 large egg, at room temperature

2 large egg whites, at room temperature

1⅓ cups all-purpose flour

1 cup ground almonds

Vegetable oil or butter for greasing the pan (optional)

¾ cup raspberry preserves

3 tablespoons slivered or chopped almonds

4   Divide the dough in half. Wrap each piece in plastic wrap and refrigerate it for at least 4 hours or up to 3 days.

5   Fifteen minutes before you're ready to prepare the bars, place a rack in the center of the oven and preheat to 350°F. Lightly grease a 9-inch square baking pan with vegetable oil or butter, or line the pan with parchment paper.

6   Pat half the dough gently and evenly over the bottom of the prepared pan. Bake the base until lightly golden but not hard, about 25 minutes. Place the base in the refrigerator for 15 minutes to cool completely. Leave the oven on.

7   While the base is baking and cooling, place the second half of the dough between two pieces of plastic wrap and, with your fingers and the palms of your hands, flatten it into a square slightly larger than the pan or roll it out with a rolling pin.

8   When the base is cool, spread the preserves evenly over it, leaving a ¼-inch strip uncovered on all sides. Peel the top piece of plastic from the remaining dough and flip the dough over the jam. Press the dough into

the sides of the pan to seal the edges. Gently peel the remaining piece of plastic from the dough and remove any excess dough that has climbed up the sides of the pan.

9   Pour the remaining egg white over the dough and tip the pan from side to side so that the white spreads evenly over the surface to glaze the dough. Pour off the excess. Sprinkle the almonds over the top.

10   Bake until the top is golden and firm, about 40 minutes. Let cool in the pan on a rack for 10 minutes. Run a frosting spatula or knife around the sides of the pan and let cool completely in the pan before cutting into pieces.

NOTE: *Leave the bars in the pan at room temperature, covered with plastic wrap, for a day, or layer them in an airtight container with plastic wrap, parchment paper, or waxed paper between the layers, and store in the refrigerator for up to 1 week or in the freezer for up to 2 weeks. Bring the bars to room temperature before eating.*

Pucker-Your-Lips Apricot Bars

* *

For me, few fruits can rival the beauty and succulent tartness of apricots, so I created these bars to highlight those attributes. I placed a mixture of dried apricots and apricot preserves over a rich pastry crust, topped it with latticework, and came up with the perfect complement for afternoon tea.

MAKES 16 BARS

1   Place a rack in the center of the oven and preheat to 375°F. Lightly grease a 9-inch square baking pan with vegetable oil or butter, or line the bottom with parchment paper.

2   Make the dough: Place the flour, sugar, salt, and lemon zest in a food processor and process to blend for 20 seconds.

3   Distribute the butter evenly over the flour and process until the mixture resembles coarse meal, 15 to 20 seconds.

4   Whisk the egg yolks together. With the processor running, pour the yolks in a steady stream through the feed tube and process just until the dough comes together, 20 to 30 seconds.

5   Divide the dough into two portions: one twice the size of the other. Pat the larger portion gently and evenly over the bottom and a scant ½ inch up the sides of the prepared pan. Pour the egg white over the dough and tip the pan from side to side so the white spreads over the surface to glaze the dough. Pour off and reserve the excess.

6   Bake the base until golden, about 30 minutes.

7   While the base is baking, roll out the remaining portion of dough between two pieces of plastic wrap to form a 9½-inch square. Place this, still sandwiched in the wrap, in the freezer while you prepare the filling.

INGREDIENTS

Vegetable oil or butter for greasing the pan (optional)

Dough

2 cups plus 3 tablespoons all-purpose flour

½ cup sugar

¼ teaspoon salt

2½ teaspoons grated lemon zest

15 tablespoons (2 sticks minus 1 tablespoon) unsalted butter, cold, cut into 15 pieces

2 large egg yolks

1 large egg white

Filling

8 ounces dried apricots, finely chopped

¾ cup apricot preserves

2 tablespoons fresh lemon juice

8   Make the filling: Place the apricots in a small saucepan and add water to cover. Bring to a boil over medium heat and boil until soft, 2 to 3 minutes. Drain the apricots and pat them dry with paper towels. Place them in a small bowl along with the apricot preserves and lemon juice, and mix together.

9   Remove the pan from the oven, and increase the oven temperature to 400°F.

10   Spread the apricot filling over the baked base.

11   Remove the remaining dough from the freezer and peel off the top piece of plastic wrap. Cut the dough into 12 strips, each about ¾ inch wide.

12   Carefully place 6 of the strips across the filling, about 1 inch apart, with the first and last strip touching the sides of the pan. Repeat the procedure with the remaining 6 strips, laying them perpendicular to the first 6.

Press the ends of the strips into the dough border on the edge of the pan. Brush the remaining egg white over the lattice strips with a pastry brush.

13   Bake until the lattice is golden, 40 minutes. Let cool in the pan on a rack for at least 2 hours before cutting into pieces, "sawing" carefully through the lattice with the tip of a sharp, thin knife.

NOTE: *Leave the bars in the pan, at room temperature, covered with plastic wrap, for up to 2 days, or layer the bars in an airtight container with plastic wrap, parchment paper, or waxed paper between the layers, and store in the refrigerator for 2 or 4 days or in the freezer for up to 2 weeks. Bring the bars to room temperature before eating.*

Chocolate Linzer Bars

* *

I'm a big fan of linzer bars and tortes, so I had fun trying out all kinds of variations. I knew that nuts and chocolate go great together, and that raspberry goes well with chocolate, so when it came to variations on a linzer bar, I put them all together, and this is the result.

MAKES 16 BARS

1   Place a rack in the center of the oven and preheat to 350°F. Lightly grease a 9-inch square baking pan with vegetable oil or butter, or line the bottom with parchment paper.

2   Using a fork, stir the whole egg, egg yolks, and vanilla together in a small cup. Set aside.

3   Place the flour, cocoa powder, baking powder, salt, and sugar in a food processor and process to blend, 5 seconds.

4   Add the almonds and process several seconds to blend.

5   Distribute half the butter over the flour mixture and process until the mixture resembles coarse meal, 15 seconds. Then repeat with the remaining butter and process for 10 seconds more.

6   With the machine running, add the egg mixture through the feed tube and process for 3 seconds. Scrape the bowl with a rubber spatula, and then process until the dough comes together, another 3 seconds.

7   Divide the dough into two portions, one double the size of the other. Pat the larger portion gently and evenly over the bottom of the prepared pan. Bake the base until firm to the touch, about 20 minutes. Then remove the pan from the oven, but leave the oven on.

8   While the base is baking, roll out the remaining dough between two pieces of plastic wrap to form a 9½-inch square. Place the dough, still sandwiched between the plastic wrap, onto a platter or baking sheet and refrigerate it for 45 minutes.

INGREDIENTS

Vegetable oil or butter for greasing the pan (optional)

1 large egg, at room temperature

2 large egg yolks

1½ teaspoons pure vanilla extract

1¼ cups plus 2 tablespoons all-purpose flour

7 tablespoons unsweetened cocoa powder

¼ teaspoon baking powder

⅛ teaspoon salt

¾ cup plus 2 tablespoons sugar

1 cup coarsely ground almonds

14 tablespoons (1¾ sticks) unsalted butter, cold, cut into 14 pieces

¾ cup raspberry preserves

1 tablespoon fresh lemon juice

1 large egg white

9 Stir the raspberry preserves and lemon juice together in a small bowl, and spread the mixture evenly over the baked base.

10 Remove the chilled dough from the refrigerator, and peel off the top piece of plastic wrap. Cut the dough into 12 strips about ¾ inch wide.

11 Carefully place 6 of the strips across the filling, about 1 inch apart, with the first and last strip touching the sides of the pan. Repeat the procedure with the remaining 6 strips, weaving them perpendicular to the first 6, in a lattice pattern (see page 335). Press the ends of the strips into the dough border on the edge of the pan.

12 Brush the egg white over the lattice strips with a pastry brush.

13 Bake until the lattice strips are firm and the filling is bubbling, 35 to 40 minutes. Let cool completely in the pan on a rack. Cut into pieces by "sawing" carefully through the lattice with the tip of a sharp, thin knife.

NOTE: *If you plan to eat them that day, leave the bars in the pan at room temperature, covered with plastic wrap. At the end of the day, layer them in an airtight container with plastic wrap, parchment paper, or waxed paper between the layers. They will stay fresh in the refrigerator for up to 3 days or in the freezer for up to 2 weeks. Bring the bars to room temperature before eating.*

Cinnamon Pecan Shortbread Bars

* *

A simple shortbread, flavored with cinnamon—the prince of spices—and covered with pecans.

MAKES 16 BARS

1 Place a rack in the center of the oven and preheat to 300°F. Have ready an 8-inch square baking pan.

2 Make the shortbread: Sift the flour, cinnamon, baking powder, and salt together into a small bowl and set aside.

3 Cream the butter and both sugars together in a medium-size mixing bowl with an electric mixer on medium speed until light and fluffy, 1 to 1½ minutes. Stop the mixer once or twice to scrape the bowl with a rubber spatula.

4 Add the flour mixture on medium-low speed and mix for 20 seconds. Scrape the bowl. Then mix on medium-high speed until the dough is light and fluffy again and comes together, 2 to 2½ minutes, stopping the mixer three times to scrape the bowl.

5 Pat the dough gently and evenly over the bottom of the pan and prick it all over with the tines of a fork.

6 Make the topping: Mix the granulated sugar with the cinnamon. Sprinkle this mixture over the dough, and then scatter the nuts over the surface.

7 Bake until the shortbread is firm to the touch, 55 to 60 minutes. While the shortbread is still hot, cut it into pieces with the point of a sharp, thin knife. Let cool completely in the pan on a rack before eating.

NOTE: *Layer the bars in an airtight container with plastic wrap, parchment paper, or waxed paper between the layers, and store at room temperature for up to 4 days. After that, store in the freezer for up to 2 weeks. Bring the bars to room temperature before eating.*

INGREDIENTS

Shortbread

1 cup plus 1 tablespoon all-purpose flour

½ teaspoon plus ⅛ teaspoon ground cinnamon

⅛ teaspoon baking powder

¼ teaspoon salt

8 tablespoons (1 stick) unsalted butter, at room temperature

3 tablespoons (lightly packed) light brown sugar

2 tablespoons granulated sugar

Topping

1 tablespoon granulated sugar

½ teaspoon ground cinnamon

¼ cup plus 1 tablespoon coarsely chopped pecans

Semolina Shortbread Bars

* *

Semolina is the flour used in pasta; here it gives shortbread a grainy texture to add to its already divinely buttery flavor. This shortbread is thick, so be sure that it's baked through and through.

MAKES 16 BARS

INGREDIENTS

1½ cups plus 2 tablespoons all-purpose flour

½ cup plus 3 tablespoons semolina flour

½ cup plus 2 tablespoons sugar

½ teaspoon salt

2 sticks (8 ounces) unsalted butter, cold, cut into 10 pieces

1　Place a rack in the center of the oven and preheat to 325°F. Have ready an 8-inch square baking pan.

2　Place both flours, the sugar, and salt in a food processor and process to blend for 5 seconds.

3　Distribute the butter over the flour mixture and process just until the dough comes together, 40 to 45 seconds. Stop the processor once to scrape the bowl with a rubber spatula.

4　Place the dough on a work surface and work it gently with your hands to bring it together. Pat the shortbread gently and evenly into the pan. Using the tines of a fork, poke deep holes over the entire surface.

5　Bake the shortbread for 45 minutes. Then reduce the heat to 300°F and continue baking until it is crisp, firm, and richly golden, about 30 minutes.

6　While the shortbread is still hot, cut it into pieces with the point of a sharp, thin knife. Then let it cool completely in the pan on a rack.

NOTE: *Layer the bars in an airtight container with plastic wrap, parchment paper, or waxed paper between the layers, and store at room temperature for up to 4 days. After that, store in the freezer for up to 2 weeks. Bring the bars to room temperature before eating.*

Noah's Scotch Shortbread Bars

* *

Back in the day, my son Noah's second-grade teacher asked the class to bring in easy-to-make international recipes to conclude her section on other cultures. We chose this utterly delicious cookie that will be enjoyed by people of all ages. It's amazing how such a delicious treat can be so easy to prepare!

MAKES 16 BARS

1 Place a rack in the center of the oven and preheat to 325°F. Have ready an 8-inch square baking pan.

2 Sift the flour, salt, and baking powder together into a small bowl and set aside.

3 Cream the butter and sugar together in a medium-size mixing bowl with an electric mixer on medium-high speed until light and fluffy, 1 to 1½ minutes. Stop the mixer twice to scrape the bowl with a rubber spatula.

4 With the mixer on low speed, add the flour mixture and blend for 10 seconds. Scrape the bowl, and then beat at medium-high speed until fluffy and the dough comes together, 2 to 2½ minutes, stopping the mixer twice to scrape the bowl.

5 Pat the dough gently and evenly into the pan and pierce the surface all over with the tines of a fork. Bake until it is crisp and golden, about 45 minutes.

6 While the shortbread is still hot, cut it into pieces with the point of a sharp, thin knife. Let cool completely in the pan before eating.

NOTE: *Layer the bars in an airtight container with plastic wrap, parchment paper, or waxed paper between the layers, and store at room temperature for up to 4 days. After that, store in the freezer for up to 2 weeks. Bring the bars to room temperature before eating.*

INGREDIENTS

1½ cups plus 1 tablespoon all-purpose flour

½ teaspoon salt

⅛ teaspoon baking powder

12 tablespoons (1½ sticks) unsalted butter, at room temperature

7 tablespoons sugar

Tosca Bars

* *

T*his crunchy shortbread bar is topped with a thin layer of raspberry or apricot preserves and a soft almond paste mixture.*

MAKES 16 BARS

INGREDIENTS

Vegetable oil or butter for greasing the pan (optional)

Base

1⅓ cups all-purpose flour

⅓ cup sugar

8 tablespoons (1 stick) unsalted butter, cold, cut into 8 pieces

1 large egg, separated

Filling

1 package (7 ounces) almond paste (not marzipan)

3 tablespoons sugar

9 tablespoons (1 stick plus 1 tablespoon) unsalted butter, at room temperature, cut into 9 pieces

2 large eggs, at room temperature

¾ teaspoon pure vanilla extract

3 tablespoons all-purpose flour

¾ teaspoon baking powder

6 tablespoons raspberry or apricot preserves

Topping

3 tablespoons unsalted butter

6 tablespoons sugar

1½ tablespoons milk

1½ tablespoons all-purpose flour

¾ cup sliced almonds

1   Place a rack in the center of the oven and preheat to 350°F. Lightly grease an 11 × 7-inch baking pan with vegetable oil or butter, or line the bottom with parchment paper.

2   Make the base: Place the flour and sugar in a food processor and process to blend for 5 seconds.

3   Distribute the butter evenly over the flour mixture and process until the mixture resembles coarse meal, 15 to 20 seconds.

4   With the processor running, drop the egg yolk through the feed tube and process just until the dough comes together, 20 to 30 seconds.

5   Pat the dough gently and evenly over the bottom and ½ inch up the sides of the prepared pan. Using a pastry brush, glaze the dough all over with the egg white. (Or you can pour the egg white over the dough and tip the pan from side to side so that the white spreads over the surface and glazes the dough. Pour off the excess.)

6   Bake until golden, 20 to 25 minutes. Remove the pan from the oven, but leave the oven on.

7   Meanwhile, make the filling: Place the almond paste and sugar in a food processor and process until the mixture resembles coarse sand, 20 seconds.

8   Add the butter and process until evenly incorporated, 5 seconds.

9   Add the eggs and vanilla, and process until evenly incorporated, 5 seconds.

10   Add the flour and baking powder, and process 5 seconds more.

11   Spread the raspberry preserves over the baked base. Then gently pour and spread the almond filling over that. Return the pan to the oven and bake until

the filling is set in the center, about 25 minutes. Remove the pan from the oven and preheat the broiler.

12   Meanwhile, make the topping: Melt the butter in a small saucepan over low heat. Add the sugar, milk, and flour, and bring to a simmer. Stir constantly over medium-low heat for about 1½ minutes. Do not boil. Remove the pan from the heat and stir in the almonds.

13   Pour the topping evenly over the filling and spread it gently with a small frosting spatula or a butter knife. Broil the bars until golden, about 2 minutes. Watch carefully! Let cool completely in the pan before cutting into pieces with a sharp, thin knife.

NOTE: *Leave the bars in the pan at room temperature, covered with plastic wrap, for a day, or layer them in an airtight container with plastic wrap, parchment paper, or waxed paper between the layers, and store in the refrigerator for up to 1 week or in the freezer for up to 2 weeks. Bring the bars to room temperature before eating.*

* *

Almond Bars

* *

H*ere is a first-class recipe from Kathleen Stewart of the Downtown Bakery and Creamery in Healdsburg, California. It's a bar made of a rich shortbread base covered with a creamy, buttery almond topping.*

MAKES 16 BARS

1   Place a rack in the center of the oven and preheat to 375°F. Lightly grease a 9-inch square baking pan with vegetable oil or butter, or line the bottom with parchment paper.

2   Make the base: Place the flour, sugar, and salt in a food processor, and process to blend for 5 seconds. Scatter the butter over the flour and process until the mixture looks like coarse meal, about 20 seconds.

INGREDIENTS

Vegetable oil or butter for greasing the pan (optional)

Base

1 cup all-purpose flour

1½ tablespoons sugar

¼ teaspoon salt

8 tablespoons (1 stick) unsalted butter, cold, cut into 8 pieces

1½ tablespoons cold water

Topping

1 cup heavy (whipping) cream

1 cup sugar

2 teaspoons Grand Marnier or amaretto

¾ cup slivered almonds

301

3   With the machine running, add the cold water through the feed tube and process just until the dough comes together, 10 to 15 seconds.

4   Pat the dough gently and evenly over the bottom of the prepared pan (it will be thin). Bake until lightly golden, about 20 minutes. Remove the pan from the oven and increase the oven temperature to 400°F.

5   Let the base cool while you make the topping: Place the cream, sugar, and Grand Marnier in a medium-size saucepan and cook over medium-low heat, whisking occasionally, until it comes to a rolling boil, 2 to 3 minutes.

6   Remove the pan from the heat, stir in the almonds, and let the mixture sit for 15 minutes. Then pour the warm topping mixture over the baked base, making sure that the almonds are evenly distributed.

7   Return the pan to the oven and bake until light golden, 25 to 30 minutes.

8   While still hot, use the point of a sharp, thin knife to free the baked edges from the sides of the pan. Then let sit for 15 to 20 minutes before cutting into pieces. Let cool completely in the pan on a rack.

NOTE: *Leave the bars in the pan at room temperature, covered with plastic wrap, for up to 2 days, or layer the bars in an airtight container with plastic wrap, parchment paper, or waxed paper between the layers, and store in the refrigerator for up to 1 week or in the freezer for up to 2 weeks. Bring to room temperature before eating.*

Almond Apricot Bars

* *

F or those of you who love almond paste as I do, these are the bars for you; a golden shortbread base topped with tart apricot preserves and a wonderfully moist, buttery almond topping.

MAKES 12 BARS

1   Place a rack in the center of the oven and preheat to 350°F. Lightly grease a 9-inch square pan with vegetable oil or butter, or line the bottom with parchment paper.

2   Make the base: Place the flour and confectioners' sugar in a food processor and process to blend for several seconds. Distribute the butter evenly over the flour mixutre and process until the dough comes together, 20 to 30 seconds.

3   Pat the dough gently and evenly over the bottom of the prepared pan. Bake the base until lightly golden, about 25 minutes. Place the base in the refrigerator for 15 minutes to cool completely. Leave the oven on.

4   Meanwhile, make the topping: Process the almond paste and sugar in a food processor until the

mixture looks like coarse sand, about 25 seconds.

5   Add the butter, eggs, almond extract, lemon zest, salt, and baking powder and process until smooth, about 20 seconds.

6   Transfer the topping to a medium-size mixing bowl and with an electric mixer on medium-high speed, beat until thick and pale yellow in color, about 1½ minutes.

7   In a small bowl, stir the apricot preserves and lemon juice together. Remove the base from the refrigerator and spread the apricot mixture evenly over it, leaving a ½-inch strip uncovered around the edges. Pour the almond topping evenly over the apricot. Tip the pan from side to side to distribute the topping evenly or use a small frosting spatula to very gently spread the

INGREDIENTS

Vegetable oil or butter for greasing the pan (optional)

Base

1½ cups all-purpose flour

6 tablespoons confectioners' sugar

12 tablespoons (1½ sticks) unsalted butter, cold, cut into 12 pieces

Topping

1 package (7 ounces) almond paste (not marzipan)

¼ cup granulated sugar

2 tablespoons plus 2 teaspoons unsalted butter, at room temperature

3 large eggs, beaten lightly with a whisk

1 teaspoon pure almond extract

1 teaspoon grated lemon or orange zest

Pinch of salt

⅛ teaspoon baking powder

½ cup apricot preserves

3 tablespoons fresh lemon juice

303

almond mixture so that it does not mix with the apricot mixture.

8   Bake until set and lightly golden, about 35 minutes. Let cool completely in the pan on a rack.

9   Cut into pieces with a sharp, thin knife that has been dipped in hot water and wiped dry before each cut.

NOTE: *If you plan to keep the bars for more than one day, chill them first, then layer them with parchment paper in an airtight container and refrigerate or freeze them for up to 2 weeks. Bring them to room temperature before serving.*

INGREDIENTS

Vegetable oil or butter for greasing the pan (optional)

Base

1 cup all-purpose flour

½ teaspoon salt

¼ teaspoon baking soda

8 tablespoons (1 stick) unsalted butter, at room temperature

½ cup sugar

1 teaspoon pure vanilla extract

1 large egg, at room temperature

Filling

12 tablespoons (1½ sticks) unsalted butter, at room temperature

Pinch of salt

½ teaspoon pure vanilla extract

6 tablespoons sweetened condensed milk

⅓ cup light corn syrup

1 large egg, at room temperature

⅓ cup all-purpose flour

* *

Gooey Butter Bars

* *

H*erein lies a tale—or two tales, to be precise. The first involves my mother-in-law, Barbara, who served us a yellow cake bar soaked through with custard so scrumptious that I couldn't help but talk with my mouth full. I asked for the recipe, only to find that she had used a cake mix, and since I had decided that cake mix would never touch my cookbook, I fought temptation and put the recipe aside. Enter tale two. On my travels, I came across the same treat in St. Louis, Missouri, where, as the story goes, a baker working during World War II mistakenly doubled the sugar in a butter cake recipe. Because sugar was rationed, he was loath to toss the cake out. So he sold it—and to his surprise, got rave reviews. The cake has assuaged the St. Louis sweet tooth ever since. I came up with my own made-from-scratch version, which has a cakey bottom with a very sweet vanilla custard topping that sinks partway into the base.*

MAKES 24 BARS

1   Place a rack in the center of the oven and preheat to 350°F. Lightly grease a 9-inch square baking pan with vegetable oil or butter, or line the bottom with parchment paper.

2   Make the base: Sift the flour, salt, and baking soda together into a small bowl and set aside.

3   Cream the butter, sugar, and vanilla together in a medium-size mixing bowl with an electric mixer on medium speed until light and fluffy, about 1 minute. Scrape the bowl with a rubber spatula.

4   Add the egg to the butter mixture and beat until smooth, 10 seconds. Scrape the bowl.

5   Add the flour mixture and beat on low speed until the dough comes together, 10 seconds, stopping the mixer once to scrape the bowl.

6   Using floured fingertips or a spatula, pat the dough gently and evenly over the bottom of the prepared pan. Set it aside.

7   Make the filling: Cream the butter, salt, and vanilla together in a medium-size mixing bowl with an electric mixer on medium speed until light and fluffy, about 1 minute. Scrape the bowl.

8   Add the condensed milk and beat on low speed until blended, 15 seconds. Scrape the bowl, then add the corn syrup and beat until blended, 10 seconds.

9   Add the egg and beat on medium-high speed until the mixture is light and fluffy again, about 1½ minutes. Scrape the bowl.

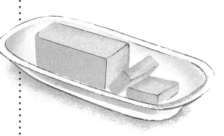

10   With the mixer on medium-low speed, add the flour and beat until mixed, 30 seconds.

11   Pour the filling evenly over the base. Bake until the edges appear set but the center is still jiggly, 25 to 27 minutes. Let cool to room temperature, then refrigerate until set, about 4 hours.

12   Cut into pieces with a sharp, thin knife, dipping it in hot water and wiping it clean before each new cut.

NOTE: *If you plan to eat them the first day, place the bars on a plate or simply leave them in the pan. After that, refrigerate overnight, covered with plastic wrap, or layer the bars in an airtight container with plastic wrap, parchment paper, or waxed paper between the layers. Store the container in the freezer for up to 2 weeks. Bring the bars to room temperature before eating.*

Cherry Crumb Bars

* *

J ust what the world has been clamoring for: a portable cherry crumb pie. Okay, maybe not clamoring, but this sure beats those commercial snack pies. It's built on a shortbread base, which is layered with a tart cherry filling, then finished off with a crunchy crumb topping.

MAKES 16 BARS

INGREDIENTS

Vegetable oil or butter for greasing the pan (optional)

Base

1 cup plus 2 tablespoons all-purpose flour

¼ cup granulated sugar

¼ teaspoon salt

8 tablespoons (1 stick) unsalted butter, cold, cut into 8 pieces

1 large egg white

Filling

2¼ cups canned pitted sour cherries, drained, 1 cup juice reserved

3 tablespoons cornstarch

¾ cup granulated sugar

¼ teaspoon salt

Topping

5 tablespoons all-purpose flour

1 tablespoon granulated sugar

2 tablespoons (lightly packed) light brown sugar

6 tablespoons quick-cooking oats

Pinch of salt

3 tablespoons unsalted butter, cold, cut into 4 pieces

1 Place a rack in the center of the oven and preheat to 350°F. Lightly grease an 8-inch square baking pan with vegetable oil or butter, or line the bottom with parchment paper.

2 Make the base: Place the flour, sugar, and salt in a food processor and process to blend for 5 seconds. Scatter the butter over the flour mixture and process just until the dough comes together, 20 to 30 seconds.

3 Pat the dough gently and evenly over the bottom of the prepared pan. Pour the egg white over the dough and tip the pan from side to side so that the white spreads over the surface to glaze the dough. Pour off the excess.

4 Bake the base until golden brown, 25 to 30 minutes.

5 Meanwhile, make the filling: Place the drained cherries in a small bowl and set aside. Combine ¼ cup of the reserved juice with the cornstarch in a small bowl and set aside.

6 Combine the remaining ¾ cup juice, the sugar, and salt in a small saucepan and bring to a boil over medium-low heat.

7 Pour the cornstarch mixture slowly into the boiling juice, whisking vigorously. Reduce the heat to low and continue whisking vigorously until the mixture turns clear and thickens, about 4 minutes. Add the mixture to the cherries and set aside.

8   Make the topping: Place the flour, both sugars, the oats, and salt in a food processor and pulse 4 times to blend.

9   Add the butter and pulse 8 to 10 times, until it is incorporated evenly. Scrape the bowl with a rubber spatula.

10   Remove the base from the oven, and raise the oven temperature to 425°F. Spread the cherry filling evenly over the base and sprinkle the topping evenly over the cherries.

11   Return the pan to the oven and bake until the topping is lightly golden and crispy, about 25 minutes. Then preheat the broiler.

12   Broil until the topping is a slightly deeper gold, 1 to 2 minutes. Watch the bars the entire time they are under the broiler.

13   Let cool completely in the pan on a rack, before cutting into pieces.

NOTE: *Leave the bars in the pan, at room temperature, covered with plastic wrap, for up to 2 days, or layer the bars in an airtight container with plastic wrap, parchment paper, or waxed paper between the layers, and store in the refrigerator for 3 to 4 days or in the freezer for up to 2 weeks. If frozen, the fruit may get a little wet in the thawing process, but the bars will still taste delicious.*

* *

Rosie's Raspberry Crumb Bars

* *

This bar is one of Rosie's bestsellers: a crunchy golden shortbread base topped with raspberry preserves and a crunchy and sweet white crumb topping. You can also make this with any good-quality jam, such as apricot or cherry.

MAKES 12 BARS

307

INGREDIENTS

Vegetable oil or butter for
   greasing the pan (optional)

Base

1¼ cups all-purpose flour

5 tablespoons confectioners'
   sugar

10 tablespoons (1¼ sticks)
   unsalted butter, at room
   temperature

Topping

½ cup plus 3 tablespoons
   all-purpose flour

5 tablespoons granulated sugar

4 tablespoons (½ stick) unsalted
   butter, cold

¾ cup plus 2 tablespoons
   raspberry preserves

1   Place a rack in the center of the oven and preheat to 350°F. Lightly grease an 8-inch square baking pan with vegetable oil or butter, or line the bottom with parchment paper.

2   Make the base: Place the flour, confectioners' sugar, and butter in a food processor and process until the dough comes together, 20 to 30 seconds.

3   Pat the dough gently and evenly over the bottom of the prepared pan. Bake the base until lightly golden, about 20 minutes. Remove from the oven and raise the oven temperature to 375°F.

4   Meanwhile, make the topping: Place the flour, granulated sugar, and salt in a food processor and process to blend for 5 seconds. Scatter the butter over the flour mixture and process just until the dough forms loose clumps, about 1½ minutes.

5   Spread the raspberry jam evenly over the surface of the base leaving a ⅜-inch strip uncovered around the edges. Sprinkle the topping evenly over the jam.

6   Return the pan to the oven and bake until the topping is golden and the jam is bubbling around the edges, about 30 minutes. Let cool in the pan on a rack before cutting into pieces.

NOTE: *Leave the bars in the pan, at room temperature, covered with plastic wrap, for up to 2 days, or layer the bars in an airtight container with plastic wrap, parchment paper, or waxed paper between the layers, and store in the refrigerator for 2 to 4 days or in the freezer for up to 2 weeks. Bring the bars to room temperature before eating.*

Orange Birthday Cake Bars

* *

This pound-cake-like bar doesn't really fit into any of the categories in this chapter, but it is an easy-to-handle and not overly sweet bar. It's great for 1- to 2-year-old's birthday parties as well as a delicious treat for grown-ups.

MAKES 24 BARS

1 Place a rack in the center of the oven and preheat to 350°F. Lightly grease a 15 × 10-inch jelly-roll pan with vegetable oil or butter, or line the bottom with parchment paper.

2 Make the cake: Sift the flour, baking soda, and salt together into a small bowl and set aside.

3 Cream the butter, cream cheese, granulated sugar, vanilla, and orange zest together in a medium-size mixing bowl with an electric mixer on medium-high speed until light and fluffy, about 2 minutes. Stop the mixer once or twice to scrape the bowl with a rubber spatula.

4 Add the eggs one at a time and beat on medium-low speed until each yolk is partially blended, 10 seconds. Scrape the bowl after each addition.

5 Fold in half the flour mixture with the spatula until partially incorporated, then turn the mixer to low speed and blend for several seconds. Repeat with the remaining flour mixture, blending with the electric mixer for 10 seconds. Finish the mixing by hand with a few broad strokes of the spatula. Spread the batter evenly in the prepared pan.

6 Bake until the cake is lightly golden, springs back to the touch, and a tester inserted in the center comes out clean, 20 to 25 minutes. Allow the cake to cool completely in the pan on a rack while preparing the glaze.

7 Make the glaze: In a small bowl, combine the confectioners' sugar, melted butter, orange juice, lemon juice, and salt and stir vigorously with a whisk until blended.

INGREDIENTS

Vegetable oil or butter for greasing the pan (optional)

Cake

2¼ cups cake flour

1 teaspoon baking soda

½ teaspoon salt

2 sticks (8 ounces) unsalted butter, at room temperature

3 ounces cream cheese, at room temperature

1¾ cups granulated sugar

2 teaspoons pure vanilla extract

1 tablespoon grated orange zest

4 large eggs, at room temperature

Glaze

1 cup sifted confectioners' sugar

4 tablespoons (½ stick) unsalted butter, melted

3 tablespoons fresh orange juice

1 teaspoon fresh lemon juice

Pinch of salt

8   Pour the glaze over the cooled cake and spread it evenly with a frosting spatula. Let the glaze harden 3 to 4 hours before cutting into pieces.

NOTE: *Leave the bars in the pan at room temperature, covered with plastic wrap, for a day, or layer them in an airtight container with plastic wrap, parchment paper, or waxed paper between the layers, and store in the refrigerator for up to 1 week or in the freezer for up to 2 weeks. Bring the bars to room temperature before eating.*

INGREDIENTS

Vegetable oil or butter for greasing the pan (optional)

Base

1 cup plus 2 tablespoons all-purpose flour

¼ teaspoon salt

5 tablespoons confectioners' sugar

8 tablespoons (1 stick) unsalted butter, cold, cut into 8 pieces

1 large egg white

Topping

2 cups fresh cranberries

½ cup light corn syrup

½ cup sugar

2 large eggs, at room temperature

2 tablespoons unsalted butter, melted

¾ teaspoon pure vanilla extract

1 tablespoon all-purpose flour

½ cup chopped walnuts

* *

Cranberry Walnut Squares

* *

P*atti Chase, an experienced Boston chef, passed the recipe for these squares on to me: a crunchy shortbread base that supports a sweet and gooey mix chock-full of walnuts and tart cranberries. They are a tribute to her talent.*

MAKES 16 BARS

1   Place a rack in the center of the oven and preheat to 350°F. Lightly grease an 8-inch square baking pan with vegetable oil or butter, or line the bottom with parchment paper.

2   Make the base: Place the flour, salt, and confectioners' sugar in a food processor and process to blend for 5 seconds.

Scatter the butter over the flour mixture and process until the dough comes together, 20 to 30 seconds.

3   Pat the dough gently and evenly over the bottom of the prepared pan. Pour the egg white over the dough and tip the pan from side to side so that the white spreads over the surface

to glaze the dough. Pour off the excess.

4   Bake the base until golden, about 25 minutes.

5   Meanwhile, make the topping: Place the cranberries in a food processor and process for 3 seconds to break them down a little. Set aside.

6   In a medium-size bowl, combine the corn syrup, sugar, eggs, melted butter, vanilla, and flour and whisk vigorously to blend. Add the cranberries and the nuts, and stir well.

7   Remove the base from the oven, pour the topping over the hot base, and return the pan to the oven. Bake until the topping is set, 40 to 45 minutes.

8   Let cool completely in the pan on a rack. Then cut into pieces, "sawing" carefully through with the tip of a long, sharp, thin knife.

NOTE: *If you plan to eat them the first day, place the bars on a plate or simply leave them in the baking pan, covered. After that, layer the cut bars in an airtight container, with plastic wrap, parchment paper, or waxed paper between the layers, and place in the refrigerator for up to 4 days or the freezer for up to 2 weeks. If frozen, the fruit may get a little wet in the thawing process, but the bars will still taste delicious.*

* *

Dating Bars

* *

*I*n my younger, sillier years, when Rosie's had just opened, *I named this bar. My co-workers and I had a good chuckle, and the name has stuck around all these years. You'll find some version of these bars in nearly every American cookbook. Two hearty, crunchy oatmeal layers with a gooey date filling in between.*

MAKES 16 BARS

INGREDIENTS

Filling

1½ cups finely chopped dates

6 tablespoons (lightly packed) light brown sugar

¾ cup water

1½ teaspoons pure vanilla extract

½ teaspoon grated lemon zest

Vegetable oil or butter for greasing the pan (optional)

Base

1½ cups plus 2 tablespoons all-purpose flour

5 tablespoons whole wheat flour

1¼ cups quick-cooking oats

½ cup plus 2 tablespoons old-fashioned rolled oats

½ teaspoon baking soda

¼ teaspoon salt

½ cup minus ½ tablespoon (lightly packed) light brown sugar

2½ tablespoons granulated sugar

12½ tablespoons (1½ sticks plus ½ tablespoon) unsalted butter, melted

1 Make the filling: Combine the dates, brown sugar, and water in a small saucepan and bring to a boil over medium heat. Reduce the heat to low and simmer until the mixture has thickened, 5 minutes.

2 Remove the pan from the heat and stir in the vanilla and lemon zest. Set aside.

3 Place a rack in the center of the oven and preheat to 350°F. Lightly grease an 8-inch square baking pan with vegetable oil or butter, or line the bottom with parchment paper.

4 Make the base: Combine both flours, both oats, the baking soda, salt, both sugars, and the butter in a medium-size bowl and toss to mix.

5 Pat half of the dough gently and evenly over the bottom of the prepared pan. Spread the date mixture over this, and then sprinkle the remaining dough evenly on top, pressing it down lightly into the dates.

6 Bake until the top is crunchy and golden, about 40 minutes.

7 Let cool in the pan on a rack for 30 minutes before cutting into pieces with a sharp, thin knife.

NOTE: *Leave the bars in the pan, at room temperature, covered with plastic wrap, for up to 2 days, or layer the bars in an airtight container with plastic wrap, parchment paper, or waxed paper between the layers, and store in the refrigerator for 3 to 4 days or in the freezer for up to 2 weeks. Bring the bars to room temperature before eating.*

Yummy Cheesecake Bars

* *

*A*nd yummy they are. I've sandwiched a cream cheese and golden raisin mixture in between two soft crumb layers. These bars taste equally good served cold or at room temperature. They will turn a bit soggy after a couple of days in the fridge, but they are absolutely delicious that way, too.

MAKES 16 BARS

1 Place a rack in the center of the oven and preheat to 350°F. Lightly grease an 8-inch square baking pan with vegetable oil or butter, or line the bottom with parchment paper.

2 Make the crumb layers: Place the flour and confectioners' sugar in a food processor and process to blend for 5 seconds.

3 Add the butter and pulse 8 times, until the mixture forms coarse crumbs.

4 Remove 1 cup of the mixture to a small bowl, add the brown sugar to it, and toss it with a fork to incorporate. Set it aside.

5 With floured fingertips, pat the remaining crumbs firmly and evenly to form a dough base over the bottom and 1 inch up the sides of the prepared pan.

6 Bake until lightly golden, 20 minutes. Remove the pan from the oven, but leave the oven on. Let the base cool to room temperature.

7 While the base cools, make the filling: Place the cream cheese, sour cream, lemon juice, lemon zest, sugar, egg, and vanilla in the food processor and process until smooth, 15 to 20 seconds. Stir in the raisins by hand.

8 Pour the filling over the cooled base and top it with the reserved crumb mixture. Return the pan to the oven and bake until the crumbs are just beginning to

INGREDIENTS

Vegetable oil or butter for greasing the pan (optional)

Crumb Layers

1½ cups all-purpose flour

6 tablespoons confectioners' sugar

12 tablespoons (1½ sticks) unsalted butter, at room temperature, cut into several pieces

2 tablespoons (lightly packed) light brown sugar

Filling

8 ounces cream cheese, at room temperature

3 tablespoons sour cream

2 tablespoons fresh lemon juice

1½ teaspoons grated lemon zest

¼ cup granulated sugar

1 large egg, at room temperature

1 teaspoon pure vanilla extract

¼ cup golden raisins

turn golden and the filling is set, 45 minutes.

9   Let cool in the pan on a rack for 1 hour before cutting into pieces with a sharp, thin knife.

NOTE: *Refrigerate the bars in the pan, uncovered, for the first day. At the end of the day, cover them. They will remain fresh in the refrigerator for 2 days. To freeze, layer the bars in an airtight container with plastic wrap, parchment paper, or waxed paper between the layers. Store in the freezer for up to 2 weeks. Serve cold or at room temperature.*

INGREDIENTS

Vegetable oil or butter for greasing the pan (optional)

Base

1 cup all-purpose flour

¼ cup confectioners' sugar

8 tablespoons (1 stick) unsalted butter, at room temperature, cut into 8 pieces

1 egg white, for glazing

Topping

10 ounces cream cheese, at room temperature

½ cup plus 1 tablespoon granulated sugar

2 teaspoons grated lemon zest

¼ cup plus 1 tablespoon sour cream, at room temperature

6 tablespoons fresh lemon juice

2 large eggs, at room temperature

1 teaspoon pure vanilla extract

* *

Lemon Cream Cheese Squares

* *

I *think of these squares as portable cheesecake for, like the best of that genre, they're rich and tart. Of course, from the baker's viewpoint, they're much easier than making cheesecake, especially with their shortbread crust and relatively short baking time.*

MAKES 12 TO 16 BARS

1   Place a rack in the center of the oven and preheat to 350°F. Lightly grease an 8-inch square baking pan with vegetable oil or butter, or line the bottom with parchment paper.

2   Make the base: Place the flour and confectioners' sugar in a food processor and process to blend for several seconds. Add the butter and process until the dough comes together, 20 to 30 seconds.

3   Pat the dough gently and evenly over the bottom of the prepared pan and about 1 inch up the sides. Pour the egg white over the dough and tip the pan from side to side so that the white spreads over the surface to glaze the dough. Pour off the excess.

4   Bake the base until golden, about 25 minutes. Place the base in the refrigerator for 15 minutes to cool completely. Leave the oven on.

5   Meanwhile, make the topping: Cream the cream cheese, granulated sugar, and lemon zest together in a medium-size mixing bowl with an electric mixer on medium-high speed until light and fluffy, 2 to 3 minutes. Stop the mixer once or twice to scrape the bowl with a rubber spatula.

6   Add the sour cream and lemon juice and beat the mixture on medium-high speed until smooth, about 1 minute. Scrape the bowl.

7   Add the eggs and vanilla and beat on medium-high speed until smooth and creamy, about 10 seconds.

8   Spread the topping evenly over the base. Bake until the top is slightly golden and a tester inserted in the center comes out clean, about 1 hour. If the topping bubbles up during baking, prick the bubbles with a toothpick or a thin knife.

9   Let cool completely in the pan on a rack. Cut into pieces with the point of a sharp, thin knife that is dipped in hot water and wiped dry before each cut.

NOTE: *Refrigerate the bars, covered, in the pan. They will remain fresh in the refrigerator for 2 days. To freeze, layer the bars in an airtight container with plastic wrap, parchment paper, or waxed paper between the layers. Store in the freezer for up to 2 weeks. Serve cold (but not frozen) or at room temperature.*

Carrot Cake Cream Cheese Bars

* *

T his bar consists of two layers of carrot cake sandwiched around a pineapple cream cheese filling. Topped with chopped walnuts, it's much easier to throw together than an actual carrot cake, and it's definitely more portable.

MAKES 16 BARS

INGREDIENTS

Topping

½ cup chopped walnuts

1 teaspoon ground cinnamon

2 tablespoons granulated sugar

Filling

8 ounces cream cheese, at room temperature

1 large egg, at room temperature

¼ cup granulated sugar

2 tablespoons unsalted butter, at room temperature

1 tablespoon cornstarch

½ teaspoon pure vanilla extract

1 can (8 ounces) crushed pineapple, drained

Vegetable oil or butter for greasing the pan (optional)

1   Make the topping: Toss the walnuts, cinnamon, and sugar together in a small bowl and set aside.

2   Make the filling: Place the cream cheese, egg, sugar, butter, cornstarch, and vanilla in a food processor and process until smooth, 10 seconds. Stir in the pineapple by hand and set aside.

3   Place a rack in the center of the oven and preheat to 350°F. Lightly grease a 13 × 9-inch baking pan with vegetable oil or butter, or line the bottom with parchment paper.

4   Make the cake: Stir the pureed and grated carrots together in a small bowl and set aside. Sift the flour, baking powder, baking soda, salt, cinnamon, and allspice together into a small bowl and set aside.

5   Cream the butter, oil, brown sugar, and vanilla together in a medium-size mixing bowl with an electric mixer on medium speed until well blended, 1 minute. Stop the mixer once to scrape the bowl with a rubber spatula. Add the lemon juice and orange juice, and blend on medium speed for a couple of seconds.

6   Add the eggs one at a time, mixing on medium after each addition until blended, 10 seconds. Scrape the bowl each time.

7   Add the flour mixture and beat on low speed for 5 seconds. Scrape the bowl. Then mix the batter by hand until the dry ingredients are incorporated.

8   Blend in the carrots with several turns of the mixer at low speed. Then add the raisins and blend on low for several seconds.

9   Spread about two-thirds of the batter in the prepared pan. Then pour the cream cheese filling gently over the batter, and using a frosting spatula, spread it evenly over the batter.

10   Drop the rest of the cake batter by spoonfuls all over the filling and use the frosting spatula to gently spread the batter. The batter will not thoroughly cover the filling (it's fine for the cream cheese to show through here and there).

11   Sprinkle the walnut topping over the cake. Bake until golden and set, about 35 minutes.

12   Let cool in the pan on a rack before cutting into pieces with a sharp, thin knife.

NOTES: *To make pureed carrots, cut 3 or 4 carrots into 1-inch chunks and steam them until tender, about 10 minutes. Then puree them in a food processor, 10 to 15 seconds.*

If you plan to eat them the first day, place the bars on a plate or simply leave them in the pan. After that, refrigerate, covered with plastic wrap, overnight, or layer the cut bars in an airtight container with plastic wrap, parchment paper, or waxed paper between the layers. Store the container in the freezer for up to 2 weeks. Bring the bars to room temperature before eating.

Cake

⅔ cup pureed cooked carrots (3 or 4 carrots; see Notes)

⅓ cup grated raw carrot

1⅓ cups all-purpose flour

¾ teaspoon baking powder

¼ teaspoon baking soda

¾ teaspoon salt

1¾ teaspoons ground cinnamon

¾ teaspoon ground allspice

5½ tablespoons (⅓ cup) unsalted butter, at room temperature

⅓ cup vegetable oil

1 cup (lightly packed) light brown sugar

1½ teaspoons pure vanilla extract

2 teaspoons fresh lemon juice

1 tablespoon plus 1 teaspoon fresh orange juice

2 large eggs, at room temperature

½ cup raisins

Berry Cheesecake Bars

* *

A luscious layer of cheesecake studded with cherries or berries atop a crunchy shortbread crust.

MAKES 12 BARS

INGREDIENTS

Vegetable oil or butter for greasing the pan (optional)

Base

1 cup all-purpose flour

3 tablespoons confectioners' sugar

7 tablespoons unsalted butter, at room temperature, cut into 7 pieces

½ teaspoon pure vanilla extract

1 egg white, for glazing

Topping

½ cup drained canned pitted sour cherries or fresh blueberries

8 ounces cream cheese, at room temperature

1 cup sour cream, at room temperature

7 tablespoons granulated sugar

2 large egg yolks

1 teaspoon pure vanilla extract

2 teaspoons all-purpose flour

1 Place a rack in the center of the oven and preheat to 350°F. Lightly grease an 8-inch square baking pan with vegetable oil or butter, or line the bottom with parchment paper.

2 Make the base: Place the flour and confectioners' sugar in a food processor and process to blend for several seconds. Add the butter and vanilla and process until the dough comes together, 20 to 30 seconds.

3 Pat the dough gently and evenly over the bottom and about 1½ inches up the sides of the prepared pan. Pour the egg white over the dough and tip the pan from side to side so that the white spreads over the surface to glaze the dough. Pour off the excess.

4 Bake the base until lightly golden, about 30 minutes. Place the base in the refrigerator for 15 minutes to cool completely. Leave the oven on.

5 Meanwhile, make the topping: Wrap the cherries, if using, in paper towels to absorb any liquid.

6 Place the cream cheese, sour cream, granulated sugar, egg yolks, vanilla, and flour in a food processor and process until blended, about 15 seconds.

7 Pour the topping evenly over the base, then arrange the cherries or blueberries evenly on the topping. Bake until set, about 1 hour. Let cool completely in the pan on a rack, then refrigerate overnight.

8 The next day, cut into pieces with a sharp, thin knife that is dipped in hot water and wiped dry before each cut. Let the bars warm to room temperature before serving.

NOTE: *Refrigerate the bars, covered, in the pan. They will remain fresh in the refrigerator for 2 days. To freeze, layer the bars in an airtight container with plastic wrap, parchment paper, or waxed paper between the layers. Store in the freezer for up to 2 weeks. Serve cold (but not frozen) or at room temperature.*

* *

Raspberry Cream Cheese Bars

* *

Here raspberry preserves separate a shortbread base from a layer of cheesecake, which is topped with glazed fresh raspberries. When you cut these bars, try to slice between the berries so they don't get bruised.

MAKES 16 BARS

1 Place a rack in the center of the oven and preheat to 350°F. Lightly grease an 8-inch square baking pan with vegetable oil or butter, or line the bottom with parchment paper.

2 Make the base: Place the flour, salt, and sugar in a food processor and process to blend for 5 seconds. Scatter the butter over the flour and process until the mixture resembles coarse meal, 20 seconds.

3 Stir the egg yolk, vanilla, and milk together in a small cup. With the machine running, pour this mixture through the feed tube and process just until it is mixed in and the dough is starting to come together, 1 minute.

INGREDIENTS

Vegetable oil or butter for greasing the pan (optional)

Base

1 cup all-purpose flour

¼ teaspoon salt

½ cup minus 1 tablespoon sugar

6 tablespoons (¾ stick) unsalted butter, cold, cut into 6 pieces

1 large egg yolk

¼ teaspoon pure vanilla extract

1 tablespoon milk, half-and-half, or heavy (whipping) cream

1 large egg white

Topping

11 ounces cream cheese, at room temperature

5 tablespoons sugar

1 teaspoon cornstarch

1 large egg, at room temperature

1 large egg yolk

¼ teaspoon grated lemon zest

¾ cup sour cream

¾ cup raspberry preserves

To Finish

1 pint fresh raspberries

⅓ cup red currant jelly

319

4   Pat the dough gently and evenly over the bottom of the prepared pan. Pour the egg white over the dough and tip the pan from side to side so that the white spreads over the surface to glaze the dough. Pour off the excess. Bake until golden, about 30 minutes. Set the pan on a rack to cool slightly. Leave the oven on.

5   Meanwhile, make the topping: Place the cream cheese, sugar, cornstarch, whole egg and yolk, lemon zest, and sour cream in a food processor and process just until blended, 15 seconds. Stop the processor once during the process to scrape the bowl with a rubber spatula.

6   Using a frosting spatula, spread the raspberry preserves over the base. Then pour the cream cheese topping over the preserves and spread it gently.

7   Bake until set, about 1 hour. Transfer the pan to the refrigerator and chill for 1 hour.

8   To finish: Top the cooled bars with the fresh raspberries, arranging them in rows (see Note).

9   Heat the jelly in the top of a double boiler placed over simmering water until liquefied. Glaze the berries by brushing the jelly over them with a pastry brush. Chill for at least 1 hour in the refrigerator so the glaze can set.

10   Cut into pieces with the tip of a sharp, thin knife, dipping it in hot water and wiping it dry before each cut.

NOTE: *Once you put the raspberries on top of these luscious bars, they can only be stored in the pan or on a plate. No stacking, please. If you want to make the bars a couple of days before serving, don't dress them with the berries. Complete the bars through step 7. When cooled, cover with plastic wrap and store in the refrigerator until the day they are to be served, then add the berries.*

Tropical Macadamia Bars

* *

Hawaii's answer to the dream bar—that traditional shortbread-based bar topped with a gooey coconut mixture that's found in every classic American dessert book. This one is chock-full of toasted macadamias as well as coconut, and it's accented with rum.

MAKES 16 BARS

1   Place a rack in the center of the oven and preheat to 350°F. Lightly grease an 8-inch square baking pan with vegetable oil or butter, or line the bottom with parchment paper.

2   Make the base: Place the flour and brown sugar in a food processor and process to blend for 5 seconds. Add the butter and process until the dough comes together, 20 to 30 seconds.

3   Pat the dough gently and evenly over the bottom of the prepared pan. Bake until golden around the edges, 20 to 25 minutes.

4   Meanwhile, make the topping: Using a whisk, beat the brown sugar, corn syrup, vanilla, rum, melted butter, eggs, flour, baking powder, and salt in a medium-size bowl until blended. Stir in the nuts and coconut with a rubber spatula.

5   Once baked, spread the topping evenly over the base. Return to the oven and bake until the top is golden and set, about 20 minutes. Let cool completely in the pan on a rack before cutting into pieces with a sharp, thin knife.

NOTE: *Leave the bars in the pan at room temperature, covered with plastic wrap, for up to 2 days, or layer the bars in an airtight container, with plastic wrap, parchment paper, or waxed paper between the layers, and store in the refrigerator for up to 1 week or in the freezer for up to 2 weeks. Bring to room temperature before eating.*

INGREDIENTS

Vegetable oil or butter for greasing the pan (optional)

Base

1 cup all-purpose flour

½ cup plus 1 tablespoon (lightly packed) light brown sugar

8 tablespoons (1 stick) unsalted butter, at room temperature

Topping

¾ cup plus 2 tablespoons (lightly packed) light brown sugar

¼ cup light corn syrup

1½ teaspoons pure vanilla extract

2 tablespoons rum

3 tablespoons unsalted butter, melted

2 large eggs, at room temperature

3 tablespoons all-purpose flour

½ teaspoon baking powder

¼ teaspoon salt

1 cup macadamia nuts, toasted (see page 272) and coarsely chopped

½ cup plus 2 tablespoons shredded sweetened coconut

Walnut Dream Bars

* *

This is a bar that refuses to compromise. It's sweet, chewy, full of butter, nuts, and coconut, and it rapidly attained cult status among Rosie's customers. Be forewarned, though: A small bite goes a long way.

MAKES 16 BARS

INGREDIENTS

Vegetable oil or butter for greasing the pan (optional)

Base

1 cup all-purpose flour

½ cup plus 1 tablespoon (lightly packed) light brown sugar

8 tablespoons (1 stick) unsalted butter, at room temperature, cut into 8 pieces

Topping

1 cup (lightly packed) light brown sugar

¼ cup plus 3 tablespoons dark corn syrup

2 teaspoons pure vanilla extract

2 tablespoons unsalted butter, melted

1½ tablespoons all-purpose flour

2 large eggs, at room temperature

1 cup coarsely chopped walnuts

½ cup shredded sweetened coconut

1   Place a rack in the center of the oven and preheat to 350°F. Lightly grease an 11 × 7-inch baking pan with vegetable oil or butter, or line the bottom with parchment paper.

2   Make the base: Place the flour and sugar in a food processor and process to blend for several seconds. Add the butter and process until the dough comes together, 20 to 30 seconds.

3   Pat the dough gently and evenly over the bottom of the prepared pan. Bake the base until golden around the edges, 10 to 12 minutes. Place the base in the refrigerator for 15 minutes to cool completely. Leave the oven on.

4   Meanwhile, make the topping: Whisk the sugar, corn syrup, vanilla, butter, flour, and eggs together in a medium-size bowl until blended. Stir in the walnuts and coconut with a rubber spatula.

5   Spread the topping evenly over the base. Return to the oven and bake until the top is golden and set, about 25 minutes. Let cool completely in the pan on a rack before cutting into pieces.

NOTE: *Leave the bars in the pan at room temperature, covered with plastic wrap, for up to 2 days, or layer them in an airtight container with plastic wrap, parchment paper, or waxed paper between the layers, and store in the refrigerator for up to 1 week or in the freezer for up to 2 weeks. Bring them to room temperature before eating.*

Pecan Bars

* *

I f you like pecan pie, you'll love this portable version: a crunchy, buttery crust with a gooey nut topping.

MAKES 16 BARS

1   Place a rack in the center of the oven and preheat to 350°F. Lightly grease a 9-inch square pan with vegetable oil or butter, or line the bottom with parchment paper.

2   Make the base: Place the flour and confectioners' sugar in a food processor and process to blend for several seconds. Add the butter and process until the dough comes together, 20 to 30 seconds.

3   Pat the dough gently and evenly over the bottom and ½ inch up the sides of the prepared pan. Pour the egg white over the dough and tip the pan from side to side to spread the white over the surface to glaze the dough. Pour off the excess.

4   Bake the base until lightly golden, about 30 minutes. Place the base in the refrigerator for 15 minutes to cool completely. Leave the oven on.

5   Meanwhile, make the topping: Gently whisk together both sugars, the corn syrup, eggs, vanilla, and salt in a medium-size bowl until blended. Stir in the melted butter, then the nuts.

6   Pour the topping evenly over the base. Return the pan to the oven and bake until the topping is set and forms a crust, about 50 minutes.

7   Let cool in the pan on a rack for 15 minutes, then run a sharp knife around the sides of the pan. Let cool completely before cutting into pieces. A cleaver or very strong knife works best.

NOTE: *Leave the bars in the pan at room temperature, covered with plastic wrap, for up to 2 days, or layer them in an airtight container with plastic wrap, parchment paper, or waxed paper between the layers, and store in the refrigerator for up to 1 week or in the freezer for up to 2 weeks. Bring them to room temperature before eating.*

INGREDIENTS

Vegetable oil or butter for greasing the pan (optional)

Base

1¼ cups all-purpose flour

½ cup plus 2 tablespoons confectioners' sugar

10 tablespoons (1¼ sticks) unsalted butter, at room temperature, cut into 10 pieces

1 large egg white

Topping

½ cup (lightly packed) light brown sugar

½ cup granulated sugar

10 tablespoons dark corn syrup

2 large eggs, at room temperature

¼ teaspoon pure vanilla extract

Pinch of salt

3 tablespoons unsalted butter, melted

1½ cups chopped pecans

Caramel Pecan Bars

* *

I *was always crazy about those little Turtle candies that came in pink-and-white-striped bags, so I decided to capture their spirit in a bar. A layer of shortbread is topped with a chewy caramel that's packed with pecans, and bittersweet chocolate is drizzled over the whole thing. You'll need a good candy thermometer to determine when the caramel is done, but otherwise the method is straightforward. They're best if you keep them refrigerated until an hour before eating.*

MAKES 16 BARS

INGREDIENTS

Vegetable oil or butter for greasing the pan (optional)

Base

1 cup all-purpose flour

½ cup granulated sugar

8 tablespoons (1 stick) unsalted butter, cold, cut into 8 pieces

1¼ cups pecans, very coarsely chopped

Caramel

¾ cup plus 2 tablespoons heavy (whipping) cream

⅔ cup light corn syrup

⅔ cup (lightly packed) light brown sugar

6 tablespoons granulated sugar

5½ tablespoons (⅓ cup) unsalted butter

¼ teaspoon salt

1¼ teaspoons pure vanilla extract

Glaze

1 ounce bittersweet chocolate

1 teaspoon vegetable oil

1   Place a rack in the center of the oven and preheat to 350°F. Lightly grease an 8-inch square baking pan with vegetable oil or butter, or line the bottom with parchment paper.

2   Make the base: Place the flour and sugar in a food processor and process to blend for 5 seconds. Scatter the butter over the flour mixture and process until the dough comes together, 20 to 30 seconds.

3   Pat the dough gently and evenly over the bottom of the prepared pan. Bake until golden, 25 to 30 minutes. Place the pan in the refrigerator for 15 minutes to cool completely.

4   Sprinkle the nuts evenly over the base and set aside at room temperature.

5   Make the caramel: Place the cream, corn syrup, both sugars, butter, and salt in a heavy 2½- to 3-quart saucepan fitted with a tight lid. Cook over medium heat without stirring for exactly 5 minutes.

6   Uncover the saucepan, reduce the heat to medium-low, clip a candy thermometer to the side of the pan (but not touching the bottom), and continue to cook, stirring very frequently, until the thermometer reads 238°F to 240°F, about 30 minutes.

7   Remove the pan from the heat and let the mixture sit for 2 minutes. Then stir in the vanilla.

8   Pour the caramel over the base and let sit at room temperature until set, about 3 hours.

9   After the caramel has set, make the glaze: Melt the chocolate in the top of a double boiler placed over simmering water. Remove the top pan from the bottom pan and vigorously stir in the vegetable oil with a small whisk. Drizzle this mixture over the caramel in whatever pattern strikes your fancy. Chill in the refrigerator for no more than 15 minutes, then let sit at room temperature for 1 hour to set. Cut into pieces with a sharp, thin knife.

NOTE: *Store the bars in the pan in the refrigerator, covered with plastic wrap, for up to 1 week. To freeze, cut and remove the bars from the pan, and layer them in an airtight container with plastic wrap, parchment paper, or waxed paper between the layers, and store for up to 2 weeks. Bring the bars to room temperature before eating.*

Pies and Fruit Desserts and Puddings

4

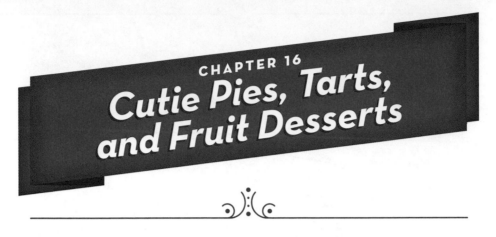

CHAPTER 16

Cutie Pies, Tarts, and Fruit Desserts

You can put nearly anything in a pie or tart. I think that's one of the reasons they're tied to the seasons more than other desserts. Some pie ingredients are good only at certain times of the year, and our bodies and palates seem to have atavistic cravings for different tastes, textures, and densities depending on the weather. So we eat dried fruit, nut, or chocolate pies with solid winter meals; rhubarb, strawberry, or chiffon pies when spring brings the first fruits; berry, peach, or cream pies as summer treats; and all the largesse of the harvest—apple and pumpkin pies—in the fall.

FEAR OF FLAKING

My friend Martha likes to say she's going to write an Anxiety Cookbook that chronicles all the things that can go wrong with a recipe. None of those soothing or rah-rah cookbooks for her; she doesn't trust them. Frankly, I don't think she'll ever get around to it (the prospect makes her too anxious), but if she does I intend to contribute a chapter about the affliction that keeps perfectly capable cooks from approaching the simplest pie. I call it "crustophobia," and I'm convinced that one day someone will discover an obscure monograph of Freud's entitled something like "Flake and Taboo" or "Civilization and Its Dishcontents."

I'm an expert on this because I'm a former sufferer, having spent years trying to make the entirely beautiful pie crust. Then, dear reader, I made two discoveries that changed my pie-baking career: First, I began using a food processor, and second, I came to understand that there's no such thing as an ugly pie crust—imperfections are what gives pies distinction. At that point, I relaxed, and pie crust became, well, as easy as pie.

THE END-OF-ANXIETY PIE CRUSTS

The recipes in this book use the following kinds of crusts, which are reliable and easy to prepare when you follow my step-by-step methods:

1. Basic Pie Crust I made with flour, butter, water, and sometimes sugar (Basic Pie Crust 2)
2. Basic Tart Crust or Pâte Sucrée made with flour, butter, eggs, sugar, and sometimes water or milk
3. Basic Shortbread Crust made with flour, butter, and sugar only (no liquid or eggs)
4. Crumb Crust (the easiest) made with butter, crushed cookies, and sometimes nuts, grated chocolate, coconut, and so on.

BUTTER VS. SHORTENING

Although many people think that crusts made with shortening are flakier, I think this is true only when they're just-baked. As soon as a shortening crust cools and sits for a while, it loses its crispness and it always lacks the extraordinary flavor of butter. If butter crusts are made correctly, they are wonderfully flaky and crisp and rich in taste.

BASIC PIE AND PASTRY CRUSTS

These crusts can be mixed in a food processor or by hand. I find the machine method reliable and easy, so I've put it first. But some people believe that when you make a crust by hand, you get a greater feel for the texture of the dough, so you may prefer that technique. For both methods, make sure that your butter is cold when you start.

MIXING WITH A FOOD PROCESSOR

1. Place the dry ingredients (such as flour, salt, and sugar) in a food processor and process for 20 seconds.
2. Mix all liquid ingredients (such as water and egg) together in a small cup and add an ice cube to chill them.
3. Cut the butter into 8 tablespoons per stick and distribute them evenly on top of the dry ingredients. Then process for 15 to 20 seconds or until the mixture resembles coarse meal.
4. Remove the ice cube from the liquid and add the liquid in a steady stream to the butter mixture while the food processor is running. Process just until it is distributed throughout the dough and the dough holds together. To test, pinch a piece the size of a marble between your thumb and forefinger; if it doesn't stick together, add more liquid.

MIXING BY HAND

1. Sift the dry ingredients into a large mixing bowl or place them directly in the bowl and stir them around with a whisk.

2. Mix all liquid ingredients together in a small cup and add an ice cube.

3. Cut the butter into 8 tablespoons per stick and distribute them evenly over the dry ingredients. Use both thumbs and forefingers to rub the butter into the flour mixture or cut it in with a pastry cutter. Continue until the mixture resembles coarse meal.

4. Remove the ice cube from the liquid and sprinkle the liquid over the dry ingredients while tossing them with a fork to distribute the moisture. When the dough can be gathered into a ball, it's ready for the next step.

ROLLING THE DOUGH

1. When a dough is the right consistency, gather it into a mass with your hands and place it on a lightly floured surface. Knead it several times with the heel of your palm so that it holds together.

2. Form the dough into a chubby disk (if the recipe requires a top crust also, make two disks). Wrap each disk in plastic wrap and chill it for 1 hour. Doughs that contain sugar, such as Basic Pie Crust 2, often can be rolled out right away.

3. When the dough is chilled, place it between two large (18 to 20 inches long)

PROBLEMS WITH PIE DOUGH

The pie crust recipes in this book are quite elastic and there really shouldn't be any problems with them if you follow the directions carefully. But if for some reason the dough cracks when being rolled, lift up the top sheet of plastic and pinch the dough together with your fingers, or cut off a little strip from another section and place it over the crack. Place the plastic wrap back over the dough and roll right over the crack.

If you should pull up a chunk of dough when you remove the plastic wrap, leaving a hole, scrape the dough off the wrap, place it on the hole, and use your fingers to pinch it back in place. Then cover the dough with a fresh piece of plastic wrap and roll over the hole. This can happen when the dough gets too warm, so it's best to then slide your dough onto a plate or platter and refrigerate it for 15 to 20 minutes before proceeding.

pieces of plastic wrap or waxed paper, or two plastic produce bags (the kind you get at any supermarket) that have been cut to make a longer sheet for rolling, and roll it out with a rolling pin. (It may be necessary to overlap pieces of plastic wrap or waxed paper to make it large enough.)

4. Roll evenly, always beginning each roll at the center. Roll the pin outward, each time in a different direction. Lift the rolling pin after each roll. Don't roll the pin back and forth.

5. After you've rolled once in each direction (north, south, east, west), peel the top

Form the dough into
a chubby disk.

Roll out the dough between
2 pieces of plastic wrap.

Make sure the pie crust still has plastic
between your hand and the crust.

piece of plastic wrap off the dough, then place it back. Flip the dough over and do the same thing on the second side. This keeps the dough from sticking to the wrap, giving it more room to expand.

6. Continue to roll out the dough, peeling off the plastic and putting it back again every four rolls until the dough is ⅛ inch thick and at least 2 inches larger than your pie pan. Don't expect a perfect round or beautiful edges. They're neither likely nor necessary.

FITTING THE BOTTOM PIE SHELL INTO THE PAN

1. Remove the top piece of plastic. Place your hand in the center of the side that still has the plastic and flip the dough over into the pie pan, making sure it is centered in the pan.

2. Press the crust gently into the pan and smooth it with your fingers, taking special care around the bottom edge of the pan

and the flutes if the pan has them. Do not stretch the dough by hand, because stretched dough shrinks during baking. When the crust is patted into place, peel off the remaining piece of plastic wrap.

3. **FOR A SINGLE-CRUST PIE:** Trim the excess dough and rough edges evenly with scissors and finish the edge decoratively.

   FOR A DOUBLE-CRUST PIE: Trim the bottom crust so that it just overlaps the edge of the pan by about ¼ inch; you can make a finished edge when you cover the pie with the top crust (see Decorative Edges for Pies and Tarts on page 334).

   FOR A TART SHELL: Roll a rolling pin across the top of the pan to cut off any excess dough. You can press some of the extra into the sides of the tart shell to make them thicker and stronger.

4. Refrigerate all pie and tart shells for at least 30 minutes if they are to be prebaked.

UPPER CRUSTS

1. Roll out the top crust in the same way you roll out the bottom one, between two pieces of plastic wrap or waxed paper, until it is ⅛ inch thick and 2 inches larger than your pie pan.

2. Peel off the top piece of plastic wrap and flip the dough onto the pie filling. Peel off the second piece of plastic.

3. Trim the edge of the dough ¾ inch larger than the bottom crust and tuck the edge of the top crust under the edge of the bottom crust all around. Make several little slits in the top crust with the point of a sharp knife so that steam can escape while the pie bakes.

TO PREBAKE BASIC PIE CRUSTS 1 AND 2

If you have two metal or disposable aluminum pie pans of the same size, I suggest the following simple method. It is a good technique for savory crusts, such as Basic Pie Crust 1, which contains no sugar, because it prevents the dough from shrinking, leaving you with a nice tall crust.

STORING PIES

You can keep any leftover fruit pie overnight under a glass dome or covered with plastic wrap. Chiffon, mousse, custard, and cream pies must all be stored in the refrigerator, but it's best to take them out of the fridge an hour before you serve them so that the flavor isn't blunted by the cold.

To keep leftover pieces of these delicate pies looking fresh, "bubble" them with plastic wrap: Insert toothpicks around the edge of the pie and a few in the center, then lower a generous piece of plastic wrap over the toothpicks and tuck it carefully under the edge of the pie dish. This bubble keeps the pie from drying out or changing color and its top from getting mushed.

Fit the dough in the pan.

Cover the dough with parchment paper and place a second pan into the first one.

Flip the pans to bake the crust.

1. Carefully fit the pie dough into the pan and refrigerate it for at least 30 minutes.

2. Once chilled, cover the dough with a piece of parchment, stack the second pan into the first, and place all on a baking sheet.

3. Flip both pans and bake the crust upside down between the two pans in a preheated 400°F oven for about 15 minutes.

4. Carefully remove the top pan but leave the crust, and continue baking it until the bottom is golden, about 5 minutes more. Take it out of the oven and replace the top pan.

5. Turn the whole thing right side up and carefully remove the empty top pan and the parchment paper.

Note: Lightly prebaking the crust: If you're going to fill this crust and bake it again, cut the step 3 baking time to 12 minutes. In step 4, stop when the crust is very lightly golden, after about 3 minutes.

PREBAKING A PIE OR TART CRUST THAT CONTAINS SUGAR

1. Fit the pie dough into a pan and refrigerate it for at least 30 minutes.

2. Remove the pie shell from the refrigerator and prick the bottom and sides in several places with a fork.

3. Line the dough with parchment paper, or aluminum foil that has been greased on the underside. Fill it with rice, beans, or pie weights (little metal nuggets available at kitchen stores).

4. Bake the crust in a preheated 400°F oven until the edge is golden and the sides seem firm enough to support themselves, about 15 minutes.

5. Remove the weights and parchment very carefully so as not to disturb the crust, and continue to bake it until it is golden brown on the inside bottom, about 5 minutes (or if the crust is to be baked a second time, 2 to 3 minutes). If the crust puffs during baking, prick it with a fork to let the steam escape.

6. Let the crust cool completely before filling. If you bake the crust again after it is filled, cover the rim with foil before you put it in the oven, to keep it from burning.

SHORTBREAD TART CRUST

Since this is an eggless, liquidless crust, you don't have to worry about overmixing. This means you can make it in a food processor or with an electric mixer without anxiety.

USING AN ELECTRIC MIXER

1. Have the butter at room temperature.

2. Cream the butter and sugar (and vanilla) with the mixer at medium to medium-high speed until light and fluffy, about 1½ minutes.

3. Add the dry ingredients with the mixer at low speed, then beat at medium speed until the dough becomes light and fluffy again. The time will vary a lot depending on the proportions of ingredients but is usually about 2 minutes.

4. Gather the dough into a ball with your hands.

5. Dip your fingertips in flour so that the dough doesn't stick to them, and pat the dough gently into a pie pan. Glaze with egg white if the base will be covered by a wet filling after prebaking.

6. Prebake the crust at 300°F without using pie weights until it is a rich golden color, 40 to 45 minutes. Shortbread rises more than regular flaky pie dough and it needs to cook slowly to create a crunchy texture and a buttery flavor.

7. Let the crust cool before adding the filling.

USING A FOOD PROCESSOR

1. Place the dry ingredients in a food processor and process for 20 seconds.

2. Add the butter (cold or at room temperature) and process until the dough comes together (1½ to 2 minutes for cold butter, 30 to 40 seconds for butter at room temperature). Then follow steps 4 through 7 of the electric mixer method.

TO MAKE AND PREBAKE CRUMB CRUSTS

1. Put the crumbs, sugar, grated chocolate, nuts, or whatever the recipe calls for in a medium-size bowl and stir them together with a wooden spoon.

2. Melt the butter and pour it into the bowl with the crumbs. Toss the mixture with two forks or your fingers until the butter is fully distributed.

3. Pat the crumbs firmly over the bottom and up the sides of a pie pan to form a crust.

4. Bake it in a preheated 375°F oven until it is crisp and golden, about 10 minutes.

5. Let the crust cool completely before filling it so that it stays crunchy. And have the filling cool, too: Pouring hot fillings into crumb crusts can easily penetrate the crust and make it soggy.

DECORATIVE EDGES FOR PIES AND TARTS

A pretty edge is a must for a well-turned-out pie or tart. As with anything to do with pastry, once you get it, it's as easy as—well, you know.

FORKED EDGE

Fold the overhanging dough under the crust at the rim of the pan to make a thick edge. Press the back of a fork into it all around, making a pattern with the tines. Dip the fork in flour before you use it and dip it again whenever it begins to stick.

Making a forked edge.

FLUTED EDGE

Fold the overhanging dough under the crust at the rim of the pan to make a thick edge. Make flutes (tiny waves around the edge of the crust) with a gentle finger-pinching motion: With the thumb and index finger of one hand, pinch the outer edge of the crust inward while, at the same time, the index finger of the other hand pushes the outer edge of the crust inward between the other two fingers. For a fancier version, dip a fork in flour and press with its back instead of your index finger.

Pinching a fluted edge.

ROPE EDGE

Fold the overhanging edge of the crust under the rim of the pan to make a thick edge. Pinch a small piece of the dough between your thumb and the first knuckle of your index finger, angling your hand slightly. Repeat this pinching motion around the edge of the crust, putting your index finger in the depression your thumb has just made.

Use the overhanging dough to make a rope edge.

LATTICE TOP

1. Roll out the dough to about 9 inches wide and 2 inches longer than the diameter of your pie. The dough should never be thicker than ⅛ inch. With a sharp knife, cut about 10 strips lengthwise ¾ inch wide.

2. Lay half of the strips across the top of the pie or tart, spacing them equally and parallel to each other.

3. To weave the lattice, start at an outer edge and fold every other strip halfway back on itself. Lay one of the remaining strips across those on the pie that aren't folded back. Bring the folded strips back down over the new strip. Now fold back the strips that weren't originally folded back. Add a second strip parallel to the first and continue weaving until half the pie is done. Repeat this process on the other side of the pie.

4. Trim any overhang from the strips. Brush the underside of the strips with milk at the point where they meet the bottom crust and press down gently with your finger to make sure they adhere.

Weaving a lattice top.

FRUIT PIES

Conquering crust is half the battle, but like books and their covers, what you put inside a pie matters, too. I'm a longtime fan of fresh fruit pies and tarts and classic desserts like brown Bettys. Each fruit has its own characteristics, though, so you'll need to take a few variables into consideration when you're shopping and baking.

FRUIT FILLINGS

I've found that because most fruit is naturally sweet, it's unnecessary to add a lot of sugar. Then, too, tart fruit provides a contrast to a sweet crumb topping or pastry crust. Lemon juice, lemon zest, and cinnamon work well to enhance a fruit's flavor, and I sometimes mix orange and lemon juices for the liquid to pour over the fruit. But in all pies and tarts, it's important to let the taste of the fruit come through, so whatever I add, I add it sparingly.

APPLES: The best apple for baking is a firm apple because it holds its shape as it cooks. In the fall when apples are at their best, I recommend Cortlands or Granny Smiths; you can put a combination of these together in a pie. After apple season, though, most of the Cortlands you find have been stored and become soft, so I suggest baking with Granny Smiths for the rest of the year. Keep in mind that Granny Smith is a tart apple and may require more sugar than the Cortlands.

I add apple cider or orange juice as well as lemon juice to the apples because, as the liquid boils, it cooks the apples more evenly. The kind of apple you use dictates how much liquid you need. Obviously, the crisper the apple, the more liquid required. For instance, if a pie made exclusively with Granny Smiths requires ¼ cup of liquid, one made with juicier apples might need only a tablespoon or two or none at all. The recipes in this chapter specify how much liquid to add, but you may need to experiment to find the right amount for the apples available to you. Keep in mind that soft apples and too much liquid will make your pie a mushy one.

PEACHES, PEARS, PLUMS, NECTARINES, AND OTHER SOFT FRUITS: Soft fruits appear in the stores at various stages of ripeness; so various, in fact, that it's hard to make any generalizations about them. When they're very ripe, they need no additional juice, other than fresh lemon juice for flavor, but with less ripe fruit, you can add any juice to the filling to get the proper consistency.

For the times when you can't find soft fruit that's ripe, rather than turn to the frozen food section for a pie, try peeling and slicing a pie's worth (6 to 8 cups) of the too-hard fruit into ½-inch-thick slices and simmering them with ½ cup of orange or apple juice in a covered saucepan. Toss the slices occasionally just until they lose their hardness, 3 to 5 minutes, then use the fruit and the juice as the recipe requires.

THICKENING: I thicken my fruit fillings with cornstarch to produce a transparent and slightly viscous juice. The juicier the fruit, the more cornstarch you need, but too little is always better than too much. As a rule of thumb, use 1½ tablespoons cornstarch for every 6 cups fruit.

BAKING TEMPERATURES FOR FRUIT PIES

In general, preheat the oven to 425°F at

least 20 minutes before you put your pie in. Bake the pie in the center of the oven for 15 minutes at this temperature. Reduce the heat to 375°F and bake it for 45 to 60 minutes (if the top crust is getting too dark, cover it loosely with a piece of aluminum foil while it bakes) until the fruit starts to bubble. You'll be able to tell when this bubbling happens with any kind of top because the juice will ooze out of the crumb topping or through the slits of a top crust. I put a baking sheet on the bottom rack of the oven or directly under the pie to catch drips, which also works as a test for doneness: When the drips look thick, the pie is done or close to it. Let your pies cool on a rack and serve them when they are still warm.

MOUSSE-, CUSTARD-, AND CHIFFON-FILLED PIES

With the exception of the Vanilla Custard Tart, these fillings are always placed in fully baked pie or tart shells. For stand-alone custards and mousses, see the Puddings and Custards chapter (page 385).

Basic Pie Crust 1

* *

A classic recipe, flaky and buttery. Remember that pastry, especially one made from butter, is easier to prepare if the kitchen is cool rather than warm.

MAKES ONE OR TWO 9- OR 10-INCH CRUSTS

INGREDIENTS

Single Crust
  (9-inch, standard or deep dish crust)

1½ cups all-purpose flour

¼ teaspoon salt

9 tablespoons (1 stick plus 1 tablespoon) unsalted butter, cold, cut into 9 pieces

3 tablespoons ice water

Double Crust
  (two 9-inch, standard or deep dish crusts)

2½ cups all-purpose flour

½ teaspoon salt

13½ tablespoons (1 stick plus 5½ tablespoons) unsalted butter, cold, cut into 14 pieces

4½ tablespoons ice water

1 Place the flour and salt in a food processor and process to blend for 20 seconds. (Or whisk them together by hand in a large mixing bowl.)

2 Distribute the butter evenly over the flour and process until the mixture resembles coarse meal, 15 to 20 seconds. (Or rub the butter into the flour with your fingertips or cut it in with a pastry blender.)

3 With the food processor running, pour the ice water in a steady stream through the feed tube and process just until the dough comes together. (Or sprinkle the water over the mixture while tossing with a fork.)

4 Knead the dough for several turns on a lightly floured surface to bring it together.

5 Shape the dough into a thick disk (or 2 disks for a double crust), wrap in plastic (if making a double crust, wrap each disk individually), and refrigerate at least 1 hour.

6 Following the instructions for "Rolling the Dough" on page 330, roll the chilled dough for the bottom crust out to a circle 2 inches bigger than the size of the pie pan. (Keep the second disk in the refrigerator until you're ready to roll it out.)

7 Fit the rolled dough into a 9-inch pie pan and trim the edges (see page 334 for decorative edges). Keep the crust in the refrigerator until ready to fill. If prebaking the crust (see page 332), refrigerate it for at least 30 minutes before baking.

Basic Pie Crust 2

* *

This crust is slightly sweeter than Basic Pie Crust 1 and has a texture that is somewhat more crunchy than flaky.

MAKES ONE OR TWO 9- OR 10-INCH CRUSTS

1 Place the flour and sugar in a food processor and process to blend for 20 seconds. (Or whisk them together by hand in a large mixing bowl.)

2 Distribute the butter evenly over the flour and process until the mixture resembles coarse meal, 15 to 20 seconds. (Or rub the butter into the flour with your fingertips or cut it in with a pastry blender.)

3 With the food processor running, pour the ice water in a steady stream through the feed tube and process just until the dough comes together. (Or sprinkle the water over the mixture while tossing with a fork.)

4 Knead the dough for several turns on a lightly floured surface to bring it together.

5 Shape the dough into a thick disk (or 2 disks for a double crust), wrap in plastic (if making a double crust, wrap each disk individually), and refrigerate at least 1 hour.

6 Following the instructions for "Rolling the Dough" on page 330, roll the chilled dough for the bottom crust out to a circle 2 inches bigger than the size of the pie pan. (Keep the second disk in the refrigerator until you're ready to roll it out.)

7 Fit the rolled dough into a 9-inch pie pan and trim the edges (see page 334 for decorative edges). Keep the crust in the refrigerator until ready to fill. If prebaking the crust (see page 332), refrigerate it for at least 30 minutes before baking.

INGREDIENTS

Single Crust
(9-inch, standard or deep dish crust)

1½ cups all-purpose flour

2 tablespoons sugar

12 tablespoons (1½ sticks) unsalted butter, cold, cut into 12 pieces

2 tablespoons ice water

Double Crust
(two 9- or 10-inch, standard or deep dish crusts)

2¼ cups all-purpose flour

3 tablespoons sugar

1 cup plus 2 tablespoons (2¼ sticks) unsalted butter, cold, cut into 18 pieces

3 tablespoons ice water

Basic Tart Crust

* *

T*his is a sturdy and tasty crust that is dependable and easy to make.*

MAKES ONE OR TWO 9- OR 10-INCH TART CRUSTS

INGREDIENTS

Single Crust
  (9- or 10-inch tart crust)

1 cup all-purpose flour

2½ tablespoons sugar

⅛ teaspoon salt

6 tablespoons (¾ stick)
  unsalted butter, cold,
  cut into 6 pieces

1 tablespoon cold water

1 large egg yolk

Double Crust
  (two 9- or 10-inch tart crusts)

2 cups all-purpose flour

5 tablespoons sugar

¼ teaspoon salt

12 tablespoons (1½ sticks)
  unsalted butter, cold,
  cut into 12 pieces

2 tablespoons cold water

2 large egg yolks

1 Place the flour, sugar, and salt in a food processor and process to blend for 20 seconds. (Or whisk them together by hand in a large mixing bowl.)

2 Distribute the butter evenly over the flour and process until the mixture resembles coarse meal, 15 to 20 seconds. (Or rub the butter into the flour with your fingertips or cut it in with a pastry blender.)

3 Whisk together the cold water and egg yolk. With the food processor running, pour the egg mixture in a steady stream through the feed tube and process just until the dough comes together, 20 to 30 seconds. (Or sprinkle the egg mixture over the flour mixture while tossing with a fork.)

4 Knead the dough for several turns on a lightly floured surface to bring it together.

5 Shape the dough into a thick disk (or 2 disks for a double crust), wrap in plastic (if making a double crust, wrap each disk individually), and refrigerate or roll it out right away.

6 Following the instructions for "Rolling the Dough" on page 330, roll the dough out to a circle 2 inches bigger than the size of the tart pan. (Keep the second disk in the refrigerator until you're ready to roll it out.)

7 Fit the rolled dough into a 9- or 10-inch tart pan and trim the edge by rolling over the top of the pan with a rolling pin. Keep the crust in the refrigerator until ready to fill. If prebaking the crust (see page 332), refrigerate it for at least 30 minutes before baking.

Shortbread Tart Crust

* *

A wonderfully crunchy crust with a buttery flavor. I use it for the Chocolate Berry Tart (page 367). It bakes at a lower temperature so that its texture is crisp throughout.

MAKES ONE OR TWO 9- OR 10-INCH TART CRUSTS

1 Cream the butter, sugar, and vanilla in a medium-size mixing bowl with an electric mixer on medium-high speed until light and fluffy, about 1½ minutes.

2 With the processor on low speed, add the flour, then increase the speed to medium and beat until the mixture is light and fluffy again, about 2 minutes.

3 Gather the dough into a ball (or 2 balls if making enough for 2 tarts). With floured fingertips, press the dough gently over the bottom and up the sides of one or two 9- or 10-inch tart pans or pie pans.

4 Place a rack in the center of the oven and preheat to 350°F. Bake until a rich, golden color, 40 to 45 minutes.

5 Let the crust(s) cool completely on a rack before filling.

INGREDIENTS

*Single Crust
(9- or 10-inch tart crust)*

9½ tablespoons (1 stick plus 1½ tablespoons) unsalted butter, at room temperature

5 tablespoons confectioners' sugar

1 teaspoon pure vanilla extract

1 cup plus 3 tablespoons all-purpose flour

*Double Crust
(two 9- or 10-inch tart crusts)*

2 sticks (8 ounces) unsalted butter, at room temperature

½ cup confectioners' sugar

1½ teaspoons pure vanilla extract

2 cups all-purpose flour

Cookie Crumb Crust

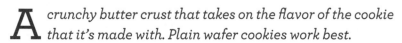

A crunchy butter crust that takes on the flavor of the cookie that it's made with. Plain wafer cookies work best.

MAKES ONE 9- OR 10-INCH CRUST

INGREDIENTS

1¼ cups cookie crumbs from any plain crunchy cookie, such as vanilla wafers, chocolate wafers, graham crackers, or gingersnaps

3 tablespoons sugar

6 tablespoons (¾ stick) unsalted butter, melted

1 Stir the cookie crumbs and sugar together in a small bowl. Add the melted butter and toss with two forks or your fingers until the butter is evenly distributed.

2 Pat the crumbs firmly over the bottom and up the sides of a 9- or 10-inch pie plate.

3 Place a rack in the center of the oven and preheat to 375°F. Bake until the crust is crisp and golden, 10 minutes.

4 Let the crust cool completely on a rack before filling.

All-American Apple Pie

* *

The apple: wedding gift for the Greek gods, instrument of Sir Isaac Newton's enlightenment, proof of William Tell's loyalty, fertility symbol in medieval times, talisman against homesickness for the American colonists, raison d'être for Johnny Appleseed, one-time gift of choice for a favorite grade-school teacher, and last, but not least, an apple a day keeps the doctor away. It's stood for practically everything at one time or another. Try this version of the classic apple pie—not too sweet, but pleasantly spicy, and contained in a buttery crust.

MAKES 8 TO 12 SERVINGS

1 Roll out both crusts. Place 1 crust in a pie pan. Refrigerate both the top and bottom crusts.

2 Place a rack in the center of the oven and a baking sheet on the bottom rack, and preheat to 425°F.

3 Place the apple slices in a large bowl with the sugar, cinnamon, nutmeg, salt, apple cider, lemon juice, and cornstarch. Toss them together with your hands to coat the apples evenly.

4 Scoop the apples into the bottom crust and dot the mixture with small pieces of the butter.

5 Cover the apples with the top crust. Seal and trim the edge; make a decorative edge. Cut 3 to 4 slits in the top crust. Using a pastry brush, brush the top with the egg glaze.

6 Bake the pie for 15 minutes. Reduce the temperature to 350°F and continue baking until the top of the pie is golden and the filling is bubbling, about 1 hour 10 minutes longer. If the top crust is getting too dark, cover it with a piece of aluminum foil and continue to bake.

7 Let the pie cool on a rack. Serve with ice cream, if desired.

INGREDIENTS

Double-crust Basic Pie Crust 1 or 2 (page 338 or 339)

8 cups peeled Granny Smith apple slices (⅜ inch thick; 6 to 8 apples)

¾ cup sugar

1 teaspoon ground cinnamon

¼ teaspoon ground nutmeg

¼ teaspoon salt

¼ cup apple cider, apple juice, or orange juice

2 tablespoons fresh lemon juice

1½ tablespoons cornstarch

1 tablespoon unsalted butter

1 large egg mixed with 2 tablespoons water or milk, for glazing

Ice cream, for serving (optional)

INGREDIENTS

Single-crust Basic Pie Crust 1 or 2
(page 338 or 339)

Filling

4 cups peeled Granny Smith
apple slices (¼ inch thick;
3 to 4 apples)

4 tablespoons (½ stick) unsalted
butter, melted

½ cup (lightly packed) light
brown sugar

1 teaspoon grated lemon zest

2 tablespoons fresh lemon juice

¼ cup golden raisins

1 tablespoon all-purpose flour

Sour Cream Topping

1¼ cups sour cream

2 large eggs, at room
temperature

½ cup granulated sugar

1 teaspoon pure vanilla extract

Sugar-Nut Topping

¾ cup chopped pecans

2 tablespoons unsalted butter,
melted

¼ cup (lightly packed) light
brown sugar

Sour Cream Apple Pie

* *

When you're in the mood for a variation on the
All-American Apple Pie, this one gilds the lily.
*Because of the extra richness created by the sour cream,
it's important that you use tart, crisp apples. I like Granny
Smith. I think of this as a harvest pie—with a little something
extra on the top.*

MAKES 8 TO 10 SERVINGS

1 Roll out the crust. Place
the pie crust in the pie pan and
refrigerate it until ready to use.

2 Place a rack in the center of
the oven and a baking sheet on
the bottom rack, and preheat to
375°F.

3 Prepare the filling: Toss the
apples with the melted butter in a
large bowl. Add the brown sugar,
lemon zest, lemon juice, raisins,
and flour and stir to coat the
apple slices.

4 Scoop the apples into the crust.

5 Bake the pie for 30 minutes.

6 Meanwhile, make the sour
cream topping: Whisk the sour
cream, eggs, granulated sugar,
and vanilla together in a medium-
size bowl.

7 After the pie has baked
for 30 minutes, pour the sour
cream topping over the apples.
Continue baking until the
topping is set, 30 to 35 minutes.

8 Meanwhile, make the sugar-
nut topping: Toss the pecans,
melted butter, and brown sugar
together in a small bowl with a
wooden spoon.

9 Crumble the nut topping
over the pie (it will not cover
the whole surface) and continue
baking until the topping bubbles,
about 10 minutes. Don't worry if
the sour cream topping rises up;
it will fall when you take it out of
the oven.

10 Let the pie cool on a rack
for an hour or two before serving.

Apple-Cranberry Tart

* *

The union of apples and cranberries produces a less-sweet filling, making this tart a nice ending to a heavy meal—Thanksgiving comes to mind. Unless you want to end up with an applesauce tart, you need to use crisp apples, such as Granny Smith. If you can't get hold of hard apples, adjust the recipe by simmering them for only a minute before adding the cranberries.

MAKES 10 TO 12 SERVINGS

1 Place a rack in the center of the oven and a baking sheet on the bottom rack, and preheat to 400°F.

2 Roll out the tart dough to 11 inches in diameter. Fit the bottom crust into a 9-inch tart pan and lightly prebake (see Note, page 333). Let cool. Leave the oven on.

3 In a medium-size saucepan, combine the apples, brown sugar, orange zest, and salt and toss to coat using a wooden spoon. Dissolve the cornstarch in the orange juice and add it to the apples. Cover the pan and simmer the apples over medium-low heat just until they begin to lose their crispness, about 3 minutes. Stir them once after 1½ minutes.

4 Stir the cranberries into the apples, cover the pan, and bring

the mixture to a simmer again. Cook just until the cranberries have softened slightly, but not so long that they pop open, about 2 minutes. Transfer the mixture to a bowl and refrigerate it while you prepare the topping.

5 Make the topping: Place the nuts, brown sugar, flour, oats, and cinnamon in a food processor and process for 5 seconds. (Or place them in a large mixing bowl and toss together with your hands or a large spoon.)

6 Transfer the mixture to a large mixing bowl (if not already in one). Add the melted butter and mix thoroughly with your hands or a large spoon.

7 Scoop the apple mixture into the tart shell and top with the nut-crumb mixture.

INGREDIENTS

Single-crust Basic Tart Crust (page 340)

3 cups peeled Granny Smith or Macoun apple chunks (¾ inch chunks; 3 to 4 apples)

½ cup (lightly packed) light brown sugar

1 tablespoon grated orange zest

¼ teaspoon salt

1 teaspoon cornstarch

⅓ cup fresh orange juice

2 cups fresh cranberries, rinsed and picked clean of stems

Topping

½ cup chopped walnuts or pecans

½ cup plus 3 tablespoons (lightly packed) light brown sugar

¾ cup plus 2 tablespoons all-purpose flour

½ cup quick-cooking oats

½ teaspoon ground cinnamon

8 tablespoons (1 stick) unsalted butter, melted

345

8   Bake the tart until the topping is a rich golden brown, 15 to 20 minutes. Drop a piece of aluminum foil lightly over the topping (do not mold or seal it) and continue baking the tart until the filling is bubbling, 25 to 30 minutes longer.

9   Let the tart cool on a rack for an hour or two before serving.

* *

Apple Pie for Passover

* *

INGREDIENTS

Crust

1 cup matzoh cake meal (*not* matzoh meal)

¼ cup granulated sugar

¼ cup light brown sugar

1 teaspoon ground cinnamon

¼ teaspoon salt

8 tablespoons (1 stick) unsalted butter, at room temperature, cut into 8 pieces

2 tablespoons ice water

½ egg yolk (see Note)

Filling

9 cups peeled Granny Smith apple slices (½ inch thick; about 8 apples)

¼ cup (lightly packed) light brown sugar

2 tablespoons potato starch

½ teaspoon salt

¼ cup apple juice or cider

3 tablespoons fresh lemon juice

Y ou will be amazed how absolutely delicious this pie made with matzoh cake meal is. My daughter, Maya, actually prefers it to regular apple pie and would be happy to eat it at any time during the year. Extra deelish when served warm. Make sure you buy matzoh cake meal, not regular matzoh meal.

MAKES 8 TO 10 SERVINGS

1   Have ready a 10-inch deep-dish pie pan.

2   Make the crust: Place the matzoh cake meal, both sugars, the cinnamon, and salt in a food processor and process to blend for 10 seconds.

3   Distribute the butter evenly over the flour mixture and pulse 12 times.

4   In a small bowl, whisk together the ice water and egg yolk. With the food processor running, pour the egg mixture in a steady stream through the feed tube and process just until evenly incorporated, several seconds.

5   Transfer the crust mixture to the pie pan and pat firmly and evenly over the bottom and up the sides. Place in the freezer while you prepare the filling.

6   Prepare the filling: Place the apple slices in a large bowl. Add the brown sugar, potato starch, salt, apple juice, and lemon juice. Toss them together with your hands to coat the apples evenly. Set aside.

7   Place a rack in the center of the oven and a baking sheet on the bottom rack, and preheat to 425°F.

8   Make the topping: Place the matzoh cake meal, potato starch, both sugars, the cinnamon, and salt in a food processor and process for several seconds to mix. Add the butter and pulse until it is incorporated and the topping comes together and forms clumps when squeezed in the hand, 1 to 1½ minutes. Set aside.

9   Pile the apple filling into the shell, then use your hands to press lightly down on the apples so they fill the pan more evenly.

10   Take the crumb topping in your hand and squeeze it so that the mixture forms generous clumps of different sizes as you distribute these evenly over the apples.

11   Place the pie on a baking sheet and lay a piece of aluminum foil loosely over the top of the pie.

12   Bake the pie for 30 minutes, then lower the oven to 375°F, remove the foil and continue baking until the pie juices are bubbling and begin to drip onto the baking sheet, and the apples in the center of the pie feel soft when poked with a tester, about 1 hour 15 minutes.

NOTE: *To get ½ yolk, crack an egg into your palm and let the egg white run through your fingers. Use a knife to gently cut through the center of the yolk, then slide the ½ yolk into a cup. (Save the other half to scramble into your kids' eggs the next morning.)*

Topping

¾ cup matzoh cake meal

¾ cup potato starch

¼ cup granulated sugar

¼ cup (lightly packed) light brown sugar

1 teaspoon ground cinnamon

¼ teaspoon salt

8 tablespoons (1 stick) unsalted butter, at room temperature, cut into 8 pieces

Apple Crostata

* *

As far as I am concerned the union of a buttery crust and baked fruit is just about as good as it gets. I love the rustic appearance of this dessert and the fact that it is baked in an iron skillet just makes it seem that much more earthy.

MAKES 10 TO 12 SERVINGS

INGREDIENTS

Crust

2 cups all-purpose flour

¼ cup sugar

½ teaspoon salt

2 sticks (8 ounces) unsalted butter, very cold, cut into 16 pieces

¼ cup ice water

Filling

5 cups peeled Granny Smith or Cortland (or a mix) apple chunks (½ inch chunks; 4 to 5 apples)

¼ cup golden raisins

3 tablespoons sugar

2 tablespoons fresh lemon juice

1 tablespoon cornstarch

Pinch of salt

Vegetable oil or butter for greasing the skillet

2 teaspoons cornmeal, for the pan

Vanilla ice cream or whipped cream, for serving

1   Make the crust: Place the flour, sugar, and salt in a food processor and process to blend for several seconds.

2   Distribute the butter evenly over the flour and pulse 25 times.

3   With the food processor running, pour the ice water in a steady stream through the feed tube and pulse 25 times. Then process just until the dough begins to come together, 10 seconds.

4   It will be easier to form this dough into a disk if you pour it into a plastic produce bag first and use the bag to help mold it. Once formed, refrigerate the dough in the bag for at least 1 hour.

5   Make the filling: Toss the apples and raisins together in a medium-size bowl. Add the sugar, lemon juice, cornstarch, and salt, and toss. Transfer the mixture to a medium-size saucepan. Cover,

bring to a boil, and simmer just long enough for the cornstarch to start thickening, 3 to 4 minutes. Transfer the fruit mixture to a bowl and refrigerate while you continue with the recipe.

6   Place a rack in the center of the oven and a baking sheet on the bottom rack, and preheat to 425°F. Grease a 9-inch cast-iron skillet with vegetable oil or butter and sprinkle the cornmeal over the bottom.

7   Roll out the dough between two pieces of plastic wrap to a circle approximately 15 inches in diameter. Peel off the top layer of plastic and flip the dough over onto the skillet, making sure it is centered in the skillet. Press down gently to mold the dough to the pan. Gently remove the remaining plastic wrap.

8   Place the fruit filling in the center of the dough. Gently fold the edges of the dough over the fruit, creating slightly overlapping folds as you rotate

the pan; there will be about a 4-inch opening left in the center, displaying the fruit filling.

9   Bake the crostata for 20 minutes. Lower the oven temperature to 375°F and bake until the crust is golden and the juices are bubbling, 15 to 20 minutes more.

10   Let the crostata cool on a rack for about 30 minutes. Serve directly from the pan, accompanied by vanilla ice cream or whipped cream.

* *

Tarte Tatin

* *

This upside-down apple tart is, hands down, my favorite dessert. I cannot remember when I first tasted this classic French treat, but whenever I see it on a menu, I cannot resist ordering it. The recipe is one of the more challenging ones in the book because you must take caution not to burn the sugar-butter mixture as you are caramelizing it on the stovetop. But once you have mastered this, the rest is easy. There is nothing that can beat the flavor of tart apples caramelized with butter and sugar. And, if the apples stick to the bottom of your pan—which they often do—fear not, just use a metal spatula to loosen them and add them to the tart. It is best eaten soon after baking, with whipped cream or vanilla ice cream.

MAKES 8 TO 12 SERVINGS

INGREDIENTS

Single-crust Basic Pie Crust 1 or 2
(page 338 or 339)

4 tablespoons (½ stick)
unsalted butter

¾ cup sugar

8 cups peeled, cored Granny
Smith apple wedges (4 to
6 chunks per apple: 6 to
8 apples)

1   Roll out the dough to about 12 inches in diameter. Refrigerate until ready to bake.

2   Place a rack in the center of the oven and a baking sheet on the bottom rack, and preheat to 425°F.

3   Place the butter and sugar in a 12-inch cast-iron skillet. Using a silicone spatula, stir the mixture constantly over medium-high heat, moving it around the pan and making sure to keep it from going up the sides of the pan. Continue stirring until the mixture is a rich caramel color. (It will become white and foamy and appear to be separating before it turns this color, about 3 minutes.) Remove from the heat.

4   Place the apples, round side down, in concentric circles in the caramel leaving a ¼-inch border between the apples and the side of the pan. Continue to mound the remaining apples evenly in a pattern over the bottom layer.

5   Peel off the top layer of plastic wrap from the dough and flip the dough over onto the skillet, making sure it is centered on the apples. Gently press the sides of the dough down around the apples to cover them. Once this is done, use your hands to gently press down on the center of the dough to slightly flatten the mound. Gently remove the remaining plastic wrap.

6   Cut 4 small slits in the dough and place the pan in the oven. Reduce the oven temperature to 400°F. Bake until the top is lightly golden and the apples in the center of the pie feel soft when poked with a tester, about 35 minutes.

7   Remove the pan from the oven. Immediately place a ceramic plate that is the same size as (or larger than) the opening of the pan over the pan and using 2 thick oven mitts, flip the pan over so that the tart drops out from the pan onto the plate. Remove any apples that have stuck to the pan and replace them in their appropriate spots.

Sour Cherry Tart

* *

*W*hen The Boston Globe *did a write-up on Rosie's cherry pie, they claimed that George Washington would have named this the best cherry pie in town if it had been around when he slept here. Prepare to pucker along with George; these sour cherries mean business. Serve with whipped cream or ice cream.*

MAKES 10 TO 12 SERVINGS

1   Roll out the bottom crust to 11 inches in diameter. Line a 9-inch tart pan with a removable bottom with the dough. Roll out the top crust as for a lattice (see page 335). Refrigerate both the bottom and top crusts.

2   Place a rack in the bottom third of the oven, place a baking sheet on the rack, and preheat to 400°F.

3   Combine ⅓ cup of the cherry or orange juice with the cornstarch in a small bowl and set aside.

4   Combine the remaining ⅔ cup juice, the brown sugar, cinnamon, mace, orange zest, and salt in a small saucepan and bring to a boil over medium-low heat.

5   Pour the cornstarch mixture slowly into the boiling juice while stirring vigorously with a whisk. Reduce the heat to low and bring the mixture to a boil again. Boil until it thickens, about 5 minutes.

6   Place the cherries in a medium-size heatproof bowl. Pour the hot syrup over them and toss to coat.

7   Remove the tart pan from the refrigerator and distribute the bread crumbs evenly over the bottom of the crust. Pour in the cherry filling and spread it evenly.

8   Cut the top crust into lattice strips and make a lattice top (see page 335). Brush the lattice and outer edges of the tart with the egg glaze.

9   Place the tart pan on the baking sheet (to catch any drips) and bake until the crust is golden, about 45 minutes.

INGREDIENTS

Double-crust Basic Tart Crust (page 340)

1 cup cherry juice (from canned sour cherries if using, see below) or 1 cup fresh orange juice (if using fresh sour cherries)

1 tablespoon plus 1½ teaspoons cornstarch

½ cup plus 3 tablespoons (lightly packed) light brown sugar

1 teaspoon ground cinnamon

Scant ¼ teaspoon ground mace

1½ teaspoons grated orange zest

⅛ teaspoon salt

4 cups drained canned pitted sour cherries, juice reserved, or 4 cups pitted fresh sour cherries

2 tablespoons plain dried bread crumbs

1 large egg mixed with 2 tablespoons water or milk, for glazing

10 Let the tart cool on a rack for 1 hour. Then push the bottom of the tart pan up slightly to loosen it from the pan before the syrup has the chance to harden over the edges. Cool the tart for 4 to 5 hours more before serving. Remove the bottom from the side of the pan. If you wish, slide a spatula under the tart and transfer it to a platter. Or if the thought of doing this stresses you out, just serve the tart on the pan bottom.

* *

Blueberry-Plum Crumb Pie

* *

A sumptuous summer pie with a tart filling and a sweet (but not too sweet) crunchy topping. Vanilla ice cream is a must.

MAKES 8 TO 12 SERVINGS

INGREDIENTS

Single-crust Basic Pie Crust 1 or 2 (page 338 or 339)

Crumb Topping

¾ cup plus 2 tablespoons all-purpose flour

6 tablespoons (lightly packed) light brown sugar

½ cup quick-cooking oats

½ cup ground almonds or walnuts

¼ teaspoon ground cinnamon

8 tablespoons (1 stick) unsalted butter, melted

Filling

3 cups blueberries

3 cups firm-ripe red plum slices (¾ inch thick; 7 to 8 plums)

6 to 8 tablespoons granulated sugar

¼ teaspoon grated orange zest

1 tablespoon plus 1 teaspoon cornstarch

2 tablespoons fresh orange juice

1 Place a rack in the center of the oven and a baking sheet on the bottom rack, and preheat to 400°F.

2 Roll out the crust. Fit the crust into a pie pan and lightly prebake (see Note, page 333). Let cool. Leave the oven on.

3 Make the topping: Mix the flour, brown sugar, oats, ground almonds, and cinnamon in a medium-size bowl. Pour in the melted butter and stir with a wooden spoon until it is fully incorporated. Set aside.

4 Prepare the filling: Place the blueberries, plums, granulated sugar, and orange zest in a large bowl. Dissolve the cornstarch in the orange juice and pour it over the fruit. Toss the mixture with your hands or a large spoon.

5 Scoop the fruit into the cooled pie shell. Use your hands to distribute the topping evenly over the fruit. Cover the edge of the crust with aluminum foil.

6   Place the pie on the baking sheet (to catch drips) and bake for 20 minutes. Lower the oven temperature to 350°F and continue baking until the pie juices are bubbling and begin to drip onto the baking sheet, about 1 hour longer (see Note).

7   Remove the pie from the oven and carefully remove the foil. Let cool on a rack for several hours before serving.

NOTE: *If at any point you feel that the top of your pie is getting too dark, loosely drop a piece of aluminum foil about the size of the pie on top of it and continue to bake. This will prevent it from getting too dark.*

* *

Peach Crumb Pie

* *

A *classic dessert that pays homage to one of the world's greatest fruits.*

MAKES 8 TO 12 SERVINGS

1   Place a rack in the center of the oven and a baking sheet on the bottom rack, and preheat to 400°F.

2   Roll out the crust. Fit it into a pie pan and lightly prebake (see Note, page 333). Let cool. Leave the oven on.

3   Make the topping: Place the flour, brown sugar, cinnamon, and salt in a food processor and process for several seconds to blend. Add the butter and pulse until the butter is completely mixed in and the topping forms large moist clumps. Set aside.

4   Prepare the filling: Place the peaches, granulated sugar, cinnamon, and salt in a large bowl. Dissolve the cornstarch in the lemon and orange juices and pour it over the fruit. Toss the mixture with your hands or a large spoon. Scoop the fruit into the pie shell and set aside.

5   Use your hands to distribute the topping evenly over the fruit. Cover the edge of the crust with aluminum foil.

INGREDIENTS

Single-crust Basic Pie Crust 1 or 2 (page 338 or 339)

Topping

1 cup plus 2 tablespoons all-purpose flour

½ cup plus 2 tablespoons (lightly packed) light brown sugar

1 teaspoon ground cinnamon

¼ teaspoon salt

10 tablespoons (1 stick plus 2 tablespoons) unsalted butter, cold, cut into 10 pieces

Filling

7 cups peeled peach slices (¾ inch thick; 6 to 7 peaches)

⅓ to ½ cup granulated sugar

½ teaspoon ground cinnamon

¼ teaspoon salt

1 tablespoon plus 1 teaspoon cornstarch

3 tablespoons fresh lemon juice

2 tablespoons fresh orange juice

353

6   Place the pie on the baking sheet (to catch drips) and bake for 20 minutes. Reduce the heat to 350°F and continue baking until the pie juices are bubbling and begin to drip onto the baking sheet, about 1 hour longer (see Note, page 353).

7   Remove the pie from the oven and carefully remove the foil. Let cool on a rack for several hours before serving.

INGREDIENTS

Single-crust Basic Pie Crust 1 or 2 (page 338 or 339)

Topping

¾ cup plus 2 tablespoons all-purpose flour

3 tablespoons granulated sugar

2 tablespoons light brown sugar

¼ teaspoon salt

Generous pinch of baking powder

5½ tablespoons (½ stick plus 1½ tablespoons) unsalted butter, cold, cut into pieces

Filling

2 cups (1 pint) fresh blueberries

1½ cups peeled peach cubes (¾ inch; 3 large peaches)

3 tablespoons granulated sugar

1 tablespoon cornstarch

1 tablespoon orange juice

1 tablespoon fresh lemon juice

½ teaspoon salt

1 cup raspberries

* *

Blueberry-Raspberry-Peach Pie

with a CRUMBLE TOP

* *

The minute summer fruit is in season I cannot wait to indulge in homemade pies. Those of you who are able to pick your own fruit will really delight in this one. As with all fruit pies, I suggest that vanilla ice cream accompany each bite.

MAKES 8 TO 12 SERVINGS

1   Roll out the crust. Fit it into a pie pan and refrigerate until chilled.

2   Place a rack in the center of the oven and a baking sheet on the bottom rack, and preheat to 400°F.

3   Make the topping: Place the flour, both sugars, baking powder, and the salt in a food processor and process for several seconds to blend. Add the butter and process until the mixture comes together, 1½ minutes.

4 Prepare the filling: Toss the blueberries, peaches, granulated sugar, cornstarch, both juices, and salt together in a large bowl.

5 Pour the fruit filling into the chilled crust then dot the top with the raspberries. Toss very lightly with the peach mixture. It is important that the berries stay as whole as possible.

6 Squeeze the crumb topping with your hands to form loose clumps from ½ inch to 1 inch in size. Distribute the topping evenly over the fruit. Cover the edge of the crust with aluminum foil.

7 Place the pie on the pan in the oven and bake for 20 minutes. Lower the oven temperature to 350°F and continue baking until the juices are bubbling and dripping onto the baking sheet and the peaches are cooked through, about 30 minutes more. Time can vary greatly depending on the ripeness of the peaches.

8 Remove the pie from the oven and let cool on a rack for 1 hour before serving.

* *

Nectarine Synergy

* *

T his dessert made its debut at a farewell dinner party for the Hamiltons, our erstwhile neighbors from England. "So what do you think?" I asked. "Fabulous," someone said, then someone else mentioned "synergy," and we were so amused by the concept that the name stuck.

MAKES 8 TO 10 SERVINGS

INGREDIENTS

Crust

Vegetable oil or butter for
  greasing the pan

1½ cups all-purpose flour

1 cup granulated sugar

½ teaspoon ground cinnamon

¼ teaspoon baking powder

8 tablespoons (1 stick) unsalted
  butter, at room temperature,
  cut into 8 pieces

Topping

¾ cup all-purpose flour

½ cup quick-cooking oats

½ cup standard white or whole
  wheat bread cubes

¾ cup (lightly packed) light
  brown sugar

8 tablespoons (1 stick) unsalted
  butter, cold, cut into 8 pieces

Filling

8 cups peeled ripe nectarine
  slices (½ inch thick; 7 to 8
  nectarines)

6 tablespoons granulated sugar

2 tablespoons cornstarch

¾ teaspoon salt

1 teaspoon ground cinnamon

3 tablespoons fresh lemon juice

1 Place a rack in the center of the oven and preheat to 400°F. Lightly grease a 9-inch square baking pan with vegetable oil or butter.

2 Make the crust: Place the flour, granulated sugar, cinnamon, and baking powder in a food processor and process to blend for 10 seconds. Add the butter and process until the mixture resembles coarse meal, 15 to 20 seconds.

3 Gather the dough into a ball. With floured fingertips, press the dough gently over the bottom and 1½ inches up the sides of the prepared pan.

4 Lightly prebake the crust (see Note, page 333) until it is golden in color, 12 to 15 minutes. Let cool. Leave the oven on and place a baking sheet on the center oven rack.

5 While the crust cools, make the topping: Place the flour, oats, bread cubes, and brown sugar in a food processor and process to blend for 30 seconds.

6 Add the butter and process until the mixture resembles coarse meal, 15 to 20 seconds.

7 Prepare the filling: Toss the nectarines, granulated sugar, cornstarch, salt, cinnamon, and lemon juice together in a large bowl.

8 Scoop the fruit mixture into the crust and sprinkle the topping over it.

9 Lower the oven temperature to 375°F and place the pan on the baking sheet. Bake until the top is light gold and crisp and the juices are bubbling, about 1 hour.

10 Open the oven door, turn the oven to broil, and cook the topping until it turns a deep gold, 2 to 3 minutes. (If your broiler is separate, remove the Synergy from the oven and place it under the broiler.) You'll need to watch carefully so it doesn't burn!

11 Allow the Synergy to cool a little on a rack. Serve it warm.

Pecan Pie

* *

T*ake a buttery crust, fill it with pecans and syrupy caramel, make sure the flavor is sweet, and you've got a classic pecan pie, unimpeded by any extraneous flavors. Make this the day before you want to serve it. Serve with ice cream or Whipped Cream (page 119).*

MAKES 12 TO 16 SERVINGS

1 Place a rack in the center of the oven and a baking sheet on the bottom rack, and preheat to 350°F.

2 Roll out the crust. Fit it into a pie pan and lightly prebake (see Note, page 333). Leave the oven on.

3 Heat the sugar and corn syrup in a small saucepan over low heat, stirring occasionally, until the sugar is dissolved, about 5 minutes. Transfer the mixture to a medium-size heatproof bowl. Stir in the butter and the salt and let the mixture cool for 8 to 10 minutes, stirring occasionally.

4 Whisking constantly, add the eggs and vanilla to the cooled sugar mixture. Stir in the pecans. Pour the filling into the pie shell.

5 Bake the pie until the top is fully risen, set, and crisp to the touch, 50 to 55 minutes. The surface will be covered with little cracks that will settle.

6 Let the pie cool completely on a rack. Cover with plastic wrap or aluminum foil and wait a day—if possible—before serving.

INGREDIENTS

Single-crust Basic Pie Crust 1 or 2 (page 338 or 339)

1 cup sugar

1½ cups plus 2 tablespoons dark corn syrup

7 tablespoons (½ stick plus 3 tablespoons) unsalted butter, at room temperature, cut into large pieces

⅛ teaspoon salt

4 large eggs, lightly beaten with a fork, at room temperature

½ teaspoon pure vanilla extract

1½ cups pecan halves

357

Chocolate-Bourbon Pecan Pie

* *

INGREDIENTS

Single-crust Basic Pie Crust 1 or 2 (page 338 or 339)

4 ounces unsweetened chocolate

1 cup sugar

1 cup dark corn syrup

4 tablespoons (½ stick) unsalted butter, at room temperature

¼ teaspoon salt

4 large eggs, at room temperature

¼ cup bourbon whiskey

1 teaspoon pure vanilla extract

1½ cups pecan halves

*F*udgy, delicious, and studded with pecans, this pie is a showstopper and oftentimes a nice substitute for the traditional pecan pie. I like to serve it on Christmas or New Year's Eve with eggnog ice cream.

MAKES 12 TO 16 SERVINGS

1   Roll out the crust. Fit it into a pie pan and refrigerate until ready to use.

2   Place a rack in the center of the oven and a baking sheet on the bottom rack, and preheat to 350°F.

3   Melt the chocolate in the top of a double boiler placed over simmering water. Set aside.

4   Heat the sugar and the corn syrup in a small saucepan over low heat, stirring occasionally, until the sugar is dissolved, about 5 minutes. Transfer the mixture to a medium-size heatproof bowl. Stir in the butter and salt and let the mixture cool for 8 to 10 minutes, stirring occasionally.

5   Whisking constantly, add the eggs and bourbon to the cooled sugar mixture.

6   Add the chocolate and vanilla and whisk vigorously until blended. Stir in the pecans. Pour the filling into the pie shell.

7   Bake the pie until the top is risen, set, and crisp to the touch, 55 to 60 minutes. The surface will be covered with little cracks that will settle. Let cool completely on a rack before serving.

Sweet-Potato Pecan Pie

* *

The sweet potato is a New World vegetable—Europeans didn't know it existed until Columbus stumbled upon it. Pecans, too, are quintessentially American, since they originally grew only in the American South. Even without such an impeccable pedigree, this would be the perfect Southern dessert, although I'm a fan of it for those long northern winters.

MAKES 8 TO 12 SERVINGS

1 Place a rack in the center of the oven and a baking sheet on the bottom rack, and preheat to 450°F.

2 Roll out the crust. Fit it into a deep-dish pie pan and lightly prebake (see Note, page 333). Let cool before filling. Leave the oven on.

3 Make the filling: Bake the sweet potatoes in the oven until they are soft, about 50 minutes. Leave the oven on and lower the oven temperature to 375°F.

4 Scoop the potatoes out of their skins into a medium-size bowl. Add the melted butter, brown sugar, eggs, lemon zest, lemon juice, cream, and salt and stir vigorously with a whisk until smooth and well blended. (This can also be done with an electric mixer on medium speed.) Set aside.

5 Make the topping: Stir the granulated sugar, corn syrup, eggs, butter, vanilla, cinnamon, and salt together in a medium-size bowl with a wooden spoon. Stir in the pecans.

6 Scoop the sweet potato filling into the pie shell, spread it evenly, and spread the topping over it. Cover the edge of the crust with aluminum foil. Bake the pie until the top rises and sets and is a rich golden color, about 1 hour.

7 Remove the pie from the oven and carefully remove the foil. Let cool slightly on a rack and serve it while it is still warm.

INGREDIENTS

Single-crust Basic Pie Crust 1 or 2 (page 338 or 339)

Filling

1¼ pounds sweet potatoes (about 2 large)

8 tablespoons (1 stick) unsalted butter, melted

¾ cup (lightly packed) dark brown sugar

2 large eggs, lightly beaten with a fork, at room temperature

1 teaspoon grated lemon zest

1½ tablespoons fresh lemon juice

¼ cup light cream or half-and-half

¼ teaspoon salt

Topping

¾ cup granulated sugar

¾ cup dark corn syrup

2 large eggs, at room temperature

1½ tablespoons unsalted butter, melted

2 teaspoons pure vanilla extract

Pinch of ground cinnamon

Pinch of salt

¾ cup pecan halves

Deep-Dish Pumpkin Pie

* *

Pumpkins are another of the foods that Americans can claim as all their own. This New World vegetable finally did get discovered by Europeans, but even then they were pretty slow in figuring out what to do with this fleshy squash. Good old Yankee ingenuity came up with this ideal fall and winter dessert. Serve it with Whipped Cream (page 119).

MAKES 10 TO 12 SERVINGS

INGREDIENTS

Single-crust Basic Pie Crust 1 or 2 (page 338 or 339)

1 can (15 ounces) unsweetened pumpkin puree

½ cup plus 3 tablespoons (lightly packed) dark brown sugar

1½ teaspoons ground cinnamon

1 teaspoon ground nutmeg

½ teaspoon ground cloves

1½ teaspoons ground ginger

¼ teaspoon salt

3 tablespoons molasses

1¼ cups evaporated milk

3 large eggs, at room temperature

1   Place a rack in the center of the oven and a baking sheet on the bottom rack, and preheat to 375°F.

2   Roll out the crust. Fit it into a deep-dish pie pan and lightly prebake (see Note, page 333). Let cool before filling. Leave the oven on.

3   Whisk the pumpkin, brown sugar, spices, and salt together in a large bowl. Whisk in the molasses, milk, and eggs, whisking vigorously until smooth.

4   Pour the filling into the pie shell. Cover the edge of the crust with aluminum foil. Bake the pie until the top is shiny and set and a tester inserted in the center comes out clean, about 1 hour.

5   Carefully remove the foil. Let the pie cool on a rack. Serve the pie warm, cold, or at room temperature.

Florida Lime Pie

* *

This southern favorite used to take its name from a kind of lime found in the Florida Keys, which turns the color of your average lime inside out—that is, the green is on the inside and the yellow is outside. Key limes are easier to find than they once were, so do look for them. If you can't find them, do use fresh limes, not bottled juice, for a better flavor.

MAKES 8 TO 12 SERVINGS

1 Place a rack in the center of the oven and a baking sheet on the bottom rack, and preheat to 350°F.

2 Lightly prebake the crust (see Note, page 333), and let cool before filling. Leave the oven on.

3 Make the filling: Whisk the condensed milk, lime zest, lime juice, eggs, and salt together in a medium-size bowl until they are completely mixed. Pour the filling into the pie shell.

4 Bake the pie until it begins to set, 10 minutes. Remove the pie from the oven and increase the heat to 425°F.

5 Make the topping: Whisk the sour cream, sugar, and salt together in a small bowl. Spread the topping over the pie.

6 Bake the pie for 5 minutes more. The topping will be loose when you remove the pie, but it will set as it cools. Let cool on a rack, then chill the pie for 6 hours before serving.

7 With a vegetable peeler, Microplane, or citrus zester, shave strands of zest from a whole lime around the edge of the pie for garnish just before serving.

INGREDIENTS

Cookie Crumb Crust (page 342) made with graham crackers

Filling

1 can (14 ounces) sweetened condensed milk

2 tablespoons grated lime zest

½ cup plus 2 tablespoons fresh lime juice (16 to 18 Key limes; 5 to 6 regular limes)

2 large eggs, at room temperature

Pinch of salt

Topping

1 cup sour cream

¼ cup sugar

⅛ teaspoon salt

Lime zest, for garnish

INGREDIENTS

Filling

6 tablespoons cornstarch

1½ cups water

¾ cup plus 2 tablespoons sugar

¾ cup fresh lemon juice
(about 3 lemons)

3 large egg yolks, lightly beaten

3 tablespoons unsalted butter, at
room temperature

1½ teaspoons grated lemon zest

Single-crust Basic Pie Crust
1 or 2 (page 338 or 339), fully
prebaked (see page 332),
or Cookie Crumb Crust
(page 342) made with
graham crackers, prebaked

Meringue Topping

3 large egg whites

1 cup sugar

Lemon Meringue Pie

* *

As American as Mom playing baseball. I see lemon meringue pie as a creature of the roadside diner, a special treat for the weary truck driver or, better yet, the handsome stranger who pulls into town and wins the heart of the good-natured waitress. Have you seen this movie, too?

MAKES 8 TO 10 SERVINGS

1   Make the filling: Dissolve the cornstarch in the water in a medium-size saucepan. Add the sugar and cook the mixture over low heat, whisking constantly until it thickens, about 5 minutes.

2   Add a couple of spoonfuls of the hot sugar mixture to the egg yolks to temper them, then stir the yolk mixture and the lemon juice into the sugar mixture and simmer, stirring occasionally, so the yolks cook, 3 minutes.

3   Strain the mixture through a sieve into a medium-size bowl and stir in the butter and lemon zest. Let cool for 10 to 15 minutes, stirring occasionally with a wooden spoon to let the steam escape.

4   Pour the lemon mixture into the cooled pie shell. Place it in

the refrigerator and allow it to set for 4 to 6 hours.

5   Place a rack in the center of the oven and preheat to 350°F.

6   Place the egg whites and sugar in the top of a double boiler over simmering water. Stir with a whisk until the mixture is opaque and the sugar is dissolved, 4 to 5 minutes.

7   Place the egg-white mixture in a medium-size mixing bowl and mix on high speed with the whisk attachment of an electric mixer until the whites resemble Marshmallow Fluff, 5 to 7 minutes.

8   Use a rubber spatula to scoop and spread the meringue over the pie. Use the back of a metal spoon to make little peaks.

9 Cover the edge of the crust with aluminum foil. Bake the pie until the tips and ridges of the meringue are golden, about 15 minutes.

10 Remove the pie from the oven and carefully remove the foil. Let the pie cool on a rack for 1 hour, then refrigerate it for at least another hour before serving. Cut the pie with the tip of a sharp, thin knife that has been dipped in hot water and wiped dry before each cut.

NOTE: *Water may sometimes form under meringue when it is baked on a water-based custard. If this occurs, after you have removed the first slice, carefully tip the pan over the sink and pour off any excess liquid or blot it out with absorbent paper towels.*

* *

Banana Custard Pie

* *

T*his custard pie is richer than Croesus, smooth and creamy, layered with bananas, and topped with whipped cream.*

MAKES 8 TO 10 SERVINGS

1 Place a rack in the center of the oven and preheat to 400°F.

2 Roll out the crust. Fit it into a pie pan and fully prebake (see page 332). Let cool before filling.

3 Place 2 cups of the milk, the sugar, and salt in a heavy medium-size saucepan and heat over low heat until almost boiling. Stir occasionally until the sugar is dissolved.

4 Dissolve the cornstarch in the remaining ¼ cup milk in a small bowl. Whisk in the egg yolks.

5 Whisking vigorously, gradually add ½ cup of the hot milk mixture to the egg yolks. Whisk this mixture back into the remaining hot milk mixture. Cook, whisking constantly, over low heat until it thickens and bubbles, about 3 minutes, then cook for 1 minute more.

INGREDIENTS

Single-crust Basic Pie Crust 1 or 2 (page 338 or 339)

2¼ cups milk

½ cup sugar

¼ teaspoon salt

¼ cup cornstarch

3 large egg yolks

3 tablespoons unsalted butter, at room temperature, cut into 3 pieces

1 teaspoon pure vanilla extract

3 ripe bananas

2 tablespoons fresh lemon juice

1½ cups Whipped Cream (page 119), for topping

The custard should form loose mounds when dropped from a spoon back into the pan.

6   Remove the custard from the heat and stir in the butter and vanilla. Transfer the custard to a small bowl and let cool for 15 minutes, gently stirring it several times to allow the steam to escape. Place a piece of plastic wrap directly on the surface of the custard and puncture the wrap in several places with the tip of a knife. Cool for 30 minutes in the refrigerator.

7   While the custard is cooling, cut the bananas into ¼-inch-thick slices and toss them with the lemon juice to prevent them from turning brown.

8   Spread half the custard in the pie shell with a metal spatula and cover it with a layer of bananas. Spread the remaining custard carefully over the bananas and arrange the remaining bananas on top. Spread the Whipped Cream over the bananas.

9   Chill the pie for at least 2 hours before serving.

* *

Coconut Custard Pie

* *

I love anything with coconut in it, so this pie is one of my long-time favorites. It starts with a simple butter crust, which I fill with thick, coconut-rich pudding, then top with meringue.

MAKES 8 TO 10 SERVINGS

1   Make the filling: Place the cream, ½ cup of the milk, and the sugar in a heavy medium-size saucepan and heat over low heat. Stir occasionally until the sugar is dissolved.

2   Dissolve the cornstarch in the remaining ¾ cup milk. Whisk in the egg yolks.

3   Whisking vigorously, gradually add ½ cup of the hot cream mixture to the egg-yolk mixture. Whisk this mixture back into the remaining hot cream mixture. Cook, whisking constantly, over low heat until it thickens and bubbles, 5 to 6 minutes. Cook, continuing to whisk, 20 to 30 seconds more. The custard should form loose mounds when dropped from a spoon back into the pan.

4   Remove the custard from the heat and stir in the vanilla. Transfer the custard to a medium-size bowl and let cool for 15 minutes, gently stirring it several times to allow the steam to escape.

5   Stir all but 3 tablespoons of the coconut into the custard. Place a piece of plastic wrap directly on the surface of the custard and puncture the wrap in several places with the tip of a knife. Let cool at room temperature for 1 hour.

6   Place a rack in the center of the oven and a baking sheet on the bottom rack, and preheat to 350°F.

7   Scoop the custard into the pie shell and use a metal spatula to spread it evenly.

8   Make the meringue topping: Place the egg whites and sugar in the top of a double boiler over simmering water. Stir with a whisk until the mixture is opaque and the sugar is dissolved, 4 to 5 minutes.

9   Place the egg-white mixture in a medium-size mixing bowl and mix on high speed with the whisk attachment of an electric mixer until the whites resemble Marshmallow Fluff, 5 to 7 minutes.

10   Use a rubber spatula to scoop and spread the meringue over the pie. Use the back of a metal spoon to make little peaks. Sprinkle the reserved coconut over the top. Bake the pie until the coconut and the meringue peaks are golden, about 15 minutes.

11   Let cool for 15 minutes, then refrigerate the pie for 1 hour before serving.

INGREDIENTS

Filling

1½ cups heavy (whipping) cream

1¼ cups milk

¾ cup sugar

6 tablespoons cornstarch

2 large egg yolks

1 teaspoon pure vanilla extract

2 cups sweetened shredded coconut

Single-crust Basic Pie Crust 1 or 2 (page 338 or 339), fully prebaked (see page 332)

Meringue Topping

3 large egg whites

1 cup sugar

Vanilla Custard Tart

* *

A double-crust tart, this is delicious sprinkled with confectioners' sugar and served with sliced berries that have been tossed with sugar.

MAKES 8 TO 12 SERVINGS

INGREDIENTS

Double-crust Basic Tart Crust
(page 340)

2 cups heavy (whipping) cream

2 cups milk

½ cup sugar

6 tablespoons cornstarch

8 large egg yolks, at room
temperature

1 tablespoon pure vanilla extract

1 large egg mixed with
2 tablespoons water or milk,
for glazing

1 Roll out both crusts to 11 inches in diameter. Refrigerate the top crust. Fit the bottom crust into a 9-inch tart pan and lightly prebake (see Note, page 333). Let the baked shell cool before filling.

2 Place the cream, 1½ cups of the milk, and the sugar in a heavy medium-size saucepan and heat over low heat, stirring occasionally, until the sugar is dissolved.

3 Dissolve the cornstarch in the remaining ½ cup milk in a medium-size bowl. Vigorously whisk in the egg yolks.

4 Whisking vigorously, gradually add ½ cup of the hot cream mixture to the egg-yolk mixture. Whisk this mixture back into the remaining hot cream mixture. Cook, whisking constantly, over low heat until it thickens and bubbles, about 4 minutes; cook for 1 minute more.

5 Remove the custard from the heat and stir in the vanilla.

Transfer the custard to a ceramic bowl and let cool for 15 minutes, gently stirring it several times to allow the steam to escape. Place a piece of plastic wrap directly on the surface of the custard and puncture the wrap in several places with the tip of a knife. Refrigerate for 15 minutes.

6 Place a rack in the center of the oven and a baking sheet on the bottom rack, and preheat to 350°F.

7 Scoop the custard into the tart shell and use a metal spatula to spread it evenly.

8 Brush the egg glaze along the edge of the tart shell. Lay the top crust over the custard and press along the edge with your thumb to seal the two crusts. Cut 3 to 4 small slits in the top crust; brush the top with the egg glaze.

9 Bake until the crust is golden, about 1 hour. Let cool completely on a rack before serving.

Chocolate Berry Tart

* *

I don't remember when I first tasted chocolate fondue, although I do remember someone ordering it for me and saying, "This'll knock your socks off." An understatement. I think of this pie as a less messy version of that fondue, and I'd like to propose a toast to the marriage of two of the world's most distinguished tastes—fresh berries and rich chocolate. May they thrive and prosper.

MAKES 8 TO 12 SERVINGS

1   Roll out the crust to 11 inches in diameter. Fit it into a 9-inch tart pan and fully prebake (see page 332). Let cool before filling.

2   Chop both the chocolates to fine flakes in a food processor, about 20 seconds. Leave the chocolate in the processor.

3   Place the cream and milk in a small saucepan and heat over low heat just to boiling, about 5 minutes. Remove it from the heat.

4   Add the egg yolks, vanilla, and espresso powder to the food processor and process to blend for about 8 seconds.

5   With the processor running, pour the hot cream mixture through the feed tube and process until the chocolate is melted. Scrape the bowl with a rubber spatula and process several more seconds.

6   Let the mixture cool to lukewarm, 10 to 15 minutes, then spread it in the tart shell. Chill the tart for at least 4 hours in the refrigerator.

7   Before serving, whip the cream until it forms firm peaks and spread it over the surface of the tart, starting at the center. Distribute the berries evenly over the whipped cream and serve.

NOTE: To get ½ yolk, crack an egg into your palm and let the egg white run through your fingers. Use a knife to gently cut through the center of the yolk, then slide the ½ yolk into a cup.

INGREDIENTS

Single-crust Shortbread Tart Crust (page 341)

Filling

1 ounce unsweetened chocolate, cut into 4 pieces

½ cup plus 2 tablespoons (4 ounces) semisweet chocolate chips

½ cup plus 2 tablespoons heavy (whipping) cream

¼ cup plus 2 tablespoons milk

1½ large egg yolks (see Note), at room temperature

1 teaspoon pure vanilla extract

½ teaspoon instant espresso powder

Topping

⅓ cup heavy (whipping) cream, cold

1 pint strawberries, rinsed and hulled, or raspberries (not necessary to rinse)

Chocolate Mousse Pie

in a TOASTED PECAN CRUST

* *

H ere's a rich, dark mousse encased in a sweet nut crust that's glazed with semisweet chocolate.

MAKES 10 SERVINGS

INGREDIENTS

Crust

2 cups chopped toasted pecans (see page 272)

½ cup (lightly packed) light brown sugar

5 tablespoons unsalted butter, melted

¾ cup (4 ounces) semisweet chocolate chips

Filling

4 ounces semisweet chocolate

2 ounces unsweetened chocolate

1 teaspoon instant coffee powder

4 large eggs, at room temperature

½ teaspoon pure vanilla extract

1½ cups heavy (whipping) cream, cold

½ ounce unsweetened chocolate, for shaving (see page 22)

1   Place a rack in the center of the oven and preheat to 375°F.

2   Make the crust: Toss the nuts, brown sugar, and melted butter together in a medium-size bowl with a fork or your hands. Pat the mixture firmly and evenly over the bottom and up the sides of a 9-inch pie pan.

3   Bake the crust until the butter and sugar begin to caramelize, 8 to 10 minutes.

4   Distribute the chocolate chips evenly over the crust, return it to the oven, and bake until the chips are softened, 1 to 1½ minutes. Remove the crust from the oven and spread the chips over the bottom and sides with a frosting spatula. Refrigerate the crust while you prepare the filling.

5   Make the filling: Melt the semisweet chocolate and 2 ounces unsweetened chocolate with the coffee powder in the top of a double boiler placed over simmering water. Then vigorously whisk in the eggs and vanilla until the mixture is smooth, 30 seconds. Transfer this mixture to a medium-size bowl and let cool for at least 5 minutes.

6   Beat the cream in a small bowl with an electric mixer on medium-high speed until it forms firm peaks, 1½ minutes. Fold two-thirds of the whipped cream into the chocolate mixture and spread the mousse in the crust.

7   Refrigerate the pie until ready to serve, 6 to 8 hours. Store the remaining whipped cream in a small bowl covered with plastic.

8   Before serving, spoon the whipped cream onto the center of the pie and spread it, leaving a 1½-inch border uncovered. Cover the whipped cream with chocolate shavings.

Crucheon's Fudge Pie

* *

*W*hen I was a student at Berkeley, I was a regular at a little restaurant called Crucheon's, mostly because it had desserts I was prepared to die for. It seems appropriate that a fudge pie would be one of my college experiences because fudge first caught on about 150 years ago at women's colleges, where students made it as an excuse to stay up late and talk. I didn't need an excuse. I kept working on this recipe until I was able to re-create the dark, chocolate filling in its butter crust. I dedicate the results to Crucheon's.

MAKES 8 TO 12 SERVINGS

1 Place a rack in the center of the oven and preheat to 400°F.

2 Roll out the crust. Fit it into a pie pan and lightly prebake (see Note, page 333). Let cool before filling. Reduce the oven temperature to 375°F.

3 Melt the chocolate and butter in the top of a double boiler placed over simmering water. Cool until the mixture is tepid.

4 Beat the eggs and sugar in a medium-size mixing bowl with an electric mixer on medium speed until the mixture is thick and pale yellow, about 80 seconds.

5 Add the chocolate mixture and mix on medium speed until blended, about 30 seconds. Scrape the bottom and sides of the bowl with a rubber spatula and mix for 15 seconds more.

6 Pour the filling into the pie crust, then cover the edge of the pie crust with a strip of aluminum foil so that it won't burn. Bake the pie until the filling is set and forms a crust on top and a tester inserted in the center comes out with moist crumbs, 35 to 40 minutes. Remove the foil from the crust after 30 minutes of baking.

7 Serve the pie warm with whipped cream.

INGREDIENTS

Single-crust Basic Pie Crust 1 or 2 (page 338 or 339)

4 ounces unsweetened chocolate

8 tablespoons (1 stick) unsalted butter

3 large eggs, at room temperature

1 cup plus 2 tablespoons sugar

½ recipe Whipped Cream (page 119), for serving

Lemon Cream Cheese Pie

* *

My version of a cream-cheese pie has quite a tart filling to enhance the variety of flavors. I've added a sour cream topping and graham cracker crust.

MAKES 8 TO 12 SERVINGS

INGREDIENTS

Cookie Crumb Crust (page 342) made with graham crackers

Filling

9 ounces cream cheese, at room temperature

½ cup sugar

1½ teaspoons grated lemon zest

½ cup sour cream, at room temperature

1 large egg, at room temperature

5 tablespoons fresh lemon juice

1 teaspoon pure vanilla extract

2 tablespoons all-purpose flour

Topping

1 cup sour cream, at room temperature

3 tablespoons sugar

1 pint raspberries, for garnish

1 Place a rack in the center of the oven and a baking sheet on the bottom rack, and preheat to 375°F.

2 Bake the crust (see page 334) and let cool before filling. Reduce the oven temperature to 325°F.

3 Make the filling: Cream the cream cheese, sugar, and lemon zest in a medium-size mixing bowl with an electric mixer on medium speed until light and fluffy, about 1 minute. Scrape the bowl with a rubber spatula halfway through and at the end.

4 Add the sour cream and mix on medium-low speed until the mixture is smooth, about 30 seconds. Scrape the bowl.

5 Beat in the egg, lemon juice, and vanilla on medium speed until blended, 30 to 45 seconds. Scrape the bowl.

6 Add the flour and mix just until blended, about 8 seconds. Pour the filling into the crust.

7 Bake the pie until the top is rounded and springs back to the touch, 45 to 50 minutes. (A tester inserted in the center will not come out clean.) Small cracks may form on the surface.

8 Let the pie cool on a rack for 20 minutes. Leave the oven on.

9 Make the topping: Stir the sour cream and sugar together. Spread it over the cream cheese filling and return the pie to the oven for 5 minutes.

10 Let the pie cool to room temperature, then refrigerate it for 4 hours. Cover the top with raspberries before serving.

Strawberry Cream Cheese Tart

* *

S trawberries and cream have probably been keeping company since the first cow wandered into a berry patch. So herewith is my contribution to that excellent combination: a crunchy, buttery tart shell holding a sweet cream cheese filling topped with whole strawberries. It's an elegant version of the classic New York cheesecake, and I like to display it on a cake pedestal for full effect.

MAKES 8 TO 10 SERVINGS

1   Place a rack in the center of the oven and a baking sheet on the bottom rack, and preheat to 400°F.

2   Roll out the crust to 11 inches in diameter. Fit it into a 9-inch tart pan and lightly prebake (see Note, page 333). Let cool before filling. Reduce the oven temperature to 350°F.

3   Place the cream cheese, sour cream, sugar, and lemon juice in a food processor and process until thoroughly blended, about 30 seconds. Scrape the bowl with a rubber spatula.

4   Add the eggs and process for 10 seconds. Pour the filling into the tart shell.

5   Bake the tart until the filling rises in the center and a tester inserted in the center comes out clean, about 40 minutes.

6   Let the tart cool on a rack at least 2 hours. Top the tart with the strawberries arranged in concentric circles.

7   Heat the jelly in a saucepan over low heat, stirring gently with a whisk just until melted. Glaze the berries by brushing the jelly over them with a pastry brush. Let the glaze set for 15 minutes. Serve the tart at room temperature.

INGREDIENTS

Single-crust Basic Tart Crust (page 340)

12 ounces plus 1 tablespoon cream cheese, at room temperature

¼ cup sour cream, at room temperature

½ cup sugar

¼ cup fresh lemon juice

2 large eggs, at room temperature

2 pints strawberries, rinsed and hulled

½ cup strawberry or red currant jelly

Linzertorte

* *

INGREDIENTS

Vegetable oil or butter for
    greasing the pan

Crust

8 ounces almonds

2 sticks (8 ounces) unsalted
    butter, at room temperature

¾ cup sugar

¼ teaspoon salt

1 teaspoon ground cinnamon

¼ teaspoon ground cloves

1 teaspoon grated lemon zest

1 teaspoon grated orange zest

1 large egg, at room temperature

2 teaspoons pure vanilla extract

1½ cups all-purpose flour

1 tablespoon unsweetened cocoa
    powder

Filling

1¼ cups raspberry preserves

2 teaspoons fresh lemon juice

¼ cup finely chopped almonds
    for sprinkling

Originally from Linz in Austria, the linzertorte has become a popular dessert in America. This beautiful lattice-topped tart is made from cookie dough rich in the flavor of ground almonds and fragrant spices. Layered between the crusts is a filling of raspberry preserves.

MAKES 12 TO 16 SERVINGS

1   Place a rack in the center of the oven and preheat to 400°F. Lightly grease an 11-inch tart pan with vegetable oil or butter.

2   Make the crust: Process the almonds in a food processor until finely chopped, about 15 seconds. Set aside.

3   Blend the butter, sugar, salt, spices, and citrus zests together in a medium-size mixing bowl with an electric mixer on medium speed just until mixed, 15 to 20 seconds. Stop once to scrape the bowl with a rubber spatula.

4   Whisk the egg in a small bowl until blended; add 2 tablespoons of the egg to the butter mixture. Set aside the remaining egg to use as a glaze. Add the vanilla to the

butter mixture and mix until incorporated, about 15 seconds. Scrape the bowl.

5   With the mixer on high speed, add the flour and the cocoa and beat just until blended, about 15 seconds. Scrape the bowl. Add the almonds on low speed and mix until blended.

6   Remove the dough from the mixing bowl and work it a bit with your hands so that it holds together. Break off about one-third of the dough, cover it with plastic wrap, and refrigerate it.

7   Press the remaining dough evenly over the bottom and up the sides of the prepared tart pan with your fingers. Wrap a strip of aluminum foil around the outside of the pan and fold it over the very top of the crust to keep it from burning.

8   Prebake the tart shell until the dough loses its sheen and is golden, about 15 minutes. Let cool on a rack. Turn off the oven.

9   While the tart shell is baking and cooling, remove the dough from the refrigerator and place it between two pieces of plastic wrap or waxed paper. Roll it out to a rectangle about 12 × 8 inches. Slip this dough, still sandwiched between the plastic, onto a platter or baking sheet and refrigerate it for 2 hours.

10   After 2 hours, preheat the oven to 400°F.

11   Carefully remove the foil strip from the tart shell and set the foil aside.

12   Make the filling: Stir the raspberry preserves and lemon juice together in a small bowl. Spread the mixture evenly over the bottom of the baked tart shell.

13   Remove the chilled dough from the refrigerator. Peel off the top piece of plastic wrap and cut the dough lengthwise into

9 strips each about ¾ inch wide. Using a frosting spatula, carefully remove the first 4 strips from the paper one at a time and place them evenly spaced across the top of the tart. Press the edges of the strips down onto the top of the baked edge and save any dough scraps that drop off. Then evenly space the next 5 strips at right angles to the first 4 across the tart. Use the scraps to fill in the spaces along the edges of the crust between the lattice strips.

14   Brush the reserved beaten egg over the lattice strips with a pastry brush. Sprinkle the crushed almonds over the entire surface of the tart.

15   Replace the foil around the top edge of the tart. Bake until the top is shiny and golden and the jam is bubbling, about 30 minutes. Let cool completely on a rack before serving.

INGREDIENTS

Dough

1 cup all-purpose flour

2 tablespoons sugar

¼ teaspoon salt

8 tablespoons (1 stick) unsalted butter, cold, cut into 8 pieces

3 tablespoons cream cheese, cold

Vegetable oil or butter for greasing the pans

Filling

½ cup (firmly packed) light brown sugar

3 tablespoons dark corn syrup

1 large egg

2 teaspoons pure vanilla extract

⅛ teaspoon salt

2 tablespoons unsalted butter, melted

Generous ¾ cup chopped pecans

Joyce Miller's Pecan Tartlets

* *

My friend Michael Miller swears by his mother's pecan tartlets, and so does his wife, Alisa. So here they are, straight from Joyce's Long Island kitchen—sweet, crunchy, portable perfections designed for pecan pie lovers.

MAKES 24 TARTLETS

1   Make the dough: Place the flour, sugar, and salt in a food processor and process to blend for 5 seconds.

2   Scatter the butter and cream cheese over the flour mixture and pulse until the mixture is the size of small peas, 20 pulses. Then process just until the mixture comes together, 15 seconds.

3   Place the dough on a piece of plastic wrap and form it into a mass. Pinch off 24 pieces of dough and roll them into balls with the palms of your hands. Place them on a plate and refrigerate, uncovered, for 30 minutes.

4   Place a rack in the center of the oven and preheat to 375°F. Lightly grease 24 mini muffin cups with vegetable oil or butter.

5   Remove the balls from the refrigerator and flatten each one with your fingers. Press them gently into the muffin cups so that the edge of each comes ⅛ inch above the rim. Make sure not to make a hole or tear the dough. Place the pan in the refrigerator or freezer while you prepare the filling.

6   Make the filling: Whisk the brown sugar, corn syrup, egg, vanilla, salt, and melted butter together in a small bowl until smooth.

7   Remove the pan from the refrigerator. Place a slightly rounded teaspoon of filling in the bottom of each cup, then spoon a generous teaspoon of nuts over the filling.

8 Bake until the pastry is a rich golden color and the top of the filling has risen and cracked (this will happen before the pastry color is right), 25 to 30 minutes.

9 Let the tartlets cool completely in the pan on a rack. Run a little frosting spatula or butter knife around the top edge of each tart, and use the knife to gently lift the tart out of the pan.

10 These are best eaten on the day they are baked. Otherwise, store them in an airtight container in the refrigerator for up to 1 week or the freezer for up to 2 weeks.

Rosy Cranberry Tartlets

* *

T *art in shape, tart in taste, these tiny pies hold a cranberry-raisin filling inside a flaky sour cream pastry. Sprinkle them lightly with confectioners' sugar before serving.*

MAKES 24 TARTLETS

1 Make the dough: Place the flour, sugar, and salt in a food processor and process to blend for 5 seconds.

2 Scatter the butter over the flour mixture and pulse until the mixture resembles coarse meal, 20 to 30 pulses.

3 Distribute the sour cream evenly over the mixture and process for 5 seconds. Scrape the bowl with a rubber spatula, then process until the liquid is evenly distributed, 10 seconds. Do not let the dough come together into a ball.

INGREDIENTS

Dough

1⅓ cups all-purpose flour

1½ tablespoons sugar

Scant ½ teaspoon salt

10½ tablespoons (1 stick plus 2½ tablespoons) unsalted butter, cold, cut into 12 pieces

⅓ cup sour cream, cold

Filling

1 tablespoon all-purpose flour

½ cup plus 2 tablespoons sugar

⅛ teaspoon salt

⅓ cup water

1 tablespoon plus 1 teaspoon cornstarch

1½ cups fresh cranberries

½ cup golden or dark raisins

1 teaspoon grated lemon zest

1 tablespoon unsalted butter

2 tablespoons fresh lemon juice

Vegetable oil or butter for greasing the pans

Topping

1 tablespoon confectioners' sugar

375

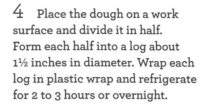

4 Place the dough on a work surface and divide it in half. Form each half into a log about 1½ inches in diameter. Wrap each log in plastic wrap and refrigerate for 2 to 3 hours or overnight.

5 Make the filling: Combine the flour, sugar, and salt in a medium-size saucepan.

6 In a small cup, stir the water into the cornstarch. Whisk the cornstarch mixture into the flour mixture.

7 Stir in the cranberries, raisins, and lemon zest. Cook, covered, over medium heat, stirring occasionally, until the cranberries start to pop and the liquid is rosy colored and bubbling furiously, 5 minutes.

8 Remove the pan from the heat and stir in the butter and lemon juice until the butter has melted. Cool the filling in the refrigerator.

9 Generously grease 24 mini muffin cups with vegetable oil or butter. Remove one log of dough from the refrigerator and cut it into 12 equal slices. Place each slice between two pieces of plastic wrap and roll them out to form rounds about 3¼ inches in diameter.

10 Remove the rounds from the plastic wrap and press them gently into the muffin cups so that the edge of each comes ¼ inch above the rim. Make sure not to make a hole or tear the dough. Repeat with the second log.

11 Place 1 slightly rounded teaspoon of the filling in each tartlet. Then fold the excess dough inward to form a ruffled crust around the edges of the cranberry mixture.

12 When all the tartlets have been made, place the pan in the freezer for 10 minutes. Place a rack in the center of the oven and preheat to 425°F.

13 Remove the pan from the freezer and bake until the pastry is a rich golden color, about 35 minutes.

14 Let the pan cool on a rack for 10 minutes. Then run a little frosting spatula or butter knife around the top edge of each tartlet and gently lift the tartlet out of the pan. Let them cool completely on the rack. Before serving, sift the confectioners' sugar over the tartlets.

NOTE: *These are best eaten on the day they are baked. Otherwise, store them in an airtight container in the refrigerator for a day or two or freeze them for up to 2 weeks. To serve, recrisp them in a preheated 400°F oven for 8 to 10 minutes, or if frozen, for 10 to 15 minutes.*

* *

Lemon Curd Tartlets

* *

H ere's a mouthful of tart lemon curd held in a sweet
pastry crust and finished off with a dollop of whipped
cream.

MAKES 18 TARTLETS

1 Make the dough: Place the
flour, granulated sugar, and salt
in a food processor and process
to blend for 20 seconds. (Or
whisk them together by hand
in a large mixing bowl.)

2 Distribute the butter evenly
over the flour, and process until
the mixture resembles coarse
meal, 15 to 20 seconds. (Or rub
the butter into the flour with your
fingertips, or cut it in with
a pastry blender.)

3 In a small cup, whisk
together the cold water and egg
yolk. With the processor running,
pour the egg mixture in a steady
stream through the feed tube
and process just until the dough
comes together, 20 to 30 seconds.
(If not using a food processor,
sprinkle the egg mixture over the
flour mixture while tossing with
a fork.)

4 Place the dough on a lightly
floured work surface and knead it
several times to bring it together.
Shape the dough into a thick
disk, wrap it in plastic wrap, and
refrigerate it for 2 hours.

5 When you are ready to
roll out the dough, generously
grease 18 mini muffin cups with
vegetable oil or butter.

6 Place the disk between
two fresh pieces of plastic wrap
and roll it out to form a 12-inch
round, a generous ⅛ inch thick.

7 Using a 2½-inch round
cookie cutter or the rim of a
glass that has been dipped in
flour, cut out approximately
14 rounds. Gather up the dough
scraps and reroll the dough to
make an additional 4 rounds.

8 Press each round of dough
into a muffin cup so that the edge

INGREDIENTS

Dough

1 cup all-purpose flour

3 tablespoons granulated sugar

⅛ teaspoon salt

6 tablespoons (¾ stick) unsalted
butter, very cold, cut into
6 pieces

1 tablespoon cold water

1 large egg yolk

Vegetable oil or butter for
greasing the pans

Curd

¼ teaspoon unflavored gelatin
powder

⅓ cup plus 1 tablespoon fresh
lemon juice

4 large egg yolks

½ cup plus 1 tablespoon
granulated sugar

1 tablespoon unsalted butter

Topping

¼ cup heavy (whipping) cream

1 tablespoon confectioners' sugar

of each comes ⅛ inch above the rim. Prick the bottoms once with the tines of a fork and place the pan in the freezer for 30 minutes.

9 Meanwhile, place a rack in the center of the oven and preheat to 375°F.

10 Bake the shells until they are a rich golden color with darker golden edges, 18 to 20 minutes. Let them cool.

11 Meanwhile, make the curd: Dissolve the gelatin in the lemon juice in a small bowl.

12 Using a whisk, stir the egg yolks and sugar together in a small bowl until blended.

13 Combine the lemon juice mixture and the egg mixture in a small heavy saucepan and stir with a whisk to blend. Place the pan over medium-low heat and, stirring constantly with the whisk, bring the mixture just to the boiling point.

14 Remove from the heat and strain the mixture through a sieve into a small bowl. Stir in the butter and let the curd cool slightly, 15 to 20 minutes.

15 Pour the mixture into the cooled shells and place the pan in the refrigerator so that the curd can set, about 2 hours.

16 Remove the tartlets from the refrigerator 1 hour before serving.

17 Fifteen minutes before serving, make the topping: Beat the cream and the confectioners' sugar in a small bowl with an electric mixer on medium-high speed until firm peaks form, 1 to 1½ minutes. Garnish each tartlet with a dollop of whipped cream.

NOTE: *Do not put whipped cream on any tarts that you plan to store. Place these tarts on a plate, cover with plastic wrap, and refrigerate for up to 2 days. For longer storage, place them in an airtight container with plastic wrap, parchment paper, or waxed paper between the layers and freeze for up to 2 weeks. Defrost the tarts and dollop with whipped cream before serving.*

Almond Raspberry Tartlets

* *

F or these miniature tarts, I fill a butter crust with an almond paste mixture and accent it with raspberry preserves.

MAKES 24 TARTLETS

1   Refrigerate but don't roll out the tart dough.

2   Place a rack in the center of the oven and preheat to 425°F. Lightly grease 24 mini muffin cups with butter.

3   Pinch off 24 rounded tablespoons of the tart dough and press them into the cups with your fingers so that the edge of each comes ⅛ inch above the rim. (There will be dough left over. This can be wrapped and frozen for future use.) Prick the bottoms once with the tines of a fork and refrigerate the shells for 15 minutes.

4   Bake the shells until golden, about 10 minutes. Let cool on a rack. Lower the oven temperature to 350°F.

5   Meanwhile, beat the almond paste, sugar, egg, flour, melted butter, and salt together in a small mixing bowl with an electric mixer on medium-high speed until thoroughly mixed, about 1½ minutes.

6   Place ¼ teaspoon raspberry jam in the bottom of each tart shell, then spoon a rounded teaspoon of almond filling over the jam.

7   Bake the tartlets until the tops are golden and a tester inserted in the center comes out clean, about 15 minutes.

8   Let the tartlets cool for 2 hours in the pans before serving.

INGREDIENTS

Single-crust Basic Tart Crust (page 340)

Butter for greasing the cups

2½ ounces almond paste (not marzipan)

5 tablespoons sugar

1 large egg, at room temperature

1 tablespoon plus 1 teaspoon all-purpose flour

2 teaspoons unsalted butter, melted

¼ teaspoon salt

2 to 3 tablespoons raspberry preserves

Maya's Pocketbooks

* *

When I was young, my aunt, Martha, always had a little dough left over when she made her fabulous fruit pies. She'd give it to me to make what I called pocketbooks, which I filled with jam, baked, and got to eat way before the pie was done. These miniature turnovers are the latter-day version of my early creations.

MAKES 40 OR MORE POCKETBOOKS

INGREDIENTS

2½ cups all-purpose flour, sifted

3 tablespoons sugar

¾ teaspoon salt

2 sticks (8 ounces) unsalted butter, cold, cut into 16 pieces

3 large egg yolks

2 tablespoons ice water

Vegetable oil or butter for greasing the baking sheets (optional)

About 1 cup fruit preserves (the thicker the better)

1   Place the flour, sugar, and salt in a food processor and process to blend for about 6 seconds.

2   Add the butter to the flour mixture and process until all the ingredients are blended, 10 to 15 seconds.

3   Whisk the egg yolks and ice water together in a small cup. While the machine is running, pour the yolk mixture through the feed tube and pulse 15 times. Process until the dough comes together, 5 seconds more.

4   Remove the dough from the machine and knead it with 6 or 7 turns. Shape the dough into 2 thick disks, wrap each in plastic wrap, and refrigerate at least 1 hour.

5   Preheat the oven to 400°F. Line several baking sheets with parchment paper or lightly grease them with vegetable oil or butter.

6   Roll out each piece of dough between two pieces of plastic wrap or waxed paper ⅛ inch thick (see page 330 for rolling technique). Using a 2¾-inch round cookie cutter, cut out 20 round cookies from each piece. Gather up the dough scraps and reroll them to make as many more rounds as possible. (On a humid day, it may be necessary to refrigerate the rolled-out dough for 15 minutes before cutting.)

7   Place 1 level teaspoon of fruit preserves on one half of each round and fold the other half over. Seal the seams by pinching the edges together. Make a fork prick in the center

of each pocketbook. Place the pocketbooks about 1 inch apart on the prepared baking sheets.

8   Bake the pocketbooks until they are golden, about 12 minutes. Let cool on a rack before serving.

* *

Apple Brown Betty

* *

*A*mong the important questions that will go unanswered *in this book are who was Betty and how did her name get attached to this crumble, which isn't particularly brown. It's something you'll want to ponder, no doubt, as you work your way through its scrumptious pecan crumb topping to the apples underneath. You may also find yourself pondering whether you even need the apples with a crust this good. Serve Apple Brown Betty with your favorite ice cream.*

MAKES 8 SERVINGS

1   Place a rack in the center of the oven and a baking sheet on the bottom rack, and preheat to 350°F. Generously grease an 8-inch square baking pan with vegetable oil or butter.

2   Place half the apple slices in the prepared pan and sprinkle them with the granulated sugar. Layer the remaining apples over the sugar.

3   Combine the flour, brown sugar, pecans, and cinnamon in a large bowl and stir them together with a wooden spoon. Work the butter into the mixture with your fingertips until it is evenly distributed. Spread the topping evenly over the apples.

4   Bake until the topping is crunchy and golden and the apples are bubbling, 55 to 60 minutes. Serve hot.

INGREDIENTS

Vegetable oil or butter for greasing the pan

7½ cups peeled Granny Smith apple slices (½ inch thick; 5 to 6 apples)

5 tablespoons granulated sugar

⅔ cup all-purpose flour

⅔ cup (lightly packed) light brown sugar

⅔ cup finely chopped pecans

½ teaspoon ground cinnamon

5 tablespoons plus 1 teaspoon (⅓ cup) unsalted butter, at room temperature, cut into 5 pieces

Ice cream, for serving

INGREDIENTS

Butter for greasing the baking dish

Filling

4½ generous cups peeled nectarine slices (½ inch thick; 4 to 5 nectarines)

4½ generous cups fresh apricot slices (½ inch thick; about 9 apricots)

¼ to ⅓ cup granulated sugar

⅜ teaspoon ground cinnamon

Slightly rounded ¼ teaspoon salt

1 tablespoon plus ¼ teaspoon cornstarch

1 tablespoon plus 1 teaspoon fresh lemon juice

Topping

2 cups all-purpose flour

¼ cup cornmeal

1 tablespoon baking powder

¼ teaspoon salt

6 tablespoons (½ stick plus 2 tablespoons) unsalted butter, cold, cut into 6 pieces

2 tablespoons (¼ stick) all-natural shortening, cut into 6 pieces

1 large egg

¾ cup milk

⅓ cup confectioners' sugar

Vanilla ice cream or Whipped Cream (page 119), for serving

Apricot Nectarine Cobbler

* *

Historically, cobblers have been made with all shortening or a combination of butter and shortening. For years I tried to create an all-butter cobbler but was always disappointed. Recently I discovered an all-natural shortening made with unhydrogenated oil that contributes to the kind of texture that a cobbler topping should have. I have added butter as well, which contributes to the flavor. It is imperative that the cobbler be served as soon as it comes out of the oven or be reheated thoroughly before serving. Vanilla ice cream or whipped cream are a must.

MAKES 8 TO 10 SERVINGS

1   Place a rack in the center of the oven and a baking sheet on the bottom rack, and preheat to 400°F. Grease a 13 × 9-inch baking dish with butter.

2   Prepare the filling: Toss the nectarines, apricots, sugar, cinnamon, salt, cornstarch, and lemon juice together in a large bowl. Transfer to the baking dish and set aside.

3   Make the topping: Place the flour, cornmeal, baking powder, and salt in a food processor and process to blend for 10 seconds.

4   Scatter the butter and shortening over the flour mixture, then pulse the mixture 6 times until the butter is in pea-size bits.

5   Whisk the egg and the milk together in a small cup until blended. With the processor running, pour the egg mixture in a steady stream through the feed tube and process until the topping just comes together, 15 pulses.

6   With your hand, grab small clumps of the topping and drop them over the surface of the fruit to cover it.

7 Bake the cobbler for 20 minutes. Lower the oven temperature to 375°F and continue to bake until the topping is golden and firm, 20 to 25 minutes.

8 Let cool for 15 minutes, then place the confectioners' sugar in a small strainer and shake it over the topping. Serve the cobbler hot with ice cream or whipped cream.

* *

Caramel Apple Casserole

* *

E ven my cousin Kate, who resists eating fats, couldn't resist this dessert. I felt a little guilty about tempting her when I made it with the apples I had picked that day—but not very guilty because even virtuous people need an occasional treat to remind them of how virtuous they're usually being.

MAKES 8 SERVINGS

1 Place a rack in the center of the oven and a baking sheet on the bottom rack, and preheat to 375°F. Lightly grease a 2-quart soufflé dish with vegetable oil or butter.

2 Make the dough: Place the flour, granulated sugar, and salt in a food processor and process to blend for 20 seconds. Add the butter and process until the dough resembles coarse meal, about 30 seconds.

3 Stir the egg yolks and water together in a small cup. With the processor running, pour this mixture through the feed tube and process until the dough comes together, 35 seconds.

4 Remove the dough from the processor and knead it for several turns. Divide the dough into quarters and shape each piece into a thick round disk.

INGREDIENTS

Vegetable oil or butter for greasing the dish

Dough

3 cups all-purpose flour

3 tablespoons granulated sugar

½ teaspoon salt

2 sticks (8 ounces) unsalted butter, cold, cut into 16 pieces

3 large egg yolks, at room temperature

2 tablespoons ice water

Apple Filling

6 cups peeled tart apple slices (¼ inch thick; 5 medium-large)

1 cup (lightly packed) light brown sugar

2 tablespoons fresh lemon juice

¼ teaspoon salt

Caramel

8 tablespoons (1 stick) unsalted butter

½ cup granulated sugar

5   Roll each disk ⅛ inch thick between two pieces of plastic wrap (see page 330 for rolling technique). Trim each disk to fit the soufflé dish. Stack the disks on a plate with plastic wrap between each layer and place them in the refrigerator while you prepare the filling.

6   Prepare the filling: Combine the apples, brown sugar, lemon juice, and salt in a large bowl and toss to evenly coat the apples. Set aside.

7   Make the caramel: Melt the butter in a small saucepan and stir in the granulated sugar. Bring the mixture to a boil over medium heat, then simmer until golden, 2 minutes. Watch closely—caramel can go from just right to burnt pretty quickly.

8   Pour two-thirds of the caramel into the prepared dish. Fit 1 pastry circle in the bottom over the caramel.

9   Place one-third of the apple mixture (2 cups) over the pastry and top with a second pastry circle. Add another one-third of the apples, top with the third pastry circle, then the remaining apples and the fourth pastry circle.

10   Pour the remaining caramel over the top and spread evenly with a frosting spatula.

11   Cover the top of the dish with aluminum foil and pierce the foil in several places with the tip of a knife.

12   Bake the casserole for 30 minutes. Remove the foil and continue baking until the top is golden and the apple mixture is bubbling, 30 to 35 minutes longer.

13   Let the dish cool on a rack. Serve warm or at room temperature.

CHAPTER 17
Puddings and Custards

Apparently, food smoothness is a universal craving, because puddings and custards show up in cooking almost everywhere in the world. Try out this richness on your tongue: mousse, charlotte, chiffon, tiramisù, baked Alaska, Persian cream, blancmange, *blote kage,* tapioca, meringue, *weinschaum, zerde,* zabaglione. And that's not even counting the wonderful names the English have for their puddings, like Poor Knights of Windsor and Grateful Pudding and, my favorite, Kiss-Me-Quick.

Now if you have a list of names a mile long for a single food, that says something about where it stands in your pantheon of pleasures, and, in fact, the British use "pudding" to signify all dessert. The children of my former neighbors would politely ask me what's for pudding when I invited them over for a meal, and it took me months to admit my cross-cultural clumsiness and ask their mother what they were talking about.

To me, pudding is custard, a fancier version of jarred baby food, though lighter and richer. I think of puddings and other chilled creations as the most seasonal of desserts (with the possible exception of pies before frozen fruit became passable). Chills and whips are the ideal dessert in the sultry summer months when you crave something sweet, but not ponderous. Others, such as Indian or bread pudding, are creatures of the autumn harvest months, and chocolate and butterscotch puddings are to me what sacrifices to the gods were for the ancients when the winter dark made them fear that the sun would never return.

PUDDING IT ALL TOGETHER

These desserts are perhaps the most delicate of all to make because they demand precision and seldom allow for a middle ground. They don't usually take too long, though, and you'll find that once you're familiar with a few basic recipes, whole worlds of mousses, crèmes, and trifles will open to you. I've divided the recipes in this chapter into two categories in order to explain some of the preparation techniques.

STOVETOP PUDDINGS

For puddings that contain liquid, sugar, cornstarch, and eggs, it is usually best to dissolve the cornstarch in a portion of the liquid and to stir in the eggs with a whisk. The remaining liquid should be heated with the sugar in a heavy saucepan over medium-low heat just to the boiling point. Then give the cornstarch mixture a final stir (it tends to settle as it sits) and add it in a stream to the boiling mixture while stirring vigorously with a whisk. The mixture is then brought to a second boil while stirring constantly and usually boiled for 10 to 30 seconds more to ensure proper thickening. It is essential for cornstarch to be brought to a boil in order for it to "clear," that is to lose its chalky taste and become less cloudy in appearance.

After the pudding has cooked, pour it into a large bowl. Let it sit for 10 minutes, stirring occasionally with a wooden spoon. Cover the surface of the custard with plastic wrap that has been punctured several times with a knife or skewer to release steam, and then refrigerate.

Curdled eggs are the biggest problem that can occur with these puddings. If this starts to happen, you can do one of two things. Either pour the mixture immediately from the pot into a cool bowl and stir it vigorously with a whisk (you can strain it to check for evidence of cooked eggs), or pour the mixture into a blender and blend on medium-high speed for 5 to 10 seconds until it's smooth. The second process is more reliable for making your pudding smooth, but it also tends to loosen it.

BAKED CUSTARDS

These desserts, which include such delights as Baked Chocolate Custard, occasionally call for some stovetop cooking, but regardless of preliminaries, they're all baked in a large baking dish or individual ramekins after the ingredients have been stirred together in a mixing bowl.

I bake my custards in a water bath, which allows them to cook more evenly and gently. To make a water bath, put the custard dish or dishes in a shallow pan on the center rack of the oven, and pour enough hot water into the pan to come about two-thirds of the way up the sides of the custard baking dish.

For more delicate puddings, such as Peaches 'n' Cream Custard and Baked Chocolate Custard, I find that individual ramekins allow the custard to bake more evenly than a large baking dish. Hearty puddings, such as the bread puddings, kugel, and Indian pudding, can be baked in large dishes with no problem.

Test if baked puddings are done by inserting a tester close to the center but not directly in it. If it comes out clean, the pudding is done. The center will continue to cook after the custard comes out of the oven. Remove the custard from the water bath as soon as it leaves the oven and let it cool to room temperature before refrigerating.

PUDDING ON THE RITZ

The desserts in this chapter are mostly hearty winter fare, but one in particular—Peaches 'n' Cream Custard—makes a perfect end to a summer meal.

Bread pudding, Indian pudding, and traditional puddings, such as Daddy's Oedipal Chocolate Pudding and Butterscotch Pudding, are stick-to-your-rib sweets and are best served piled generously in a dessert bowl with whipped cream and in some cases a heavier bourbon or vanilla sauce.

Up until not so long ago, fancy restaurants would serve anything before they would use the word "pudding" on a dessert menu. It sounded so—heaven forbid—family style. But now they've learned what smart cooks knew all along—the proof is in the pudding.

Daddy's Oedipal Chocolate Pudding

* *

INGREDIENTS

3 ounces unsweetened chocolate

1½ cups heavy (whipping) cream

2¼ cups milk

½ cup plus 2 tablespoons sugar

¼ cup cornstarch

2 large egg yolks

2 tablespoons unsalted butter, cut into 2 pieces

Whipped Cream (page 119), for serving

*M*y father, the champion dessert eater, has never been much of a dessert maker, but this pudding is all his own. *For those who prefer their comfort food on the rich, indulgent side, this one's for you!*

MAKES 8 TO 10 SERVINGS

1   Melt the chocolate in the top of a double boiler placed over simmering water.

2   Combine the cream, 1½ cups of the milk, and the sugar in a large saucepan. Heat over medium heat, stirring twice during this time, until almost boiling, about 5 minutes.

3   In a small bowl, dissolve the cornstarch in the remaining ¾ cup milk. Whisk in the egg yolks.

4   Whisk the melted chocolate vigorously into the hot cream mixture. Cover and heat over very low heat to blend, about 2 minutes. Uncover the saucepan and whisk again vigorously until the mixture is uniform in color and all specks of chocolate have disappeared.

5   Increase the heat to medium-low. Measure out 1 cup of the hot chocolate mixture. Whisking vigorously, pour it in a stream into the yolk mixture. (If the mixture should curdle, place it in a blender and blend it on low speed until smooth, 5 to 10 seconds.)

6   Bring the chocolate mixture remaining in the saucepan just to the boiling point over medium-low heat. Whisking vigorously, add the yolk mixture to it in a stream. Cook, stirring constantly over low heat, until the mixture thickens and forms loose mounds when dropped from the whisk back into the pan, 30 seconds.

7   Strain the pudding through a sieve into a medium-size bowl and gently fold in the butter until it is completely incorporated.

8   Let cool for 10 minutes, stirring gently several times to release steam. Lay a piece of plastic wrap directly on the surface of the pudding and puncture it in several places with a knife or skewer. Refrigerate the pudding until chilled, 4 to 6 hours before serving.

9   Spoon into a bowl or martini glass and serve topped with Whipped Cream.

* *

Butterscotch Pudding

* *

*I*t must have been sometime during my high school years that I indulged myself almost daily with butterscotch pudding. This is an especially creamy version of that adolescent pleasure.

MAKES 4 TO 6 SERVINGS

1   Combine 1¼ cups of the milk, the cream, brown sugar, and salt in a heavy medium-size saucepan. Heat over medium heat, stirring twice during this time, until almost boiling, about 5 minutes.

2   In a small bowl, dissolve the cornstarch in the remaining ¾ cup milk. Whisk in the egg yolks.

3   Measure out 1 cup of the hot cream mixture. Whisking vigorously, pour it in a stream into the yolk mixture. (If the mixture should curdle, place it in a blender and blend it on low speed until smooth, 5 to 10 seconds.)

4   Bring the cream mixture remaining in the saucepan just to the boiling point over medium-

INGREDIENTS

2 cups milk

1 cup heavy (whipping) cream

1 cup plus 2 tablespoons (lightly packed) dark brown sugar

⅛ teaspoon salt

¼ cup plus 2 teaspoons cornstarch

2 large egg yolks, at room temperature

3 tablespoons unsalted butter, cut into 3 pieces

1½ teaspoons pure vanilla extract

Whipped Cream (page 119), for serving

low heat. Whisking vigorously, add the yolk mixture in a stream. Cook, stirring constantly over low heat, until the mixture thickens and forms loose mounds when dropped from the whisk back into the pan, 1½ minutes.

5 Strain the pudding through a sieve into a medium-size bowl and gently fold in the butter and vanilla until they are completely incorporated.

6 Let cool for 10 minutes, stirring gently several times to release the steam. Lay a piece of plastic wrap directly on the surface of the pudding and puncture it in several places with a knife or skewer. Refrigerate the pudding until chilled, 4 to 6 hours before serving.

7 Spoon into a bowl or martini glass and serve topped with Whipped Cream.

* *

Creamy Stovetop Rice Pudding

(FOR ELIOT)

* *

INGREDIENTS

1¾ cups plus 2 tablespoons water

½ cup plus 3 tablespoons long-grain white rice

½ teaspoon salt

2 tablespoons unsalted butter

½ cup raisins

1 cup milk

1 cup heavy (whipping) cream

4 large eggs, at room temperature

7 tablespoons sugar

1 teaspoon ground nutmeg

1½ teaspoons pure vanilla extract

This recipe took a lot of attempts to perfect, for it had a penchant for curdling. The method that I came up with, to my relief, is foolproof. The custard is cooked first so that if it curdles it can be put in the blender and made smooth again before adding the rice. Eliot, my business partner, is such a devotee of my rice pudding that he would drive miles to my house to eat it each time I tested the recipe.

MAKES 8 SERVINGS

1   Bring the water, rice, and salt to a simmer in an uncovered, medium-size saucepan over medium-high heat. Cover the pan and simmer over low heat until the rice is tender, about 15 minutes. The water should be completely absorbed by the rice.

2   Remove the pan from the heat and stir in the butter and raisins. Cover the pan and let the rice sit while you prepare the custard.

3   Vigorously whisk the milk, cream, eggs, sugar, and nutmeg together in a large heavy saucepan until well blended.

4   Cook the mixture over low heat, whisking constantly, until it is thick enough to coat the back of a wooden spoon, 10 to 15 minutes. (The time may vary considerably depending on the pan and the stove.) Immediately remove the pan from the heat, stir in the vanilla, and then add the rice by large spoonfuls, stirring gently after each addition. (If the pudding should curdle before adding the rice, place it in a blender and blend on low speed until smooth, 5 to 10 seconds. Then pour the custard into a large bowl and add the rice.)

5   Let the pudding sit for 30 minutes, then cover and refrigerate until ready to serve. It can be served warm or cold.

* *

Peaches 'n' Cream Custard

* *

A rich and flavorful baked custard topped with fresh peaches that have been lightly sautéed in bourbon. It is best to prepare the topping right before serving. If you prepare it earlier, heat it slightly before spooning it over the custard.

MAKES 8 SERVINGS

INGREDIENTS

Vegetable oil or butter for
  greasing the ramekins

Custard

2¼ cups milk

¾ cup heavy (whipping) cream

1 cup plus 2 tablespoons
  (lightly packed) light
  brown sugar

5 large egg yolks

3 large eggs, at room
  temperature

2¼ teaspoons grated lemon zest

1¼ teaspoons pure vanilla extract

½ teaspoon salt

¾ teaspoon ground cinnamon

Topping

4 cups unpeeled peach slices
  (½ inch thick; 4 medium-size
  peaches)

2 tablespoons (lightly packed)
  light brown sugar

3 tablespoons fresh orange juice

Pinch of salt

2 tablespoons plus 2 teaspoons
  bourbon

1   Place a rack in the center of the oven and preheat to 350°F. Lightly grease eight ½-cup ramekins with vegetable oil or butter.

2   Make the custard: Combine all the ingredients in a large bowl and stir vigorously with a whisk until completely blended.

3   Pour the custard mixture into the ramekins. Place them in a shallow baking pan in the oven. Pour enough hot water into the baking pan to come two-thirds of the way up the sides of the ramekins.

4   Bake the custard until it is loosely set and a tester inserted close to but not in the center comes out clean, about 35 minutes.

5   Let the custard cool to room temperature, then cover with plastic wrap if you plan to refrigerate it. The custard should be at room temperature when served.

6   Prepare the topping: Combine the peaches, brown sugar, orange juice, and salt in a medium-size skillet. Bring to a simmer over medium-high heat; simmer until most of the liquid is absorbed but the peaches still hold their shape, 2 to 3 minutes.

7   Remove the skillet from the heat, add the bourbon, and toss gently.

8   Spoon the peaches on top of each custard and serve.

Baked Chocolate Custard

* *

This dark chocolate custard is delicious served warm or cold with—not surprisingly—whipped cream. The texture when warm is custardlike and when cold, more dense. Thank goodness the custard is baked in individual ramekins—meaning it's portion controlled—so I really can't justify eating more than one . . . can I?

MAKES 6 SERVINGS

1 Place a rack in the center of the oven and preheat to 325°F. Lightly grease six ½-cup ramekins with vegetable oil or butter.

2 Combine the cream, milk, and both chocolates in the top of a double boiler. Heat over simmering water, whisking occasionally, until the chocolate is melted, 8 to 12 minutes. Then stir the mixture very briskly with the whisk until any specks or strands of chocolate are dissolved and the liquid is uniformly brown. Turn off the heat but leave the top pan over the bottom one.

3 Beat the egg yolks in a medium-size mixing bowl using the whisk attachment of an electric mixer on medium-high speed until thick and pale in color, 3 to 4 minutes.

4 Whisking vigorously, gradually add the chocolate mixture to the egg yolks. Blend in the vanilla.

5 Strain the mixture through a sieve into the prepared ramekins. Place the ramekins in a shallow baking pan in the oven. Pour in enough hot water to come two-thirds of the way up the sides of the ramekins.

6 Bake the puddings until a tester inserted close to but not in the center comes out clean, about 1 hour 20 minutes.

7 Remove the ramekins from the water bath and serve the pudding warm or cold with Whipped Cream.

INGREDIENTS

Vegetable oil or butter for greasing the ramekins

2 cups heavy (whipping) cream

¾ cup milk

1 cup (6 ounces) semisweet chocolate chips

½ ounce unsweetened chocolate, cut into 4 pieces

6 large egg yolks, at room temperature

2 teaspoons pure vanilla extract

Whipped Cream (page 119), for serving

Truffle Soufflé

* *

In a book of recipes notable for their richness, this one probably takes the cake. It's loaded with butter and chocolate, and although it's flourless, you can slice it into pieces like a cake. But it works better scooped out like a pudding.

MAKES 6 TO 8 SERVINGS

INGREDIENTS

Vegetable oil or butter for greasing the dish

4 ounces unsweetened chocolate, chopped

4 ounces semisweet chocolate, chopped, or ⅔ cup chocolate chips

1 cup sugar

2 teaspoons instant espresso powder

½ cup boiling water

4 large eggs, separated

2 teaspoons pure vanilla extract

2 sticks (8 ounces) unsalted butter, melted and cooled to tepid

Whipped Cream (page 119), for serving

1 Place a rack in the center of the oven and preheat to 300°F. Lightly grease a 6- to 8-cup soufflé dish with vegetable oil or butter.

2 Place both chocolates, ¾ cup of the sugar, and the espresso in a large bowl. Add the boiling water and stir until the chocolate melts. Let the mixture cool to tepid.

3 Whisk the egg yolks and the vanilla together in a small bowl. Add the butter and whisk until the mixture is silky and smooth, about 10 seconds.

4 Beat the egg whites in a medium-size mixing bowl with an electric mixer on medium-high speed until frothy, about 30 seconds. Gradually add the remaining ¼ cup sugar and continue beating until the whites form firm peaks, 1 minute.

5 Stir the yolk mixture into the chocolate mixture. Fold in the egg whites.

6 Pour the soufflé batter into the prepared dish and place the dish in a shallow baking pan in the oven. Pour enough hot water into the baking dish to come two-thirds of the way up the sides of the soufflé dish.

7 Bake the soufflé until the top rises up and cracks, about 1½ hours. (A tester inserted in the center will not come out clean. When checking for doneness, be sure to open and close the oven carefully.) Turn the oven off and allow the soufflé to set for 1 hour in the water bath, in the oven. Serve the soufflé hot or warm, garnished with Whipped Cream.

Banana Rum Bread Pudding

* *

H old the piña coladas, just give me a hunk of this instead, right from the oven with a spoonful of Boston pastry chef Nicole Coady's caramel sauce and a big dollop of whipped cream. This dessert should be served while it is still warm. It is irresistible and is really easy to throw together: The caramel sauce can be made ahead of time and reheated before serving, and all the pudding ingredients can be prepared earlier and put in the oven an hour before serving.

MAKES 6 TO 8 SERVINGS

1 Make the pudding: Vigorously whisk the cream, milk, rum, eggs, salt, and ½ cup plus 3 tablespoons of the brown sugar together in a large bowl until blended. Add the bread and bananas and toss with a large wooden spoon to evenly soak.

2 Refrigerate the mixture overnight or for several hours, tossing occasionally with the spoon to make sure all the cubes are fully soaked. You can pull a few pieces apart with your fingers to check.

3 Fifteen minutes before baking, place a rack in the center of the oven and preheat to 350°F. Grease a 9-inch soufflé dish with vegetable oil or butter. Scoop the bread mixture into the baking dish. Sprinkle the remaining 2 tablespoons brown sugar over the top.

4 Bake until the top is crisp and golden and risen in the center, about 1 hour. Let the pudding cool for 30 minutes.

5 Meanwhile, make the caramel sauce: Whisk the granulated sugar and water in a small heavy saucepan. Place the saucepan over medium heat and bring the mixture to a gentle boil. Boil until the mixture reaches 350°F on a candy thermometer or until it turns a rich caramel color, 7 to 8 minutes. Take care not to

INGREDIENTS

Pudding

1½ cups heavy (whipping) cream

1 cup milk

¼ cup dark rum

5 large eggs

¼ teaspoon salt

½ cup plus 5 tablespoons (lightly packed) light brown sugar

5 cups bread cubes (1-inch cubes)

2½ cups sliced (generous ¼ inch thick) bananas

Vegetable oil or butter for greasing the dish

Caramel Sauce

½ cup granulated sugar

2 tablespoons water

2 tablespoons unsalted butter, cut into pieces

5 tablespoons heavy (whipping) cream

let it burn because it can go from perfect to burnt in an instant.

6   Remove from the heat and add the butter pieces, stirring to mix. Slowly add the cream and stir to incorporate. The mixture will continue to boil for quite a few minutes while you complete this entire process.

7   Serve the bread pudding with the hot or warm caramel sauce on top.

* *

Chocolate Bread Pudding

* *

C*ertainly not your average bread pudding, this is more of a rich chocolate dessert with bread in it. It is great served hot or cold with whipped cream or vanilla ice cream. I like to use challah, which makes it a bit richer.*

MAKES 8 TO 10 SERVINGS

INGREDIENTS

1¾ cups plus 2 tablespoons heavy (whipping) cream

1½ cups milk

6 tablespoons sugar

1½ cups (9 ounces) semisweet chocolate chips

⅛ teaspoon salt

3 large eggs, lightly beaten with a fork

3 cups cubed (1 inch) challah

Vegetable oil or butter for greasing the dish

1   Place the cream, milk, sugar, chocolate chips, and salt in a medium-size saucepan and heat over low heat, whisking occasionally, until the chocolate is completely melted and all the chocolate specks are gone, 3 to 4 minutes. Remove the pan from the heat.

2   Vigorously whisk in the eggs.

3   Place the cut-up bread in a large bowl and pour the chocolate mixture over the bread. Toss with a large wooden spoon to evenly soak. Refrigerate the mixture for 2 to 3 hours, tossing the mixture occasionally with the spoon to make sure all the cubes are fully soaked. You can pull a few pieces apart with your fingers to check.

4   Fifteen minutes before baking, place a rack in the center of the oven and preheat to 350°F. Generously grease a 6- or 8-cup soufflé dish with vegetable oil or butter.

5   Scoop the pudding into the prepared dish. Bake until the top is crisp, about 40 minutes. Then lay a piece of aluminum foil loosely over the surface of the pudding and bake until the pudding is set and a tester inserted close to but not in the center comes out clean, 30 minutes more. Let cool slightly before serving.

* *

Bourbon Bread Pudding

* *

T his dessert melts in your mouth from its crunchy topping down through its custard filling, with or without the sauce. You can make it with crusty French bread (see Note), but I think that croissants make it extra special. Serve it warm on the first day and right out of the refrigerator thereafter.

MAKES 8 SERVINGS

1   Vigorously whisk the cream, milk, eggs, vanilla, bourbon, ½ cup of the sugar, the nutmeg, and salt together in a large bowl until blended. Add the croissant cubes and the raisins and toss with a wooden spoon to evenly soak.

2   Refrigerate the mixture for at least 2 hours, tossing with the large spoon occasionally to make sure all the cubes are fully soaked. You can pull a few pieces apart with your fingers to check.

3   Fifteen minutes before baking, place a rack in the center of the oven and preheat to 350°F. Lightly grease an 8-inch square baking dish with vegetable oil or butter.

4   Scoop the pudding mixture into the prepared baking dish

INGREDIENTS

1 cup heavy (whipping) cream

1 cup milk

4 large eggs, at room temperature

1 teaspoon pure vanilla extract

¼ cup bourbon

½ cup plus 2 tablespoons sugar

¼ teaspoon ground nutmeg

¼ teaspoon salt

4 cups croissant cubes (½ inch; 3 or 4 croissants)

⅓ cup dark raisins

Vegetable oil or butter for greasing the dish

Bourbon Sauce (recipe follows; optional)

397

Pies and Fruit Desserts and Puddings

and sprinkle the remaining
2 tablespoons sugar over the top.

5   Bake the pudding until
the top is crisp and golden
and has risen in the center,
about 50 minutes.

6   Let cool 30 minutes before
devouring or, if you wish, while
you make the bourbon sauce.

NOTE: *If you'd prefer to use
French bread, you'll need about
½ baguette. Split it lengthwise,
butter generously, and cut into
½-inch cubes until you have
4 cups.*

Bourbon Sauce

INGREDIENTS

½ cup sugar

2 large egg yolks

5 tablespoons bourbon

4 tablespoons (½ stick) unsalted
   butter, cut into 4 pieces

*This sauce is like the icing
on the cake. Just drizzle it
over each serving, and if
you are really in the mood
to indulge, top off the bread
pudding with a dollop of
ice cream.*

MAKES ¾ CUP

1   Pour water to a depth of
¾ inch in the bottom pot of a
double boiler and bring it to a
simmer over medium-low heat.

2   Place the sugar and egg yolks
in the top of the double boiler
(not yet over the simmering
water) and stir vigorously with a
whisk until light in color.

3   Whisk in the bourbon and
place the top of the double
boiler over the simmering water.
Cook, whisking vigorously, until
the mixture is hot and slightly
thickened, 3 to 4 minutes.

4   Strain the mixture through a
fine-mesh sieve into a small bowl.
Add the butter and stir until it
melts.

5   Serve the sauce warm over the
bread pudding. If you prepare the
sauce ahead of time, reheat it in a
double boiler over hot water.

Apple Bread Pudding

with VANILLA SAUCE

* *

Just a little twist on the classic version. The apples introduce both a texture and flavor that makes the pudding different. I like to serve this at the end of autumn when the apples are divine and the weather is starting to turn chilly.

MAKES 8 SERVINGS

1 Vigorously whisk the cream, milk, whole eggs, egg yolks, brown sugar, salt, vanilla, and ¼ teaspoon of the cinnamon in a large bowl until blended.

2 Add the bread cubes, apples, and raisins and toss with a large wooden spoon to evenly soak.

3 Refrigerate the pudding for at least 2 hours, tossing the mixture occasionally with the spoon to make sure the cubes are fully soaked. You can pull a few pieces apart with your fingers to check.

4 Fifteen minutes before baking, place a rack in the center of the oven and preheat to 350°F. Lightly grease an 8-inch square baking dish with vegetable oil or butter.

5 Scoop the pudding into the prepared baking dish. Mix the granulated sugar and the remaining 2 teaspoons cinnamon together and sprinkle it over the bread pudding.

6 Place the baking dish in a shallow baking pan in the oven. Pour enough hot water into the larger pan to come two-thirds of the way up the sides of the baking dish.

7 Bake the pudding until the top is golden and crisp and has risen in the center, about 50 minutes.

8 Remove the pudding from the water bath and let cool for 30 minutes while you make the sauce.

INGREDIENTS

1 cup heavy (whipping) cream

1 cup milk

2 large eggs, at room temperature

2 large egg yolks

⅓ cup (lightly packed) light brown sugar

¼ teaspoon salt

1 teaspoon pure vanilla extract

2¼ teaspoons ground cinnamon

⅓ to ½ French baguette, split lengthwise, generously buttered, and cut into ½-inch cubes (4 cups)

2 cups peeled tart apple cubes (½ inch; about 3 apples)

⅓ cup golden raisins

Vegetable oil or butter for greasing the dish

1 tablespoon plus 1 teaspoon granulated sugar

Vanilla Sauce (recipe follows)

INGREDIENTS

½ cup plus 2 tablespoons heavy (whipping) cream

½ cup plus 2 tablespoons milk

¼ cup sugar

¼ teaspoon salt

1 tablespoon cornstarch

3 tablespoons unsalted butter, cut into 3 pieces

1½ teaspoons pure vanilla extract

½ teaspoon ground nutmeg

Vanilla Sauce

This creamy sauce with a hint of nutmeg accents both the flavor and texture of the Apple Bread Pudding.

MAKES 1¼ CUPS

1 Combine the cream, ¼ cup plus 2 tablespoons of the milk, the sugar, and salt in a heavy medium-size saucepan and heat over medium heat until almost boiling.

2 Dissolve the cornstarch in the remaining ¼ cup milk in a small cup. Stir it into the hot cream mixture.

3 Bring the mixture to a boil over low heat, whisking constantly. Continue boiling and whisking until the sauce thickens, about 3 minutes.

4 Remove the pan from the heat and stir in the butter, vanilla, and nutmeg. Let the sauce cool slightly before serving.

Indian Pudding

* *

The Puritan women learned how to make this dark, spicy dessert from the Indians, and it has remained a New England favorite ever since, probably because it warms the cockles and sticks to the bones during those long winters. My partner, Eliot, can't get enough of it. He likes it served warm with heavy cream spooned over the top, so this recipe is for him.

MAKES 10 SERVINGS

1   Place a rack in the center of the oven and preheat to 325°F. Lightly grease a 6- or 8-cup soufflé dish with vegetable oil or butter.

2   Heat the milk in a medium-size saucepan over medium-low heat until almost boiling.

3   While the milk is heating, pour the cream into a medium-size bowl and stir in the cornmeal, sugar, molasses, salt, cinnamon, nutmeg, cloves, and ginger.

4   Add the cornmeal mixture to the hot milk and cook, whisking constantly, over medium-low heat until the pudding has thickened to the consistency of syrup, about 5 minutes. Remove it from the heat.

5   Beat the eggs in a small bowl with a whisk. Whisking vigorously, beat ½ cup of the hot cornmeal mixture into the eggs. Then vigorously whisk the egg mixture back into the remaining cornmeal mixture. Add the butter and stir until it melts.

6   Pour the pudding into the prepared baking dish. Place the dish in a shallow baking pan in the oven. Pour enough hot water into the larger pan to come two-thirds of the way up the sides of the baking dish.

7   Bake the pudding until it is set and a tester inserted close to but not in the center comes out clean, about 1 hour 15 minutes.

8   Remove the pudding from the water bath and let cool slightly. Serve the pudding warm.

INGREDIENTS

Vegetable oil or butter for greasing the dish

2 cups milk

1 cup heavy (whipping) cream

½ cup yellow cornmeal

½ cup (lightly packed) light brown sugar

½ cup molasses

1 teaspoon salt

2 teaspoons ground cinnamon

¼ teaspoon ground nutmeg

¼ teaspoon ground cloves

¼ teaspoon ground ginger

4 large eggs, at room temperature

4 tablespoons (½ stick) unsalted butter, cut into 4 pieces

Conversion Tables

APPROXIMATE EQUIVALENTS

1 stick butter . . . . 8 tbs / 4 oz / ½ cup

1 cup all-purpose presifted flour
   or dried bread crumbs . . . . 5 oz

1 cup granulated sugar . . . . 8 oz

1 cup (packed) brown sugar . . . . 6 oz

1 cup confectioners' sugar . . . . 4 ½ oz

1 cup honey or syrup . . . . 12 oz

1 cup grated cheese . . . . 4 oz

1 cup dried beans . . . . 6 oz

1 large egg . . . . *about* 2 oz or about 3 tbs

1 egg yolk . . . . *about* 1 tbs

1 egg white . . . . *about* 2 tbs

Please note that all conversions are approximate but close enough to be useful when converting from one system to another.

WEIGHT CONVERSION

US/UK	Metric	US/UK	Metric
½ oz	15 g	7 oz	200 g
1 oz	30 g	8 oz	250 g
1 ½ oz	45 g	9 oz	275 g
2 oz	60 g	10 oz	300 g
2 ½ oz	75 g	11 oz	325 g
3 oz	90 g	12 oz	350 g
3 ½ oz	100 g	13 oz	375 g
4 oz	125 g	14 oz	400 g
5 oz	150 g	15 oz	450 g
6 oz	175 g	1 lb	500 g

LIQUID CONVERSION

US	Imperial	Metric
2 tbs	1 fl oz	30 ml
3 tbs	1 ½ fl oz	45 ml
¼ cup	2 fl oz	60 ml
⅓ cup	2 ½ fl oz	75 ml
⅓ cup + *1 tbs*	3 fl oz	90 ml
⅓ cup + *2 tbs*	3 ½ fl oz	100 ml
½ cup	4 fl oz	125 ml
⅔ cup	5 fl oz	150 ml
¾ cup	6 fl oz	175 ml
¾ cup + *2 tbs*	7 fl oz	200 ml
1 cup	8 fl oz	250 ml
1 cup + *2 tbs*	9 fl oz	275 ml
1 ¼ cups	10 fl oz	300 ml
1 ⅓ cups	11 fl oz	325 ml
1 ½ cups	12 fl oz	350 ml
1 ⅔ cups	13 fl oz	375 ml
1 ¾ cups	14 fl oz	400 ml
1 ¾ cups + *2 tbs*	15 fl oz	450 ml
2 cups (*1 pint*)	16 fl oz	500 ml
2 ½ cups	20 fl oz (*1 pint*)	600 ml
3 ¾ cups	1 ½ pints	900 ml
4 cups	1 ¾ pints	1 liter

OVEN TEMPERATURES

°F	Gas Mark	°C	°F	Gas Mark	°C
250	½	120	400	6	200
275	1	140	425	7	220
300	2	150	450	8	230
325	3	160	475	9	240
350	4	180	500	10	260
375	5	190			

Note: Reduce the temperature by 20°C (68°F) for fan-assisted ovens.

Index

* *